THE HERO OI

The Hero of Italy examines a salient episode in Italy's Thirty Years' War with Spain and France, whereby the young duke Odoardo Farnese of Parma embraced the French alliance, only to experience defeat and occupation after two tumultuous years (1635–1637). Gregory Hanlon stresses the narrative of events unfolding in northern Italy, examining the participation of the little state in these epic European events.

The first chapter describes the constitution of Cardinal Richelieu's anti-Habsburg alliance and Odoardo's eagerness to be part of it. A chapter on the Parman professional army, based on an extraordinary collection of company roster-books, sheds light on the identity of over 13,000 individuals, soldier by soldier, the origin and background of their officers, the conditions of their lodgings, and the good state of their equipment. The next chapter follows the first campaign of 1635 alongside French and Savoyard contingents at the failed siege of Valenza, and the logistical difficulties of organizing such large-scale operations. Another chapter examines the financial expedients the duchy adopted to fend off incursions on all its borders in 1636, and how militia contingents on both sides were drawn into the fighting. A final chapter relates the Spanish invasion and occupation which forced duke Odoardo to make a separate peace. The volume includes a detailed assessment of the impact of war on civilians based on parish registers for city and country. The application of the laws of war was largely nullified by widespread starvation, disease and routine sex-selective infanticide. These quantitative analyses, supported by maps and tables, are among the most detailed anywhere in Europe in the era of the Thirty Years' War.

The Hero of Italy

*Odoardo Farnese, Duke of Parma,
his Soldiers, and his Subjects
in the Thirty Years' War*

GREGORY HANLON

OXFORD
UNIVERSITY PRESS

OXFORD
UNIVERSITY PRESS

Great Clarendon Street, Oxford, OX2 6DP,
United Kingdom

Oxford University Press is a department of the University of Oxford.
It furthers the University's objective of excellence in research, scholarship,
and education by publishing worldwide. Oxford is a registered trade mark of
Oxford University Press in the UK and in certain other countries

© Gregory Hanlon 2014

The moral rights of the author have been asserted

First published 2014
First published in paperback 2019

All rights reserved. No part of this publication may be reproduced, stored in
a retrieval system, or transmitted, in any form or by any means, without the
prior permission in writing of Oxford University Press, or as expressly permitted
by law, by licence, or under terms agreed with the appropriate reprographics
rights organization. Enquiries concerning reproduction outside the scope of the
above should be sent to the Rights Department, Oxford University Press, at the
address above

You must not circulate this work in any other form
and you must impose this same condition on any acquirer

Published in the United States of America by Oxford University Press
198 Madison Avenue, New York, NY 10016, United States of America

British Library Cataloguing in Publication Data
Data available

Library of Congress Cataloging in Publication Data
Data available

ISBN 978–0–19–968724–4 (Hbk.)
ISBN 978–0–19–884703–8 (Pbk.)

Links to third party websites are provided by Oxford in good faith and
for information only. Oxford disclaims any responsibility for the materials
contained in any third party website referenced in this work.

I dedicate this book to the passionate intelligence and industry of three local historians, the fruits of whose labours will serve us all for many years to come:
Federica Dallasta, Mario Zannoni, Giuseppe Bertini

Acknowledgements

This book springs from my encounter with Odoardo Farnese's company rosters conserved in the Archivio di Stato of Parma. Years ago, local scholar Mario Zannoni volunteered to put the military papers of the duchy into order, and future historians of military questions will all be in his debt. Federica Dallasta and Giuseppe Bertini helped with this project and others concerning early modern Parma in multiple ways. The former director of the Archivio di Stato, Mariella Loiotile, has also been very helpful, in Parma while Massimo Baucia ensured that the work at the Biblioteca Comunale Passerini-Landi in Piacenza was both more agreeable and efficient. Another local historian, Carlo Dabene of Valenza, welcomed this project with open arms and opened the door to the parish archive there, while Alberto Menziani introduced me to the rich Modenese holdings. Military history is not immediately associated with Italian academic historiography, but the field includes some real experts who are laying the parameters of future scholarship, in particular Davide Maffi in Milan, Luciano Pezzolo in Venice, Paola Bianchi in Turin, and a promising newcomer, Giovanni Cerino Badone, in Milan. A whole group of Lombard historians at the Università degli Studi di Pavia—Mario Rizzo, Renzo Corritore, and Giovanni Vigo—have been an invaluable sounding board over the years, as has Giovanvittorio Signorotto in Modena (who correctly intuited how much I would discover in Florence), Angelantonio Spagnoletti in Bari, and Giovanni Muto in Naples. These historians in particular have demonstrated the surprising resilience of Spanish Italy. Guido Alfani, a young Milanese historian, is presently regenerating the rural economic and demographic history of northern Italy, following the path of Marzio Achille Romani and Marco Cattini, all of whom have been very helpful. Marco Costa, a psychologist specializing in military affairs at Bologna has influenced this study, and I hope many historians will read his work.

The French historical establishment is my principal *port d'attache*, and I am proud to fly its banner. In Paris, the historians who have been instrumental in this research have been Yves-Marie Bercé, Denis Crouzet, Olivier Chaline, Lucien Bély, Hervé Drévillon, Jean-Michel Sallmann, and Robert Descimon. Serge Brunet in Montpellier and Gilles Bertrand in Grenoble have also been helpful. Readers will discern how much the British military history tradition has informed this book as well as my more recent research, and I have had the pleasure more recently of encountering some of these British military historians first hand, in particular Jeremy Black, David Parrott, Toby Osborne, Hamish Scott, and Christopher Storrs. My contacts in North America are more fleeting, but I am happy to have discussed this project with William Caferro, Jamel Ostwvald, Brian Sandberg, and Mathew Vester. And finally, several of my graduate students in Halifax have explored important aspects of regional history with enthusiasm and competence: Laura Hynes, Brad Meredith, and Colin Rose in Parma, and Cheryl Bradbee in Piacenza.

Table of Contents

List of Figures, Tables, and Maps ... xi

Introduction: The Other Thirty Years' War ... 1

1 The Moth and the Flame ... 7
The Farnese Gran Giustizia of 1612 ... 7
A boy-warrior in dangerous times ... 20

2 Duke Odoardo's Army ... 42
Officers and gentlemen ... 42
Army cadres ... 54
The rank and file ... 58
Weapons and tactics ... 78
Auxiliary forces ... 84

3 The Duke of Parma's Great Adventure ... 88
Odoardo over the brink ... 88
The siege of Valenza ... 96
Odoardo and his army part ways ... 123

4 Parman Sideshow ... 129
The sinews of war ... 129
The duchy stranded ... 140

5 The Deluge ... 164
The Deluge ... 164
How brutal was the Thirty Years' War in Italy? ... 190

Conclusion ... 210

Sources and Bibliography ... 216
Index ... 237

List of Figures, Tables, and Maps

FIGURES

1.1 Parma and its citadel *c*.1650; The sixteenth-century fortifications are depicted here with multiple ravelins, a covered way and a counterscarp, added on the occasion of the war. The river Parma would have been near-empty for most of the year. *Biblioteca Palatina Parma* Ms Parm. 3711, f.45.   18

1.2 Piacenza's Palazzo Gotico town hall, seat of the city government. The equestrian statues emphasize the town's subjection to the Farnese dynasty. *Biblioteca Comunale Passerini-Landi di Piacenza*, Ms Pallastrelli 162, vol.2, p.5.   18

1.3 Piacenza and its citadel *c*.1650. This sketch includes the all-important citadel on the top right, and the Farnese palace at bottom centre. The Po river shown on the lower right is much too narrow. *Biblioteca Palatina Parma* Ms Parm. 3711, f.46.   19

1.4 Casale Monferrato and its citadel *c*.1650. This city and its powerful citadel, taken over from the Mantuan ally, served as France's threatening advanced base in Italy for most of the 17th century. *Biblioteca Palatina Parma*, Ms Parm. 3711, f.41.   29

2.1 Callot: the pay muster, *c*.1633. The scribe at the extreme right referred to company roster-books similar to those available in Parma. *Musée Lorrain, Nancy* 2006.0.1846.   60

2.2 Callot: the firing squad, *c*.1633. Severe measures such as these were meted out in a punishment parade. They did little to stem desertion. *Musée Lorrain, Nancy* 2006.0.1856.   60

2.3 Piacenza city hospital, *c*.1750. *Biblioteca Comunale Passerini-Landi di Piacenza*, Ms Pallastrelli 162, vol.2, p.5.   76

3.1 Snayers, siege of Valenza in 1635. The painting depicts multiple episodes of the siege, flattening the topography and removing much of the vegetation at the top for clarity. The painter was working from sketches made by others. Parman quarters were at the top right. Note the French redoubts encroaching on the fortified perimetre, well-defended to stave off counter-attacks. The batteries fired from the rear. *Deutsches Historisches Museum, Berlin*, Gm 94/2.   98

3.2 Snayers, siege of Valenza (detail). Note the multitude of labourers moving earth or collecting materials to make fascines, with soldiers' huts in the background. *Deutsches Historisches Museum, Berlin*, Gm 94/2.   99

3.3 Snayers, detail, camp scenes at Valenza. Note the men excreting along the earthworks not far from the tents. It is doubtful European armies dug latrines. *Deutsches Historisches Museum, Berlin*, Gm 94/2.   100

3.4 Promiscuous culture Parmigiano. This lush landscape, stable in north-central Italy until after 1950, made it difficult to spot troop movements from afar. I.F. Ravenet "Vue topographique du Po, et des environs de Sissa", sanguine drawing, Raccolta di Mappe e Disegni vol.19/19, *Archivio di Stato Parma*.   102

xii *List of Figures, Tables, and Maps*

3.5 Parma: farmhouse with hayloft. Each of these numerous farms stocked precious supplies of fodder for horses and oxen. Raccolta di Mappe e Disegni, vol.66, 214-2, *Archivio di Stato Parma*. 103

3.6 Callot: the cavalry skirmish, c.1633. Squadrons of horse broke up on contact to permit close-quarter fighting until one or both sides disengaged to regroup. *Musée Lorrain, Nancy*, 2006.0.1847. 110

3.7 Callot: collecting deserters, c.1633. Troops herd captured deserters back to camp. Few would suffer severe punishment. *Musée Lorrain, Nancy* 2006.0.1853. 111

4.1 Merchants' seat in Piacenza, c.1750. Located at the edge of the city square. Merchants were among the principal victims of Odoardo's dreams of glory. *Biblioteca Comunale Passerini-Landi di Piacenza*, Ms Pallastrelli 162, vol.2, p.5. 131

4.2 Farnese palace in Piacenza, c.1750. The late 16th-century residence served as a refuge for the ducal couple, together with their military advisors. *Biblioteca Comunale Passerini-Landi di Piacenza*, vol.1, p.28. 131

4.3 Borgo Taro, c.1640. This is a fanciful depiction of the town fortifications. At the foot of a mountain, the town was almost defenseless against an enemy with large cannon. *Biblioteca Palatina Parma*, Ms Parm 3711, f.42. 153

5.1 Cover page, mortuary register. This pen-and-ink sketch serves as title-page to the parish burial register. The war's human toll is revealed here, in hundreds of entries concerning humble people. Parish of San Benedetto in Parma. 165

5.2 Callot: soldiers burning a village, c.1633; Note the armed villagers dug in around the church, daring the soldiers to come closer. *Musée Lorrain, Nancy* 2006.0.1851. 172

5.3 Cortemaggiore castle, c.1780. Castles like these would resist for days if the assailants lacked heavy artillery. Raccolta di Mappe e Disegni, *Archivio di Stato Parma*. 175

5.4 Callot, peasants ambushing soldiers, c.1633; Troops relied on local guides to lead them to hidden treasures, with predictable consequences. *Musée Lorrain, Nancy* 2006.0.1861. 184

5.5 Spanish blockade of Piacenza, late 1636. Spanish troops have erected batteries on the island in the Po across from the city, 24 dic. 1636. *Civica Raccolta delle Stampe Achille Bertarelli, Castello Sforzesco, Milan*. 185

5.6 Birds'-eye view of Castel San Giovanni, c.1900; Scene of a forgotten tragedy. Author's collection. 200

TABLES

2.1 Age of non-coms and ranks 61
2.2 Attrition levels in peacetime army 75
5.1 Mortality by parish in the 1630s 202

MAPS

1.1	Northern Italy in 1635	17
1.2	French and allied fortresses in northern Italy	28
2.1	French and foreign recruits	67
2.2	Recruitment in north-central Italy	68
2.3	Recruitment in southern Italy	69
2.4	Recruitment in Farnese territories	74
5.1	Castles occupied by Spanish troops	177
5.2	Rural mortality in the Farnese duchies	200

Introduction
The Other Thirty Years' War

A young Italian scholar once lamented to me that his compatriot colleagues would not take his military history project seriously.[1] Anyone working on military history must be somehow arrested in adolescence, they would object. What did he mean by that? In order to learn something about the state of military history in Italy, I visited the online website of a well-known publisher of the genre, Ermanno Albertelli.[2] There were, first of all, books with lurid cover illustrations, containing abundant colour drawings, and sometimes with sketched figures. A series of books on blade weapons and firearms, often in English, covered every period from antiquity to the present. Another series highlighted ships and aircraft, tanks and other war materiel used in Italian armed forces past and present, and those of other countries too. There was a rich list of Napoleonic titles, on weaponry, on uniforms, and a comic-book chronicle of his campaigns of Italy containing hundreds of drawings. Albertelli sold a disturbing number of titles dealing with the armed forces of Mussolini's Repubblica Sociale, and still others devoted to famous units of the Nazi SS. A rapid review of the titles on offer seemed to justify the critics, so far. There were also books on the great defeats of Italian armies, Custozza, Adowa, Caporetto, with no countervailing titles that might have shown the Italian armies in a better light. These last seemed to be true works of scholarship, judging from the description given on the website. There was one serious-looking book on the Napoleonic-era military encampment of Montechiari. The only other title I encountered for the early modern period, was a brief booklet on the Battle of Guastalla in 1734; according to the website its 46 pages contained, 'a very documented reconstruction of the event, which gives a perfect view of the manner of living, fighting and politicking in this period. It describes the routine of life in the army, the techniques of combat, the layout of the camps, and of military engineering.'[3] What these titles have in common is their appeal to people one might call military buffs, who are fairly numerous in Anglo-Saxon countries and in Britain in particular, where the best of them are a respected part of the academic world. British and American authors write traditional military history without complexes, probably because they have never experienced a fascist regime or suffered conquest and occupation. Many modern studies—I am thinking in particular of those of

---

[1] Maurizio Arfaioli is the author of a valuable study of early sixteenth-century soldiering, *The Black Bands of Giovanni: Infantry and Diplomacy during the Italian Wars (1526–1528)* (Pisa, 2005).
[2] See the Albertelli website at www.tuttostoria.it.
[3] Andrea Santangelo and Corrado Re, *Una battaglia per il trono della Polonia* (2003).

John Keegan and his imitators—are multidisciplinary and theoretically quite sophisticated, in the positive sense of that word.[4]

It is still widely thought in Italy that military history carries some unhealthy political baggage, a kind of crude militarism best kept on a short leash. Albertelli's catalogue gives some grounds for thinking this is true. However, there is at bottom a sophism:, that whoever studies the wars of the past, is an indiscriminate apologist for wars of the present or the future. Wars have shaped Italian history as much as any other country, beginning with the struggles of medieval city states to control their rural hinterlands and to carve out zones of influence. During the Habsburg domination of the sixteenth and seventeenth centuries, Italians continued to play important leadership roles in Flanders, in Hungary, in France, and throughout the Mediterranean.[5] Fascist authors once celebrated the protagonists of these struggles, and, because of this, the corporation of university historians went out of their way to ignore these figures. It is true that fascist propagandists wrote many egregious idiocies, but their claims were not false in each and all of their components. The upshot is that if critical minds ignore these periods and these questions, much of Italian history will remain in the shadows, or, worse, the vacuum will be filled by less scrupulous writers.

Military history has stagnated outside the main currents of modern historiography in most of the West, although those who deride its study often invoke ethical imperatives, which are irrelevant or even detrimental to historical understanding.[6] Still, no one could deny the institutional importance of armies, or that their organization constituted a legitimate area of investigation. Two pioneering works that shed much new light on the organization of early modern armies appeared in Germany and France in the 1960s.[7] They were soon followed by a number of British titles in the 1970s, led by the historian Geoffrey Parker, who explored the administrative and financial papers of the Spanish Habsburgs hitherto ignored by scholars. In their wake, Italians and Spaniards began to find military matters more interesting, and in recent years there has been an important revival of some kinds of military history in southern Europe.[8] There is still, in those countries, a strong taboo against what the French call '*histoire-bataille*'.[9] It is licit to study diplomacy,

---

[4] John Keegan, *The Face of Battle: A Study of Agincourt, Waterloo and the Somme* (New York and Harmondsworth, 1976), 54.

[5] For an overview of this important presence, and a periodization of its decline, see my book *The Twilight of a Military Tradition: Italian Aristocrats and European Conflicts, 1560–1800* (London and New York, 1998).

[6] Peter Paret, 'The Annales School and the history of war', *The Journal of Military History*, 73 (2009): 1289–94.

[7] André Corvisier, *L'Armée française de la fin du XVIIe siècle au ministère de Choiseul: le soldat*, 2 vols. (Paris, 1964); Fritz Redlich, *The German Military Enterpriser and his Work Force: A Study in European Economic and Social History*, 2 vols. (Wiesbaden, 1965).

[8] Piero del Negro, 'La Storia militare dell'Italia moderna nello specchio della storiografia del Novecento', *Cheiron*, 22 (1995): 11–33; Enrique Martinez-Ruiz, 'La eclosion de la historia militar', *Studia Historica, Historia Moderna*, 25, (2003): 17–25; Claudio Donati, 'Il "militare" nella storia dell'Italia moderna, dal Rinascimento all'età napoleonica', in *Eserciti e carriere militari nell'Italia moderna*, ed. C. Donati (Milan, 1998), 7–40.

[9] Enrique Martinez-Ruiz, 'La eclosion de la historia militar'.

military institutions, finance and provisioning, the careers of officers and so on, but on the '*guerra guerreggiata*' of early modern times there has been close to nothing written in the past half-century. Most recent titles on Italy reveal both the virtues and the defects of Italian historiography: they promote the close study of archival documents (mostly administrative), but authors usually study international issues through a strictly local lens.

The unfortunate consequence of the state of infancy of Italian military history is that we lack even a basic history of the Thirty Years' War in Italy. This 'other' Thirty Years' War has been historically neglected in general narratives, and no author has ever attempted to synthesize the conflict and its impact on the peninsula.[10] This is astonishing given its status as the most important event in Italian history between the Council of Trent and the French Revolution. The interminable war conditioned the steep decline of the entire country's urban manufactures and prepared the way for the plague pandemics of 1630 and 1656. War, and the urgent need for men and money, undermined the royal state in the Mezzogiorno (southern Italy) and enhanced the absolute rule of the other Italian princes, but it simultaneously reduced them to the level of minor satellites of the great powers. For all we know, the war might have been responsible for a marked shift of landed property to the aristocracy and the Church, and it might also have led to a durable decline in the living standards of a population that was increasingly rural and polarized between rich and poor. All of these themes are crucial to a basic understanding of early modern Italy, but have never been systematically explored. A complete history of the war should probably begin in 1613 with the first challenge to the House of Austria by the ambitious House of Savoy, and conclude with the Peace of the Pyrenees in 1659, almost a half-century of conflict that was intermittently fought over most of the peninsula and the islands, but which became entrenched (literally) in Piedmont and Lombardy. A proper history of Italy at war would have to combine the papers of all the capitals of Italy with the reports sent to foreign sovereigns and conserved today at Paris, Simancas, and Vienna. Peter H. Wilson points to the ways one might intermix military and diplomatic history with the subjective vision of the phenomenon derived from its witnesses and its participants. To do that, we would have to unearth from the archives the private letters and the hundreds of chronicles of Italians who described what they saw. We would have to examine the paintings commissioned by generals to document their exploits, and include the ex-voto images, still hanging in rural or urban sanctuaries, left by soldiers and civilians who were thankful for having escaped some great peril. And, above all, we would have to measure the local impact of the war by studying closely the surviving

---

[10] Carla Sodini, 'L'Italie et la Guerre de Trente Ans', in *Nouveaux regards sur la guerre de Trente Ans*, ed. Philippe Bonnichon (Vincennes, 1998), 37–56; Robert Oresko and David Parrott, 'Reichsitalien and the Thirty Years War' in *1648: War and Peace in Europe*, ed. K. Bussmann and H. Schilling, 2 vols. (Munster-Osnabruck, 1998), vol. 1, 141–60; Peter H. Wilson's recent magisterial narrative account of the great war only briefly alludes to fighting in Italy, *Europe's Tragedy: A History of the Thirty Years War* (London, 2009).

parish registers, which, for the most part, remain dispersed in thousands of individual churches.[11]

Since we are nowhere close to having the materials necessary to write a synthesis of the Thirty Years' War in Italy as Peter H. Wilson has recently done for Germany, in this book I will commit the same offence I deplore on the page above, that is, examining it locally. However, *this* local study will attempt to examine *in piccolo* the big picture as ascertained from multiple points of view. The experiences of Duke Odoardo Farnese of Parma are our window onto turbulent times. The young duke's misadventures span fewer than five years of the long Thirty Years' War in Italy, but, as other historians have already noticed, war derives much of its significance from its interaction with other spheres, like politics and diplomacy, economics and social stratification.[12] It is opportune to adopt the view from one of the mid-sized Italian principalities. They were not quite sovereign, but rather '*soprani*' in the nice term of the seventeenth-century political scientist Gregorio Leti. Italian princes and the leaders of adjacent republics were all mindful of Spanish and French power, and of the ambiguous status of the Catholic Church in the peninsula. While analysing the impact of the war on Italian history, it is fitting that, from time to time, a historian should recount afresh the great events that beset the peninsula during this era, for they are not well known among modern Italians, and still less so among non-Italians. Therefore, this book will proceed through narrative to describe the political and military context of the 1630s, and will halt occasionally to explain particular phenomena in short vignettes.

Of course, it is unfair as well as inaccurate to present the period in Italy as a tabula rasa. We know that the wars in Italy never caused the terrible effects on the population that we see in Germany, but it remains true that the country's overall population declined by about 15 per cent over its duration. We know nothing about the demographic impact of the war in the zones where it was fought, although the work of Guido Alfani has given us some solid reference points for the beginning of the crisis.[13] We will need to learn how people died in the war, as well as how many. John Keegan, who has rehabilitated the importance of campaign or battle history more than anyone, has deplored the weight of tradition in describing war, which often descends into a 'pornography of violence'. We know that there were not, in Italy, great battles engaging tens of thousands of combatants on each side, as in Germany, so it is easy to avoid the typical vices of that genre.[14] But we still know very little about how operations unfolded on the terrain. These seem to have been dominated by skirmishes and engagements involving only parts of the

---

[11] Peter H. Wilson, 'New perspectives on the Thirty Years War', *German History*, 23 (2005): 237–61; also David A. Meier, 'An appeal for a historiographical Renaissance: lost lives and the Thirty Years' War', *The Historian*, 67 (2005): 254–74.

[12] Jeremy Black, *War in European History 1494–1660* (Washington, DC, 2006), 9.

[13] Guido Alfani, *Il Grand Tour dei Cavalieri dell'Apocalisse: L'Italia del 'lungo Cinquecento' (1494–1629)* (Venice, 2010).

[14] Keegan, *The Face of Battle*, pp. 28–9; Yves-Marie Bercé, 'Les guerres dans l'Italie du XVIIe siècle', in *L'Italie au XVIIe siècle*, ed. Yves-Marie Bercé, Jean-Claude Waquet, Jean-Michel Sallmann, and Gérard Delille (Paris, 1989), 311–31.

field army. We know very little about how those battles were fought, notwithstanding half a century of debate on the military revolution of the seventeenth century.[15] There were, on the one hand, few large-scale sieges, but, on the other, there were countless small-scale operations against towns and castles. We know that many fortified cities contained large garrisons, sometimes for many years; but we do not know much about the interaction of garrison soldiers with civilians or their degree of integration.[16] Notwithstanding some very suggestive pages by Geoffrey Parker and David Parrott, we are still at an early stage of discovering something about the composition of armies in Europe, both with regard to the aristocracy who commanded it at various levels, and to the rank and file.[17] Studies elsewhere on the Thirty Years' War in Europe have revealed that both civilians and soldiers understood that they were bound by a set of 'rules' observed, most of the time, by both sides.[18] These rules tended to limit the scale of devastation, but nobody has ever taken the measure of the damage done to Italy during the great struggle.[19] The war demanded much of the loyalty of the subjects of Italian and foreign princes, but we yet know little or nothing about the enthusiasm or reluctance of subjects to make sacrifices for their rulers. The most recent generation of Italian historians, of whom Davide Maffi is perhaps the most important exponent, is starting to make inroads into these important issues.[20]

The scale of our ignorance makes the contents of the Archivio di Stato in Parma more exciting. It contains, first and foremost, about seventy company rosters in the collection of the *Collatereria Generale*, indicating the names, the place of origin, the age, the physical description, and usually even the destiny of more than 13,000 soldiers. The books are almost complete for the army of 1635. To my knowledge, this is the most comprehensive collection of rosters anywhere in Europe before the eighteenth century. Minutes after I examined these on a recommendation by Mario Zannoni, I was ready to drop all other projects and write this book, in part through an understandable fear that they would be discovered by some other, likely British, historian. These rosters are complemented by a wide variety of internal reports, ranging from work on fortifications, to finance, to army administration,

---

[15] Luciano Pezzolo, 'La "Revoluzione militare": Una prospettiva italiana 1400–1700', in *Militari in età moderna: la centralità di un tema di confine*, ed. A. Dattero and S. Levati (Milan, 2006), 15–64.

[16] This has been explored in Spanish Galicia, and an account of it is contained in the article by Enrique Martinez-Ruiz, 'La eclosion de la historia militar'.

[17] Geoffrey Parker, 'The universal soldier', in *The Thirty Years War*, ed. Geoffrey Parker et al. (London, 1984), 191–208. More detailed work on the Spanish army can be found in articles by Antonio Espino Lopez, 'La historiografia hispana sobre la Guerra en la epoca de los Austrias: Un balance, 1991–2000', *Manuscrits*, 21 (2003): 161–91; and Lorraine White, 'Spain's early modern soldiers: origins, motivations and loyalty', *War and Society*, 19 (2001): 19–46.

[18] Barbara Donagan, *War in England 1642–1649* (Oxford and New York, 2008); also Trintje Helfferich and Paul Sonnino, 'Civilians in the Thirty Years War', in *Daily Lives of Civilians in Wartime Europe, 1618–1900*, ed. L. S. Frey and M. L. Frey (Westport, CT, and London, 2007), 23–58.

[19] Some of these problems are developed in the yet-unpublished doctoral thesis of Giovanni Cerino Badone, 'Le Seconde Guerre d'Italia (1588–1659): Storiografia, Temi, Fonti' (Università degli Studi del Piemonte Orientale, 2012).

[20] Davide Maffi, *Il baluardo della corona: Guerra, esercito, finanze e società nella Lombardia seicentesca (1630–1660)* (Florence, 2007).

and even drill manuals. In historical research, as in police work, one thing usually leads to another. I have consulted the surviving dispatches between the Duke of Parma and the French court, as well as the correspondence between the French ambassador to the Italian theatre of war and Cardinal Richelieu, which also contain reports from the field commanders and junior diplomats. Similar correspondence exists on the Spanish side, that is, reports from the governor of Milan and his principal collaborators to Madrid, which are conserved in the archives in Simancas, and copies of which were made available to me by Mario Rizzo in Pavia. We have a number of precious chronicles from Parma and Piacenza, but also from the cities on the Spanish side, like Valenza and Alessandria. Other shorter chronicles come from the towns and villages on both sides that bore the weight of the troop lodgings. The parish registers available from the dioceses of Parma and Piacenza make it possible to study the impact of the war across a large number of towns and villages during and immediately after the conflict. A detailed census from Parma helps us determine the social background of the local soldiery, and a hospital register for Piacenza depicts the care given to sick and wounded soldiers. We have an excellent and very detailed biography of Duke Odoardo himself by a well-informed courtier and participant. I have consulted published accounts not only by local contemporaries eager to leave a close account of the event, but also the analyses fashioned by a generation of talented seventeenth-century historians who spanned the entire spectrum of political allegiance. To sum up, few accounts of the Thirty Years' War are as well-documented and as well-rounded as this one. What follows will incite other historians, I hope, to widen the research on this crucial era of Italian and European history. That way, someone will be able to write the missing synthesis on Italy during the Thirty Years' War.

1

The Moth and the Flame

THE FARNESE GRAN GIUSTIZIA OF 1612

On the morning of Saturday 19 May 1612, Parma's great bell, whose tolling marked every capital execution, began to ring in the city square. In the days preceding carpenters had erected a high platform onto which the reluctant principals of the ceremony could be brought out of the tall windows of the tribunal palace. Three blocks were fixed on the platform, and a little parapet along one side prevented the victims from seeing the spectacle of the preceding earlier beheadings and the headless corpses. Along the front edge of the stage workers set eight spikes onto which the heads of the victims would be planted one after another. In the square below workmen erected a gallows with three emplacements and nooses. Duke Ranuccio's chief functionaries arranged that several hundred infantry soldiers blocked all four entrances into the great piazza, while a company of mounted arquebusiers from Piacenza were deployed in the square itself. The supporting cast, the horse guards (*cavalleggieri*) and the company of ducal archers under their officers, then took their places around the stage. At ten hours after sunrise the *sbirri* or police bullies began to strong-arm the doomed principals convicted of plotting to kill the duke through the window of the courthouse, the first being Barbara Sanvitale, Countess of Colorno and erstwhile mistress of Duke Vincenzo of Mantua. Without saying anything her attendants made her kneel at the first block and one of the two executioners quickly struck off her head. She was followed to the block by her husband, Count Orazio Simonetta, and then by her son, Girolamo Sanvitale, and finally by five other members of leading houses of Parma. The executioner then hanged three non-noble accomplices in the plot on the gallows nearby. At the end of the bloody spectacle, a Jesuit, Father Albrizzi, climbed a ladder next to the gallows and exhorted the people standing in the square and pressed up against the windows to obey their prince. The executioner's helpers removed the naked bodies one by one for burial in the nearby chapel of San Giovanni Decollato, sepulchre of executed criminals. The day's eleven victims were not the last. Ducal magistrates watched the hanging of two ecclesiastics involved in the alleged plot against the duke's life in the same square later, on 11 August. Another suspect, Count Teodoro Scotti, died as a result of excessive torture without confessing. Duke Ranuccio spared the lives two more aristocratic suspects, Benedetta Pio and Girolamo da Correggio, but let them languish for years in the palace dungeon. About 20 other persons, mostly noble, remained in prison without being tried, and hundreds of other nobles their followers were subjected to secret surveillance.[1]

Arnaldo Barilli, who was one of the few historians to examine all the papers extant from the trial, including those moved to Naples in the eighteenth century, concluded that the spectacle thereafter known as the Gran Giustizia looked very much like judicial murder, hatched by Ranuccio himself and his unscrupulous secretary and right-hand man Bartolomeo Riva. In exchange for money and favours, some of the witnesses perjured themselves. Riva transferred far from Parma lawyers for the defendants and the confessors assigned to the prisoners. Magistrates subjected the accused to unlawful torture lasting hours in order to extract confessions from them. Most European states (including Britain and France) practiced similar judicial murder in the early modern period, though never on this scale, for desperate measures such as this were fraught with uncertainties. The duke skilfully presented the Gran Giustizia of 1612 as the last-minute thwarting of an attempt against his life by unpopular feudatories, who began to be arrested in June of the previous year. For good measure the judges variably charged them with theft, witchcraft, rape, sodomy, and incest.[2] The duke confiscated the considerable properties of his victims and added them to the Farnese dynastic assets, whose patrimonial revenues were *quadrupled* thereby.

This spectacular and noisy event, which provoked criticism from many quarters in Italy, drew much of its context from the dynastic weakness of the House of Farnese. Ranuccio had married a papal niece, Margherita Aldobrandini, in 1600, but she had not borne an heir to the throne. The duke sired a bastard boy, Ottavio, who he legitimized shortly afterwards, by the daughter of a judicial official. In the absence of legitimate heirs Ottavio was groomed for succession, but it was unlikely that the Pope would have consented to such a thing; he would probably use this as a pretext to extinguish the principality and reincorporate it into the Papal States governed from Rome. Pope Clement VIII Aldobrandini had ejected the Este dynasty from Ferrara and occupied the city in 1598 for that very reason. The first Farnese duke, Pier Luigi, was the legitimized bastard of Pope Paul III, and his son and heir, Duke Ottavio married Emperor Charles V's bastard daughter, Margherita of Austria. The Farnese were interlopers in Parma and Piacenza, never quite legitimate in the eyes of their subjects. Nobles in Parma were heard to grumble that these Farnese bastards were not the descendants of ancient and illustrious lineages like their own. Duke Ranuccio had been ruling the Farnese duchy for 20 years and had been married for over ten, but still lacked a son and legitimate heir. Duchess Margherita Aldobrandini finally bore him a son in 1610, baptized Alessandro, but the parents quickly discovered that he was deaf–mute and incapable of inheriting

---

[1] For a description of the event, see Biblioteca Palatina Parma (hereafter BPPr) Ms Parmense 1558, '*Memorie antiche della città di Parma*', an anonymous chronicle, 17th century, f.41; for modern analysis, Gian Luca Podestà, 'Dal delitto politico alla politica del delitto (Parma, 1545–1611)', in *Complots et conjurations dans l'Europe moderne*, ed. Y.-M. Bercé and E Fasano Guarini (Rome, 1996), 679–720; Romano Canosa, *I Segreti dei Farnese* (Rome, 2001), 202–16.

[2] Arnaldo Barilli, 'La congiura di Parma del 1611 e le confessioni dei congiurati', *Archivio Storico per le Province Parmensi*, series 3 vol. 1 (1936): 105–50.

the throne. Only on 28 April 1612, with the birth of a second son, Odoardo, three weeks before the bloody executions in the city square, did Ranuccio have a possible alternate heir. Still, for some years afterwards, worthy friars subjected poor Alessandro to exorcisms and other trying ceremonies intent on casting off his affliction.[3]

The feudal nobility as a social class was still formidable in late Renaissance northern Italy not only by virtue of the country fiefs over which they held sway, but by their urban preponderance too. Before the arrival of the Farnese, Piacenza's four principal houses—the Anguissola, Landi, Scotti, and Fontana—formed competing 'teams' of city councillors and virtually blocked access to the levers of municipal government from wealthy families not in their sway. Urban feudatories often formed political consortia that diverted the public revenues into their family coffers, and they held great influence over urban assemblies for centuries after papal governors introduced reforms in 1535 to reduce their power. The papal reforms opened up access to representation by other families in the assembly in a timid way, but the teams of noblemen persisted and their patronyms continued to dominate city government for generations.[4] The Farnese interfered with the mechanisms of these municipal institutions in Parma and Piacenza and increasingly ruled by decree and favour, in order to curtail the traditional autonomy of urban elites. The same families dominating the city assemblies also held multiple fiefs in the rural hinterland of each of the cities, ruling them like statelets from the shadow of their strong castles. The first duke, Pier Luigi, challenged aristocratic political and social preponderance head-on with his customary brutality. The thick new walls and bastions of Piacenza, his capital, prevented the city's capture by outside powers. Pier Luigi placed his confidence in a great citadel, which he commenced on the model of the Medici stronghold erected in Florence in 1545.[5] Citadels were powerful fortresses built on the edge of a city, not with the aim of protecting it from an external enemy, but rather as a means of allowing a fairly small number of soldiers in the prince's pay to control the town and arrest troublemakers with impunity. To erect his in record time, Pier Luigi mobilized men and animals amongst the peasantry through violent and forcible methods that deeply alienated both high-born and low-born subjects.[6] The project entailed tearing down churches, monasteries, and private houses to clear space for the fortress and its field of fire, and, in the meantime, the duke lodged unruly soldiers in the dwellings of private citizens. Pier Luigi also ordered the compilation of a new cadastre that would serve as the basis for an unprecedented level of direct taxation. After months of patient plotting, members

---

[3] Ugo Benassi, 'I Natali e l'educazione del duca Odoardo Farnese', *Archivio Storico per le province Parmensi*, 9 (1909): 99–227.

[4] W. Cesarini-Sforza, 'Il consiglio generale e le classi cittadine in Piacenza nel secolo XVI', *Bollettino Storico Piacentino*, 5 (1910): 71–82.

[5] Nicola Soldini, 'Strategie del Dominio: la Cittadella nuova di Piacenza (1545–1556)', *Bollettino Storico Piacentino*, 86 (1991): 11–69; Letizia Arcangeli, 'Feudatari e duca negli stati farnesiani (1545–1587)', in *Il Rinascimento nelle corti padane: Società e cultura*, ed. Paolo Rossi (Bari, 1977), 77–96.

[6] Biblioteca Comunale Passerini-Landi di Piacenza (henceforth BCPLPc) Ms Pallastrelli 162, D. Giulio Gandini, 'Compendio Storico di Piacenza' (post-1750), 28.

of the leading noble houses of Piacenza, the Anguissola, Landi, and Pallavicino, turned on the prince and his guards in a savage ambush on 10 September 1547. The plotters had previously obtained permission to proceed from the Spanish governor of Milan, Ferrante Gonzaga, who rushed into the city with his pre-deployed troops on the pretext of restoring order. The emperor, Charles V, completed the citadel and his son Philip II kept it firmly in hand until 1585.[7]

Having lost Piacenza, Duke Ottavio, Pier Luigi's son, kept Parma and its duchy against both the Habsburg emperor and the Pope in 1555, but only with French military assistance. He then rallied to the Spanish alliance to recover Piacenza too by the Treaty of Ghent the following year. His long reign (1547–86) witnessed a slow conflict of attrition against the powers that would have ejected the Farnese dynasty from northern Italy. Ottavio was justifiably wary of plots against his house, and he used fair means and foul to usurp the lands of the leading feudatories, the Pallavicino and the Landi. Duke Ottavio seized all of the Pallavicino fiefs south of the Po, and the last autonomous duke, Alessandro Pallavicino, was put in chains at his capital Busseto and carted off to the dungeon fortress of the Rocchetta in Parma in 1587.[8] Claudio Landi, a leading force behind the assassination plot against Duke Pier Luigi, obtained the mountain fief of Borgo Taro from the emperor in 1547 in order to consolidate his presence outside Piacenza. When his vassals rebelled against him there in 1578, Duke Ottavio marched soldiers and cannon into the town and annexed it to Farnese territories. Claudio Landi lost no time in preparing his revenge with the help of other feudatories in Piacenza, but the duke's men uncovered the plot and five aristocrats—an Anguissola, a Scotti, a Volpe, and two Landi—were subsequently decapitated in Parma in 1580.[9] Ottavio could not rule against the nobility by force alone, however, for the number of paid soldiers in the duchy of Parma was very small. The Farnese employed only about 400 men, who were more like security guards than professional soldiers; of these, they posted 89 to Borgo Taro, 137 to Parma, and 243 to Piacenza, with a mere 13 German guards remaining for the person of the duke.[10] However, a newly established peasant militia enabled Duke Ottavio to overpower non-cooperative feudatories who were disinclined to marry his bastards or attend his court. All the castles and fortified places belonging to these feudatories had to be placed at the duke's disposal when needed, and a few strategically situated strongholds like Montechiarugolo became Farnese fiefs.[11] In the plain, Ottavio forced feudal courts to give up the

---

[7] Emilio Ottolenghi, *Storia di Piacenza, dalle origini sino all'anno 1918* (Piacenza, n.d.), 60–76.

[8] Vito Ghizzoni, 'Sorprusi dei Farnese ai danni dei Pallavicino nella seconda metà del '500', *Archivio Storico per le Province Parmensi*, 19 (1967): 149–61.

[9] Riccardo De Rosa, 'La congiura di Claudio Landi contro i Farnese e i suoi riflessi sulla questione di Borgo Val di Taro', *Bollettino Storico Piacentino*, 97 (2002): 131–50.

[10] Marzio Achille Romani, 'Finanza pubblica e potere politico: il caso dei Farnese (1545–1593)', in *Le Corti farnesiane di Parma e Piacenza (1545–1622)*, ed. Marzio A. Romani, vol. 1 (Rome, 1978), 3–85.

[11] Letizia Arcangeli, 'Giurisdizioni feudali e organizzazione territoriale nel Ducato di Parma (1545–1587)', *Le Corti farnesiane di Parma e Piacenza (1545–1622)*, ed. M. A. Romani, vol. 1 (Rome, 1978), 91–148; Pietro Castignoli, 'Caratteri della feudalità nel ducato di Parma durante il secolo XVII', *Archivio Storico per le Province Parmensi*, 18 (1966): 317–24; Arcangeli, 'Feudatari e duca negli', 77–96.

most serious crimes to the jurisdiction of ducal judges, and in key fiefs he had the right of veto over local magistrates. In the late sixteenth century, about two thirds of the duchy was still in the hands of feudatories jealous of their autonomy, and ducal functionaries were still quite rare in the periphery. The governor of Parma, who headed the ducal administration, appointed about 150 judges and local *podestà* and constables throughout the city's surrounding territory in 1589.

While Duke Ottavio recovered Piacenza (but not the control over its citadel) through an agreement with Philip II in 1556, he still had little property he could call his own with respect to the great families, whom he had to treat tactfully when force would not work. European princes customarily raised their profile with respect to feudatories and urban elites by establishing opulent courts that would place members of high-ranking families on public view and in positions of responsibility. Whenever Ottavio was able to recover a fief, for whatever reason, he decided to award it to a new recipient, generally from among the circle of his closest collaborators. Ottavio's court was relatively modest and some of the feudatories, like the opulent counts Rossi of San Secondo, lords over multiple fiefs, opted to live in the countryside or even Milan. There was no ducal palace in Parma, the principal seat after 1547, but Ottavio eventually moved from the bishop's palace to a large house with a great garden, inside the city ramparts. The transformation of the medieval castle in Piacenza near the Po into a proper palace did not begin in earnest until 1589, and it was Margherita's project, not Ottavio's, for she could not bear to reside with her relatively low-born, pleasure-seeking husband after her return from Flanders, where she managed that troubled province as governor-general.

Ottavio's only legitimate son, by virtue of his marriage with Margherita of Austria, was a nephew of King Philip II of Spain. A hero of the great Battle of Lepanto against the Turks in 1571 at the tender age of 16, Alessandro Farnese became the most successful general of his age, appointed commander-in-chief of the Spanish army of Flanders after 1579, until his death in 1592. He came tantalizingly close to quelling the great rebellion in the Netherlands in 1587, before King Philip ordered him to divert his efforts against England, and then France. Alessandro succeeded to the throne of Parma at his father's death in 1586, but left its administration in the hands of his son, Ranuccio.

Farnese success in rallying their new vassals owed much to a policy of not taxing their subjects proportionately to their wealth, and by leaning heavily upon the original Farnese fiefs in the Papal States and the kingdom of Naples in order to provide revenue for Parma and Piacenza. They pressed those faraway vassals for more taxes wherever they were feudal lords, and they purchased territories inside Emilia and elsewhere in Italy to increase their patrimonial revenues, as opposed to public tax receipts. Ranuccio launched the first great '*estimi*' or fiscal assessments used as a basis for direct taxation that drew revenue not only from land but from business capital too.[12] Duke Alessandro and his son Ranuccio supervised the

---

[12] Paola Subacchi, 'L'imposizione fiscale in età farnesiana: formazione degli estimi piacentini', *Archivio Storico per le Province Parmensi*, ser. 4, 44 (1992): 151–73.

construction of the citadel of Parma, which they astutely presented as a relief project for the poor of the town and countryside during the great famine of 1590–1. Much of the new revenue they spent on their court, which, with 226 officeholders in 1593, was fairly small by Italian ducal standards. Court employment was a worthwhile objective for an up-and-coming city notable, and the gentlemen receiving stipends there constituted the flower of the local aristocracy.[13]

Numerous nobles of Parma and Piacenza followed Alessandro Farnese in a generation of military expeditions under the aegis of Spain, first at Lepanto (1571) and then in Flanders (1572–1609). They were not so much officers holding long-term commissions rewarded with gradual promotion, as warriors attaching themselves as clients to the commander-in-chief and serving until incapacity or other interests motivated them to return home. They expected that a grateful prince would reward their service as soon as an opportunity arose. The Farnese continued to pursue projects that would vault them still higher in the hierarchy of princes, knowing that their neglect of this ambition might place them at a disadvantage with respect to other dynasties like the Medici, the Este, or the Gonzaga. Higher status enabled them to make more prestigious marriages and be treated with greater consideration in other courts in Europe.[14] Alessandro, for example, was a candidate to the throne of Poland in 1587. Between 1608 and 1614 Ranuccio, like his rival Italian dukes, listened to projects that promised to make him King of Albania, but he understood that he must first obtain consent from Philip III of Spain.[15]

Italy's great fortune in the later sixteenth century was that religious strife in France, beginning in 1561, forced the latter's monarchs to postpone their ambitions of conquest in the peninsula. Spain had already acquired the upper hand under Emperor Charles V, but Philip II was mindful to guarantee the existing social orders and respect local customs and institutions throughout Italy.[16] The Catholic kings, as the Spanish monarchs were called, distributed garrisons to hold secure the most strategic locations. Given the King of Spain's concern for peace and quiet in the peninsula, and his unrelenting crusade against the Turks and Protestants abroad, princes and feudatories saw him in a mostly positive light. The Farnese spent much of their revenues in the furtherance of the Spanish interest, but this was not a mark of altruistic devotion to higher values. All the princes operated towards the furtherance of their own interests, which included the hopes of expansion against their smaller neighbours, or at least in the maintenance of the balance of power and the preservation of their estates.[17] The Italian political system lacked

[13] Romani, 'Finanza pubblica e potere politico', 3–85.
[14] Daniela Frigo, ' "Small states" and diplomacy: Mantua and Modena', in *Politics and Diplomacy in Early Modern Italy: The Structure of Diplomatic Practice 1450–1800*, ed. Daniela Frigo (Cambridge, 2000), 147–75.
[15] Arnaldo Barilli, 'La candidatura di un duca di Parma al trono d'Albania', *Aurea Parma*, 3 (1915): 11–24.
[16] Giovanni Muto, 'Noble presence and stratification in the territories of Spanish Italy', in *Spain in Italy: Politics, Society and Religion 1500–1700*, ed. T. J. Dandelet and J. A. Marino (Leiden, 2007), 251–97.
[17] Gualdo Priorato, *Il guerriero prudente e politico* (Venezia and Bologna, 1641), ed. Angelo Tamborra (Naples, 2002), 39.

a recognized higher power that served as a final appeal in disputes between autonomous states, a role played by the emperor in Germany both before and after the Thirty Years' War. The Spanish peace therefore put an end to centuries-old infighting among Italian principalities and republics that previous leagues and global peace agreements among the principal territorial states had been unable to achieve.[18] By the early seventeenth century, Italy only contained 11 superior states (most of which were not technically *sovereign*—that is, free of higher authorities), and 18 smaller ones, which were equal in rights to the large ones. These all enjoyed the ability to issue money, fashion laws, create officials, administer justice and pardons, and make war and peace.[19] These republics and princes could award titles and honours to notable families on their own authority, in order to gratify the nobility. Italian princes like the Farnese, the Gonzaga, and the Medici became Philip's most prestigious clients, who could be gratified with Imperial fiefs in northern Italy or with Spanish fiefs located in the kingdom of Naples when they became vacant. The king favoured the consolidation of those states most closely allied with him, and would protect them from any encroachment by their neighbours, but he would not allow one state to grow at the expense of another.[20] Spain offered recruiting subsidies, advantageous marriages, titles, honours, and other pensions to keep the princes happy, but also remembered to gratify members of other leading families in all the key cities. One favoured instrument was the collar of the Golden Fleece, which admitted the beneficiary to an exclusive club of Catholic princes and dignitaries: another honour was the title of Grandee of Spain. Both of these gifts gave princes and important feudatories precedence and privileges at the Spanish court. Philip II awarded the Golden Fleece to Alessandro Farnese in recognition of his stellar services in the Low Countries theatre, and, simultaneously, authorized his father, Duke Ottavio to recover control over the citadel of Piacenza. King Philip III held out the same collar to Ranuccio I, after the prince participated in an aborted attack on Algiers in the company of 200 noble subjects from his territories, in 1601.[21]

---

[18] Riccardo Fubini, 'Aux origines de la balance des pouvoirs: le système politique en Italie au XVe siècle', in *L'Europe des Traités de Westphalie: Esprit de la diplomatie et diplomatie de l'esprit*, ed. Lucien Bély (Paris: 2000), 111–22.

[19] The superior princes were the Pope, the King of Spain, the Grand Duke of Tuscany, the Duke of Savoy, the Duke of Mantua, the Duke of Parma, the Duke of Modena, the republics of Venice, Genoa, and Lucca, and the Prince Bishop of Trent; the minor princes in 1675, when Italy's foremost political scientist, Gregorio Leti, was writing were the Vizzini dukes of Bracciano, the Chigi Princes of Farnese, the Colonna Princes of Pagliano, and the Barberini princes of Palestrina in Lazio; the Ludovisi princes of Piombino in Tuscany; the Pico dukes of Mirandola, the Gonzaga dukes of Novellara and the Gonzaga dukes of Guastalla, and the Aldobrandini marchesi of Meldola, all in Emilia; the Doria marchesi of Torreglia, Bardi, and Compiano; the Cibo marchesi of Massa Carrara and the Grimaldi princes of Monaco in Liguria (this last family still reigning today); the Gonzaga Marchesi di Castiglione, the Gonzaga princes of Bozzolo, and the Medina Las Torres princes of Sabbioneta in Lombardy; the Ferreri princes of Masserano in Piedmont, and finally the Republic of San Marino in the Marches (which also survives).

[20] Angelantonio Spagnoletti, *Principi italiani e Spagna nell'età barocca* (Milan, 1996), 10–12.

[21] Giovanni Drei, *I Farnese: Grandezza e decadenza di una dinastia italiana* (Rome, 1954), 175.

Secure in the Pax Hispanica, Italian states flourished and prospered as never before in an atmosphere of *peaceful* rivalry. The absence of a French threat enabled governments to invest a sort of 'peace dividend' in productive enterprises and prestigious embellishment. As much as any other prince in his time, Duke Ranuccio I displayed some remarkable administrative gifts during the 30 years of his rule. Most of these benefited Parma in particular, which the dynasty elected as its principal capital over Piacenza. In addition to the large residence Ottavio built in the gardens adjacent to the north wall, Ranuccio transformed the old Visconti fortress and Rocchetta prison on the Parma river into a proper palace, the Pilotta. The complex became the public stage for a modern court, with its many specialized officials and its exclusive festivities revolving around the prince and his family. In 1618 the Farnese transformed the great hall, built originally to display weapons and practice using them, into one of Europe's great baroque theatres. Duke Ottavio and then Ranuccio established three Jesuit-run educational institutions for the benefit of the upper and upper-middle classes—a college dispensing secondary education in Latin, another adjacent college for the formation of noblemen, and a proper university with its own medical school. The dynasty spent lavishly on urban churches and convents in its active patronage both in the city and its hinterland. Late sixteenth and early seventeenth-century Parma was a busy building site with multiple military, civil, and ecclesiastical monuments that ornament the townscape today. Largely as a result of the assassination of Duke Pier Luigi, Piacenza remained the second city of the duchy despite its superior size and industriousness relative to Parma. There, work continued for several decades on Margherita of Austria's palace near the Po river, but ceased when the edifice was still only one-third of its projected size. The city's compensation for the loss of political status came principally from a quarterly fair of international bankers, most of whom hailed from northern Italy. Vast sums of credits and debits circulated there among the participants, along guidelines established by the principal bankers of Genoa, whose loans and investments bankrolled the entire Spanish Empire. At their height around 1610, the fairs of Piacenza were probably the single most important financial forum in the world.[22]

In the weeks leading up to the Gran Giustizia in May 1612, and immediately before the birth of Prince Odoardo, Ranuccio decided to embellish Piacenza with a more symbolic display of Farnese prowess, in the form of a pair of equestrian bronze statues planted in the city's main square before the medieval town hall: one of his illustrious father, and another of himself, both bedecked with the Golden Fleece. The technology for creating large bronze statues was still in its infancy and the statues had already cost a great deal by the time the first one, that of himself, was unveiled with a great display of martial pomp and ceremony in 1620.[23] Well-drilled soldiery celebrated the military virtues of the dynasty, and their movements

---

[22] Fernand Braudel, *The Mediterranean and the Mediterranean World in the Age of Philip II* (New York, 1967), vol. 1, 504–9.

[23] BCPLPc, Ms Pallastrelli 313, 'Relatione delle allegrezze fatte... nel discoperte la Statua di bronzo da essa città (1620)'.

were said to delight the thousands of citizens and invited dignitaries who were present. The cardinal regent Odoardo Farnese, Ranuccio's younger brother, finally erected Duke Alessandro's statue, adjacent to it, in 1625.[24]

Ranuccio died suddenly of a heart attack on 5 March 1622, at the age of 53. His contemporaries considered him a politician of no little acumen, able to elicit the respect, if not affection, of his subjects with his concern for justice, his liberality towards the poor, and his generosity towards men of letters. He was especially munificent towards the clergy and its two leading orders, the learned Jesuits and the more theatrical, threadbare Capuchin friars. In the opinion of contemporaries, Ranuccio was severe towards the nobility in order to repress their *prepotenza* (arrogant and high-handed behaviour) towards the lower classes, and was inclined to punish them without respite.[25] But as partial compensation for this severity, he increased the size of his court to more than 350 people on the public payroll by the time of his death, and began to distribute patents of nobility to loyal families of the city elites of both Parma and Piacenza, totalling 50 such promotions between 1596 and 1620. The duke reserved the most prestigious and lavishly remunerated honours for the closely watched feudatories.[26] Another aspect of Ranuccio's legacy was more crassly pecuniary, in the form of a vast wealth of property and furnishings valued at 5 ½ million scudi (30 or 40 scudi was a typical revenue for a peasant family in the seventeenth century). Another 800,000 scudi, which translated into almost 6 million lire, equal to over a year's tax revenue, filled a great chest locked away in the Rocchetta palace dungeon, guarded by Swiss mercenaries.[27] Cardinal Odoardo Farnese took the reins of power until Ranuccio's son, Odoardo, came of age. Like his brother, Cardinal Odoardo was a conscientious administrator well versed in the arts of government. The regent removed the surveillance bearing on the feudatories with the death of his suspicious brother Ranuccio, but he still expected its members to turn out at dynastic functions, and he created special martial companies of gentlemen for ceremonial purposes. The Farnese also continued to interfere in the marriage projects of the aristocracy, arranging such important alliances themselves.[28]

It was not long before the King of Spain called upon the dynasty to revisit its military exploits as it was facing a moment of great peril. In late 1624 the Duke of Savoy, Charles Emanuel I, in alliance with France, launched a powerful and completely unprovoked invasion of the neighbouring Republic of Genoa, in order to deprive Spain of its financial support and its convenient corridor for the easy dispatch of Spanish soldiers to Milan and beyond. A combined Dutch and English

---

[24] BCPLPc, Ms Pallastrelli 126, 'Croniche o Diario del Rev.o Sgr. Benedetto Boselli, rettore della chiesa di San Martino di Piacenza, 1620–1670', 60.

[25] BCPLPc, Ms Pallastrelli 162, Gandini, 'Compendio Storico di Piacenza', 144.

[26] Roberto Sabbadini, *La Grazia e l'Onore: Principe, nobiltà e ordine sociale nei ducati farnesiani* (Rome, 2001), 64–8.

[27] BPPr Ms Parmense 737, Hippolito Calandrini, 'L'Heroe d'Italia, overo Vita del Sereniss.o Odoardo Farnese il Grande, quinto duca di Parma e di Piacenza', 93; see also Podesta, 'Dal delitto politico', 679–720.

[28] Ugo Benassi, 'Governo assoluto e città suddita nel primo Seicento', *Bollettino Storico Piacentino*, 12 (1917), 193–203, and 13 (1918), 30–8.

fleet set sail to strike the helpless republic from the sea, but it fell upon Cadiz instead and local forces drove it off ingloriously. Neapolitan and Sicilian contingents conveyed by sea to Genoa saved the city from immediate occupation and threatened to turn the tables on the invaders. Spain expected its Italian satellites to fulfill their commitments to their defensive alliance by sending contingents of professional soldiers to Lombardy where they would join Spanish and Imperial troops and strike the French and Savoyards from the rear.[29] As a loyal ally, Cardinal Odoardo proceeded to designate noblemen who would lead the new contingents into battle and protect Piacenza, which was perilously close to the theatre of operations. Why noblemen? These often considered military leadership to be a special prerogative of their class, but more practical reasons no doubt prevailed: princes expected loyal noblemen to employ their own financial resources and social relations in order to find soldiers in a hurry and to train them for action. The state would reimburse them or reward them in other ways later, after the crisis had passed.[30] A group of five companies, perhaps about 600 men in total, served as a garrison for nearby Cremona, thereby releasing the Spanish soldiers there for field duty. The cardinal raised more men for garrison service in Piacenza, and hired 3,000 peasants under the direction of the engineer Carlo Soldati to erect earthen ravelins, and a covered way at the foot of the bastioned walls. A Roman cousin, Don Francesco Farnese, led an expeditionary force of 2,000 men to join the Spanish troops in the field. They came very close to engaging the Savoyards directly and served as support in the Battle of Ottaggio. Farnese troops served at the siege of the Piedmontese fortress of Verrua overlooking the Po river, 'with more courage than good fortune'. Francesco Farnese died of wounds received during the siege, and the cardinal regent disbanded the remaining soldiers after four months in the field. The threat to the rear of French and Savoyard positions forced Cardinal Richelieu to cut his losses and sign a truce with Spain; this was followed by the Peace of Monzón in 1626, which restored the status quo ante. Cardinal Odoardo was reportedly frustrated with the way the Spanish commander, the Duke of Feria, allegedly mishandled the duchy's contingent, and, like the other princes, he was unhappy with the peremptory way that Spain's new chief minister, Count Duke of Olivares, treated his junior allies.

With the end of hostilities in early 1626, the cardinal regent, Odoardo, continued to pay a great deal of attention to the military preparedness of Parma and especially Piacenza, whose fortifications he continually upgraded. Much of Europe was on a war footing in those years, and tensions focused around competing access to the Valtellina valley and the passes leading from Lombardy into Switzerland.[31] The citadel of Piacenza was a dangerous asset, one that Olivares would have dearly

---

[29] Hanlon, *The Twilight of a Military Tradition: Italian Aristocrats and European Conflicts, 1560–1800* (London and New York, 1998), 106–10.

[30] Archivio di Stato di Parma (henceforth ASPr), Governo Farnesiano, Milizie 1: *Lettera informativa da Orazio Scotti per scegliere e creare ufficiali, 15 aprile 1625*.

[31] A concise and elegant analysis of this question is contained in an article by Yves-Marie Bercé, 'Rohan et la Valteline', in *L'Europe des traites de Westphalie. Esprit de la diplomatie et diplomatie de l'esprit*, ed. Lucien Bély (Paris, 2000), 321–36.

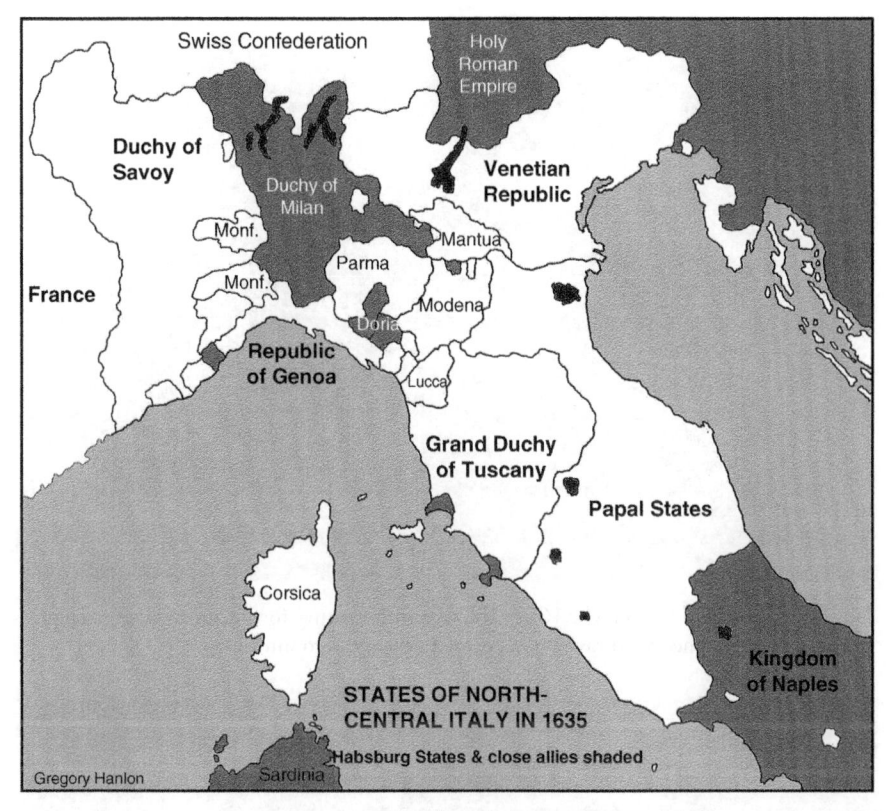

Map 1.1. Northern Italy in 1635

liked to hold, and, in 1625, the governor of the citadel was still someone whose appointment had to be ratified by the Spanish Crown. The cardinal regent was careful now to dismiss many of the Milanese garrison soldiers there, whose loyalties might have been incompatible with Farnese direction.[32] David Parrott considers citadels of the size of Piacenza and Parma to be 'white elephants', strategically more useful to a foreign occupier than to the dukes themselves.[33] A large ducal garrison for such a fortress was only of the order of about 200 men, barely enough to keep the powerful families in subjection, and far too few to hold against a European power. The fortresses were, nevertheless replete with arms, ammunition, and war materiel of all kinds. The French Prince de Condé was impressed with the 100 cannon on the ramparts of the city and citadel of Parma, together with the abundance of good weapons for both infantry and cavalry in the magazines.[34]

---

[32] Benassi, 'Governo assoluto e città suddita nel primo Seicento', *Bollettino Storico Piacentino*, 12 (1917), 193–203, and 13 (1918), 30–8.
[33] David Parrott, 'The utility of fortifications in early modern Europe: Italian princes and their citadels', *War in History*, 7/2 (2007): 127–53.
[34] Giorgio Cusatelli and Fausto Razzetti, *Il Viaggio a Parma: Visitatori stranieri in età farnesiana e borbonica* (Parma, 1990), 50.

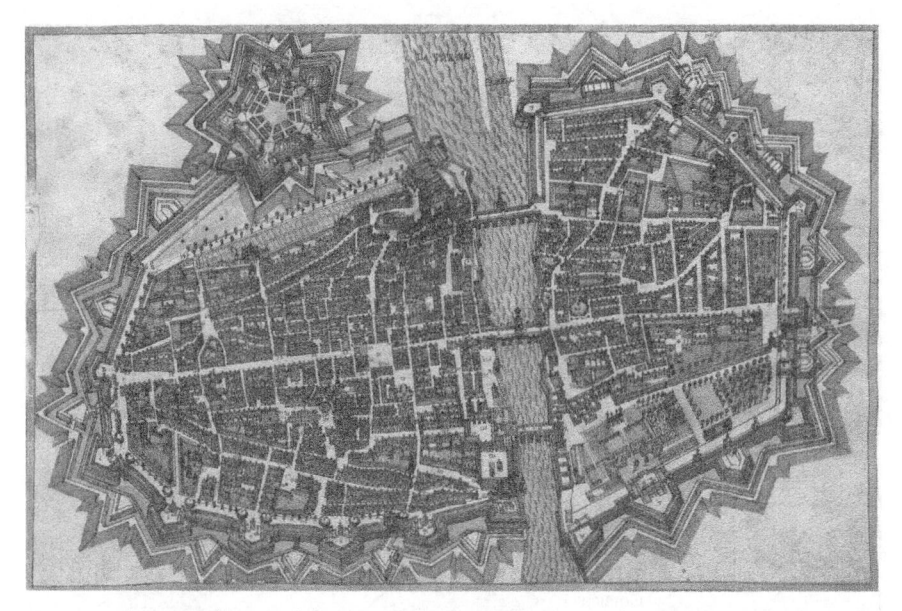

Fig. 1.1. Parma and its citadel *c.*1650; The sixteenth-century fortifications were strengthened with ravelins, a covered way and a counterscarp.

Fig. 1.2. Piacenza's Palazzo Gotico town hall. The equestrian statues emphasize the town's subjection to the Farnese dynasty.

The cautious cardinal died in 1626 and the regency passed to Duke Odoardo's mother, Margherita Aldobrandini, who, like her late husband and brother-in-law, was a solid Habsburg client. Her brother in Bologna, Cardinal Pietro Aldobrandini was a source of sound advice, and a conduit to the important papal curia in Rome. A new crisis erupted in northern Italy in 1628 with the succession crisis

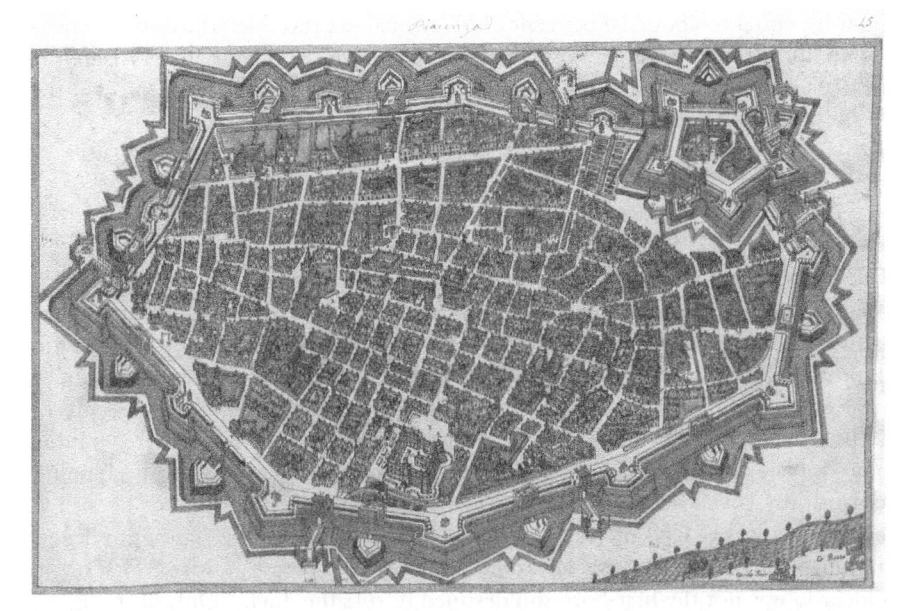

Fig. 1.3. Piacenza and its citadel *c.*1650. The citadel is on the top right, and the Farnese palace at bottom centre. The Po river shown on the lower right is much too narrow.

in nearby Mantua, whereby a French branch of the Gonzaga dynasty established itself on the ducal throne without the requisite Imperial consent. Spain rightly feared that Mantua and Casale Monferrato would become French bases in Italy, threatening Milan and, by extension, its vital access through Germany to the Spanish Netherlands. Olivares, whose policies openly sought to maintain Spanish hegemony in Europe, fashioned a shaky alliance with Duke Charles Emanuel I of Savoy. A Spanish army based in Milan laid siege unsuccessfully to Casale, stubbornly defended by a garrison of mostly French soldiers, while in 1629 a German Imperial army descended into Italy to lay siege to Mantua. The Gonzaga dukes of Mantua were long-time rivals of the House of Farnese. Odoardo and his mother determined to prevent the French-born duke Charles of Mantua from dispatching from Mantua reinforcements to relieve his threatened citadel of Casale. Odoardo raised a powerful militia force of 15,000 men to build earthworks along their common border, thereby preventing the Gonzaga duke from building a boat bridge across the Po.[35] The new prince, who assumed full powers on 24 August 1629, also tried to avoid paying contributions to the Imperial army under Marshal Aldringhen, arguing that as a vassal of the Pope he was exempt from such impositions. Powerful defensive works around the two principal cities served to keep foreign troops out of urban areas, but the countryside was helpless. The German soldiers were determined to seize what the duke would not supply, so Odoardo resigned himself to pay large subsidies of 18,000 lire per week for five

---

[35] BPPr Ms Parmense 737, Calandrini, 'L'Heroe d'Italia', 345.

months, equal to about 10 per cent of his annual tax revenue. The only compensation for Parma's trouble was when Spain allowed Odoardo to garrison the strategic fortress town of Sabbioneta with his own nominally neutral forces at the death of its Gonzaga duke.

A BOY-WARRIOR IN DANGEROUS TIMES

Peace was always a fleeting pause in Europe for the entire generation after 1618, although contemporaries could not have known this in advance. The great contest between Catholics and Protestants in Germany and the Low Countries drew in almost all the bystander states caught between belligerent powers, but these junior princes were sometimes very willing participants. Odoardo Farnese gave precocious signs that he would not be an inactive bystander while others were winning glory on the battlefield. We have a very long panegyric on Odoardo by Ippolito Calandrini, a well-informed eyewitness whose accuracy on points of detail has been verified by Ugo Benassi, working from administrative correspondence, although the courtier did not always respect the chronological order.[36] First of all, Odoardo was not the first-born son destined to rule the duchy. Only at the age of seven or eight did his parents focus their attentions on him as the presumptive heir. From Odoardo's very early years, Duke Ranuccio confided his education to the young nobleman Cremona Visdomini, a Piacenza feudatory whose family had been a fixture at the palace for generations. This courtier daily informed the duke of every detail concerning the young prince's education. At age four Odoardo was introduced to the alphabet and to the rosary. At five his father gave him a retinue of twelve noble pages, and in their company he began to learn the simpler ceremonies of the palace and church. On the Jesuit model favoured by the Farnese, the little prince learned reading and writing, the catechism, and a bit of Latin, seven days a week. Also on the Jesuit model, he learned to dance as part of a bodily discipline he would develop in other forms later on. It was clear by age six that, like his mother, he would become obese. Ballet helped keep his weight down and enhanced his agility, as did his fencing lessons, which were also designed, in the seventeenth century, to develop physical *sprezzatura* and grace in movement. Odoardo was reportedly a very nimble fencer, according to his biographer Calandrini, and his equestrian skills also elicited admiration from fawning courtiers.[37]

The little prince was a headstrong playmate, excessively interested in war and the punctilious vanities of *cavalleria* or chivalric honour that demanded satisfaction. Odoardo did not lack self-esteem, we would say today. With his first child-scale sword he manifested the deep hatred he bore for his half-brother Ottavio, the bastard, who was on increasingly strained terms with his suspicious father. His uncle,

---

[36] Benassi, 'I Natali e l'educazione', 99–227.
[37] Benassi, 'I Natali e l'educazione', 180; for the importance of corporeal control for a prince, see Hervé Drévillon, 'Le Roi-cavalier: les savoirs du corps dans l'éducation de Louis XIII', in *Le Savoir du Prince: du Moyen-Age aux Lumières*, R. Halévi (Paris, 2002), 147–73.

the cardinal-regent, Odoardo, and Vicedomini wanted to inculcate in the boy a love of peace, but Odoardo was inclined to discuss military honour from the tender age of seven, as he listened to his mother read news of foreign wars. This fierce and unrelenting desire to seize any occasion to make a name for himself as a soldier, 'to open the path of glory with his sword', as Calandrini phrased it, was something Odoardo manifested from a tender age.[38] The child prince dug up the palace garden to erect fortifications he would storm for play, with aristocrat playmates in his wake. When he was barely ten years old, the Spanish ambassador admonished him for his bold talk of making war on the House of Habsburg, and for being too intent on his warlike path. As a youth in the company of his cardinal uncle, he inspected the soldiers of the citadel of Piacenza and admired the weapons massed there, then watched as horses harnessed to a winch turned the mills grinding grain there (for a besieger was likely to block the canals providing water to conventional mills). In 1625, as hostilities raged in nearby Lombardy and Liguria, the adolescent Odoardo toured the province to inspect the peasant militia, dismissing the invalid soldiers and enrolling new ones in their place. This peasant force, reasonably well armed and periodically drilled by veterans of foreign wars, was held to number 36,000 infantrymen and 800 cavalry troopers before the great plague of 1630, a huge proportion of the adult males relative to other states in Italy and abroad.[39] Raising money for the militia motivated the cardinal regent to violate the privileges and exemptions of the clergy, which provoked a bishop's interdict on Piacenza. This too provoked a violent outburst from the young duke, directed now towards Rome and the new Pope, Urban VIII Barberini.

The adolescent prince experienced considerable anguish during the long and complex negotiations leading up to his marriage to a Florentine Medici princess, for he was in competition with the queen of France, Maria de' Medici, who sought a bride for the king's younger brother Gaston d'Orleans, and little Parma was not even remotely in the same league. Fortunately for him, the French project came to naught. On the eve of his wedding with Margherita de' Medici in 1628, with his violently pro-French inclinations and his bellicose speech, the 16-year-old duke frightened his Tuscan in-laws, who recommended that he support the pro-Spanish policy of his ancestors. When the court finally invested Odoardo with full ducal power on 24 August 1629, at age 17, his mind was set. He was actively looking for any pretext to break with Spain and to ally himself with France, in preparation for a great war in which he would play an important role. His ostensible model was his famous grandfather Alessandro, but the example he wished to follow was that of Charles Emanuel I, Duke of Savoy, who had challenged Spanish hegemony in Italy with some success.[40] But the specific political context was merely a cover for more personal reasons, made explicit very soon after his death by the historian Pietro Giovanni Capriata: 'The causes Odoardo gave in his published apology (for going to war) were so flimsy and of such small import that they were considered pretexts.

---

[38] BPPr, Ms Parmense 737, Calandrini, 'L'Heroe d'Italia', 160.
[39] BPPr Ms Parmense 737, Calandrini, 'L'Heroe d'Italia', 136.
[40] Benassi, 'I Natali e l'educazione', 221.

The commonly given reason was that the orphan duke grew up with very exalted and convoluted ideas, that the alliance of his ancestors with Spain was mere servitude, and that the sovereignty of Italian princes was only subjection. He aspired with his entire being to a more absolute liberty, and to greater status by increasing his territory.'[41]

With his duchy finally at his command, Odoardo dreamed of accomplishing great deeds that would force admiration from all of Europe. All princes appointed councillors whose task was to prevent them from acting impulsively or otherwise committing the state to rash policies. Odoardo's gifted namesake uncle was now dead, and he paid no attention to his mother. What he wanted in a minister was a facilitator of his own choosing who could realize his warlike ardour to its fullest. Odoardo listened to two new ministers who flattered these ambitions. Count Fabio Scotti, the scion of one of the principal noble Piacenza houses, and the lowborn Jacques Gaufridy, son of a Provençal notary who was the duke's French-language instructor before being appointed as his private secretary, were the architects of the new policy. People assumed that both were in the pay of Cardinal Richelieu, the French minister of state. Fabio Scotti's eldest son, Ascanio, became a member of Louis XIII's personal guard in Paris, while another was an ecclesiastic upon whom the King of France bestowed abbeys and other pensions drawn from the French Catholic Church.[42] What would war do for the young duke, quite apart from the important aim of making a name for himself among the concert of European princes, someone whose views and projects would have to be contended with? This first ambition, a quest for status, might have been the most important in his mind. Military success enhances the prestige of a political leader, which is something of a human universal.[43] Second, a successful war with its concomitant territorial acquisition would raise the House of Farnese above its nearby rivals, the ducal House of Este in Modena and the more dangerous Gonzaga rulers in Mantua. It would have the effect of rendering impotent the plotting Doria–Landi dynasty, whose Imperial fiefs in the Apennines the Farnese coveted, and perhaps even place Parma in the position of controlling the strategic Lunigiana valley, which connected the Po valley with the Mediterranean coast. Both the Doria and the Malaspina lords in the Lunigiana were firmly supported by Spain, as were all the minor princes with Imperial fiefs bordering the state of Milan.[44] Territorial expansion would then lift the Farnese up into the more select ranks of the House of Savoy and the Medici grand dukes of Tuscany. War might also create more durable bonds between the upstart Farnese dynasty and the great feudatory families in Parma and Piacenza, for Odoardo would surely reward their persons and their purses for their active support. Victory would bring expansion, booty, a

---

[41] Pietro Giovanni Capriata, *Dell'Historia delli movimenti d'armi successi in Italia* (Genova, 1649). vol. 2, 125.

[42] Capriata, *Dell'Historia*, vol. 2, 125–8. The historian's claims can be corroborated in Spanish state papers Archivo General Simancas (henceforth AGS), Estado 3343, no. 96, dispatch of Don Antonio Sarmiento, 28 June 1635.

[43] John Keegan, *A History of Warfare* (New York, 1993), 25.

[44] Spagnoletti, *Principi italiani e Spagna nell' età barocca*, 60.

larger population and tax base, enhanced political cohesion, and less risk of attack by rival Italian states.[45] But, more than anything else, a successful war would loosen the chains of papal feudal tutelage over Parma and Piacenza themselves. This issue, at the origin of the Farnese principality, was aggravated by an annoying tendency of the Barberini Pope, Urban VIII, to tell the young duke how he should navigate European waters, and that he should subordinate his policy to Roman direction. War would help make Odoardo a *sovereign* prince, theoretically equal in status to the kings of France and Spain.

Contemporaries were struck by Odoardo's passion for war. It was sensible for them to base their expectations of his rule on his character, for, in the political system of princes, power was personalized to a great extent. Today we deplore the concentration of political authority in a single individual with the power of life and death over all his subjects. Even though Odoardo was not quite a sovereign prince, he was an absolute one, that is, he had sole initiative over the creation of laws, and could suspend the application of any law by intervening in the workings of his own administration in order to confer some private exemption, pardon, or favour. We can legitimately consider the typical absolute prince as someone who functioned as an arbiter of competing factions and local powers, guided by cautious ministers experienced in the ways of men and of the world.[46] This marked a real progress over the feudal potentates and fractious republics of earlier periods, where power lay in the interested hands of kinship factions. But so much depended upon the *gravitas*, or the lack thereof, of the person in charge. Observers agreed that the Duke of Parma had a quick mind, was articulate and cultivated, and had a seriousness of purpose that incited his subjects to obey him. But he could not control his temper, nor would he take sound advice from other people.[47] Until 1631, Spain hoped that Odoardo would follow his ancestors as a loyal client, and it made overtures it hoped the youngster would accept. Two diplomats based in Milan, Count Rabatta and Count Villani, relayed Olivares' proposition that the duke should command a force of 6,000 men in Flanders raised at his own expense. Spain would also provide garrisons for Sabbioneta and the citadel of Piacenza for the duration of the war. The maladroit proposal from Milan triggered a violent outburst by the youngster, who resolved instead to serve the interests of France in Italy.[48] Perhaps the Spanish emissaries were unaware that Louis XIII, King of France, and his cardinal-minister, Richelieu, had contacted the adolescent duke secretly in 1625, letting him know that France held him in high regard, and promising to defend him with their own men and money should he ever become a client of that Crown.[49] Odoardo

---

[45] These arguments in favour of winnable war are also largely universal. See Marco Costa, *Psicologia militare: elementi di psicologia per gli appartenenti alle forze armate* (Milan, 2003), 54.

[46] Gregorio Leti, *L'Italia regnante, overo Nova Descritione dello Stato presente di tutti Prencipati e Republiche d'Italia*, 4 vols.(Genoa, 1675–6), 242.

[47] Emilio Nasalli Rocca, *I Farnese* (Piacenza, 1969), 160; Andrea Riggi, 'Le imprese militari di Odoardo Farnese', *Aurea Parma*, 13 (1929): 49–56, 28–36, 32–8. Riggi cites the character sketch of Odoardo drawn by the eighteenth-century Piacenza chronicler Poggiali, which the observations of people who dealt with the duke confirm amply.

[48] Leti, *L'Italia regnante*, 335–6.

[49] BPPr Ms Parmense 737, Calandrini, 'L'Heroe d'Italia', 160.

decided soon after the stormy interview with the Spanish ministers to raise four companies of mercenary soldiers that would guarantee his cities from seizure. Then he distributed arms to the citizen militia of Piacenza, whose members he reviewed on the city square.[50] Fabio Scotti and Jacques Gaufridy set to work to forge a concrete agreement with Richelieu, with the aid of Ascanio Scotti, Fabio's warrior son in Paris.[51] Odoardo became the first Italian prince to actively seek an alliance with France, concretized by a secret treaty signed on 20 April 1633.[52]

Here we need to leave Parma for Paris, where the King of France, Louis XIII, and his chief minister, Cardinal Richelieu, plotted to end the preponderance of the Habsburg dynasty in Europe. These two great monarchies of France and Spain had stood in constant opposition to each other for almost two centuries, but France was more often the initiator of hostilities.[53] Richelieu's first efforts were focused on concluding over two generations of religious strife in France itself, by forcibly disarming the Protestant minority. This policy was highly popular in a kingdom where Catholics made up about 95 per cent of the population. Richelieu's scheme to seize Genoa with the help of Savoy, England, and the Dutch Republic in 1625 was a complete failure, but, after signing the Peace of Monzón with Spain the next year, he had time to lay siege to the Protestant stronghold of La Rochelle. Once the starving city capitulated in 1628, Richelieu and Louis XIII were able to give financial and moral support to the Duke of Mantua in his unequal struggle against Spain and Austria, from 1628 to early 1630, first by pressuring the Duke of Savoy to quit his alliance with the Habsburgs. The French cardinal felt that there was a profound anti-Habsburg current in Italy that he could exploit to France's advantage. He dealt with the Italian princes, like their German counterparts, *as if* they were sovereign entities free to make alliances in their own names. He professed to act in the guise of a 'liberator' of Italy, and promised to reward his Italian allies with any spoils taken from Spain and its satellites like the Republic of Genoa.[54] Richelieu's policy of confrontation with the House of Austria was far from uniting the political elites in France itself. The influential Queen Mother, Maria de' Medici, felt that, instead of opposing the Habsburgs in their hitherto successful war against Protestants in Europe, France should be helping them. At the very least, she and her minister, Marillac, would have preferred a long internal peace in which much-needed reforms would restore efficiency to the royal administration. Louis XIII was torn between the warlike orientation of his chief minister, who proposed to aid the Protestants, and the peaceful policy aims of his devoutly Catholic mother, until the fateful day of 10 November 1630 when he finally made up his mind to back the cardinal.[55]

[50] BCPLPc, Ms Pallastrelli 126, 'Croniche o Diario', 96.
[51] BPPr Ms Parmense 737, Calandrini, 'L'Heroe d'Italia', 400.
[52] Drei, *I Farnese*, 204.
[53] Alain Hugon, 'Des Habsbourg aux Bourbons: le combat espagnol pour la conservation de l'hégémonie européenne (milieu XVe-fin XVIIe siècle)', *Bulletin de la Société d'Histoire Moderne et Contemporaine*, 3–4 (2000): 34–55.
[54] Sven Externbrink, '"Le cœur du monde" et la "liberté d'Italie": aspects de la politique italienne de Richelieu 1624–1642', *Revue d'histoire diplomatique*, 114 (2000): 181–208.
[55] Georges Pagès, 'Autour du "grand orage": Richelieu et Marillac, deux politiques', *Revue historique*, 179 (1937): 63–97.

Louis XIII, a shy and insecure king, came into his element in war; he was a 'roi de guerre' in Joël Cornette's phrase.[56] The socially awkward French monarch was comfortable in the company of his soldiers; he enjoyed roaming his kingdom and its borders with his army, sleeping in makeshift quarters. Like his father, Henri IV, he learned the art of war as a boy, and placed himself at the head of his troops as soon in life as he was able. He was happiest when on campaign, showing off his technical military skill to his mother and his queen, who followed him in the field against Protestants after 1621. When compelled to choose between a policy of peace and reform operated under the auspices of devout Catholic ministers, and a policy of open warfare against the Habsburgs of Spain and Austria, which would have the consequence of a Protestant victory in Europe, Louis chose war and left its management to his able minister.[57] Louis stayed loyal to Richelieu to the end, in the face of huge resistance at all levels of French society. The king and the cardinal proposed to occupy the southern Low Countries, Lorraine, the Franche-Comté of Burgundy, and Savoy, all of which spoke French. These would constitute a great bulwark of territories that could protect the French heartland from invasion.[58] Richelieu swore that France was not interested in Italian conquests, but King Louis never renounced the 'rights' of his house to the kingdom of Naples or Milan in Italy, for the rights of kings never die.[59] The cardinal did indeed have a '*grand dessein*' to defeat the House of Austria and to confiscate many of its territories. Richelieu felt that war was justified even if complete victory was not in the cards, for the king would thereby win '*réputation*' by force of arms that would serve afterwards to intimidate potential adversaries.[60] He could not anticipate that the war he provoked would continue for a quarter of a century.

Richelieu's nemesis was the *valido* or chief minister of the King of Spain, Philip IV, the Count-Duke of Olivares, whose primary concern after 1630 was simply to maintain Spanish positions in Europe and the world, after a decade of waging aggressive war against the Protestant powers.[61] Unlike Richelieu, minister of a single national state that had a tendency to centralize power in Paris, Olivares wished to transform the elites of the multitude of autonomous states that made up the Catholic king's great empire into a kind of service nobility. He expected them to finance and personally lead troops in all the territories threatened by French

---

[56] Joël Cornette, *Le Roi de guerre: Essai sur la souveraineté dans la France du Grand Siècle* (Paris, 1993).

[57] A. Lloyd Moote, *Louis XIII the Just* (Berkeley and London, 1989), 126.

[58] Marie-Catherine Vignal Souleyreau, *Richelieu et la Lorraine* (Paris, 2004), 155.

[59] Cornette, *Le Roi de guerre*, 141–5; also David Parrott, 'The causes of the Franco-Spanish war of 1635–1659', in *The Origins of war in Early Modern Europe*, ed. J. Black (Edinburgh, 1987), 72–111.

[60] Françoise Hildesheimer, 'Guerre et paix selon Richelieu', in *Esprit de la diplomatie et diplomatie de l'esprit*, ed. L. Bély (Paris, 2000), 31–54.

[61] John Elliott, *Richelieu and Olivares* (London and New York, 1984); also John Elliott, 'Managing decline: Olivares and the Grand Strategy of Imperial Spain', in *Grand Strategies in War and Peace*, ed. P. Kennedy (New Haven, 1991), 87–104; also Miguel Angel Ochoa Brun, 'La diplomatie espagnole dans la premiere moitié du XVIIe siècle', in *L'Europe des traités de Westphalie: Esprit de la diplomatie et diplomatie de l'esprit*, ed. L. Bély (Paris, 2000), 537–54.

ambition.⁶² Paradoxically, he could only achieve this policy of conservation by facing up to Spain's adversaries, and producing resounding military victories that would keep other potential enemies at bay. Like a modern 'domino theory' this policy of '*reputaciòn*' led Olivares into taking a more confrontational policy towards the new Duke of Mantua in 1628 than was necessary. It was Olivares' great failure that the Spanish troops could not capture Casale Monferrato in northern Italy in 1629 and 1630; it was defended by a French garrison under the talented Marshal Toiras in the service of Duke Charles of Mantua. However, the successful defence of Casale effectively reduced the Duke of Mantua to a French client with no room for manoeuvre.⁶³ France would never relinquish the great stronghold to him without solid guarantees of continued good conduct.

During one of the French army's forays into Piedmont, the fortress of Pinerolo fell to Marshal Créquy, ensuring an easy French avenue into northern Italy in the future. The peace agreement with Spain hinged upon the return of Pinerolo to Savoy before the Habsburg troops were withdrawn from the theatre of war, but Richelieu had purchased the compliance of the Savoyard governor of the place, who had hidden French soldiers in the bowels of the fortress. These emerged and ejected the Savoyard garrison as soon as the Spanish had retired. Feeling unready to confront the House of Austria, and quite content to subsidize the King of Sweden and the Dutch Republic to fight it out by proxy, Richelieu crafted the secret Treaty of Cherasco in 1631 with his hapless Italian satellites. France compensated Piedmont for its loss by awarding the duchy a few dozen villages and small towns in the Monferrato taken from Mantuan territories there.⁶⁴ The initiative of war or peace in Italy lay entirely with Louis XIII and his cardinal minister, for Spain would never consent to durable peace while France retained Pinerolo.⁶⁵ The Duke of Mantua also refused to recognize the legitimacy of the same treaty, by which his territories were transferred to Savoy without compensation. The Duke of Mantua needed French support to retain his jurisdiction in the Monferrato, but the Duchess of Mantua, sister of the Duke of Savoy, became an ardent supporter of Spain.⁶⁶

---

⁶² Jean-Frédéric Schaub, 'La crise hispanique de 1640: le modèle des "révolutions périphériques" en question', *Annales; Histoire, Sciences sociales*, 49 (1994): 219–40.

⁶³ David Parrott, 'A "prince souverain" and the French crown: Charles de Nevers 1580–1637', in *Royal and Republican Sovereignty in Early Modern Europe: Essays in Memory of Ragnhild Hatton*, ed. R. Oresko, G. C. Gibbs, and H. M. Scott (Cambridge, 1997), 149–87.

⁶⁴ Claudio Rosso, *Il Piemonte sabaudo: Stato e territori in età moderna* (Turin, 1994), 223.

⁶⁵ The most detailed and erudite account of the Mantuan succession crisis is by Romolo Quazza, *La Guerra per la successione di Mantova e del Monferrato (1628–1631)*, 2 vols(Mantua, 1926). For an update, see Robert Stradling, 'Olivares and the origins of the Franco-Spanish war, 1627–1635', *English Historical Review*, 101 (1986): 68–94.

⁶⁶ Guido Amoretti, *Il Ducato di Savoia dal 1559 al 1713*, vol. II, *dal 1610 al 1659* (Turin, 1985), 69–71; see also a published transcription of a contemporary chronicle, GianDomenico Bremio, 'Annali Casalesi (1632–1661) di GianDomenico Bremio speciaro di Casale Monferrato', ed. Dott. Giuseppe Giorcelli, *Rivista Storica Alessandrina*, 18 (1909): 381–9; César Du Plessis Praslin, *Memoires du Maréchal Du Plessis: Memoires pour servir à l'histoire de France depuis le XIIIe siècle jusqu'à la fin du XVIIIe siècle*, vol. 7, ed. J. Michaud and J. Poujoulat (Paris, 1838), 358.

France threatened its enemies principally by establishing fortified bridgeheads deep in foreign territory. Richelieu aimed to disarm the minor powers on France's borders and to convert their fortified cities into advance bases for further expansion. This was applied first in Lorraine, in part because the duke Charles IV actively supported the many malcontents in France who were opposed to the general thrust of the cardinal's policies.[67] In 1632 and 1633 French armies in Lorraine seized key fortresses and built new ones, while demolishing the fortifications of the places left in the hands of the hapless duke Charles. Outright annexation of the duchy at the first convenient opportunity was Richelieu's ultimate goal. French armies then occupied neighbouring Alsace in short order, on the pretext of protecting it from devastation by Swedish and Imperial armies. Richelieu intended to do the same to the new Duke of Savoy, Victor Amadeus I, who, in 1619, had married Princess Marie-Christine, sister of Louis XIII. The seizure of Pinerolo, and its retention by ruse in violation of the truce with Spain was the clearest sign that France intended to invade Italy, but it simultaneously reduced the Duke of Savoy to client status too.[68] It made feasible the extension of French military might clear across northern Italy, from the Alpine passes to Casale Monferrato and eventually Mantua, which bordered on the friendly Venetian Republic.[69] Odoardo's three fortresses, Piacenza, Parma, and Sabbioneta, were conveniently situated along this axis of advance. With viable bases in northern Italy, Richelieu could then call Italian princes and republics to join him in a powerful alliance intended to restore the 'liberty' of Italy, or, conversely, he could occupy those states with little interference.

The French cardinal first sought to reduce Duke Victor Amadeus to client status by offering him enticements. 'You can never swindle an honest man', it is said. Richelieu knew how easy it would be to corrupt Victor Amadeus with promises of territorial expansion and dynastic aggrandizement. The dukes of Savoy were as inclined as any European princes to increase their states by conquering their neighbours, and the previous duke, Charles Emanuel, had employed both legitimate and spurious claims to invade, at different periods, Dauphiné and Provence, Liguria, the Monferrato, and Protestant Geneva.[70] To induce Victor Amadeus to consent to the loss of Pinerolo, Richelieu offered a powerful enticement in the form of recognizing Savoy's claim to a royal title that would raise the duchy above its Italian rivals. European states focused ever increasingly on the outward trappings and titles of princes, republics, cardinals, and ambassadors from the late sixteenth century onwards, and by the 1620s and early 1630s this trend towards ceremoniousness erupted into serious conflicts between states with competing claims.[71]

---

[67] Stéphane Gaber, *La Lorraine meurtrie* (2nd edn, Nancy, 1991), 25; Vignal Souleyreau, *Richelieu et la Lorraine*, 155–81.

[68] Jacques Humbert, *Le Maréchal de Créquy, gendre de Lesdiguières (1573–1638)* (Paris, 1962), 190–201.

[69] Yves-Marie Bercé, 'Les guerres dans l'Italie du XVIIe siècle', in *L'Italie au XVIIe siècle* (Paris, 1989), 311–31.

[70] Toby Osborne, *Dynasty and Diplomacy in the Court of Savoy: Political Culture and the Thirty Years' War* (Cambridge and New York, 2002), 28–35.

[71] Maria Antonietta Visceglia, 'Il cerimoniale come linguaggio politico: su alcuni conflitti di precedenza alla corte di Roma tra '500 e '600', in *Cérémonial et rituel à Rome (XVIe–XIXe siècles)*, ed. M. A. Visceglia and C. Brice (Rome, 1997), 117–76.

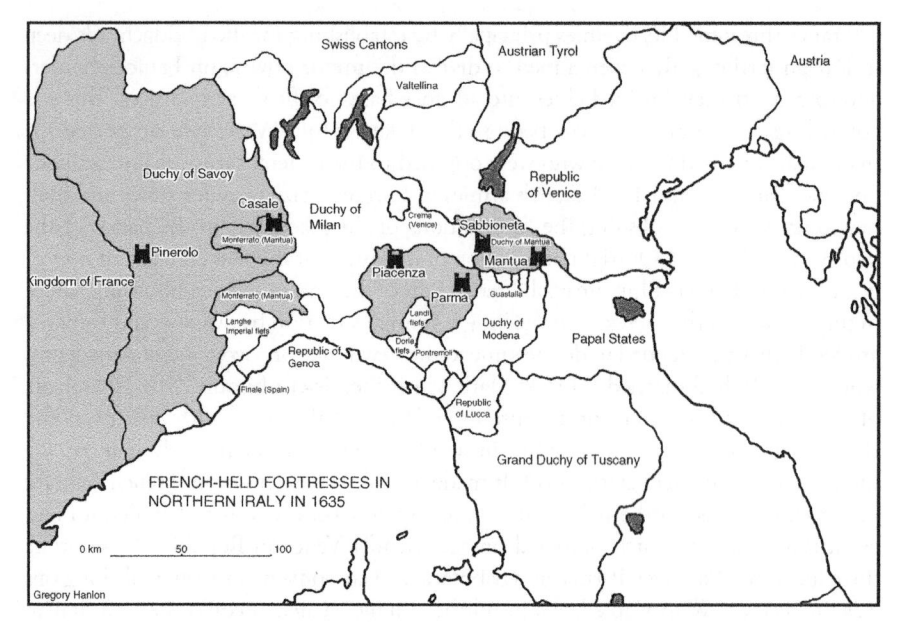

Map 1.2. French and allied fortresses in northern Italy

Territorial aggrandizement served to justify claims to higher status too. The cardinal promised to return Pinerolo to Victor Amadeus after three years if France did not assist him in conquering Genoa and the Ligurian coast, which was a long-standing ambition of the Duke of Savoy, who thought the title of King of Upper Liguria would elicit more recognition than the hypothetical claim to the kingdom of Cyprus.[72]

An offensive treaty with Savoy was just the first step in creating a league of Italian states that would strike Spanish Italy with overwhelming force from several directions simultaneously. We find already operating in modern form a network of diplomatic officials who enjoyed the cardinal's trust and who channelled detailed information on Italian courts back to Paris.[73] Richelieu instructed his special envoy, President Bellièvre, to create a league of Italian princes against Spain, ostensibly to restore the liberty of Italy.[74] They entailed discussions in January 1633 with the Grand Duke of Tuscany, Ferdinando II de'Medici, and the young duke, Francesco I d'Este, in Modena, both of whom were Odoardo's brothers-in-law.[75] From 1631, the French army aristocrat César Du Plessis Praslin also began to visit Italian dukes

---

[72] Salvatore Foa, *Vittorio Amedeo I* (Turin, 1930), 244.
[73] Daniela Frigo, 'Prudence and experience: ambassadors and political culture in early modern Italy', *Journal of Medieval and Early Modern Studies*, 38 (2008): 15–34.
[74] De Mun, *Richelieu et la Maison de Savoie: L'ambassade de Particelli d'Hémery en Piémont* (Paris, 1907), 27–30.
[75] AGS, Estado 3338, Consulta 26 January 1633.

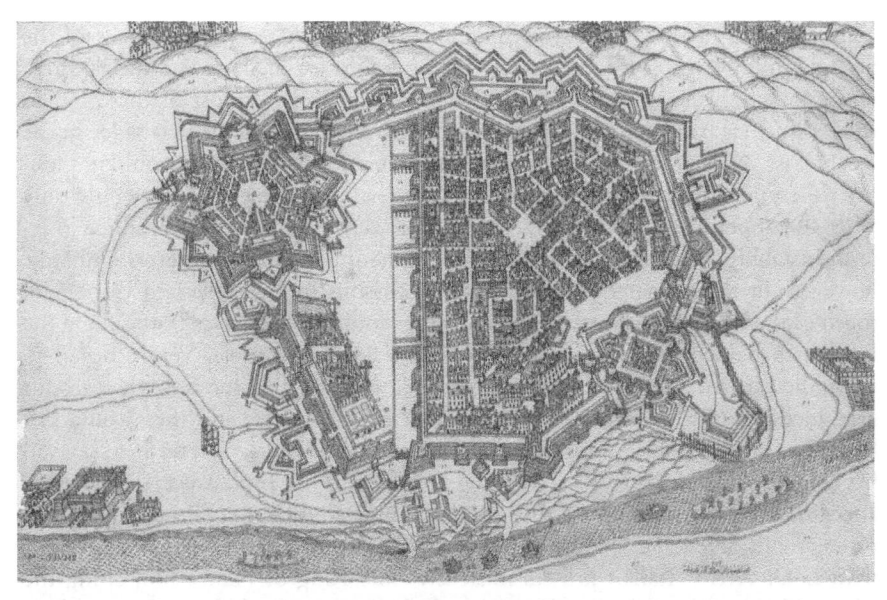

Fig. 1.4. Casale Monferrato and its citadel c.1650. Taken over from the Mantuan ally, Casale served as France's threatening advanced base in Italy for most of the 17th century.

to disburse compliments and promises. Richelieu posted him as ambassador to the Duke of Savoy in Turin, with instructions to alienate the duke entirely from the Spanish cause. Marshal Créquy replaced Du Plessis as ambassador in Rome in January 1633, where he worked to cement as many states as possible into this anti-Habsburg alliance.[76] In Rome, Cardinal Richelieu sought to obtain an annulment of Louis XIII's marriage to his Spanish wife, Anne of Austria, still childless after almost 20 years (for the French king was a closet homosexual). The papal Barberini nephews, who were not above dynastic ambition either, might also consent to join the league. In exchange for papal intervention in its favour, France would favour the reconstitution of the old duchy of Urbino in central Italy (suppressed only in 1630 when the last Della Rovere duke died without a son), under the direction of the papal nephew Taddeo Barberini.[77] Pope Urban VIII remained aloof from committing himself to a military alliance, however. In addition to the ambassadors, who were subject to ceremonial niceties and public scrutiny, Richelieu dispatched to Italy some discreet emissaries, like Nicolas Bachelier, who toured the duchies of Modena, Mantua, Parma, and Tuscany in April of the same year. He sent another emissary, Louis de Briançon, *sieur* de La Saludie on a tour of Italian capitals in March 1634 to assure everyone that France had no hegemonic interests in the

---

[76] Humbert, *Le Maréchal de Créquy*, 207; also Du Plessis Praslin, *Memoires du Maréchal Du Plessis*, 358ff.

[77] AGS, Estado 3832, letter from the Conde de La Roca in Venice, 4 June 1633.

region.[78] Both of these men were military officers with recent experience of the fighting in Italy, who could make convincing claims for the king and the cardinal; however, they were unable to overcome the misgivings of most of these Italian rulers.[79] Venice had been close to open war with the House of Austria twice in the recent past. While the republic feared Spanish intentions in Italy, it would not join such a league either, for it considered that a French conquest of Milan would only whet the appetites of Italian princes for more territories and so introduce long-term instability. The republic opposed strengthening Spain in eastern Lombardy, however, for the monarchy already posted garrisons in Guastalla and Correggio, south of the duchy of Mantua, and the former could impede river traffic along the Po, which helped feed the lagoon city.[80] Anticipating trouble, Venice began to strengthen its fortress cities in the Terraferma. Most Italian states might harbour grievances against Spain or the specific policies of Olivares and they would not have been unhappy if the King of Spain were weakened there.[81] Nevertheless, given his colossal commitments in a far-flung empire and his endless war in Germany and the Low Countries against the Dutch Republic and German Protestants, most princes considered the Spanish king, Philip IV, to be a more benign neighbour than Louis XIII.[82] Italian princes mistrusted the King of France too, citing the fable of Aesop, where the lion hunted with the lesser animals, promising to share the prey, before devouring each of them in turn.[83]

When the French marshal, Créquy, passed through Parma at the end of October 1632, Odoardo was able to greet him with a militia army of 5,000 foot and 1,200 horse, together with his noble ceremonial guard, the Company of the Cornetta Bianca, and another company of foot raised from noblemen of his states. To levy money in order to pay, equip, and feed his new soldiers, Odoardo instructed the chief accountant, Picoleti, to use the treasure amassed in the Rocchetta dungeon.[84] These actions placed Odoardo publicly in the French camp. But he also considered extracting important concessions from the King of Spain, without any quid pro quo. In 1631 Odoardo petitioned Madrid to award him one of four recompenses, in recognition of his dynasty's faithful service in the past. Three of these were territorial. The first was the Lombard city of Novara, which had been a Farnese fief until 1603, when the governor of Milan, Count Fuentes, forced Ranuccio to relinquish it under threat of military action. In addition to being a rich and populous city in Lombardy, sending substantial revenues to Parma, it was a fortress of considerable strategic importance on the border with Piedmont. Instead of Novara,

---

[78] Antonio Panella, 'Una lega italiana durante la guerra dei Trent'anni', *Archivio Storico Italiano*, 94 (1936): 3–36.

[79] Madeleine Haehl, *Les Affaires étrangères au temps de Richelieu: le secrétariat d'Etat, les agents diplomatiques (1624–1642)* (Brussels, 2006), 276–82.

[80] AGS, Estado 3316, no. 47, letter of 25 June 1633.

[81] Capriata, *Dell'Historia*, vol. 2, 120; Du Plessis Praslin, *Memoires du Maréchal Du Plessis*, 358; Niccolo Barozzi and Guglielmo Berchet, *Relazioni degli Stati Europei lette al Senato dagli Ambasciatori Veneti nel secolo XVII*, vol. 2: *Spagna (1634)* (Venice, 1856–78), 38–50.

[82] Spagnoletti, *Principi italiani e Spagna nell'età barocca*, 12–17.

[83] *Memoires de François de Paule de Clermont, Marquis de Montglat*, vol. 1 (Paris, 1727), 115.

[84] BPPr Ms Parmense 737, Calandrini, 'L'Heroe d'Italia', 406.

Odoardo suggested Spain could award him control over the Imperial fief of Pontremoli, which was a small town at the head of the Lunigiana corridor leading from Parman territory down to the Mediterranean coast. This was one of the routes by which Spanish troops arrived in northern Italy en route to Germany. The third possibility put forward was to award Odoardo the town of Casalmaggiore and its jurisdiction, just across the Po from the duchy of Parma, and the eastern limit of Spanish jurisdiction. This was a substantial territory in the richest part of Lombardy, and with it Odoardo could exercise control over navigation along the busy Po river. Moreover, in Farnese hands it would provide a convenient path connecting Parma to the adjacent fief of Sabbioneta, where Odoardo hoped to transform his temporary wardship into permanent annexation. Suspecting that the Spanish Crown would dismiss his request for expansion into such strategic territories, Odoardo suggested a fourth concession, of a different kind. He proposed that Spain offer the Farnese dynasty the 'royal treatment': this was a set of titles and addresses given only to Savoy and Tuscany in Italy, both of which would greatly resent the intrusion by an upstart minor state like Parma.[85] The Spanish ministers rejected all four requests, and so replied only with flowery words and general declarations of esteem.

Most Italian princes politely rebuffed the siren proposals of the emissaries of Cardinal Richelieu, with the notable exception of the young Duke of Parma, who urged France to intervene in Italy immediately.[86] In June 1633 Odoardo could no longer contain his impatience and began frenzied troop recruitment, something Spain considered a '*nobedad muy impensada*'.[87] Other Italian states, like Venice, were also astonished at the Duke of Parma's temerity.[88] At first Madrid thought that this just reflected the duke's unpopularity in Piacenza, where the high taxes on merchants and the troop expansion had seen the banking fairs move to Genoese territory. But noting how Odoardo was listening to 'evil' ministers who fed his vanity and his presumption, Spanish ministers watched the new troop levies with increasing apprehension. French soldiers began arriving in Parma through the Republic of Genoa, which polarized the political climate in that unstable state.[89] Spain was remarkably well informed of these developments, notably by the duke's maternal uncle, Cardinal Aldobrandini, who passed on information from his sister to the Spanish Crown, and who tried to influence the duke from Bologna. Spain also took a fresh interest in the welfare of Odoardo's illegitimate half-brother, Ottavio. The erstwhile prince, once groomed for succession before Odoardo was born, had been languishing in the Rocchetta palace prison for over a decade.[90]

---

[85] AGS, Estado 3673, Consulta of 24 May and 14 July 1631.
[86] Bibliothèque Nationale de France Ms Fr 16929, vo.528–604, 'Rélation de M. d'Esmery de ses negotiations en Piedmont en 1635 etc.', fo. 528.
[87] AGS, Estado 3339, Consulta 19 June 1633.
[88] AGS, Estado 3316, 25 June 1633.
[89] AGS, Estado 3339, Consulta 23 June 1633.
[90] AGS, Estado 3832, Consulta 4 July 1633: the document indicates that Prince Ottavio was held in the Rocchetta of Piacenza. Troublesome notables were customarily incarcerated in the Rocchetta prison, which was part of the Pilotta palace complex in Parma.

In hindsight, Odoardo's contemporaries considered his reasons for making war to be foolish.[91] But Spanish ministers thought that the Pope was complicit in Odoardo's posturing all along, possibly fomenting a 'diabolical plot' with some of the cardinals to eject the House of Austria from all of Italy. Urban VIII was, they felt, culpable for not having reined in the young prince, who was after all a papal vassal.[92] Odoardo raised many Italian troops in the summer of 1633 from Farnese fiefs in Lazio, not far from Rome itself, with tacit papal consent. The Pope purportedly dismissed the ability of Spain to defend Milan in the face of a French invasion.[93] Urban VIII certainly sent out mixed signals. The supreme pontiff deplored hostile relations between Catholic powers just when the Protestants were on the verge of being crushed in much of Europe. His overriding interest, however, was the long-term advantage of his family, the Barberini, whose establishment required steering papal policy around the shoals of great power interests. He also thought that a balance of power between Spain and France was most likely to conserve the power of minor Italian states. Urban VIII's passivity and his lack of reaction to French subterfuge in Piedmont strengthened France's position in Italy and gave Louis and Richelieu a free hand.[94] Urban himself wished to create a league of Italian states not allied with either power, for the defence of the peninsula's 'liberty'. He was close enough to France for Madrid to fear a military intervention against Habsburg interests, and there was some correspondence with Naples about the feasibility of an attack of the southern kingdom from Rome.[95] But the principal thrust of papal diplomacy was to keep the peace between the two principal Catholic powers. Urban sent his most able diplomat, Giulio Mazzarini, to Paris in 1634 as extraordinary nuncio, to argue the merits of a defensive league of Italian states; however, the future cardinal, Jules Mazarin, was already pro-French and would quickly become the instrument of Richelieu.[96]

Odoardo left the mechanics of the negotiations with France up to his minister Fabio Scotti, who advised the lad in 1633 to rein in his warrior spirits until a more propitious moment arrived.[97] In 1634 the French resident in Genoa, the Sieur de

---

[91] Galeazzo Gualdo Priorato, *Historia delle guerre del Conte Galeazzo Gualdo Priorato* (Venice, 1642), Libro XI, 306; Capriata, *Dell'Historia*, 125; Girolamo Brusoni, *Dell'Historia d'Italia, dall'anno 1625 sino al 1660* (Venice, 1661), 107–8.

[92] AGS, Estado 3832, Consulta 4 July 1633.

[93] AGS, Estado 3833, Consulta 18 February 1634, discussing a letter from Cardinal Borja dated 8 December 1633.

[94] Michel Devèze, *L'Espagne de Philippe IV (1621–1665): Siècle d'or et de misère*, 2 vols.(Paris, 1970), vol. 1, 142–9; Jaitner, 'The popes and the struggle for power during the sixteenth and seventeenth centuries', in *1648: War and Peace in Europe*, ed. K. Bussmann and H. Schilling, 2 vols. (Munster-Osnabruck, 1998), vol. 1, 61–7.

[95] Auguste Leman, *Urbain VIII et la rivalité de la France et de la Maison d'Autriche de 1631 à 1635* (Paris, 1920), 312.

[96] Devèze, *L'Espagne de Philippe IV*, vol. 1, 149.

[97] Vittorio Siri, *Memorie recondite di Vittorio Siri dall'anno 1601 fino al 1640*, 8 vols. (Lyons, 1677–9), vol. 7, 772; Siri (1608–85) was born in Parma and entered the Benedictine monastery there in 1625. Transferred to Venice to study mathematics, he took an interest in contemporary politics and began collecting documents. A client of Richelieu after 1640, and *historiographe du roi* from the time of Mazarin, Siri became one of Europe's principal historians. He enjoyed access to French diplomatic papers, and later served as Parman ambassador to the court at Versailles.

Sabran paid a call to Parma to remind the duke of Louis XIII's esteem and loyalty, but this was a preamble to the news that the king would appoint Victor Amadeus of Savoy as the general-in-chief of French armies in Italy. Richelieu promised that if France could ever raise two armies to operate in Italy, he would place the second of them under Odoardo's command. Notwithstanding this keen disappointment, Odoardo never swerved from his hostile policy to Spain, and his feelings in this regard were quite public. One symbolic act publicizing his anti-Habsburg stance was to remove the insignia of the Golden Fleece from the equestrian statues in the Piacenza square.[98] The arrival of the first French soldiers in Piacenza in the winter of 1634 created even more disruption. On 14 February 1634 the new French sergeant major in Piacenza tried to impose a tax on merchant vendors in the city square, and chased from the place those who would not comply.[99] The taxes the duke levied on merchants frequenting the currency exchange fair at Piacenza effectively killed that venue, which would not revive until 1685.[100] Odoardo was keen for the war to begin and he deplored the lack of unity among the Italian princes who, he felt, should have joined him in embracing the French cause. Their selfish interests, he complained, only maintained the status quo.[101] In March 1634, the first attempts by the King of Spain to sweet-talk the young duke and to assuage his vanity began, through the good offices of his mother and the Cardinal Aldobrandini. But Spain would not offer much in the way of tangible rewards to an untrustworthy client. In the Farnese territories themselves, it was not permitted for people to voice their apprehensions about the military escalation, but we hear echoes of their discontent all the same. Andrea Pugolotti's hugely informative diary records the assembly of all the mercenary infantry in the ducal garden of Parma on 22 October 1634, and the mustering of the cavalry the following day to welcome Marshal Créquy en route to Rome. Odoardo went out to meet the French general with all the nobility and cavalry of Parma, while guns fired from the citadel, and both the mercenaries and the militia lined the streets. 'Pray God that the arrival of the Signor Chirichi (Créquy) will not be the ruin of these states and peoples…'[102]

From 1631, then, when Richelieu violated the truce with Spain by retaining Pinerolo, France was on the road to war with the House of Austria. Louis XIII and Richelieu expected that an irresistible France could launch multiple armies in all directions against a penniless Spanish monarchy encumbered by colossal debts.[103] Richelieu justified his warlike policy by claiming that Habsburg territories encircled and threatened France, a subtle piece of propaganda that assumed that the

---

[98] Giuseppe Bertini, 'Il Farnese e il Toson d'Oro: L'ideale cavalleresco dei duchi di Parma', in *I Farnese: corti, guerra e nobilta in Antico regime*, ed. A. Bilotto, P. Del Negro, and C. Mozzarelli (Rome, 1997), 267–88.

[99] BCPLPc, Ms Pallastrelli 126, 'Croniche o Diario', 100.

[100] Drei, *I Farnese*, 207.

[101] Panella, 'Una lega italiana', 34.

[102] BPPr, Ms Parmense 461, 'Diario di Andrea Pugolotti, scritte per mia satisfazione e anco per curiosità di chi havesse gusto di leggerla', 24.

[103] Parrott, 'The causes of the Franco-Spanish war', 72–111; Stradling, 'Olivares and the origins of the Franco-Spanish war', 68–94.

Austrian branch acted in lockstep with their Spanish cousins.[104] Spaniards saw in France a Catholic country which unscrupulously allowed the Protestant cause to triumph. Richelieu's policy of internal pacification, while depriving the Huguenots of their fortresses and their troops, permitted the public toleration of the minority confession, which was something no other large state condoned and was extremely rare in Europe. Louis also encouraged jurists to make legal arguments of his 'rights' in Europe, which could never be extinguished by treaty. One jurist, Besian d'Arroy, concluded in 1634 that Louis XIII was within his rights to restore the entire empire of Charlemagne on his person, which would include all Germany, Italy, and even Spain.[105] A French army had largely dispossessed the legitimate Duke Charles of Lorraine by 1633, and Richelieu now actively solicited Italian princes to join a great anti-Spanish league that would replace Spanish hegemony in the peninsula with a French one. But only the Duke of Parma was a willing instrument of this policy.

Richelieu was the king's enabler, who built up supplies for an entire army in Pinerolo, and then placed French garrisons in the duchy of Mantua, the Swiss Grison canton, and in Piacenza and Parma, actions all reported by the King of Spain's informers.[106] Pinerolo and Casale Monferrato were good bases of operations, but only the active participation of the Duke of Savoy in the project would give the plan a chance of succeeding. Richelieu had very severe secret intentions towards Savoy proper, which was part of the Holy Roman Empire. The cardinal wished to annex it outright, by transforming it first into a fief owing vassalage to the French king.[107] Victor Amadeus I was not the scheming and unpredictable prince his father, Carlo Emanuel I, had been, but the dukes of Savoy had their own interests to protect, and they too were focused on expansion and the acquisition of a royal crown that would set them apart from junior princes in Italy. Until the very end of the 1620s, the House of Savoy was often in the Spanish clientèle. The dynasty's Spanish penchant was offset by Victor Amadeus's marriage to Louis' sister, Christine of France. The heir to the duchy was substantially older than his bride, and was an active and valiant soldier who executed, with some ability, the quixotic projects of his father. In 1625 he served in the field against Spanish troops and shared the dangers of the soldiery at the siege of Verrua.[108] A pro-Spanish policy for the new duke after 1630 was not inconceivable: Victor Amadeus was the son of a Spanish princess, and, as a child, he spoke to her in Castilian. His father sent him and his brothers to Spain for two years as an adolescent, where his uncle

---

[104] Jean Bérenger, 'La collaboration militaire austro-espagnol aux XVIe–XVIIe siècles', in *L'Espagne et ses guerres. De la fin de la Reconquête aux guerres d'Indépendance*, ed. A. Molinié and A. Merle (Paris, 2004), 11–33; also Jean Bérenger, 'Le conflit Franco-Espagnol et la guerre du Nord', in *Guerre et Paix dans l'Europe du XVIIe siècle*, ed. Jean Bérenger, Lucien Bély, and André Corvisier (Paris, 1991), 309–40.
[105] Cornette, *Le Roi de guerre*, 141.
[106] AGS, Estado 3834, Consulta of 15 February 1634.
[107] Humbert, *Le Maréchal de Créquy*, 210; Rosso, *Il Piemonte sabaudo*, 223–34.
[108] Oresko, 'The House of Savoy and the Thirty Years War', in *1648: War and Peace in Europe*, 3 vols., ed. K. Bussmann and H. Schilling (Munster-Osnabruck, 1998), vol. 1, 142–53.

king Philip III, treated him with affection. His brother, Emanuele Filiberto, later returned to Spain, and became viceroy of Sicily before his early death in 1624.[109]

Richelieu and Mazarin laid a trap for Victor Amadeus in order to entice him into the French alliance, after having tricked him out of control of Pinerolo. They promised him peace and friendship with France, and held out three prizes the dynasty had been coveting for many years: the recovery of Geneva (which had broken away in 1534 and joined the Swiss Confederation), the conquest of Genoa and the Ligurian Riviera, and the concession of a royal title, which the ambitious duchess ardently desired, for her two sisters were queens of England and Spain. The duke was under the thrall of his wife, despite her infatuation with Count Filippo d'Agliè, which made tongues wag concerning the true paternity of the ducal heir. Marie-Christine's lavish spending also alienated the duke's unmarried sisters, who lived like nuns in the Turin palace. Faced with the fierce partisanship of his wife for the French cause, Victor Amadeus's two brothers, Cardinal-Prince Maurizio and Prince Tommaso warned him that Richelieu wished to lay the burden of war against Spain on Piedmont, so that he might concentrate French resources on the Low Countries instead. Any territorial concessions accorded by Richelieu, they argued, France could easily take away at a convenient opportunity. Their sister Margherita, viceroy of Portugal, left Turin for Mantua in 1634, where she animated a pro-Spanish faction at that court.

French ambassadors in Turin—Du Plessis, Bellièvre, and Particelli d'Hémery—were not content to offer enticements, but threatened that France would annex Savoy if the duke was not compliant, and would occupy his fortresses exactly as it had done in Lorraine.[110] Victor Amadeus finally resolved to make the most of a bad bargain with his larger neighbour. The negotiations between the Duke of Savoy and Richelieu in 1634 and 1635 revolved around the use of the royal address, whereby the dukes and duchesses would become 'their royal highnesses' (different from the royal treatment, which only added a layer of symbolic honours to court receptions), which France recognized and Spain would not, and the promise of an advantageous distribution of spoils in northern Italy. France would award Victor Amadeus rich and densely populated areas taken from Spain and her allies in northern Italy, such as the Monferrato or the duchy of Milan, while giving up poor and mountainous Savoy to France. The exact designation of the territorial transfers to each of the participants of the alliance was never established. In order to allay his fears that he would be devoured in turn by the French lion, Louis XIII conferred upon Victor Amadeus command of the large French field army operating in Italy, though he was expected to take advice from the field marshal, Duke de Créquy. Richelieu nominated this general to command French troops in that theatre in part because the duke and duchess did not approve of him, and in part because he and his late father-in-law were very influential in Dauphiné and he could provide a steady stream of recruits from those districts bordering on Italy. At no time did

[109] Foa, *Vittorio Amedeo I*.   [110] Amoretti, *Il Ducato di Savoia*, 69–96.

Créquy consider himself to be a subordinate of the Victor Amadeus of Savoy, since he commanded the larger contingent, and he did not put much trust in the duke's good faith.

Richelieu customarily asked for a finger only as the first step towards taking an arm. For every concession granted by Victor Amadeus, Richelieu made new demands, such as the expansion of French territory to include a wide swath of Piedmont at the foot of the Alps, in order to supply French troops in Italy. In the final phases of negotiation just before the war, Richelieu demanded that the duke recognize the region of Savoy itself as part of French suzerainty (instead of Imperial), and that he held its ducal crown at the pleasure of the King of France. Victor Amadeus refused absolutely to agree to this clause, forcing Richelieu to withdraw that article. The cardinal's emissary, the Capuchin friar Père Joseph, then tried to convince his Italian ally to carry the principal load in the war against Spain in Italy, so that France could place its resources elsewhere. This was precisely the scenario that Victor Amadeus feared.[111]

'*A fourbe, fourbe et demi*'. The House of Savoy was famous for keeping its options open and for not being easily outmanoeuvred. Victor Amadeus's brother, Tommaso, left Turin for the Franche-Comté and Lorraine in April 1634, and not long after he appeared in Brussels, where Olivares invested him with the command of the Spanish field army in the Low Countries. While no historian has ever found evidence that the Duke of Savoy ordered his sibling to serve in the Spanish camp, it appears that the two brothers corresponded thereafter, with Tommaso calling on Victor Amadeus to jettison the French alliance and join Spain. Cardinal-Prince Maurizio moved to Rome where he served as cardinal protector of the interests of the Holy Roman Emperor. The triple defection to the House of Austria of the duke's siblings was so sudden, that observers thought the duke consented to it.[112] Certainly Cardinal Richelieu suspected double-dealing. The duke proved uncooperative in fulfilling other engagements in a way that would compromise a French victory. The pact stipulated that the Duke of Savoy would provide the artillery for the invading army, since these heavy tubes and their 'impedimenta' had to be otherwise hauled over Alpine passes, which could not be crossed by wheeled vehicles until Napoleon's time. However, he provided only about a dozen great guns to the field army, a number which was woefully inadequate to lay siege to a respectable fortress. Richelieu assumed that Savoy would supply forage and other supplies to the French army too, but the duke soon forbade his subjects to supply grain to French storehouses, with an especially strict order that nothing at all be sold to Pinerolo. The French special envoy to the duke, Michel Particelli d'Hémery, brought 700,000 *livres* to Victor Amadeus to launch the campaign as quickly as possible. The duke lamented that the sum was impossibly small, and used this as a

---

[111] Gustave Fagniez, *Le Père Joseph et Richelieu (1577–1638)*, 2 vols.(Paris, 1894), vol. 2, 221 and 275.

[112] Amoretti, *Il Ducato di Savoia*, 92; Rosso, *Il Piemonte sabaudo*, 234; Prince Tommaso complained that he never had the complete trust of the King of Spain and his powerful *valido*: Fernando Gonzalez de Leon, *The Road to Rocroi: Class, Culture and Command in the Spanish Army of Flanders, 1567–1659* (Boston and Leiden, 2009), 225.

pretext to delay his departure on campaign.[113] Savoy's own military capabilities were by no means negligible. The combined population of the duke's territories was slightly over a million people before the plague of 1630.[114] Past experience showed that the duchy could field an army of 12,000 to 15,000 men, and occasionally more, but such large numbers were a heavy drain on the treasury and could not be maintained for long.[115] So even when appearing to join the French alliance, and holding the position of commander-in-chief of the French army, the Duke of Savoy resolved to acquire some room for manoeuvre. This would have a profound impact on all the military operations of the theatre.

Spain had ample warning by 1634 that something was afoot in northern Italy, and although hard-pressed in the Netherlands and committed to help their Austrian cousins fight the Swedes in Germany, Olivares and Philip IV were not about to make concessions to Richelieu, especially after the great victory the combined Imperial and Spanish troops had won over the Swedes and their German Protestant allies at Nördlingen on 6 September of that year. In the latter half of the 1630s, the Spanish Empire was still able to maintain about 150,000 professional soldiers in its various theatres of war, between the field armies, the garrisons, and the fleet escorts.[116] If France's long-term strategy relied on obtaining offensive bridgeheads located beyond its borders, Spain developed a practice of defence based on 'bastions', whereby some peripheral provinces had the mission of protecting more central ones. The duchy of Milan served this purpose in Italy, barring access of invaders to the kingdom of Naples. To maintain the system it was enough to place garrisons in the main towns and their citadels, and hold the passes over the Apennines leading to Genoa and the Ligurian naval base of Finale, by which seaborne reinforcements would arrive.[117] Milan was a crossroads of strategic waterways, and warlike supplies floated down canals from the Alpine lakes.[118] Firmly ensconced in Lombardy, with about 15,000 men even at their weakest, Spanish forces effectively controlled the entire peninsula. The great citadel of Milan rarely contained more than 500 or 600 men, principally Spanish, but that was enough to hold the city of almost 100,000 people firmly in hand. Non-threatened fortresses only needed small garrisons of about 100 men or fewer.[119]

---

[113] De Mun, *Richelieu et la Maison de Savoie*, 55.

[114] Foa, *Vittorio Amedeo I*, 150; Piedmont's population was given as 700,000, Savoy 400,000.

[115] Claudio De Consoli, *Al soldo del duca: L'amministrazione delle armate sabaude (1560–1630)* (Turin, 1999), 196–200; with its population and revenues basically stable 50 years later, Gregorio Leti gives similar figures for 1685, *Il Cerimoniale historico e politico* (Waesberge, 1685), 166.

[116] Davide Maffi, 'Il potere delle armi: la monarchia spagnola e i suoi eserciti (1635–1700): Una revisitazione del mito della decadenza', *Rivista Storica Italiana*, 118 (2006): 394–445.

[117] Luis Antonio Ribot Garcia, 'Milano, piazza d'armi della monarchia spagnola', in *Millain the Great. Milano nelle brume del Seicento*, ed. Aldo de Maddalena (Milan, 1989), 349–63; also by Luis Antonio Ribot Garcia, 'Las Provincias italianas y la defensa de la Monarquìa', in *Nel sistema imperiale l'Italia spagnola*, ed. A. Musi (Naples, 1994), 67–92; Mario Rizzo, ' "Ottima gente da guerra": Cremonesi al servizio della strategia imperiale', in *Storia di Cremona: L'Età degli Asburgo di Spagna (1535–1707)*, ed. G. Politi (Cremona, 2006), 126–45; Davide Maffi, 'Un bastione incerto? L'Esercito di Lombardia tra Filippo IV e Carlo II (1630–1700)', in *Guerra y Sociedad en la Monarquia Hispanica*, ed. E. Garcia Hernan and D. Maffi, 2 vols.(Madrid, 2006), vol. 2, 501–36.

[118] Bercé, 'Les guerres dans l'Italie', 315.

[119] AGS, Estado 3342, Consulta no. 58, August 1635.

Preparations for hostilities quickened on both sides, beginning in 1635. The first operations took place in the Valtellina corridor, where the Duke de Rohan led a force of French and Swiss Grison Protestant soldiers to seize the valley and its key fortified towns in April. That same month, Odoardo was requisitioning horses and boats around Piacenza for hauling supplies. He did not trust his Italian contingents very much, and wished to acquire as many French soldiers as he could. Odoardo also wished to acquire the services of France's most talented general, the Maréchal de Toiras, who was a personal enemy of Richelieu, living in Rome. He had no intention of following his advice, but merely wished to enhance his own status by having a famous French field marshal serving under his command.[120] Meanwhile, he posted agents in the Apennines border stations to welcome French recruits as they arrived, and escort them to their billets in the plain.[121] These men arrived in little parties of up to 50 men, '*alla sfilata*', carrying only swords and daggers, and with their rucksacks full of food. Some marched through Genoese territory from the Monferrato. Others embarked on small boats at Voltri near Genoa, and stepped ashore farther east at Lerici, then proceeded up the valley roads to the Parman border. Genoese authorities were far from united on a proper response to this traffic. The passage of troops across neutral territory was a customary procedure in early modern Europe, and statesmen considered it unobjectionable if they paid their way and avoided plundering villages and farms along their route. Consequently, the Genoese simply provided commissioners to watch over the troops on their march. When Spanish galleys intercepted a Genoese vessel transporting some of these soldiers in July, the republic protested the violation of its neutrality and obtained their quick release.

Spanish preparations mostly reacted to those of France. They were exceedingly well informed via their ambassadors in Venice, Rome, and Genoa. Cardinal Albornoz, the new governor of Milan, was utterly untutored in military matters, and Madrid quickly realized that he would have to be replaced by a career soldier.[122] In the meantime, he deferred to his military commanders on important points, although Albornoz and his senior military adviser, Don Carlos Coloma, tussled with each other over jurisdiction and appointments.[123] By the spring of 1635 they were sending itemized company-by-company tallies of their troops to Madrid, and listing the size of their garrisons. Native Spanish *tercios* were the most in demand for their quality, although Coloma deplored the increasing tendency for the king and Olivares to award high rank to peninsular officers on the grounds of their high birth.[124] A *tercio* was a large infantry formation of pikemen and musketeers

---

[120] Toiras eventually rallied the court of Turin, where he became Victor Amadeus' chief military advisor. He remained the only French officer the Duke of Savoy fully trusted. See Foa, *Vittorio-Amedeo I*, 223.

[121] AGS, Estado 3343, Consulta no. 111, 14 July 1635.

[122] Davide Maffi, *Il baluardo della corona: Guerra, esercito, finanze e società nella Lombardia seicentesca (1630–1660)* (Florence, 2007), 154.

[123] Guill Ortega, 'L'Assedio di Valenza del 1635, estratto da Carlos Coloma 1566–1637: Espada y pluma de los Tercios', *Valensa d'na vota*, 23 (2008): 25–52, trans. Carlo Dabene.

[124] Gonzalez De Leon, *The Road to Rocroi*, 167.

composed of multiple companies (between 10 and 15) with a paper strength of 3,000 men, but, in reality, their consistent strength was rarely more than half that.[125] There were barely 2,000 native Spanish troops in service in Lombardy early in 1635, although more were on their way. Most of the troops available were Italians recruited in both northern and southern Italy. Neapolitan troops sometimes demoralized the generals. Dispatches to Madrid claimed that apart from the officers and nobles, the southerners were '*la mas vil soldadesca que Don Carlos (Coloma) ha visto en su vida*', although apart from their tendency to desert it is difficult to understand exactly why.[126] At the Battle of Nördlingen, which was the gold standard of battles in the Thirty Years' War by the juxtaposition of units both from northern and southern Europe, Neapolitan *tercios* were in the thick of the fighting throughout, right alongside the Spanish units, neither of which would cede their positions to the 'Swedes' (mostly Scots and north Germans). The Neapolitan cavalry of Gambacorta that pinned down the Swedish right flank contributed significantly to the triumph as well.[127] In the impending war against France and Savoy, the Neapolitan officers and men would play a conspicuous part.[128] Coloma recognized the inferiority of his cavalry to those of the French, which made field battles risky, but northern Italy, with its dense promiscuous agriculture, presented few districts where cavalry could operate freely, compared to the open-field landscape of the Low Countries and Germany.[129] Early in the year 1635, Spanish forces in Italy amounted to about 20,000 professional soldiers, of whom a minimum of 6,000 would be required to serve in fortresses. The remainder would have to watch over the Duke de Rohan in the Valtellina, provide a screen of forces along the border with Mantua and Parma, and comprise two additional field forces, one north of the Po protecting Milan, and one south of the Po to guard the vital communications with the Riviera ports, Finale in particular. These scattered contingents could not prevent a confederate assault on the major cities of the duchy. Albornoz had sent money off to Tirol and Germany in order to raise regiments of dragoons, who were infantrymen mounted on horseback, but they would not be available for almost a year.

Albornoz and Coloma were encouraged by the loyal response of the Milanese aristocracy, who offered to raise troops at their personal expense in exchange for a command and visibility. Cardinal Gian Giacomo Teodoro Trivulzio, a soldier-priest with estates along the Po near Piacenza, played the leading role. Born into one of the leading feudatory families of Lombardy, King Philip III awarded him

---

[125] Maffi, *Il baluardo della corona*, 82–7; Julio Albi de la Cuesta, *De Pavìa a Rocroi: los tercios de infanteria española en los siglos XVI y XVII* (Madrid, 1999), 46–51.

[126] Maffi, *Il baluardo della corona*, 97; AGS, Estado 3837, letter of Carlos Coloma, 28 August 1635.

[127] Eduardo de Mesa, *Nordlingen 1634: Victoria decisiva de los tercios* (Madrid, 2003); for an account in English see William Guthrie, *Battles of the Thirty Years War: From White Mountain to Nordlingen* (Westport, CT, and London, 2002), 264–84.

[128] Angelantonio Spagnoletti, 'Onore e spirito nazionale nei soldati italiani al servizio della monarchia spagnola', in *Militari e società civile nell'Europa dell'età moderna, sec. XVI–XVIII*, ed. Bernhard Kroener and Claudio Donati (Bologna, 2007), 211–53.

[129] Maffi, *Il baluardo della corona*, 91.

the habit of the Knights of Santiago at the age of nine. He had become a priest while still a young man, upon the death of his wife in 1620, and progressed quickly to the rank of cardinal in 1629. He was also one of the leading creditors of the Spanish Crown, which no doubt motivated Philip IV to award the Golden Fleece to his adolescent son, Ercole, in 1634. As a man of influence with estates directly threatened by the hostilities, the cardinal raised thousands of men from his territories, augmented by recruits he enticed away from Duke Odoardo's army in nearby Piacenza. He also sent to Milan and Madrid proposals to build field fortifications in vulnerable places along the Po to prevent raids from Parman troops into the richest part of Italy.[130] Pompeo Targone, a Milanese engineer who contributed greatly to the fall of Protestant La Rochelle in 1628, proposed an intriguing new secret weapon, a horse-mounted small cannon that could spray enemy cavalry with grapeshot.[131] Troilo Rossi, Count of San Secondo, a major Parman feudatory serving in the entourage of the cardinal-infante (brother of King Philip IV and one of the victorious generals at the battle of Nördlingen), proposed to raise a company of horse. In addition to the professional troops, the Milanese aristocracy mobilized thousands of militiamen from their estates. The peasant militia in Lombardy was created in 1615 during the Monferrato war against Piedmont, but its military usefulness was very limited and the men were not considered to be worth the supplies they consumed. Demobilized in 1617, the militia was reconstituted in a multitude of district companies in 1635.[132] Most Italian states already had similar auxiliary forces in being.

While Lombardy mobilized, Olivares intended to strike a pre-emptive blow against France by sending a fleet of galleys under the Marques de Santa Cruz to attack the coast of Provence in the spring of 1635, with the hope of seizing a major port like Marseille or Toulon. Galleys and their transport ships habitually navigated close to shore, so the plan entailed seizing ports or islands that would serve as bases. This would allow them to interdict shipping along the Italian Riviera. Spanish amphibious troops would also tie down French soldiers in towns and castles along the French coast as far as Marseille. However, near Corsica and Elba, a great storm beset these galleys on their cruise northwards from Naples and some of them were lost. The crews and troops of the damaged vessels disembarked on Corsica, where many of the oarsmen (often convicts or slaves from North Africa) fled into the interior, aided by the inaction of the Genoese authorities. It would take months before the flotilla was ready to resume its project, which would, of necessity, be less ambitious.[133]

---

[130] AGS, Estado 3837, Consulta 27 July 1635, letter of Cardinal Trivulzio; Gianvittorio Signorotto, *Milano Spagnola: Guerra, istituzioni, uomini di governo (1635–1660)*(2nd edn, Milan, 2001), 127.

[131] AGS, Estado 3341 no. 7, letter from Pompeo Targone of Milan, 15 October 1633.

[132] Mario Rizzo, 'I cespiti di un maggiorente lombardo del Seicento: Ercole Teodoro Trivulzio e la milizia forese', *Archivio Storico Lombardo*, 120 (1990): 463–77; Sara Pedretti, 'Ai confini occidentali dello Stato di Milano: l'impiego delle milizie rurali nelle guerre del Seicento', in *Alle frontiere della Lombardia: Politica, guerra e religione nell'età moderna*, ed. C. Donati (Milan, 2006), 177–200.

[133] AGS, Estado 3837, Consulta of 18 June 1635; Stradling, 'Olivares and the origins of the Franco-Spanish war', 68–94.

Clearly the initiative lay with Cardinal Richelieu and Louis XIII, regardless of the mutual deployment of armies and fleets in the first half of 1635. The league of Italian states that French diplomacy tried to bring into being was largely stillborn, since the Pope, the Grand Duke of Tuscany, the Republic of Venice and, by the end, the Duke of Modena wished to have no part of it. That left two unwilling allies in the dukes of Savoy and Mantua, and Odoardo Farnese, who chafed with impatience for the war to begin.

2
Duke Odoardo's Army

Robert Wright, in his book *Nonzero*, describes the ways in which war compels people into greater cooperation. War appears in Wright's telling as a zero-sum game (where one side wins, and the other loses proportionally) that generates non-zero-sum games of mutual cooperation for the greater benefit of each side. Conflict with an outside group pushes people who regularly interact with each other more tightly together into organic solidarity. So, if war creates a situation of zero-sum contention between the two belligerents, it has a paradoxically rallying effect at lower levels, uniting people into the service of the cause.[1] The unifying effect of war operates something like a 'general law of history'. This theory, which is graceful in its simplicity, holds up rather well in the case of Odoardo's little duchy.

OFFICERS AND GENTLEMEN

Odoardo's war mobilized the duchy's aristocracy like no other cause. Inducing the region's social elites to serve them voluntarily had been one of the principal aims of Farnese policy since the dynasty's establishment in northern Italy. The dukes, since the inception of the dynasty in 1545, expected their feudatories to stand behind the throne to better reflect its splendour. The so-called plot against Ranuccio I mentioned at the beginning of Chapter 1 was the work of a socially homogeneous group of interrelated feudatory families without deep roots in the city elite, whose strategic castles and extensive lands the duke coveted. The Gran Giustizia of 1612 ended all possibility of a successful coup by disgruntled and uncooperative aristocrats against the Farnese dynasty, and served as a watershed episode in relations between the prince, the feudatories, and the urban patriciate, especially as the judicial murder of the plotters and the confiscation of their estates reinforced the power of the Farnese considerably.[2] Ranuccio I, in the immediate aftermath of the sacrifice of Parman lords, created two companies of noble ceremonial guards—the Cornetta Bianca—one for Parma and the other for Piacenza. Cardinal Odoardo kept the nobles in hand by multiplying prestigious functions at court, and he created companies of ceremonial guards and gentlemen for this purpose. These functions, some of which were no sinecure, provided the members of titled

---

[1] Robert Wright, *Nonzero: The Logic of Human Destiny* (New York, 2000), 54–64.
[2] Jean Boutier, 'Trois conjurations italiennes: Florence (1575), Parme (1611), Gênes (1628)', *Mélanges de l'Ecole Française de Rome: Italie & Méditerranée*, 108 (1996): 370.

houses with stipends, a continuous presence at court, and visibility on ceremonial occasions.[3] The dynasty did not permit nobles to reside outside the state without permission, and it expected them to rally around the duke whenever he called upon them. It entrusted court dignitaries with diplomatic assignments, whose expenditures of representation were not always reimbursed. The personalization of the prince's power at the court *required* a continuous and conspicuous presence of the most senior nobility if they were not to become invisible. The power of the prince was also expressed in the lavish lifestyle at the court, which the nobles were forced to reflect at their own expense.[4] Fierce competition among noble houses for conspicuous visibility ruined many ancient families across much of Italy, particularly outside the capital cities where they did not enjoy much direct access to the prince.[5]

Princes might browbeat their nobility into subordination, but recent research over the past few decades has demonstrated that rulers could not easily direct unwilling societies to obey them. It was more to the prince's advantage if he could come to some understanding with local notables; in exchange for obedience and loyal service, they could obtain preferment and special treatment in the way of material recompense and political influence.[6] Nobles in Piacenza before and during the Farnese era constituted about 5 per cent of the city's population, but they were anything but homogenous. The oldest and richest houses constituted about a quarter of the 176 noble families in the 1540s, and a civic nobility, comprised of judicial and mercantile urban elites, made up the remainder. Only the prince could sort out conflicting claims of precedence among these new and old, titled and tacit nobles.[7] The oldest nobility clearly enjoyed preferential treatment when it came to lucrative roles at the court.[8] Alongside the feudatories, the Farnese wished to promote the city elites, something Duke Ranuccio I did systematically between 1596 and 1620, by creating 29 *cavalieri* (whose nobility lapsed when they died), 15 hereditary nobles of Parma, and 6 hereditary nobles (or *patrizi*) in Piacenza. Once the dynasty recognized their promotion officially, these *patrizi* could hope to climb into the ranks of the feudatories, although they could not expect to hold more than one fief.[9] What historians once disparagingly called a process of

---

[3] Marco Boscarelli, 'Appunti sulle istituzioni e le campagne militari dei ducati di Parma e Piacenza in epoca farnesiana', in *I Farnese: corti, guerra e nobilta in Antico regime*, ed. A. Bilotto, P. Del Negro, and C. Mozzarelli (Rome, 1997), 561–78.

[4] Cesare Mozzarelli, 'Principe, Corte e governo tra Cinque e Settecento' in C. Mozzarelli, *Antico regime e modernità* (Rome, 2008), 153–65.

[5] For a description on the 'déclassement' of this turbulent aristocracy and their rapid decline see Giorgio Politi, *Aristocrazia e potere politico nella Cremona di Filippo II* (Milan, 1976), 223.

[6] Jeremy Black, *War: A Short History* (London and New York, 2009), 74; for groundbreaking research into just such a pact, Beik, *Absolutism and Society in Seventeenth-century France: State Power and Provincial Aristocracy in Languedoc* (Cambridge and New York, 1989).

[7] Ugo Benassi, 'Governo assoluto e città suddita nel primo Seicento', *Bollettino Storico Piacentino*, 12 (1917): 193–203, and 13 (1918): 30–8.

[8] Carlo Emanuele Manfredi, 'La nobiltà piacentina alla Corte Farnesiana', in *I Farnese: corti, guerra e nobilta in Antico regime*, ed. A. Bilotto, P. Del Negro, and C. Mozzarelli. (Rome, 1997), 33–46.

[9] Roberto Sabbadini, *La Grazia e l'Onore: principe, nobiltà e ordine sociale nei ducati farnesiani* (Rome, 2001), 64–74.

retrograde 'refeudalization' was, in fact, just the Italian version of the domestication of the nobility unfolding simultaneously in France and other monarchies.[10] Noble houses let themselves be domesticated by these new offices and functions because, by the 1620s, the economic conjuncture had soured considerably, reducing revenues of all kinds and the value of the assets behind them.[11] In Piacenza, by the early decades of the seventeenth century, families with mercantile activities and assets had already shifted these towards the ownership of land. The famine of 1629 and the great plague of 1630, which killed perhaps as much as a third of the population, accelerated this transfer, for peasants needed to sell their holdings to survive. Hard times changed the make-up of the social elites in Emilia and reduced their margin of manoeuvre with respect to the ruling dynasty.[12]

Young Duke Odoardo, who was hypersensitive to issues of honour and status, paused this process of diluting the traditional nobility with an influx of new families. According to the index of the patents of nobility issued by the dynasty prior to 1646, Duke Ranuccio I delivered 10 letters of *famigliarità*, which gave the beneficiaries access to court ceremonies, alongside the 26 knighthoods or *cavalieri*, while Odoardo in his entire reign issued only one patent of *famigliarità* and no knighthoods.[13] The mercantile families and the new nobles crowded into the ranks of the aristocracy and the feudatories under Odoardo's son, Ranuccio II, starting in 1648, after which, in Piacenza, more than one family entered their ranks every year, and half of these obtained a feudal title.[14] Similarly, in Parma there was no mechanism which prevented families who were doing well socially from participating in the municipal assembly and obtaining greater visibility thereby. If Odoardo did not rush to ennoble upwardly mobile families (the term *nobiltà* was not used before 1660), he might have been expecting to see first some sign of their adhesion to his cause. Noble status was only one of the special favours the duke could bestow on deserving applicants. The ducal *patenti* or letters patent cover a great variety of situations where the duke authorized something in his prerogative his subjects desired, beginning with those who were already rich and influential. The duke could award someone a pension, he could confirm their hold over a fief, or he could appoint a judicial official there who was the feudatory's client. He could grant nobles permission to carry weapons, to hunt on reserved lands, and he could legitimize their bastards. The duke could authorize nobles to sell their

---

[10] Gregory Hanlon, 'In praise of refeudalization: princes and feudatories in north-central Italy from the sixteenth to the eighteenth century', in *Sociability and its Discontents: Civil Society, Social Capital and their Alternatives in Late Medieval and Early Modern Europe*, ed. Nicholas Eckstein and Nicholas Terpstra (Turnhout, 2009), 213–25.

[11] Marco Cattini, 'Congiunture sociali e dinamiche politiche nei consigli municipali di Parma e Piacenza in età moderna', in *Persistenze feudali e autonomie communicative in stati padani fra Cinque e Settecento*, ed. G. Tocci (Bologna, 1988), 59.

[12] Paola Subacchi, *La Ruota della Fortuna: Arricchimento e promozione sociale in una città padana in età moderna* (Milan, 1996), 17 and 122.

[13] ASPr, Indice Patenti, vol. 3, Patenti of famigliarità and of cavaliere.

[14] Emilio Nasalli Rocca, 'Il patriziato piacentino nell'età del principato', in *Studi di Paleografia, Diplomatica, Storia e Araldica in onore di Cesare Manaresi* (Milan, 1953), 227–57; also Pietro Castignoli, 'Caratteri della feudalità nel ducato di Piacenza durante il secolo XVII', *Archivio Storico per le Province Parmensi*, 18 (1966): 317–24.

harvests outside the state for a higher price, which was normally prohibited. He could appoint these noblemen and their wives to the court in some capacity. For families not yet noble, the duke could admit them to citizen status that taxed them on the (lower) city rate, and exempted them from dealing with feudal judges by committing their lawsuits and their criminal actions to city magistrates. Most people of property managed lawsuits and juggled mortgages and debts. The duke could intervene at any moment to protect someone from their creditors by arranging some compromise. There are patents for all of these situations in the records. This does not take into account the thousands of petitions that the duke and his functionaries received every year from subjects of every status, requesting a vast array of exemptions and derogations of the law in their favour.[15]

Successful prosecution of a war required bringing the aristocracy, especially the feudal aristocracy, onside, for they were people of influence and means who could lay their swords at Odoardo's feet. For centuries the principal feudatories led contingents of mercenary soldiers in the service of the dukes of Milan and of Parma. They might use the argument of the natural 'generosity' of the nobility, but, of course, nothing is free. The aristocrats rallied to his service because it was advantageous for the prestige of their house, even though the duke would draw upon their purses heavily, and put many of them in harm's way for the duration of the campaign.[16] A report to the cardinal-regent in 1625 clearly exposes the rationale for choosing noble officers. Spain called upon the duchy to respect its treaty obligation to raise contingents to operate in the field with Spanish forces. The cardinal also required some professional troops to adequately garrison Piacenza and Parma and to safeguard the dynasty's control over the duchy in an era of instability. Orazio Scotti's report to the cardinal in April 1625 described the potential officers who might be appointed, and why they would be appropriate and willing to serve.[17] The report began with the names of captains living outside the duchy with military experience and the money and connections enabling them to raise and outfit a company of soldiers for Farnese service. Since Parma mobilized troops in the framework of the Spanish alliance, ducal agents did not need to go farther than Cremona or Milan to find captains, but Urbino and Gubbio in the Marches retained the reputation for having good soldiers, and the author hoped that the Pope would consent to allow recruitment there and in the Romagna. Scotti continued his report with a list of names of likely candidates living in Piacenza and Parma who had military experience under their belts, and enough money in the family—often in the hands of their fathers—to put men in the field. A number of these were already serving the House of Austria in Flanders and in Germany, like the brothers Francesco

---

[15] Cristina Nubola, 'Supplications between politics and justice: the northern and central Italian states in the early modern age', *International Review of Social History*, 46 (2001): 35–56; also Paola Ripetti, 'Scrivere ai potenti: Suppliche e memoriali a Parma (sec. XVI–XVIII)', *Sogittura e Civiltà*, 24 (2000): 295–358. See also the study by Colin Rose, 'Grace from Above: Petitions and Appeals in Farnese Parma 1631–1727' (MA thesis, Dalhousie University, 2010).

[16] Maria Nadia Covini, *L'Esercito del duca: Organizzazione militare e istituzioni al tempo degli Sforza (1450–1480)* (Rome, 1998), 93–102.

[17] ASPr, Governo Farnesiano, Milizie 1: Lettera informativa per scegliere e creare ufficiali, da Orazio Scotti, 15 April 1625.

and Marcello Marazzani, but he hoped that they would drop everything and rally to the duke's service. Some good prospects were unwilling to accept the command of infantry detachments, and therefore he put forward their names for command of a cavalry squadron instead. Some of them could not come home because they had outstanding warrants for their arrest from ducal tribunals, or because they were on inimical terms with other feudatories. In both cases Scotti urged the cardinal regent to use his power to iron out these impediments. People without experience of war were also considered, (the report continued), if they had good social standing and adequate financing: 'Giovan Francesco Valera, brother in law of the marchesino, is a gentleman of good breeding (*garbo*), wealthy, he has friends and I know he thinks were are considering him to make a company to serve outside the state, and I believe he will accept. Giovan Battista Asinelli is also of good breeding, and his father is rich with 3,000 scudi of revenue.'

Aristocrats had excellent practical reasons for wishing to please the duke, for serving him in high-profile military capacities asserted their social and political leadership too. Ongoing war is indeed a negative-sum game, costly to everybody. But *this* war was going to be easy, and grateful Italians were going to acclaim Odoardo as a liberator. Did the nobles respond to his call for support? Examining the rosters of ducal subjects in the invasion army of 1635 and in the reconstituted army of the following year, the answer is a resounding yes. We find 263 names of *native* noblemen in the army lists and other chronicles dealing with the war, but this is still incomplete. We lack the names of the Parman noblemen admitted to the honour guard of the Cornetta Bianca (probably a couple of dozen individuals). We do not have much information on the garrison of Piacenza or its citadel, nor do we know the commanders of the city gates of Parma. We do not have the names of most of the commanders of militia companies, nor the castellans of most of the castles and walled towns considered to be strategic enough to garrison. There are, in addition, families whose noble status was unclear in 1635 or whose nobility has escaped our notice. So a more realistic number of noble vassals in the active military service of Duke Odoardo would be 300 or perhaps even more, out of an entire noble population of three or 4,000 individuals of both sexes, young and old, lay and ecclesiastic.[18] Despite the long internal peace, Italy's aristocrats had, for generations, offered their services in foreign wars, and they still defined their status in military terms. In the period of the Thirty Years' War, as I have written elsewhere, the pool of willing participants was still very large.[19]

Not all noblemen were equally inclined to fight, however. The great feudatory dynasties with stout rural castles and a long military pedigree contributed more than the others, especially in Piacenza. Eight high-profile dynasties contributed 62 individuals, and 42 of them came from the leading four, the Scotti, Anguissola,

---

[18] For detailed information on the families concerned here, see Giorgio Fiori, *Le antiche famiglie di Piacenza e i loro stemmi* (Piacenza, 1979); Maurizio de Meo, *Le antiche famiglie nobili e notabili di Parma e i loro stemmi*, 3 vols.(Parma, 2000).

[19] Gregory Hanlon, *The Twilight of a Military Tradition: Italian Aristocrats and European Conflicts, 1560–1800* (London and New York, 1998); for a regional sample, see Gregory Hanlon, 'The demilitarization of an Italian provincial nobility: Siena 1560–1740', *Past & Present*, 155 (1997), 64–108.

Pallavicino, and Arcelli. These were the same families which, for generations, had provided officers and soldiers to foreign states like Savoy.[20] Piacenza, with 166 of 260 identified noble origins, was clearly the city that was more focused on military matters, while Parma figured only 91 times.[21] The duke was careful to admit to noble status a handful of families from Borgo San Donnino, and three more families gave their place of origin as villages or small towns. It is possible that I have erred by including among the nobles some commoners who shared some patronyms which were widespread in the region, like Bianchi or Ferrari. But alongside families whose names figured in the rosters of senior municipal magistrates or persons admitted to the court, there were other families not included here whose nobility everyone considered 'tacit'. Many of these additional names are the patronyms of the brides or mothers of the noblemen figuring in the company books; these men were usually imported from authentic noble families of other Lombard cities. So the participation of social elites in Odoardo's army would include scores of families just under the threshold of official noble status, many of which would obtain that rank in the reign of Ranuccio II. On the face of its participation alone, the involvement of the dynasty's elite is quite astonishing and fully validates historian Jean Boutier's claim that the Gran Giustizia was a watershed.

Not all the noblemen were serving at a rank which reflected their exalted status, for there were not enough officer positions to satisfy everyone with a fine pedigree. The duke restricted the admission to his honour guard of the Cornetta Bianca to the leading families of each major city, which included the major court officials or their close relatives able to participate on campaign. Other nobles of diverse status he designated commanders of companies, or else ensigns or lieutenants, but, as we will see later in this chapter, the duke was careful to fill some of these roles with people with some experience. There were two additional guard companies, one of horse and another of foot that were packed with noblemen who served alongside experienced soldiers of various extraction. By concentrating these people in units kept close by the duke's person and commanded by him, the noblemen retained a fair degree of visibility. But even this was not sufficient to accommodate all of them, and some aristocrats were willing to serve at any cost. Another 116 noblemen, perhaps without any military experience to draw upon, served as rank and file in various other units over the two campaigns, and four others served as non-commissioned officers. About 60 per cent of those (66 of 116) served in the cavalry, or started out as infantrymen and then graduated soon after to become cavalry troopers. Two Piacenza families of considerable prominence, the Mancassola and the Nicelli, provided four men each, none of whom held a commission or even a berth in a guards company. Teodoro Nicelli signed on as a simple cavalry trooper at age 50. Teodoro Landi signed up as a cavalry trooper too, but this smooth-faced youth of 17 was soon sent home.

---

[20] De Consoli, *Al soldo del duca: L'amministrazione delle armate sabaude (1560–1630)* (Turin, 1999), 48.

[21] On the military engagement of Piacenza noblemen, and the relative dominance of the feudatories, see Gustavo di Gropello, 'La nobiltà piacentina e la funzione militare', in *I Farnese: corti, guerra e nobiltà in Antico regime*, ed. A. Bilotto, P. Del Negro, and C. Mozzarelli (Rome, 1997), 47–52.

Powerful peer pressure sufficed to induce all of these men to perform well. Noblemen like these would have gone out of their way to stand out from the common soldiery, already evident by their keenness to serve in the cavalry. In the era before uniforms and standardized weapons, they would have brought their own finery, armour and arms, and perhaps their own horse too, kept in the baggage train at their own expense.[22] In the army, there was a great deal of pressure for the officers and nobles of every rank to maintain an ostentatious lifestyle in order to gain and keep the respect of their peers and underlings, and to remind their superiors of their eligibility for higher office.[23] One might think that these spontaneous careers were part of social posturing, but noblemen in service could hardly avoid the hardships of campaigning, although they might petition the duke to go home. Of the more than 200 gentlemen in our rosters, only five deserted, while ten were killed or died on campaign. Ducal tribunals sentenced two more to death for flinching in the face of danger, and one paid with his life for a moment's loss of nerve. The same social pressures pushing them to join the colours worked powerfully to keep them in line.[24]

Noble birth in itself did not always suffice to acquire an officer's commission from the duke. I have found 109 commissions or *patenti* issued by Odoardo from 1629 until 1636, involving 96 different individuals, from elite cavalry to militia infantry captains, and to commissioners who oversaw troop lodgings on rural communities.[25] These do not comprise the totality of officers' commissions handed out, and it is interesting that there were no lieutenants, or ensigns among them (or commissions for *cornetta*, the most junior officer of cavalry). This means that the colonels, sergeant majors, captains, or adjutants enjoyed some authority to appoint the junior officers serving with them. The absence of commissions awarded to French officers is also conspicuous, which leads me to suspect that French colonels and captains received their commissions from Louis XIII, and that the Duke of Parma merely paid for the maintenance of their companies. Odoardo conferred only two commissions on French officers in 1634, and the remaining ten he issued after the siege of Valenza, when he hired captains to recruit troops in France and present them in Casale Monferrato the following spring for service in his army.

The *patenti* identified the positions that were vacant and then often stated the reasons why the duke conferred them upon the persons named. One might immediately think that he would reward his principal courtiers for loyal service. For example, Cremona Visdomini, a capable mathematician of Piacenza and Odoardo's personal tutor as a child, was rewarded with a company of horse and command of a castle. Orazio Pallavicino, created captain, had taught the young prince how to

---

[22] Paolo Pinti, 'Le Armi dei Farnese', in *I Farnese: Corti, Guerra e nobiltà in Antico regime*, ed. A. Bilotto, P. Del Negro, and C. Mozzarelli (Rome, 1997), 493–508.

[23] John Lynn, *Giant of the 'Grand Siècle': The French Army 1610–1715* (Cambridge, 1997), 239; also Hervé Drévillon, *L'Impôt du sang: le métier des armes sous Louis XIV* (Paris, 2005), 103–8.

[24] For a comparable situation in the Spanish army, see Lorraine White, 'Spain's early modern soldiers: origins, motivation and loyalty', *War and Society*, 19 (2001): 19–46.

[25] ASPr, Patenti. The archivation of the *patenti* defies understanding. Of the many volumes containing manuscript copies of these documents, only four volumes contain significant numbers of military commissions; vols 7, 28, 31, and 41 bis.

ride and wield a sword.[26] But only about 10 per cent of the commissions specifically mention faithful service at court or the beneficiary's status there, like page, *cameriere* (attendants of the bedchamber), or ambassador. We might include among the courtiers a number of guards from the company of *Arcieri*, who performed security functions at the palace, and about half of whom claimed to have military experience, but they were definitely not aristocrats. The commissions assigned responsibilities to them that were not all prestigious. Five or six beneficiaries were entrusted with the difficult task of sorting out the lodgings and foraging for infantry and cavalry while they waited for the campaign to begin. To others Odoardo confided the guard of city gates, in command of a handful of paid soldiers and a larger number of militiamen. Still other beneficiaries, sometimes noblemen, were placed at the head of village militia companies or, in two cases, were entrusted with coordinating large numbers of militiamen who patrolled the border areas to oppose enemy looting parties.

A good pedigree and a rich family gave young nobles some advantage in obtaining good posts in the new army, but there was a premium for expertise too. Twenty-seven of the beneficiaries of these commissions claimed military experience, extending as far back as the 1580s in the case of Galvano Anguissola, who followed the great duke Alessandro to Flanders. About a third of them cited service in Flanders and Germany since 1620. An equivalent number mentioned serving in the wars against Piedmont since 1615, and a number of them fought in the 1625 campaign in the Parman contingent under Don Francesco Farnese. All four of Odoardo's regimental commanders could boast considerable experience commanding men in action. The irony was that the great majority of the experienced officers forming the cadres of Odoardo's army, like those of other Italian armies, had done so in the defence of the Habsburg Catholic cause.[27] Fulvio Clerici spent the better part of his career in Spanish service in Flanders. The handful of other officers citing military experience referred to garrison duty in Venetian territories, or else in tranquil papal garrisons. The subjects of Odoardo were not numerous among these. Eighteen of these commissioned officers (at least) were not natural subjects of the duke, but hailed instead from all over northern and central Italy, and Corsica too, and one of them, Giovan Battista Cislago from Alessandria, came from enemy territory subject to the King of Spain. Some could boast of injuries acquired on campaign, at the bitter siege of Vercelli in 1617 (Francesco Serafini) or at Verrua (Scipione Colla) in 1625. Ricciardo Avogadri was a Brescian cavalry officer serving as lieutenant-colonel in the German regiment of Ottavio Piccolomini at the fateful Battle of Lützen in 1632, who led repeated cavalry charges against

---

[26] BPPr, Ms Parmense 737, Hippolito Calandrini, 'L'Heroe d'Italia, overo Vita del Sereniss.mo Odoardo Farnese il Grande, quinto duca di Parma e di Piacenza', 62; the noblemen from Piacenza were particularly salient in Odoardo's reign. See Manfredi, 'La nobiltà piacentina alla Corte Farnesiana', 35–46.

[27] Nobles in the Papal States who sought active military service enlisted in several of the Catholic armies operating in Germany; Giampiero Brunelli, *Soldati del Papa: Politica militare e nobiltà nello Stato della Chiesa (1560–1644)* (Rome, 2003), 206.

superior numbers and so prevented a Swedish victory.[28] Avogadri suffered a near-fatal musket wound in that desperate fight. The wounds officers received during these exploits constituted a kind of diploma reflecting their hands-on experience of war.

Few states possessed the resources to maintain troops in war and peace, and so the number of *tercios* or regiments swelled and contracted according to necessity. The standard practice for raising a *tercio* entailed designating the senior officers first. The King of Spain first appointed a colonel or maestro de campo, and a given number of captains, each with recruiting powers. The great majority of the *tercio* commanders in Spanish service were aristocrats, and no fewer than 40 of the 49 Lombard colonels were feudatories. In Piacenza and Parma, these colonels, like those elsewhere in Europe, possessed both the military and administrative command of a formation numbering about ten or twelve companies. They oversaw the behaviour of the officers below them, and applied general discipline through specialized judicial officers acting in their name. The colonels also served as Odoardo's 'general staff' and advised him on plans for the campaign and the best means of their execution. Regiments also employed a sergeant major, who supervised drill and occasionally mustered and manoeuvred the entire regiment in the field. Odoardo's invasion army of September 1635 included a colonel of cavalry, Marino Badoero from Venice, two colonels of Italian infantry, the Luccan Francesco Serafini and Fausto Melari, a Sienese nobleman residing in Piacenza who had served at the great siege of Breda under Ambrogio Spinola in 1625, a triumph immortalized in the painting by Velasquez. Alongside the Italians were two French colonels dispatched by Cardinal Richelieu from their native Dauphiné: Jean de la Roquette and Claude Vernatel. At the end of the siege of La Rochelle, Louis XIII disbanded all but the oldest regiments in French service, making many officers redundant, before ramping up recruitment again at the onset of the Thirty Years' War. Vernatel would formally command a French regiment for the army of Italy in December 1635, after the first campaign, so his Parman service might have been an interim posting.[29] Johann Werner Moralt, the captain of the large Swiss company, functioned virtually as a colonel, and employed a sergeant major too. There were few occasions, however, when colonels and sergeant majors mustered an entire regiment in the field, because most operations required only a handful of companies.

In October 1631, in the aftermath of the quarrel with the emissaries of the King of Spain, Odoardo came to Piacenza to raise soldiers in the wake of the news that the French might invade Italy. On 18 November he awarded five recruiting patents to significant noblemen residing in Parma and Piacenza, expecting each to raise

---

[28] In addition to the *patenti* themselves, some details can be gleaned from manuscript compilations on noble families; Clerici in the BPPr Ms Parmense 656, Padre Andrea da Parma, Cappuccino: 'Opere diverse di storia parmense, Appunti sulla nobiltà parmense' (sec. XVIII), 227; on Avogadri, see the anonymous manuscript in the Biblioteca Estense Modena (henceforth BEM), Ms Sorbelli 1410, Vite e morti di personaggi illustri (*c.*1650), 43–4.

[29] Louis Susane, *Histoire de l'ancienne infanterie française*, vol. 4 (Paris, 1852), 137; on demobilization and refoundation, Jean Chagniot, *Guerre et société à l'époque moderne* (Paris, 2001), 103.

large infantry companies of 200 men on the Spanish model.[30] The captains were the 'fathers' of their companies; they chose the subordinate officers and recruited the troops.[31] In the Spanish system practised in Italy, whenever a prince issued a recruiting contract, he advanced a sum of money to the captain to offset the expense of gathering and outfitting the men, along with a signing bonus of one month's pay, minus something for the cost of the clothes and the arms.[32] Or, alternately, he recognized that he owed the captain that sum from the treasury, to be paid either in cash or by some other compensation. European recruitment systems of the period were all reliant on some commitment of the personal resources of officers, to varying degrees.[33] Ducal officials in Piacenza sought the services of noblemen who had connections outside the Farnese states to find soldiers, and the cash reserves to hire them. Odoardo gave Ferrante Paveri of Piacenza a fief and a title, in exchange for raising a company of 200 infantry at his personal expense.[34] Not all of these beneficiaries held estates in the duchy, and war could be the source of social promotion. One of the first men appointed to raise a company, Francesco Serafini, was not noble at all: one author claimed he was a barber's son from Lucca who joined the Spanish army in Sardinia, before it was posted to Lombardy. His career progressed quickly after Don Francesco Farnese hired him in 1625. After various adventures Serafini became a sergeant major at Piacenza and rose to become colonel in command of the garrison of the castle in 1634, easily the most important and sensitive position in the duchy.[35]

Duke Odoardo issued seven new contracts in April 1633, to Ferrante Paveri Fontana, Francesco Arcelli, and Alessandro Scotti, all of Piacenza; to Francesco Serafini and Corneglio Palmia of Parma; and to two French officers, Captain Jacques de Roquebrune and François Nicart, a Huguenot sergeant major from Grenoble. A summary of the contract tucked inside the cover of one of these specified that the captain promised to raise 200 men for the sum of 800 ducatoni (7,200 lire in 1633). The captain could unfurl the banner of the unit once he presented 50 men to ducal officials in Piacenza, and his pay would commence from that moment. The captain was to reimburse the duke for every man under the 200 limit. The captains arranged for their own lodgings and the lodging of their men too, for which they would keep accounts. An important proviso stipulated that the captain was not to recruit anyone who lived in Parma or Piacenza or who had family members living there.[36] Such was the attraction of the duke's impending war that one Piacenza

[30] BCPLPc, Ms Pallastrelli 126, Croniche o diario del Rev.o Sgr Benedetto Boselli, rettore della chiesa di Santo Martino di Piacenza (1620–70), 94.

[31] Barbara Donagan, *War in England 1642–1649* (Oxford and New York, 2008), 285.

[32] Davide Maffi, *Il baluardo della corona: Guerra, esercito, finanze e società nella Lombardia seicentesca (1630–1660)* (Florence, 2007), 101; for the procedure in Spain itself, Julio Albi de la Cuesta, *De Pavia a Rocroi: los tercios de infantería española en los siglos XVI y XVII* (Madrid, 1999), 32.

[33] David Parrott, *The Business of War: Military Enterprise and Military Revolution in Early Modern Europe* (Cambridge and New York, 2012), 21.

[34] BCPLPc Ms Pallastrelli 126, Croniche Boselli, 16 April 1633, 96.

[35] R. Meli Lupi di Soragna, 'Vita di Francesco Serafini, mastro di campo del Ser.o Duca di Parma, castellano di Piacenza', *Atti e Memorie delle R.R. Deputazioni di Storia Patria per le Provincie modenesi e parmensi*, ser. 3, 5 (1888): 1–29.

[36] ASPr, Collatereria Generale 340.

noble, Ferrante Portapuglia, offered to raise a company of troops entirely at his own expense, if he might be allowed to command it.[37] Just before the war began, Odoardo made a decree calling all his subjects, feudatories, and even bandits to report back to the duchy, on pain of confiscation of their property.[38] All but a few native aristocrats responded to his call, although these last were significant exceptions. The Count of San Secondo, Troilo Rossi, forfeited estates worth 10 million lire, 14,000 scudi in annual revenue, and jurisdiction over about 7,500 vassals by remaining faithful to Spanish service.[39] Baron Francesco Marazzani, a colonel under Wallenstein, was also conspicuous by his absence in the Farnese order of battle, and Odoardo almost certainly placed him under surveillance in Piacenza.[40]

Seventeenth-century armies were composite constructions, something John Lynn calls an 'aggregate contract army', made up of different contingents, each having a different understanding with the warlord who hired them.[41] In addition to awarding recruiting contracts to local captains, the prince could also pay an entrepreneur for delivering a certain number of men to a designated place. This last in the Spanish service was called an *asientista*, a specialized contractor in soldiers who knew where he could locate men immediately.[42] The Holy Roman Emperor and his Protestant adversaries turned to these 'military enterprisers' on a large scale, for they placed their own private credit at the prince's disposal.[43] In theory, one should not expect much loyalty from foreign adventurers, yet in practice even mercenaries had good reasons to prove their worth to their employers, and they were, indeed, effective in the field.[44] Both France and Spain hired such foreign professionals, who recovered their initial outlay by levying contributions on areas they occupied, by padding the numbers on the payroll or adding a markup on equipment they provided, or in a myriad of legitimate or underhanded ways. Odoardo, like his contemporaries, turned to foreign professionals as he expanded his army in preparation for the long hoped-for war. He never contracted for an entire regiment, but he did have recourse to these contractors for individual companies. The largest of these was a company of 300 Swiss raised in the Catholic canton of Lucerne by Johan Werner Moralt, which arrived in Piacenza after 20 March 1635. A condition was that the Swiss were not to be incorporated into any other

[37] BCPLPc, Ms Pallastrelli 126, Croniche Boselli, 17 July 1635, 109.
[38] BPPr, Ms Parmense 1261, Storia di Parma, dell'abbate Gozzi, 1113.
[39] Sabbadini, *La Grazia e l'Onore*, 153; Rossi's estates were confiscated for treason, by ducal decree on 3 January 1636, ASPr, Gridario 32/42.
[40] Giovanni Pietro Crescenzi Romani, *Corona della nobiltà d'Italia, ovvero compendio dell'istorie delle famiglie illustri*, 2 vols. (Bologna, 1639–42), vol. 1, 73.
[41] Lynn, *Giant of the 'Grand Siècle'*, 6.
[42] Luis Antonio Ribot Garcìa, 'El reclutamiento militar en España a mediados del siglo XVII. La "composicion" de las milicias de Castilla', *Cuadernos de Investigacion Historica*, 9 (1986): 63–89.
[43] The term was coined by the pioneering historian of the question, Fritz Redlich, *The Military Enterpriser and his Work Force*, 2 vols (Wiesbaden, 1964).
[44] David Parrott, 'From military enterprise to standing armies: war, state and society in Western Europe, 1600–1700', in *European Warfare 1350–1750*, ed. F. Tallett and D. J. B. Trim (Cambridge and New York, 2010), 74–95; Parrott, *The Business of War*, 17; and Geoffrey Mortimer, 'War by contract, credit and contribution: the Thirty Years' War', in *Early Modern Military History*, ed. G. Mortimer (Basingstoke, 2004), 101–17.

regimental structure, and Odoardo promised to observe all the privileges and exemptions customary for Swiss troops in the service of other nations, specifically the French.[45] Several cavalry companies recruited from the Venetian Terraferma just before the onset of the first campaign also appear to fall into this category.

Very few French officers appear among the *patenti*, which leads me to believe that these men received their commissions and their recruiting money in France. They would have been raised to what Brian Sandberg calls 'warrior pursuits' in a country wracked by civil strife for generations before 1630, in striking contrast to most parts of Italy where military training was becoming a special calling. French nobles still lived in rural castles furnished with well-stocked weapons storerooms, and trained at arms from an early age.[46] King Louis often left the appointment of subalternate officers up to these captains, who recruited their relatives, clients, and neighbours. Such captains do not fit the urban patrician pattern discernible among the Italians, and not all of them were Catholic, notwithstanding their influence in Odoardo's entourage. While they commanded units and entire detachments of the ducal army on campaign or in garrison, they were not really the duke's men at all. More ominously, they might have been something of a fifth column in the state, looking to take control of the citadel of Piacenza or of the fortress of Sabbioneta if they could. That would reduce Odoardo to a puppet of French policy, as Richelieu had done to Duke Charles of Mantua by having French troops defend Casale Monferrato.

In the months and weeks leading up to the onset of the first campaign in September 1635, Odoardo restructured this army in two important ways. By the 1630s, the European trend was to reduce the size of the companies from 200 men to only 100 and to consider 'full' companies of even smaller size. Odoardo, perhaps following French suggestions, added seventeen new companies to his order of battle, staffed in part with new arrivals from France and Italy, and in part by shifting men from the original seven companies to the new units. These he designated either 'French' or 'Italian' companies, but only a few of the French ones were ethnically homogenous. The others mixed and matched recruits and placed them under officers of equally diverse backgrounds. The second important development was the creation of seven cavalry companies, four of which Odoardo placed under the command of officers from Venetian territories. These resemble military enterprisers, who brought a portion of their troopers and their officers with them. The duke then augmented these by blending cavalry militiamen from Farnese territories and some French troopers into the same companies. Cavalry was ruinously expensive to maintain, so officials mobilized the first company only in March 1635, with four more established the following May, and the final two in July and August, just before the beginning of operations.

So despite the enthusiastic rush of aristocratic subjects to offer their swords to the duke, the officer corps was no mirror of the local nobility. If we include both

---

[45] ASPr, Governo Farnesiano, Milizie 2: Obblighi del Cap.o Vernerio Moralto Svizzero, 22 March 1635.

[46] Brian Sandberg, *Warrior Pursuits: Noble Culture and Civil Conflict in Early Modern France* (Baltimore, 2010), 35–48 and 203.

the *patenti* or commissions and the officers designated in the two armies of 1635 and 1636, we reach a total of about 300 appointments, although many of the individuals appear two or three times, serving for both campaigns, or transferred from one unit to another. In 1635, only 43 of 152 identified individuals (a mere two are unidentifiable) were subjects of the duke—a low third. An equal number were subjects of King Louis XIII, the principal ally, to whom one can append four Savoyards and two Monferrini, subjects of allied princes. Another third, 45 individuals, were subjects of neutral Italian states, principally the Papal States and the Republic of Venice, where mercenary captains recruited much of the Italian soldiery. Six officers were Swiss, all but one serving in the large company raised in the German-speaking Catholic canton of Lucerne. And seven more were Italians hailing from territories under Spanish rule, principally from the neighbouring state of Milan. Some hard lessons were learned in the first campaign, so there was a significant shift in the composition of the 149 officers in 1636, of whom 145 could be identified. Half of them (74) had served as officers in the previous campaign, which meant that half the corps was new to war. Of these 145, only 39 were subjects of Duke Odoardo, alongside only 24 Italian neutrals, reflecting the unreliability of those troops and the duke's frustration with them. On the other hand, 68 subjects of the King of France and five Monferrini and Piedmontese, together formed practically half the cadres. The Swiss provided five more, while four officers from enemy territories continued in Farnese service. If practically none of the duke's noblemen fled the field, the same is not quite true of the officers. During the two campaigns, 12 officers fled, only one of them being a subject of the duke, and none of them French. These deserters were all junior officers, ensigns (eight), or lieutenants (four). Officers were often in harm's way, since flight or wavering was less admissible on their part. However, only one is recorded as a fatality of the siege of Valenza, the general of cavalry Avogadri, and only two more died at Casale in November 1635 in the aftermath of the siege. The campaign of 1636 was far more perilous, with about 10 per cent of the officers (12) dying of wounds or illness, a rate probably higher than the fatalities among the rank and file. With vacancies being opened up by wounds and death on campaign, there was some room for mobility. But social mobility via the officer corps (starting at ensign or *cornette*) was more the exception than the rule, and none of the beneficiaries were commoners from Farnese territories. Only eight people moved from the rank and file or from the sergeants and quartermasters (*forieri*) to become ensigns or lieutenants, and six of those were Frenchmen in predominantly French units.

ARMY CADRES

Once they had their recruiting permit in hand, the new captains needed to find not only willing recruits, but, what was much harder, an adequate number of experts who could transform the footloose volunteers into a disciplined unit. Companies belonging to colonels contained some specialized functionaries like a surgeon, a regimental scribe, and a quartermaster or *foriere*. This last official, who existed both in mercenary and in militia units, received all the munitions, weapons, clothing, and pay for their distribution through the ranks. It was his task to organize lodgings and provisions for troops on the march, and to supervise the contents and the movement of the baggage. He also inspected the march path himself, having recourse to local guides if he needed them.[47] Regiments would normally include a provost or army magistrate with a couple of helpers (*fanti*) to arrest and punish delinquents. Soldiers had good reason to mistrust the impartiality of civilian magistrates towards their sort, and so professional judges staffed every regiment and meted out martial law, whose statutory severity was only moderated by the individual colonel's clemency.[48]

There was no boot camp or other institution where the recruits might learn the art of war, and, since they signed up in dribs and drabs, they would need to be taken in hand by the non-commissioned officers and instructed individually. Many, or even most, of the new soldiers would have had some militia training with firearms, but this did not prepare them for marching and fighting in formation. In northern Europe there were many drill books in the hands of noblemen and other military enthusiasts, but literacy was not as widespread in Italian cities and it is doubtful that many people would have had experience of these.[49] Whether the captains and ensigns read the manuals or not, there was no substitute for experienced non-commissioned officers. Francesco Serafini's recruiting contract, or *contratto di leva*, instructed him, beginning from 21 April 1633, to appoint to his company a sergeant and eight corporals, as well as two drummers. At full strength, each of the corporals would become instructor to 25 recruits. The pay these men received, 72 lire monthly for a sergeant and 54 for a corporal, was only a fraction of that which the officers enjoyed (360 lire for the captain and 135 lire for the ensign), but pay for the rank and file was 36 lire, or about a lire every day, once the sums for the weapons and clothing had been deducted.[50] There is a striking lack of research on these cadres for the seventeenth century, relative to the work on officers, with only a lone article by Robert Chaboche to serve as the basis for comparison with Farnese data.[51] We have almost all the company rosters for the army of 1635, in which 7 Italian cavalry sergeants (exactly one per company) and 37 infantry sergeants appear, alongside 4 cavalry and 30 infantry sergeants of French origin. The following year, there were 2 cavalry sergeants and 30 infantry sergeants

---

[47] ASPr, Governo Farnesiano, Milizie 1: Istruzione per la fanteria di milizia; these are instructions to officers, published 23 November 1616; Bartolomeo Pelliciari, a Modenese colonel, describes the foriere's tasks in his 'avvertimenti militari', BEM, Miscellanea Estense Ital. 635, Avvertimenti militari di quello che vole havere un buon soldato di pratica e un buon caporale et un sargente et un Alfiero et un capitano (*c.*1641).

[48] The most suggestive pages on this point will be found in the book by Donagan, *War in England*, 167–70; there are informative pages in the encyclopedic work by Enrique Martinez-Ruiz, *Los Soldados del Rey: Los ejércitos de la Monarquía Hispánica (1480–1700)* (Madrid, 2008), 943–53.

[49] Donagan, *War in England*, 37.

[50] ASPr, Collatereria Generale 340: Contratto di leva.

[51] Robert Chaboche, 'Le recrutement des caporaux et sergents de l'armée française au XVIIe siècle', in *Recrutement, mentalités, sociétés: Actes du colloque Internationale d'Histoire Militaire* (Montpellier, 1974), 25–43.

of Italian origin and 1 French cavalry and 55 infantry sergeants. Scribes recorded less frequently the ages of non-commissioned officers relative to the rank and file, but when they signed on with Duke Odoardo, their mean age was 32.4 for the Italians and 32.2 for the French, an insignificant difference. Corporals were more numerous, 180 for the Italians and 198 for the French (combining infantry and cavalry), and their ages were slightly lower, at 30.3 for the Italians and 30.5 for the French. Since soldiers enlisted on average around the age of 23, we can conclude that these were men experienced in army service, though we cannot gauge the extent of their experience of combat. There were three corporals for every sergeant among the Italians and only two for every sergeant among the French, which indicates not a higher degree of control among the Italians, but rather a higher rate of desertion. Only about a third of the Italian non-coms and a mere sixth of the French served the duke during both campaigns.

Judging from the English experience (of which we have more information) the sergeants managed the company from day to day with regard to both its training and discipline, and liaised with the officers. Colonel Pelliciari recommended hiring sturdy and authoritative subjects who possessed enough psychological finesse to serve as a conduit between the soldiers and the officers, the captain, but also the ensigns, who administered everyday discipline. The natural authority of a good sergeant would motivate soldiers to obey him without question, but he would benefit too by closing his eyes and ears occasionally and showing a bit of patience with new soldiers. He would keep a list of each section of his company and note the presence and the state of each man's armour and weapons, and be capable of forming up the unit for battle with the capabilities of each man in mind.[52]

The corporals paid special attention to training each soldier in weapons handling and sentry duty, for they were responsible for the soldiers' preparation for action. While commanders hoped that corporals would teach the ropes to recruits patiently, they were authorized, in the heat of the moment, to strike soldiers, as the latter did not consider jail to be punishment and feared only blows. These non-commissioned officers kept a close watch on their charges in their quarters in order to nip disturbances in the bud, and to prevent the bullying of newcomers. They also oversaw the re-establishment of sick soldiers once they had recovered.[53] It was not unheard of for unsatisfactory sergeants and corporals to be demoted (17 cases of the 589 non-commissioned officers over the two campaigns), but, in general, these men were a precious resource who could not easily be replaced. However, dissatisfied with the service, they might desert. Over a quarter of the French cavalry non-commissioned officers did so, but only 12 of 274 among the infantry, although the rosters for 1636 might not have been kept faithfully. Among the Italians, 14 of 54 cavalry petty officers fled their units over the two campaigns, and 55 of 247 infantry non-coms fled, or left camp and neglected to return as promised. Non-commissioned officers may not have suffered a higher proportion of casualties

---

[52] Ms Misc. Estense Ital. 635, Avvertimenti militari, ff. 30–5.
[53] Ms Misc. Estense Ital. 635, Avvertimenti militari, ff. 20–9; see also Donagan, *War in England*, 286–7.

relative to other groups; only two Italians died and a lone Frenchman as a result of the campaign of 1635, while six Italians and seven Frenchmen died the following year, though it is by no means certain that these fatalities were the result of combat. The rate of fatality among these men was, in fact, quite low, 16 of 589, which, even if the rosters of 1636 under-recorded the losses, looks more like bad luck than a serious professional hazard.

The most precious capital of a company was its complement of veterans.[54] Ideally, captains and sergeants would inject new recruits among the men who had experienced combat in previous campaigns. The proportion of veterans in a company or regiment was probably the best indicator of its reliability in battle, for the ranks trusted their officers enough to remain with them, and the men developed a unit pride and a bond with comrades beside them. It was not possible to improve new companies quickly by injecting veterans among the inexperienced rank and file, for that put their lives at greater risk and gave them good reasons to desert. Veterans also knew how to take better care of themselves in the field, how to avoid sleeping on the cold ground, or how to avoid dysentery.[55] David Parrott speculates that veterans might also have built up immunity to some of the epidemics so lethal in peace as in war.[56] It is impossible to know how many of the soldiers in Odoardo's army were true veterans of combat, as opposed to long-term garrison soldiers, but we can safely venture that they were far inferior to the recommended 30 per cent minimum.[57] The solution was to designate, in addition to the corporals, a number of experienced soldiers, called the *vantaggiati*, to pass on their superior skills to the soldiers with whom they resided. Ethnic Spanish and Italian companies in Habsburg service were reputedly composed of tight bands called *camerata* of ten or twelve men who ate and slept together, and where the more experienced soldiers brought the newcomers up to speed, but the term never appears in the Parman documents.[58] French rosters rarely designate these bonus-pay soldiers as such, but the captains received extra money every month in order to reward worthy prospects, and similar '*chambrées*' were known to exist in French armies too.[59] The single French list we have that designates them by name (the company of Gratien de la Roquette) reveals that their mean age was close to 29 years, almost equal to that of the corporals. Italian company rosters sometimes listed the *vantaggiati* by name too, either in isolation or in lists, for they earned a quarter or a third more than the remaining 90 per cent of common soldiers. The reason for giving these men a bonus is never clarified and we should not assume that they were veterans.

---

[54] Luciano Pezzolo, 'Professione militare e famiglia in Italia tra tardo medioevo e prima età moderna', in *La Justice des familles: Autour de la transmission des biens, des savoirs et des pouvoirs*, ed. A. Bellavitis and I. Chabot (Rome, 2011), 341–66.

[55] Eric Gruber von Arni, *Justice to the Maimed Soldier: Nursing, Medical Care and Welfare for Sick and Wounded Soldiers and their Families during the English Civil Wars and Interregnum, 1642–1660* (Aldershot and Burlington, VT, 2001), 176.

[56] Parrott, *The Business of War*, 172.

[57] David Parrott, *Richelieu's Army: War, Government and Society in France, 1624 to 1642* (Cambridge, 2001), 40–2.

[58] Albi de la Cuesta, *De Pavia a Rocroi*, 69.

[59] Frank Tallett, *War and Society in Early Modern Europe* (London, 1992), 135.

Whenever we encounter a very young specimen, we should suspect they were the captain's clients, like the 16-year-old Pellegrino Biella, a lad of semi-noble status whose elder brother was an ensign. In Ferrante Portapuglia's company, which he raised at his own expense, half of the *vantaggiati* were natives of the captain's city of Piacenza, which leads me to suspect that they were his clients. In the companies of Brasilio Marchi and Giovanni Maria Coggia, most of the *vantaggiati* shared the captains' Corsican origins, but this might have served to tighten a unit drawn heavily from the island. Captain Giovanni Innocenzo Ceva's company was drawn from all over central Italy and beyond, like the *vantaggiati* he appointed. Companies like this one came apart easily and the *vantaggiati* deserted like the rest. Captains might also have appointed as *vantaggiati* people whose status raised them above the common soldier. These might have been 'natural' soldiers who were drawn to armies by temperament, and the love of comradeship and adventure.[60] In the company of Fausto Melari we find Fabio Corti, a young Sienese nobleman who fled that city after stabbing another youth in a game of football.[61] He moved not long after to become a trooper in Aloisio Scotti's company of horse, and then figures as a captain in 1636. True veterans were probably thin on the ground.

THE RANK AND FILE

Historians of the Thirty Years' War usually find very little pertaining to the consistency of the armies in the field, beyond global evaluations of troop numbers, which were always guesstimations. Before the advent of regular recruiting records in the eighteenth century, armies were mysterious things whose existence filled the chronicles, but whose consistency escaped close scrutiny due to lack of sources. The Parman archives contain what looks like the majority of company rosters for the duke's mercenary army, enabling us to identify most individual soldiers by name, age, place of origin, physical description, and, most importantly, by destiny. The records of the Collatereria Generale begin with the first alarm in nearby Lombardy and Liguria in 1625, when the Cardinal Regent Odoardo beefed up his garrison in Piacenza. The records follow, day by day, the augmentation of the force destined to invade the duchy of Milan in 1635, and then begin afresh in 1636 as Odoardo raised a new army to defend the duchy from Spanish retaliation. The rosters record the building of a new army in 1641 as our duke responded to the papal annexation of his Lazio fiefs, a crisis which culminated in the Castro war of 1642–4. I have not encountered in my reading any similar set of comprehensive rosters existing elsewhere during the period of the Thirty Years' War, although about 100 Spanish ones exist for the complete span of the reigns of Philip II and Philip III (1555–1621), and a similar set of muster rolls exist for the army of Lorraine during the entire

---

[60] Gwynne Dyer, *War* (2nd edn, Toronto, 2004), 53.
[61] Corti's misadventure is recounted in a celebratory compendium of Sienese nobility, Ippolito Ugurgieri Azzolini, *Le pompe sanesi, overo relazione delli huomini e donne illustri di Siena e suo stato*, 2 vols. (Pistoia, 1649), vol. 2; for the context of these impromptu careers, see Hanlon, 'The demilitarization of a provincial military aristocracy', 64–108.

span of the Thirty Years' War, although they do not indicate the destiny of Duke Charles's men.[62] So the Parma registers appear to be the most complete collection of documents pertaining to the rank and file anywhere in Europe before the late seventeenth century.

Attracting the men and keeping track of them proved an absorbing task for the new captains. Some 7,200 men signed on with the duke after April 1633, biding their time in garrison at Piacenza, and, to a lesser extent, Parma. Typically, these soldiers served for a few months or a year until they grew tired of waiting and moved on, or administrators struck them off the roll for illness or absence. The peacetime army itself is worthy of study, for its companies were each very different in origin or general composition, making it hard to generalize. With the exception of the Swiss mercenaries, who received 45 lire every month, Italian and French soldiers both received 36 lire each, equivalent to a month's wages for a city artisan, or perhaps more, for artisans did not find paid work every day. This amount was more than adequate for their subsistence, given that they were mostly single men; the rate of pay was much higher relative to soldiers of the Napoleonic era. Each of them received a new suit of clothing, ate at subsidized rates, and paid nothing for their lodging. While the soldiers paid for their clothes and their kit on instalment, this was limited to 2 lire per month. Odoardo promised to pay the captain 40 ducatoni (360 lire) per month for their services, but a good portion of this was employed to keep the men content and his company up to strength, or else served to reimburse the officer for money already invested in the unit. The secretary inscribed the names and ages and places of origin of each of the recruits. Under the name of each was a brief physical description, not so much a check against desertion, as a means of certifying that the man receiving his pay from the paymaster's table resembled the description on the page. The physical descriptions are not without interest, although they were not universally applied, and they did not record the same features for each recruit. Regimental or company scribes marked down what they saw in a short phrase, replete with abbreviations, placed under the name of the recruit. It emphasized, obviously, the physical characteristics that could not easily be modified; their scars and other markings, their height and corpulence, their eye and hair colour, the presence or absence of beards (which were reliable age markers), and any other salient feature, which could include traces of smallpox on the face (just under 10 per cent) or sometimes simply their general physiognomy like a 'melancholy air' or 'ugly face'.[63] On the page across from this information the company scribe indicated the destiny of each man, that is, the date of desertion or an indication of why the man had been struck from the roster. Historians of Spain have found that soldiers there were primarily young men, the great majority aged between 20 and 25. Mercenaries joining the Duke of Parma were significantly older on average. Infantry soldiers who were

---

[62] Anthony Thompson, 'El soldado del Imperio: una aproximaciòn al perfil del recluta español en el Siglo de Oro', *Manuscrits*, 21 (2003): 17–38; Jean-Charles Fulaine, *Le Duc Charles IV de Lorraine et son armée, 1624–1675* (Metz, 1997).

[63] For problems of identifying people in the era before bureaucracy and statistics, see Valentin Groebner, *Who Are You? Identification, Deception and Surveillance in Early Modern Europe* (New York, 2007).

Fig. 2.1. Callot: the pay muster, *c*.1633. The scribe at the extreme right refers to company roster-books similar to those in Parma.

Fig. 2.2. Callot: the firing squad, *c*.1633. Severe measures such as these, meted out in a punishment parade, did little to stem desertion.

subjects of the duke, Italian neutrals, French subjects, or even subjects of the King of Spain, tended to have a mean age of 27, with rare teenagers being offset by plenty of men in their thirties or older.[64]

Finding accommodation for thousands of soldiers and feeding them regularly was a serious headache for ducal officials. Again, we can draw a general impression from documents concerning the mobilization in 1625, when a committee of

[64] Paul Delsalle, 'De l'interêt anthropologique des rôles de recrutement au XVIIe siècle', in *Hommes d'armes et gens de guerre du Moyen Age au XVIIe siècle: Franche Comté de Bourgogne et comté de Montbéliard*, ed. Arnold Preneel and Paul Delsalle (Besançon, 2007), 177–82.

Table 2.1. Age of non-coms and ranks

Age of non-coms and ranks	number	number		
Italians	cavalry	infantry	mean age	age sample
Sergeants	9	67	33.5	13
Corporals	45	180	30.6	38
Buglers	14		40	5
rank & file (3 company sample)	292	383	31 cav/24.6 inf	675
French	cavalry	infantry	mean age	age sample
Sergeants	5	85	30	3
Corporals	9	189	30.5	64
Buglers	1			
rank & file (3 company sample)	55	324	28.6 cav/25.6 inf	379

specialized officials in Piacenza (the Eight for War) printed the regulations. Quartermasters issued soldiers with tickets (*boletta*) bearing their names and identifying the house where they would live. They were not allowed to change or exchange their lodging without permission. Administrators assigned captains a modest house designed to lodge his page, servants, and other attendants, complete with beds and bedding and other walnut furniture, good linen and kitchen furnishings. Junior officers received small houses and similar furnishings in smaller quantities. Sergeants were just given a room with a bed, a poplar-wood table, and kitchen implements. 'For the soldiers, the lodging will have box beds and palliasses, and in the same building there will be as many soldiers as one can conveniently fit box beds.'[65] Soon there was no more room in the citadel barracks or abandoned houses for soldiers to live, so the duke ordered the ground-level colonnade of the Piacenza city hall bricked up in order to provide quarters.[66] Space was only one requirement. Another document, undated, listed the items to be allocated to the soldiery so that they might be comfortable in their quarters. A complete bed, one for two men, came with sheets and covers, but each soldier would also require serviettes and towels. The rooms would require a table and stools, and a chest for each recruit. Soldiers needed an appropriate numbers of pots and pans, platters, bowls and jugs of terracotta, drinking glasses, a spoon for each man, basins for washing, candlesticks and oil lamps, fireplace implements, and a roasting spit. Since they would be cooking, they needed ladles and sieves, a salt dish, mortar and pestle, and (this was Italy), a cheese grater. Cavalry soldiers required stalls, feeding troughs, pitchforks, and other stable implements for tending horses. Soldiers also needed 40 faggots of kindling each month and a considerable quantity, 375 Parma pounds (123 kg), of firewood each.[67] As Odoardo gathered the multiple contingents together on the

---

[65] ASPr, Gridario 27/64, 9 May 1625.
[66] Giuseppina Piccinini, *Il Palazzo Gotico: Le Vicende del Palazzo Pubblico di Piacenza dal 1281* (Piacenza, 1998), 52.
[67] ASPr, Governo Farnesiano, Milizie 4: Lista delle mobilie di consignarsi a ciascuno de' soldati, n.d.; on the comforts of soldiers in their city quarters, Geoffrey Parker, 'The war in myth, legend and history', in G. Parker (ed.), *The Thirty Years' War* (London, 1997), 297.

eve of the campaign, in Piacenza, he issued a new decree on the lodging of the soldiers and announced the means by which he would distribute this considerable burden more equitably among the public. The usual fiscal exemptions applying to magistrates and militiamen in the countryside were eliminated, and the prince introduced new taxes to meet the expenditures.[68]

The initial recruiting commissions Odoardo issued prohibited the enlistment of men from Parma and Piacenza, although he later waived this proviso in the interest of fleshing out the companies in the face of unstoppable desertion. Foot soldiers who were direct subjects of Duke Odoardo on 1 September 1635, numbered 391, merely 10 per cent of those for whom we have a sure origin! Most of them hailed either from Piacenza or from Parma, and, with those coming from the other principal towns, the 'urban' portion amounts to three quarters. This meant that the entire contingent of ducal subjects, infantry and cavalry combined, was no more than 13 per cent of the army. Those from the Lazio fiefs probably numbered fewer than 20, despite the ambitious policy of raising hundreds of men there by force.

It is clear that the duke intended that the fighting core of his forces should be made of willing volunteers from wherever possible. More warlike Italian princes, like Duke Charles Emanuel of Savoy, did not hesitate to hire soldiers from wherever the recruiters might find them, for they intended that their wars should be short and the army be dispersed as quickly as it was assembled.[69] Our knowledge of the origin of seventeenth-century soldiery in the era before standing armies is so sketchy that we cannot determine if this was the exception or the rule. The Duke of Lorraine's army, for example, comprised of the prince's subjects for both the officers and the rank and file (*circa* 76 per cent, principally from the towns), with most of the foreigners coming from France and the Spanish Netherlands or Franche-Comté.[70] The soldier-historian Galeazzo Gualdo Priorato, writing of the ideal warrior prince in 1640, noted that foreign troops followed their personal interests exclusively; moths attracted by the glimmer of silver. These soldiers would be very costly, and if they became disgruntled they would not hesitate to join the enemy. However, the prince's subjects were worth conserving, for they worked the land and attended to their trades. 'Whoever loses the foreigner, loses only the expenditure; whoever loses the subject, loses the capital.'[71]

Foreigners consisted of anyone not a direct subject of Duke Odoardo, whether from Italy or farther away. Italian recruits from neutral territories comprised over a quarter of the infantry, but the 'Italian' infantry companies contained some exotic elements too. Infantry colonels Fausto Melari of Siena and Francesco Serafini from Lucca were already established in Piacenza when they received a recruiting

---

[68] ASPr, Gridario, t.2, f.6, 16 July 1635.
[69] De Consoli, *Al soldo del duca*, 196–200; see also Nicola Brancaccio, *L'Esercito del vecchio Piemonte: gli ordinamenti, parte 1: dal 1560 al 1814*, Rome, 1923, which is furnished with tables designating regiments by ethnic origin, and the period served; for an overview see Paola Bianchi, *Sotto diverse banidere: L'internazionale militare nello Stato sabaudo d'antico regime* (Milan, 2012), 51–3.)
[70] Fulaine, *Le Duc Charles IV*.
[71] Galeazzo Gualdo Priorato, *Il guerriero prudente e politico (1640)* (Venice and Bologna, 1641), ed. Angelo Tamborra (Naples, 2002), 35.

commission, but they sought men far and wide. Serafini in particular drew a good number of soldiers from Lucca and its rural hinterland. The Roman prince Ceva, who lived in Parma, held lands in Lazio near the Farnese ancestral fiefs west of Viterbo, and drew other men from farther up the Tiber valley. An undated report inserted in the letters sent from Milan to the Council of State in Madrid gives some detail about this process, confirming, meanwhile, that the Spaniards were remarkably well informed. Odoardo decreed that from his 14 sparsely populated fiefs around Castro, 305 soldiers would be raised '*a forza*', to march thereafter to Piacenza, hundreds of kilometres to the north. The duke decreed, moreover, that 825 soldiers should be levied from 11 more fiefs in the Roman periphery. This could be accomplished by pardoning outlaws even of enormous crimes, in exchange for enlisting in the duke's army, without troubling to reach some prior accord with the families of their victims. The duke instructed the small town of Ronciglione alone to raise 500 soldiers, a huge number relative to its population. Pardoning outlaws in exchange for military service was a time-honoured practice in Italy and it appealed not only to criminals from the Farnese fiefs, but also to people who had fled Rome to evade capture. This would give Pope Urban VIII good reason to consent to the duke's recruitment, for it would remove hundreds of troublemakers from the Papal States. Rumours that Duke Odoardo intended to raise 4,000 men in Lazio between his own states and those of the Pope, to march in three weeks' time to Piacenza, flew around. Spies spotted the influential cardinal, Antonio Barberini, prowling about Viterbo, quite near the Farnese fiefs, with 11 Frenchmen. The cardinal and his secretary had moved incognito from one Farnese fief to another with these Frenchmen, presumed to be officers preparing a future campaign against Spain in Italy. In the nearby city of Orvieto, Farnese recruiters purportedly raised three infantry companies of 300 men each, under captains Marabutti, Mazzocchi, and one Count Vincenzo, along with 60 cavalrymen. The sergeant Sebastiano Parmegiano had a licence to recruit men secretly, raising 35 men in the nearby estates belonging to Duke Altemps. Duke Odoardo's auditor-general, Giovan Francesco Pavonio, who hailed from Ronciglione, brought a Parman colonel with him to Lazio to help him raise soldiers. However, it was one thing to entice the soldiers to enlist with money and clothes, and another to keep them. 'Many soldiers, even the subjects, ran away, and nobody goes of their own free will, but they make them go.'[72] We have a copy of the marching orders given to a recruiting sergeant who brought his 20 men to Piacenza from Ronciglione in June 1633. The sergeant was to march them 'unarmed' (with swords and daggers only), by the main roads through Umbria and Romagna to Bologna. They were to behave themselves en route, and show their papers to the papal authorities. However, Odoardo's ministers instructed the sergeant to avoid any encounters with the Neapolitan cavalry, who were also on the move, and always lodge apart from them. I doubt they feared that the men would brawl with the Neapolitans: rather, the King of Spain drew a good portion of his cavalry from southern Italy, and they

---

[72] AGS, Consejo de Estado 3832; letters of 14 June and 4 July 1633.

moved north by the same roads en route to Milan, and from there to Germany and Flanders. Neapolitan officers were keen to enlist troopers from likely prospects they found along the way, and Odoardo's new infantry soldiers might be enticed by the higher pay and prestige of the cavalry. If they deserted again before they reached their destination, they might well be able to sell the horse that carried them to freedom.[73]

Volunteer soldiers usually signed up with more alacrity, and the dynamics of their recruitment reveal some of the initial enthusiasm, although officials reckoned that a large portion of them would desert soon after receiving the signing bonus.[74] Army recruitment during the Thirty Years' War triggered a considerable migration of free men, whatever their personal motivations. Of these, a large portion would never return home, even if they survived the rigours of campaigning.[75] Nothing permits us to conclude that a particular social group had a special propensity to become soldiers. There is a tenacious legend that sixteenth and seventeenth-century soldiers were victims forced by circumstance to fight wars in order to survive.[76] Apart from the defect of exaggerating the risks and the hardships experienced by most soldiers, such sociological explanations tend to ignore the psychological diversity of personalities and inclinations that was as rich then as it is now. It would require much labour to track single individuals from Parma and Piacenza in Odoardo's army to verify their social status, but one document permits an approximation. The Parman census of 1636 designates 67 inhabitants of the city as soldiers, together with their families. Of the 16 men who were gate guards, 3 bore the title of *signore* or *ser* (typically a notary), while 11 more were *maestri*, a title of respect typically borne by artisans. Another five were militiamen, only one of whom enjoyed the honorific *maestro* and an occupation (tailor). Of the remaining 45 soldiers identified by name, 2 were *signori* and 11 were *maestri*. The specific occupations of those without any honorific title spanned a wide range, from a professional gunner, to the husband of the ducal laundress, two silk workers, a tailor, and a couple of *braccianti*, or day labourers.[77]

Mass armies of the nineteenth and twentieth centuries learned that it was possible to conscript just about any male and turn him into a soldier in just a few weeks, probably because warrior instincts do exist and can be fostered by specific training.[78] Nevertheless, army recruiters have always been on the lookout for the natural soldier, whose assertive personality oriented him to seek out adventure and risk. Marco Costa, an army psychologist, has summarized some of these traits

---

[73] ASPr, Governo Farnesiano, Milizie 1: Ordini di marcia, 6 June 1633.
[74] ASPr, Governo Farnesiano, Milizie 1: Lettera informative per scegliere e creare ufficiali, 15 April 1625.
[75] Daniel Roche, *Humeurs vagabondes: De la circulation des hommes et de l'utilité des voyages* (Paris, 2003), 266–9.
[76] Erik Swart, 'From "landsknecht" to "soldier": the Low German foot soldiers of the Low Countries in the second half of the 16th century', *International Review of Social History*, 51 (2006): 75–92; Frank Tallett's depiction of these men is more finely nuanced; *War and Society in Early Modern Europe*, 88–95.
[77] ASPr, Comune 1934, Censimento di Parma 1636.   [78] Dyer, *War*, 32–6.

today: patriotism, a need to conform, easy acceptance of authority and a need for recognition, commitment to institutions, a weak sense of alienation towards society, strong career motivation. Easily bored, such characters often actively seek out excitement, and enjoy physical activity and competitive sport, even if dangerous. They tend to extroversion and do not cope well with solitude. Beyond their military garb, soldiers adopt attitudes and postures that express physical dominance, power, and mutual support. Their weapons are status symbols as much as instruments of death, which they carry wherever they are authorized to do so. Veteran soldiers emphasize these same behaviours, since they consider themselves to be an elite, and expect deference from their military peers and civilian underlings.[79] Armies composed primarily of mercenaries could not be expected to embrace Duke Odoardo's cause, but he had no trouble finding men to serve. However, garrison duty in Piacenza and the daily routine of soldiering probably induced many men to quit once the original shine had worn off. The ones who remained were loyal not to the duke, but to the soldiering trade and to each other. Loyalty to the group, the company, or the regiment was the glue that held the men together, as was the need to prove themselves to their peers.[80] Odoardo's war was largely a pretext.

Tightly knit ethnic units were ideal fighting societies as they provided a large amount of mutual assistance. Odoardo's disparate Italian companies never qualified for that definition, but, within each formation, handfuls of men bore allegiance to each other. These companies were their homes, where their friends were.[81] On 3 May 1633, five men in their early twenties, all from San Colombano Lodigiano (close by in the Spanish duchy of Milan) signed on with Count Ferrante Pavera in Piacenza. One of them changed his mind quickly, and deserted four days later. Three others deserted together on 23 May, leaving only one of the group of friends and neighbours behind. A few days previously, no fewer than 21 young men from a small cluster of hillside villages near the Mediterranean coast around La Spezia and Sarzana (in the neutral Genoese Republic), joined up with Pavera's company on the same day. Men like these were engaged in an intense commercial traffic between the Po valley and the seacoast, conveying goods of all kinds on the backs of their donkeys and mules. About a third of them would desert over the next few months, leaving only a residue of men in the ducal army. When men signed on together, they would have resented breaking up their little group. Three men from Brisighella in the Romagna, two of them brothers, enlisted in the company of Cornelio Palmia on 2 June 1633. One of them was struck from the rosters for an unspecified reason about a month later, which action then helped motivate the desertion of the brothers soon after.

The degree of insertion of these little bands into company *camarate* or small groups of room-mates who messed together, probably influenced the desire of the

---

[79] Marco Costa, *Psicologia militare: elementi di psicologia per gli appartenenti alle forze armate* (Milan, 2003), 173, 279, and 295.
[80] Richard Holmes, *Acts of War* (2nd edn, London, 2003), 285–301.
[81] Bernhard R. Kroener, ' "The soldiers are very poor, bare, naked, exhausted": The living conditions and organizational structure of military society during the Thirty Years' War', in *1648: War and Peace in Europe*, ed. K. Bussmann and H. Schilling (Munster-Osnabruck, 1998), 285–91.

soldiers to remain or leave. Bartolomeo Pelliciari emphasized the fact that these bonds were paramount; these men had to live together in harmony and to establish a tight consensus in everything they did. Their purpose was to help each other like brothers.[82] This sensitivity to small-group psychology helped men adjust to and accept the drudgery of garrison life and the hazards of war. The men looked out for each other, the experienced soldiers taught the ropes to the newcomers, the men shared their food and their windfall cash. Messmates quickly asserted a common ethos to which each individual was expected to adhere, on pain of ostracism.[83]

Most of northern and central Italy provided men for the recruiting captains like Francesco Pepoli of Bologna, who drew his men from Emilia, the Romagna, and the more distant valleys of the Marches and Umbria. People from these districts and the area around Rome comprised over half the contingent of Italian 'neutrals'. Two Corsican captains drew a substantial number of islanders to the continent, along with town-dwellers and villagers from much of Liguria. Like the migrant cavalry troopers, the great majority of Italian infantrymen from neutral territories declared themselves to be townsmen, about half originating from the large cities of more than 10,000 inhabitants, while another quarter came from smaller urban centres where a good portion of the population lived '*civilmente*'.

These soldiers do not seem, for the most part, to have been pushed into joining by misery, for the mountain dwellers were relatively few, apart from Corsicans who were the Swiss mercenaries of Mediterranean Europe, and Ligurians who were traders on land and sea. Most of the mainland mountain dwellers in the army lived along the trade corridors connecting the sea with the Po valley. Corsicans and Ligurians constituted about a third of the recruits coming from neutral territories. On 2 June 1633, eight Corsicans from Bastia and some villages nearby joined up together in the company of Francesco Serafini, and none of them deserted before the war began, more than two years later.

Even the enemy joined this army. An important contingent of Italians arrived from Habsburg territory, a number of them having previously served in the army of the King of Spain, who moved his troops around regularly. Spain raised a number of *tercios* in the kingdom of Naples and in Lombardy early in 1633, destined to march with the Duke of Feria into Germany during August of that year. The younger brother of King Philip IV, the Cardinal Infante Ferdinando arrived from Spain in May bringing still more troops. Thus, the roads of northern Italy were thick with soldiers destined for the most active theatre of war. Duke Odoardo's recruiters enticed 891 subjects of the King of Spain to join his army, mostly in May and June of 1633—a whole *tercio*! The ease with which the duke enlisted them reveals that he expected the campaign to be a military walk in the park. Two-thirds of these were Lombards, including numerous young men living in the towns along the border like San Colombano, Casalpusterlengo, Sant'Angelo, and Codogno, only a couple of hours leisurely walk from the village of Fombio, a small piece of

---

[82] BEM, Ms Misc. Estense Ital. 635, Avvertimenti militari, f. 13.
[83] Edward J. Coss, *All for the King's Shilling: The British Soldier under Wellington, 1808–1814* (Norman, OK, 2010), 20.

Duke Odoardo's Army 67

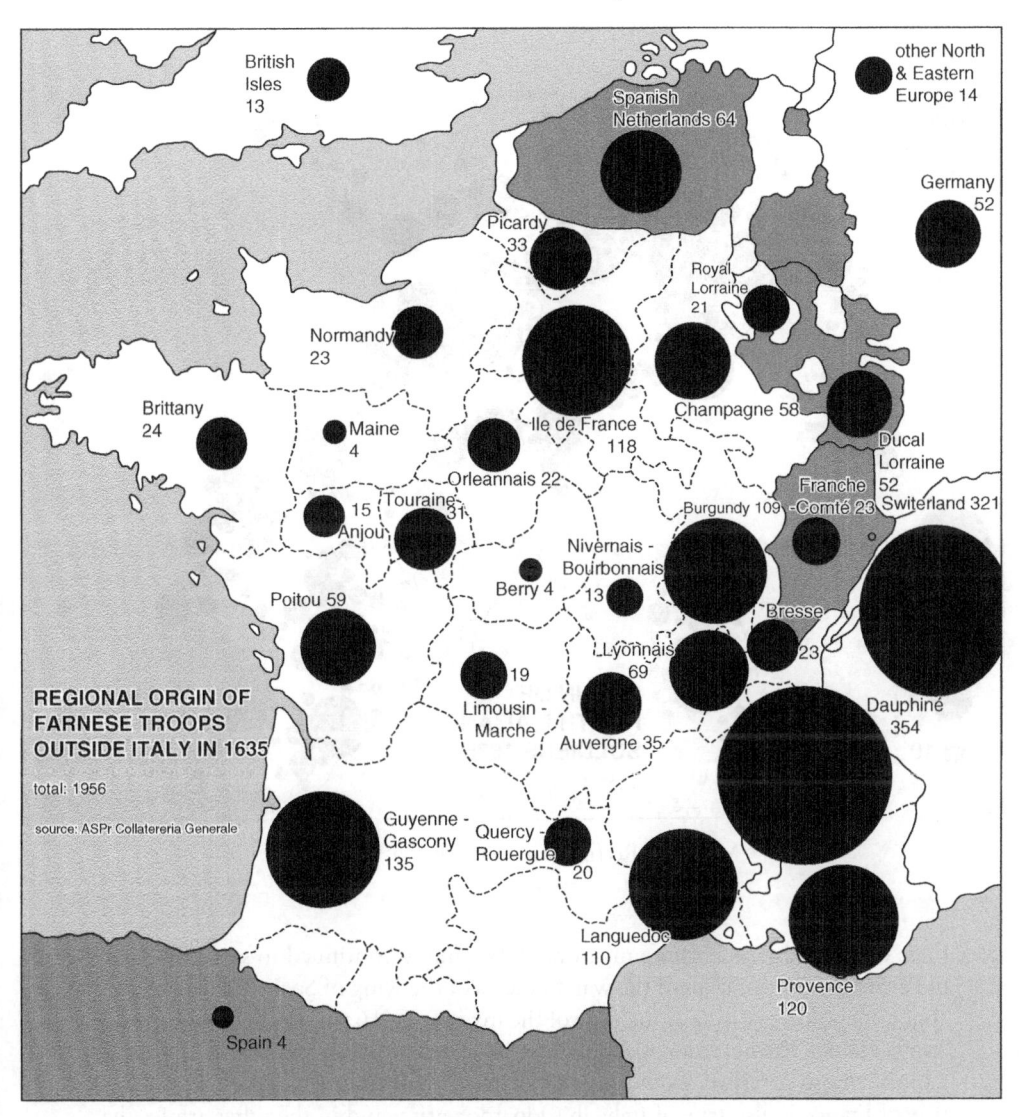

Map 2.1. French and foreign recruits

Farnese territory north of the Po near Piacenza. Men from Cremona and the town of Casalmaggiore, both river ports, signed on in nearby Parma. These may often be men paid to join the Spanish army but who thought to take the Parman signing bonus too, for a war that would take place later, if at all. The remaining third of the Italian subjects of the Catholic king trekked north from Naples or arrived by sea near Genoa. It was rare for Sicilians to be among them, and non-existent for Sardinians. The Neapolitans often claimed as their place of origin the papal enclave of Benevento, in Campania, but this was a fiction surely. After the summer of 1633

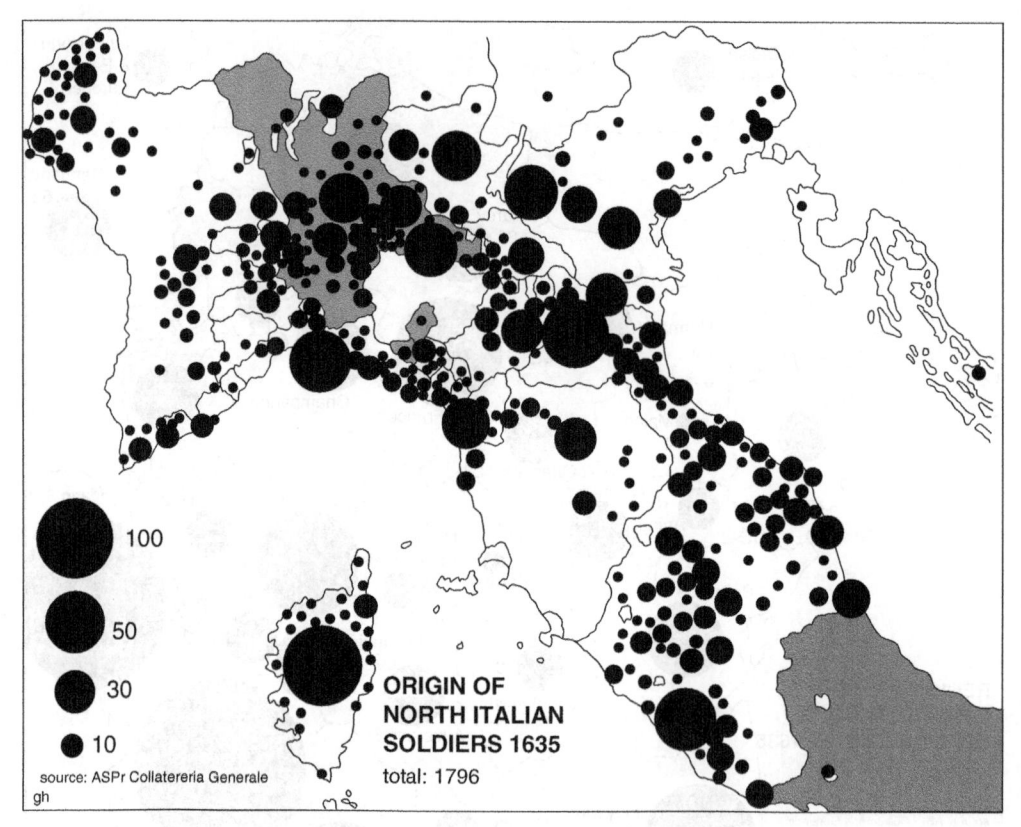

Map 2.2. Recruitment in north-central Italy

these enemy subjects become much rarer, but many continued to serve the Duke of Parma for the duration of the war. Subjects of the King of Spain still constituted about one soldier in nine at the time of the invasion in 1635. Writing of the French army, Daniel Roche emphasizes how it brought together men from the entire nation, whose survivors would resettle far from their point of departure. What is true of France is also true of Italy, in Odoardo's army and in the other armies that raised companies and *tercios* of Italian soldiers.[84] If one were to discover similar rosters for companies in the service of Spain, Venice, and Piedmont, it would be possible to evaluate the attraction of armies across the country. Ninety-one other men deserted the King of Spain's territories farther away beyond the Alps to enlist with his enemies in Italy: about two thirds of them came from the Low Countries, and most of the remainder from the Franche-Comté, the large territory wedged between the French duchy of Burgundy and French-speaking Switzerland. A mere four recruits were from Spain itself, and a lone individual came from the Castilian

---

[84] Roche, *Humeurs vagabondes*, 266–7.

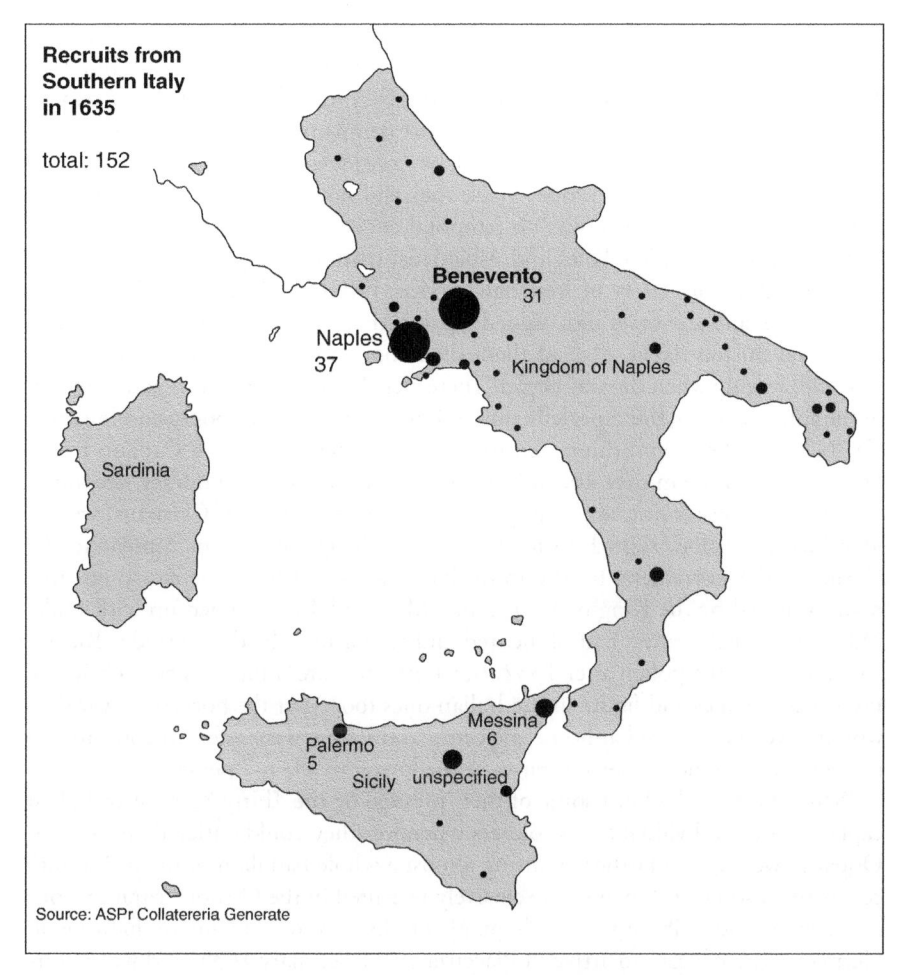

Map 2.3. Recruitment in southern Italy

heartland. Whatever their provenance, like the new recruits elsewhere these young men often joined the army in little groups of three or four, all of the same age and geographical origin, sometimes brothers or cousins signing up together.[85]

Historians are often struck by the international aspect of most seventeenth-century armies, which attracted experienced soldiers from far and wide. Over 200 of the 3,458 men signing on with the first companies were subjects of the Duke of Savoy (Piedmontese primarily), or the Duke of Mantua (mostly from the Monferrato). This latter part of Italy had been a fulcrum of intermittent war from 1613

---

[85] The desertion of the Neapolitans en route for Germany in 1633 and 1634 is described in Leon van der Essen, *Le Cardinal Infant et la politique européenne de l'Espagne, (1609–1641)* (Brussels, 1944), 336.

onward, with full-scale hostilities raging there in 1625–6 and again in 1628–30. On 9 May 1635, three 28-year-old men from the village of San Salvatore in the Monferrato signed up with Alessandro Scotti. They must have had fighting experience, for Duke Odoardo placed them in his company of guards not long after. Another couple of hundred men could be considered professional mercenaries hailing from over half of Europe. These men did not sign on in groups of larger than four or five, and there was no temporal concentration. Here we see about a dozen Englishmen, a few Poles and Albanians, with some *cappelletti* or Serbs and Croatians probably lately of Venetian service. Five of the Englishmen, all aged between 22 and 26 years old, signed up together in the company of Cornelio Palmia on 30 July 1634. One of them died about a year later, but all the others were still serving when the war began. There were lots of Swiss from a good portion of the confederation, but especially the Catholic cantons like Fribourg and Lucerne. On 11 December 1634, three men from Fribourg signed up with Captain Paveri Fontana, two of them over 40, and therefore probably old war buddies, accompanied by a youngster not, apparently, related to them. Scores of Germans, weakly identified by region, signed up for war with a change of scenery. Similar to the Germans, the Lorrainers, mostly from ducal Lorraine (that is, territory not formally annexed by the King of France, like Metz and Toul), signed up with Duke Odoardo. French armies had plundered and subjugated the duchy under Richelieu's annexationist policy after 1632, but Lorrainers are numerous enough in the French companies and figure in the Italian ones too. After the horrors of war they would have encountered at home, Piacenza and Parma were safe and comfortable postings, and so their desertion rate was the lowest of all, at 7 per cent.

While the Swiss had lost some of their prestige by the Thirty Years' War, Italian captains hired individual Swiss soldiers whenever they could entice them to join. Odoardo went a step farther by hiring almost a whole battalion of them. Moralt's company of some 300 men was exclusively recruited in the Catholic rural cantons of Lucerne and Fribourg, though many of them were veterans of fighting in Germany. These began to arrive in Piacenza on 11 February 1635, and we are fortunate that they left a longer paper trail than the others.[86] These Swiss seemed to be the last remnants of the sixteenth-century *landsknechts*, who resembled companies of skilled artisans plying the soldiering trade, and who enjoyed some contractual power with respect to their captain.[87] Johan Werner Moralt signed his final contract with Francesco Serafini on 22 March, which bore mention of the amount they were paid (5 ducatoni per man, or 45 lire), though officials deducted some of this for the bread furnished daily by the *impresario*. The duke distributed weapons to the soldiers free of charge, to be returned at the end of their service. The interesting contract noted specifics on care for sick soldiers and stipulates that even healthy men were entitled to periodical leaves of ten days. The Swiss observed the Imperial articles of war, which were part of their special privileges and autonomy the duke

---

[86] BCPLPc Ms Pallastrelli 126, Croniche Boselli, 104; ASPr, Governo Farnesiano, Milizie 2: Obblighi.
[87] Reinhard Baumann, *I Lanzichenecchi: la loro storia e cultura dal tardo medioevo alla Guerra dei Trent'anni* (Turin, 1996), 134.

promised to observe. Moralt's company saw itself as autonomous and free of amalgamation into some other regiment, just as it would have been if it were hired by another employer, like the King of France.[88] Just as interesting as the contract between Moralt and the duke was the contract of obedience between the soldiers and their captain, who all swore to serve him and the Farnese commanders as soldiers of honour at the risk of their lives. A long list of promises to observe the discipline followed, and many of the infractions were punishable by death. These mercenaries swore to uphold Roman Catholicism and to venerate the Virgin Mary and the saints, for example. That resolve was soon tested, when the company placed the sexagenarian soldier Philip Luser on trial for blasphemy. While on patrol with his squad in Piacenza, Luser vented his scorn for Catholic traditions, such as presenting arms passing before each building on consecrated soil; 'I shit, I shit on all the saints!', he was reported to exclaim, and then exhorted his comrades to become Lutheran, to whose doctrines he had become exposed a few years previous while prisoner of the Swedes. Moralt arrested Luser and tried him by a court martial composed of officers, non-commissioned officers, and other ranks of his company, who sentenced him to death after considering some alternative punishments. His execution was duly noted in the company roster, proving that even mercenary soldiers had principles.[89] There was some nervousness that the Farnese army contained a fair portion of bad Catholics, and there were certainly many Calvinists among the recruits hailing from France.[90]

The French soldiers in the duchy arrived first in little parties in the guise of merchants or pilgrims, together with their clandestine colonels and captains, bringing cash in their pouches. In Piacenza they no doubt kept together in little groups of affinity, perhaps having joined the army together. I suspect this was the case for three men in their mid-20s, all from Noyon in Picardy, whose names follow each other in the roster. It is impossible to know whether these men had served previously in the Italian theatre of war or in Lorraine, or in the French civil wars of the 1620s. Frenchmen signing on outside the two companies of François de la Guette and Jacques de Roquebrune were quite rare until February 1634, when the flow intensified. French nationals eventually comprised 35 per cent of the ducal infantry, most of them enlisting in companies composed overwhelmingly of French-speaking soldiery under their own officers. Most of the recruits, like their officers, were Dauphinois, Lyonnais, or Burgundians, hailing in large part from the cities and small towns of eastern and southern France, where the French commander of the Italian theatre, the Marshal de Créquy, enjoyed an extensive network of clients and

---

[88] The same contract emphasized this autonomy; '*si intenda franca e libera di commando e di giustizia, e non sia aggregata ad altra nazione*'. On the Imperial articles of military discipline, see Fritz Redlich, *De Praeda Militari: Looting and Booty 1500–1815* (Wiesbaden, 1956), 9–10.

[89] ASPr, Governo Farnesiano, Milizie 2: Ristretto o sommario del processo contro Filippo Luser col veto di morte, come giudicato reo di orrende e sagrileghe parole in spregio della Divina Maestà e suoi santi, 23 July 1635.

[90] Heretics figuring in Odoardo's army included the very influential sergeant major Nicart. They reappeared during the Castro War in 1642. See the anonymous pamphlet, *La Mercuriale de Parme contre le Lutheranisme: raisonnement d'Ulric Groisberg, Alleman, soldat en l'armée de Parme, avec le Père Girolamo de Plaisance, confesseur et prédicateur de l'ordre des Recollects du couvent de Parme* (n.p., c.1643).

political clout.[91] A significant number originated from Languedoc, Guyenne, and Poitou, a continuous area known as the Huguenot Crescent. One of the rare studies of the social origins of French soldiers has noted that they were disproportionately urban, and the data for Parma reflects that finding. About a third of them came from cities of more than 10,000 people, and half that proportion again came from the dense network of smaller cities and towns where one could live with decorum. Not all the French soldiers served in these ethnically homogeneous units. Many signed up to predominantly Italian mercenary companies, in which they comprised only a small portion.

The companies raised in 1633 were subject to constant depletion and so the recruiting never ceased even after the unit was considered 'full'. The overall depletion rate for the Italian companies was roughly half for the two years leading up to the war, which is not particularly high relative to armies serving in the field. The French companies declined by less, roughly a third, although depletion due to death was one of the highest rates, at 5.6 per cent. Desertion accounted for just over 500 cases, or, in other words, only 15 per cent of the army's depletion was due to soldiers deserting, dying, or being struck off the list for other causes. For the subjects of the duke or of the King of France, the level was only about 10 per cent. Those most prone to desertion were the subjects of the King of Spain: 22 per cent, which, spread over two years of peace, was not a crippling rate. Odoardo and his colonels considered desertion to be a serious problem and multiplied menacing decrees against it. To underscore the seriousness of the message, they hanged three deserters in front of the troops in the Piacenza square in May 1633, only weeks after forming the first companies, something no one had ever seen before; however, it had no dissuasive effect. Another man, who encouraged his fellows to desert, took refuge in a church, but military constables dragged him from it unceremoniously and hanged him at dawn. This was a flagrant violation of ecclesiastical immunity and the bishop excommunicated the ducal judges and scribes for having authorized and facilitated it.[92] There was a season to desertion, which intensified with the return of warm weather in April and May, and remained steady until August. It dropped off completely in November when the soldiers would have welcomed indoor accommodations. The spring and summer were also hiring seasons for other armies too, which meant that a vagabond ex-soldier was liable to find a bonus and at least the promise of pay almost immediately in some other army. Most of the first few thousand recruits would never see action, many of them deserting soon after joining, once they became bored with the easy life of a garrison soldier. As time went on, the duke softened the rule concerning the enlistment of his local subjects. The chronicler Gozzi lamented that recruiters raised soldiers *'per amore o per forza'* and that magistrates seized people on trumped-up charges that they dropped upon the enlistment of their prey.[93]

[91] Stéphane Gal, *Lesdiguières: Prince des Alpes et connétable de France*, (Grenoble, 2007), 271–2.
[92] BCPLPc Ms Pallastrelli 126, Croniche Boselli, 7 July 1633, 98.
[93] BPPr Ms Parmense 1261, Storia di Parma dell'abbate Gozzi, 1113.

There were several other reasons why captains removed names from their company list. More frequent than desertion during the peacetime build-up was when a soldier was 'broken' for some reason, not often stipulated, as happened in precisely 900 cases. Some of the men had requested permission to leave the company for a specified period to go home, and then neglected to return to their unit. Captains or colonels sent a few men away for thievery or indiscipline, which implies that their personal relations had broken down inside their own companies (for citizens constantly complained of soldiers stealing from them, with little result). A pair of soldiers from the small town of Cisternino in the kingdom of Naples who enlisted together were struck from the lists simultaneously, one for thieving and the other for being 'insolent', which probably implies complicity with his comrade. We find little trace of another common abuse in larger armies, where officers passed off their servants as soldiers on payday, an offence which appears only twice. Officers were notified to be on the lookout for men who changed their names or their place of origin, but, given the small size of the entire army and its lengthy wait in Piacenza for action, it would have been difficult to keep this type of abuse secret for very long.[94] Many more men were sent away for reasons of ill health, which made them useless for service. Swiss soldiers in the company of Johann Werner Moralt were entitled to two months' continuous sick leave before they were dismissed, which appears to be one of their privileges.[95] Paymasters were keen to remove all these men from the roster. No doubt illness was the most frequent pretext for striking someone off the list, a consequence of cramming thousands of men whose hygiene was never more than approximate, into tight spaces. The seasonality of illness was almost the converse of desertion, for the spring months from March to June had the fewest instances of it, while large numbers were struck from the roster between late August and December.

The long wait in garrisons sometimes killed soldiers. It is difficult to know what the normal morbidity was for adult men in cities, in the era before barracks. Of the first 4,000 or so men hired, 158 of those still on the company rosters died before the onset of the campaign. At least 30 of the men in these first companies died violent deaths, two-thirds of them at the hands of their peers or of civilians, and military judges hanged or shot the remaining third for desertion or murder. Soldiers were notorious for sneaking off to convenient places to fight duels, and even issuing a challenge (the *mentita*) was grounds for flogging or expulsion.[96] As war grew more certain in the spring and early summer of 1635, desertion dropped off and there was a marked decline in the turbulence of the soldiery. Scores more died of disease. The discontinuous register of the hospital of San Giuseppe of Piacenza allows us to see a constant flow of men entering and leaving the institution for the better part of a year, beginning in the summer of 1634, and again for the spring

---

[94] ASPr, Governo Farnesiano, Fabbriche Ducali e Fortificazioni 4: Ordini da Osservarsi dalli soldati del Castel di Piacenza, 4 November 1635.
[95] ASPr, Governo Farnesiano, Milizie 2, Obblighi.
[96] ASPr, Governo Farnesiano, Fabbriche e Fortificazioni 4: Ordini da osservarsi, articles 3, 10, and 14.

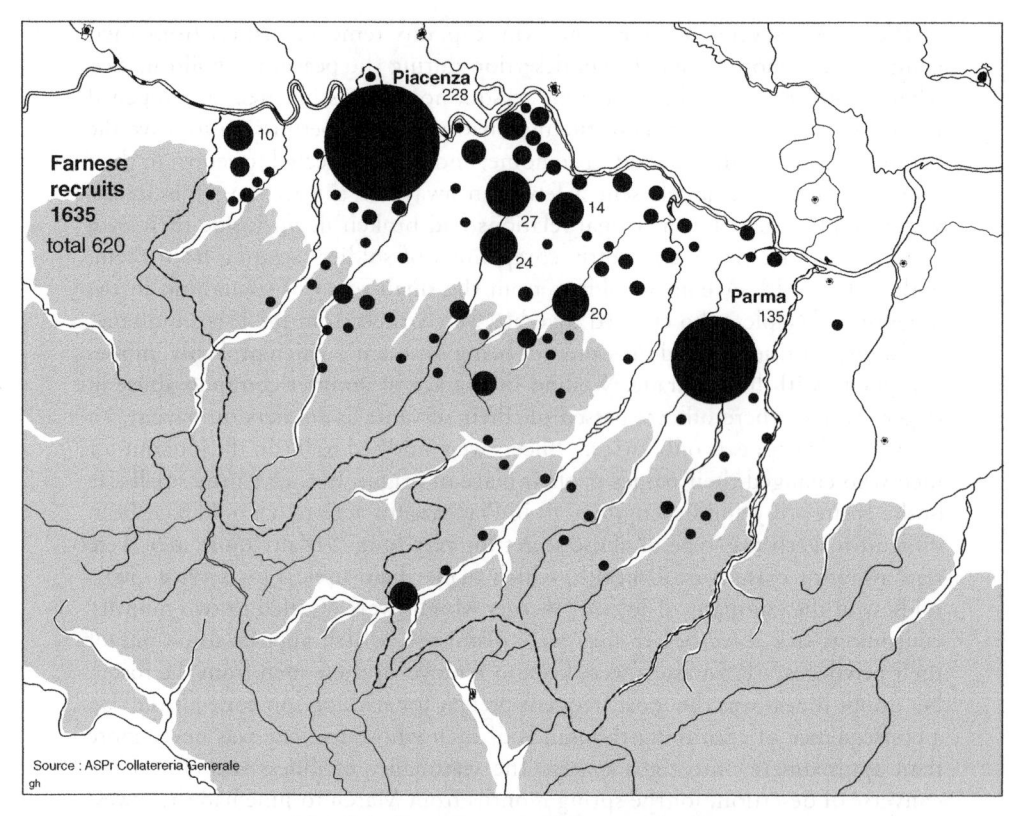

Map 2.4. Recruitment in Farnese territories

and summer of 1635 before the onset of the war.[97] Normally the hospital was an important centre of medical attention for people with no fixed address in the city, or people whose wounds were too dire to be treated at home. The institution also collected foundlings and employed wet nurses for them. During the long mobilization, however, most of the people recorded entering the institution were soldiers. The great majority of them were single men without friends in the city, and while there were enough French comrades to help most of the foreigners communicate, some north Europeans coped by using Latin. Soldiers were uneasy guests in a city where very few of them had family ties (none of the subjects of the duke died a violent death), and they may not have been good with money. Hospital records list the articles of clothing soldiers gave up when they took to bed, in which they wore only their shirts. In contrast to the odd wounded soldier who entered hospital wearing fine clothes, like Angelo Tavano from Corsica, whose tunic sleeves were made of silk and whose breeches of striped cloth were completed by silk blue

[97] Urban parish registers are accessible for Piacenza thanks to the Mormon project of microfilming them. See reel number 2201061, San Giuseppe di Piacenza.

Table 2.2. Attrition levels in peacetime army

Desertions

January	February	March	April	May	June	July	August	September	October	November	December	Total
19	13	7	51	89	46	61	57	34	32	15	12	436

Struck from Roster

January	February	March	April	May	June	July	August	September	October	November	December	Total
62	64	54	29	57	55	74	55	93	92	115	75	825

Fig. 2.3. Piacenza city hospital, *c.*1750.

stockings with gold lace, most of the other soldiers' clothes were listed by the scribes as dirty or worn, and often described as mere rags. Most soldiers went to the hospital because they were stricken with fever, but there was no shortage of men with wounds that other men had inflicted with swords and knives, and fully half the men who died in the hospital perished of such wounds. Very little work has been done on military hospitals, which were still very novel in the first half of the seventeenth century. If we may rely on the work done on English examples of the era, hospitals offered a controlled stress-free environment with a regime of rest, sleep, food and drink, excretion and retention.[98] Large hospitals tended by lay confraternities, such as those existing in all the large Italian cities, were an improvement over the cramped lodgings the soldiers shared in the city. Most soldiers spent only a few days in the hospital before they left with their belongings, but they were probably allotted a longer period of recovery in which they could receive their pay while they were incapacitated.

Hospital scribes sometimes recorded the names of the wives of soldiers treated in hospital or who died there, and, in German contingents, the wives and other womenfolk following the soldiers could be fairly numerous. I doubt that this was the case in Piacenza, for soldiers' women almost never figure in our documents, and if they

---

[98] Gruber von Arni, *Justice to the Maimed Soldier*, 3.

were common in the city, they should have figured among the people admitted to the hospital, or else appear in the parish burial registers. It is not easy to determine what the relations between soldiers and women would have been without mining the criminal archives and the baptismal records, which, for Piacenza, do not survive for many parishes. Physicians treated only 3 of the 271 soldiers in our hospital register for '*la purga del mal francese*'. They expelled Cesare Romano from Naples from the hospital for having smuggled a prostitute into his bed. Piacenza's hospital seems to have been a place for mutual support among the soldiers, where comrades kept an eye on the attendants, and kept their Protestant comrades from the clutches of ardent confessors seeking converts.[99] Illness and hospitalization activated the solidarities of friends and messmates like few other predicaments.[100]

The vast majority of the men we encounter from the spring of 1633 were foot soldiers, for Odoardo avoided raising cavalry for as long as possible, given that it was necessary to provide for both men and horses (whose daily upkeep cost several times that of a man). The first of the five companies of horse whose statistics we can trust, under Alessandro Scotti, was formed only in early March 1635. In the six months leading up to the war, its complement fell by half due to desertion, death, and other causes (not including transfer). This was the company with the largest portion of foreign Italians and the smallest number of ducal subjects. Cavalrymen hailing from Piedmont, Monferrato, and enemy territories dispersed very quickly, and there were few Frenchmen to take their place. For the remaining companies it seems that Odoardo had recourse now to military entrepreneurs from the Venetian Republic. The cavalry officers Ricciardo Avogadri of Brescia, Marino Badoero of Venice, and Antonio Maria Sarego of Verona drew troopers from the great plain, almost half of whom hailed from the Venetian Terraferma. Cavalry troopers from the Italian neutral states made up a large third of the whole, while others were French nationals (13 per cent), the subjects of allied princes from Piedmont or Monferrato, along with a handful of subjects of the King of Spain.

The burden of raising cavalry lay in the considerable quantities of forage they required, which cost roughly four times the maintenance of infantry.[101] Consequently, the horses would have to be distributed farther afield to graze, where they competed with precious cows and oxen. The parish priest of the little town of Colorno recorded on 27 April the arrival of 120 cavalrymen with their mounts, spread out among a number of villages in the district. This was something completely novel for these villagers, who were instructed to provide straw, feed, hay, and stalls with the appropriate equipment to care for the horses. Green pastures were not enough to have horses fit for service; they needed oats, barley, and pulses in their diet too.[102] While these foreigners, generically called Bersani (i.e. from

---

[99] Anon., *La Mercuriale de Parme contre le Lutheranisme*, 4; *Ospedale San Giuseppe di Piacenza*, reel no. 2201061 one Fermin Tessier from Languedoc converted on his deathbed in April 1635.

[100] For a good look at the morbidity of soldiers, see Coss, *All for the King's Shilling*, 103–6.

[101] Paul Azan, *Un tacticien du XVIIe siècle* (Paris, 1904), 71.

[102] Peter Edwards, 'Les chevaux et les guerres civiles anglaises au milieu du XVIIe siècle', *Le Cheval de guerre du XVe au XXe siècle*, in *Le Cheval et la guerre du XVe au XXe siècle*, ed. D. Roche and D. Reytier (Paris, 2002), 243–9.

Brescia) and their numerous grooms were considered bandits, the duke dutifully paid for all the expenses they incurred and his paymaster arrived punctually every month, so that nobody could complain. 'The Signor Collaterio Cantelli told me and others that the king of Spain did not dispose of such a fine company as we had, neither in men nor in horses, and all so finely outfitted.'[103] Certainly Odoardo made short shrift of tax privileges and exemptions claimed by the clergy, and before long he was on a collision course with the papacy on these grounds.

While foreign entrepreneurs provided the experienced nucleus of these cavalry companies, a good portion of the cavalry troopers appear to be village worthies pressed into service, for scribes sometimes marked that troopers were serving in place of their fathers, or could go home upon finding a willing replacement. Over 40 per cent of the horsemen in September 1635 were the duke's direct subjects, recruited for the most part in the lush dairy country along the Po river, where large livestock grazed. Cavalry militiamen were a distillation of both the urban and rural elite who were well-off enough to provide their own horses. No doubt the prince expected them to pay something towards the animals' grooming and upkeep, for a roster of militiamen from the village of Caorso before the war recorded the financial ability of each of the troopers to serve.[104] It specified a number of the troopers as gentlemen, who lived part of the year in their Piacenza palazzo, and the rest of the year on their country estates, while others were referred to disparagingly as peasants rich enough to serve. Ten such companies of militia horsemen, totalling some 700 troopers, existed early in the seventeenth century, and these notables apparently made up a fair portion of Odoardo's cavalry in 1635.[105] Cavalry troopers were the oldest of all the soldiers, with a mean age well over 30, and were often in their late 40s or even older. Professional cavalrymen from outside the duchy then fleshed out the militiamen, and, combined with them, formed professional-looking units.

WEAPONS AND TACTICS

While they waited for the duke to commit them to war, the soldiers carried out their routine duties of standing guard in the citadel, and patrolling the streets and fortifications of Piacenza, and, to a lesser extent, Parma. Sentry duty, routine patrol, and weapons drill were undemanding tasks but they required attention from the officers that they be carried out diligently, such that it was necessary to reiterate the punishments meted out to lazy or quarrelsome individuals, with much of the responsibility for inspecting the soldiery lying with the corporals.[106] Mercenary soldiers were, in the great majority, outsiders who understood that the duke required their services and that they would have considerable leeway in the city.

---

[103] D. Costantino Canivetti, *Memoria di Colorno (1618–1674)* (n.p., 1635); also the analysis of the manuscript version by Cristina Trombella, 'La 'Memoria' di Colorno (1612–1674) di Don Costantino Canivetti; parte prima 1612–1658' (Thesis, Università degli studi di Parma, 1997–8).
[104] ASPr, Governo Farnesiano, Milizie 3: Notta per la Compagnia di Cavorso, n.d. (1615?).
[105] Boscarelli, 'Appunti sulle istituzioni'.
[106] ASPr, Governo Farnesiano, Fabbriche Ducali e Fortificazioni 4: Ordini da Osservarsi.

Their many abuses resulted in a decree on 18 April 1633 that listed the articles that soldiers must observe with respect to citizens. The regulations designated blasphemy, bad language, gambling, and petty thieving in the barracks as situations that required constant vigilance. Soldiers challenged each other to duels, or bullied citizens, or embarrassed or shamed the women of the city. Piacenza clergy sounded the alarm once as soldiers were caught plundering a church, and in Parma some cavalry troopers lodged in the monastery of San Martino stole sacred objects, gradually returned to the monks as pious citizens repurchased them.[107] Francesco Serafini's instructions to the garrison late in 1635 threatened harsh punishment for a wide variety of offences, and he thought it a wise precaution to forbid soldiers from walking about town in numbers greater than five without a proper officer to supervise them.[108]

Some of the soldiers' time would have been taken up with weapons drill, which was being critically modernized in these very years. Instruction may have occupied no more than one day every week in garrison, dispensed by the corporal or a veteran to the new recruits.[109] According to legend the Dutch introduced drill in the late sixteenth century and transformed the large phalanx of pikemen into shallower formations with a wider frontage devised to maximize the growing firepower of the arquebus or the matchlock musket. The next phase saw Gustavus Adolphus of Sweden introduce a devastating salvo fire that could stop an army in its tracks. Soldiers needed to be drilled daily to almost machine-like efficiency and be taught that composure under fire was the chief virtue in war. The same legend claims that armies comprised of automatons led to a durable superiority of north European armies over those of Spain and Austria after 1630. A generation of closer research has worn down this sharp contrast a great deal, for few worthwhile innovations remain long neglected by the enemy. Spanish troops were quick off the mark to augment the proportion of musketeers to pikemen, and if the greater firepower of the Swedes was decisive over the German Habsburgs at Breitenfeld in 1631, the more highly motivated Catholic troops utterly destroyed the same Protestant army at Nördlingen in 1634.[110]

By 1635 all the major armies seem to have adopted similar infantry and cavalry tactics. Infantrymen were equipped with just two weapons that had to be used together to maximum effect. The principal infantry tactic of the sixteenth century was just an updated version of the phalanx of antiquity, where a great mass of armoured soldiers pressed forward with sharp poles, attempting to disperse a similar force of enemy foot. These pikes, of about 16 feet in length, made the same

---

[107] ASPr, Carteggio Farnesiano Interno 383; letter by D. Bernardo Bianchi, abbot of the monastery to the duchess, 2 October 1635.
[108] ASPr, Governo Farnesiano, Fabbriche Ducali e Fortificazioni 4: Ordini da Osservarsi.
[109] Giovanni Cerino Badone, 'Le Seconde Guerre d'Italia (1588–1659): Storiografia, Temi, Fonti' (PhD thesis, Università degli Studi del Piemonte Orientale, 2011, 202.
[110] Recent books designed for a popular North American market, whose authors apparently only read English, still exalt the Dutch and Swedish innovations without looking too closely at the outcome of battles. I am thinking in particular of the illustrated work by Christer Jörgensen, Matthew Bennett, Michael Pavkovic, and Rob S. Rice, *Fighting Techniques of the Early Modern World: Equipment, Combat Skills, and Tactics* (New York, 2005).

infantry invulnerable to cavalry, for a horse could not be trained to impale itself on its point. By the early sixteenth century these pikemen already enjoyed the support of a number of soldiers equipped with firearms, first the arquebus, and later the heavier musket, which was reasonably accurate at approximately 100 metres. These weapons were much slower to reload than the medieval bow or even the more powerful crossbow, but the improvements in armour technology could not keep pace with the increasing muzzle velocity and the penetrating ability of the lead shot. Troops armed with these firearms could pepper enemy columns with shot, and, when menaced by horse or foot, they would scurry to find shelter behind the pikemen. Dutch and Spanish drill innovations at the end of the sixteenth century refined these early tactics. Pikemen were taught to spread out, leaving at least one metre between each man, in order to wield their weapon to best effect, but still remain close enough to prevent gaping holes in the company that the enemy could exploit. They were to present a straight array of sharpened points towards the enemy, with only the first several ranks able to come into contact with the enemy. The pikemen behind them, up to a total depth of ten, would step forward and fill the gaps due to losses. Parties of musketeers stood on each side of the pikemen or else arrayed themselves in front and fired at their opposite numbers or at the enemy pike. If pressed, they could withdraw into the pike formation, and re-emerge with loaded weapon from the mass to fire into the enemy formation. Drill manuals provided a number of different deployments colonels could adopt to utilize the two weapons to the best effect, although the strongest and best-trained soldiers were generally the pikemen, many of whom still wore breastplates and helmets. In a melee, the soldiers could lay down either weapon, and use swords and daggers instead, and musketeers could wield their firearms as clubs.

In 1635 it was not apparent that clockwork tactics were superior to large bodies of men well skilled in the use of their weapons, but the proportion of musketeers to pikemen increased everywhere two to one.[111] Firepower was just beginning to dominate the battlefield during the Thirty Years' War. It was difficult to reduce the proportion of pikemen further because of the cumbersome reloading process of the muskets, which took up to two minutes even for the best-trained man, and misfires constituted about a fifth of every shot even in dry weather, and more like half after prolonged firing. These firearms were too heavy (7 to 10 kilograms) to fire unaided, so the soldier carried a forked stand to support the barrel. The weapon was 2 metres long and fired a heavy ball that could penetrate armour and still be effective up to 130 metres. Soldiers carried flasks of gunpowder and a dozen measured gunpowder vials on a bandolier, and a pouch containing lead shot, generally no more than 20 rounds. To load their musket they pushed the powder into the smooth barrel of the weapon and tamped it down to the base before dropping in the bullet, and priming the external firing mechanism with a little more powder. They also carried a lit wick that would be applied to the firing mechanism, igniting

---

[111] David Parrott, 'Strategy and tactics in the Thirty Years' War: the "military revolution" revisited', *Militargeschichtliche Mitteilungen*, 38/2 (1985): 7–25; a Spanish reform of 1632 stipulated that two-thirds of the foot were to be armed with muskets; see Albi de la Cuesta, *De Pavia a Rocroi*, 46.

the powder at the base of the barrel through a touch-hole, ejecting the lead ball. The operation was awkward, due to the necessity of holding the musket, its support, and the lit wick simultaneously, but fairly reliable. Over time warlords phased out the heavy musket and reintroduced the matchlock musket, a slightly shorter weapon that weighed five or six kilograms, could be reloaded more quickly, required no support, fired a lighter ball, but was accurate only to 60 metres. The barrels of these firearms were smooth bore, permitting the balls to slide in quickly. This meant that the explosion at the base of the barrel bounced the ball in unpredictable ways down the tube, and some of the air escaped around it, which reduced the velocity of its exit and gave it an unreliable trajectory once it emerged from the muzzle. The principal concern for commanders was for the musketeers to keep up a sufficient *volume* of shot to keep the enemy at bay, for every forward step they took increased the probability that their own men would be hit.[112]

The Dutch improved the rate of fire by means of the countermarch, in which a soldier who discharged his musket (either together with others in the front row in a salvo, or individually) marched to the rear to reload, while the man behind him stepped forward with loaded musket to take his turn. The depth of the unit would reflect how quickly it took each man to reload his weapon. In 1600, bodies of musketeers were commonly ten men deep, while after 1630 they might be reduced to eight or even six. This enabled the company or battalion to produce a volley of shot every 15 or 20 seconds. The lethality of this fire would depend upon their proximity to the enemy. Naturally, the enemy would return fire at something close to the same rate, if their training was comparable. Good troops were those who could hold their fire until the last possible moment, or absorb the greatest number of losses without flinching, breaking ranks, or falling back. As it became possible to increase the rate of fire, the units did not need to be as deep as before; the trend was to reduce the size of each company from 200 men in 1600 to 100 in 1635, to merely 50 by 1660, although this increased the proportion of officers to ranks and perhaps facilitated the maintenance of discipline. In the noise of battle, soldiers were trained to listen to the different drumbeats ordered by the officers.[113]

Lieutenants, sergeants, and corporals in Piacenza and Parma were well aware of all these techniques and did their best to instruct both the professional soldiers and militiamen in the details. These manoeuvres would have to be undertaken quickly while the unit was under fire, and it was important that those in charge learn how to deploy the men, dress their lines, and change formation. There were dozens of individual commands for manoeuvring the pikes in unison in the desired formation, and many more for the musketeers, to load their weapon, to step forward, to aim at the centre of their target man (*a mezzo huomo*), to fire on the order, and then

---

[112] For the Spanish army, see Lorraine White, 'The experience of Spain's early modern soldiers: combat, welfare and violence', *War in History*, 9 (2002): 1–38; also Albi de la Cuesta, *De Pavía a Rocroi*, 89–98; for England, Donagan, *War in England*, 75; for Germany, William Guthrie, *Battles of the Thirty Years War: From White Mountain to Nordlingen* (Westport, CT, and London, 2002), 4–7.

[113] Perhaps the best description of the large-unit tactics is found in William Guthrie, *The Later Thirty Years War: From the Battle of Wittstock to the Treaty of Westphalia* (Westport, CT, and London, 2003), 16–19; on the importance of being steadfast see Lynn, *Giant of the 'Grand Siècle'*, 458–77 and 514.

to withdraw to the right to the end of the file, and to reload.[114] Reloading and firing the muskets without burning themselves or the men beside them with the lit wick were complicated tasks and no doubt resulted in many accidents. Veterans knew how to do this, and even militiamen were trained in the basics fairly often.[115] Despite the complexities of the drill, the new infantry weapons no longer required either great physical strength or long apprenticeship in their use. The conversion to pikes and muskets over the course of the sixteenth century entailed a deskilling process for the individual soldier, where just being able-bodied was enough to start with.[116] But one still needed veterans in order to win wars.

The Farnese dynasty also instructed citizens as well as soldiers in the use of cannon. In Parma, the bombardier school practised gunnery on the ramparts every Sunday after mass. Both fortress and field artillery required some mathematical calculation so that educated civilians were more skilled than soldiers in its employ. Marcello Manacci, a Roman gunner employed as captain of the Parman bombardiers, has left us a printed manual dedicated to Prince Ranuccio, giving instruction in its use. Cannon came in many different varieties and dimensions, each with a different name.[117]

As for the weaponry, the manufacturing cities of the great Po valley transformed the ores mined not far away into a variety of lethal instruments. Forges in Brescia and its mountain hinterland probably supplied both sides. Spanish Milan produced considerable quantities of armaments from the mining and metallurgical valleys on the edge of the duchy near Bergamo, to the extent that the Duke of Rohan made them a special target. Less exposed city workshops in Milan, but also Pavia, Alessandria, and Novara produced arms and armour of many kinds.[118] It is unclear from where the Duke of Parma drew his arms and weapons, although there was a steady supply of saltpeter (for gunpowder) from Salsomaggiore, and there were iron and copper mines in the Apennines at Ferriere, south of Piacenza. At Ponte dell'Olio nearby, an atelier produced musket barrels for the militia, and workshops in Piacenza produced other weapons from the sixteenth century onwards.[119] Duke Odoardo possessed a foundry for casting artillery near the Parma palace, established in 1559, and kept his own ample stock of armour and weapons locked up in the two citadels of Parma and Piacenza. Before the war (1622), the

---

[114] Luciano Pezzolo, 'La "Revoluzione militare"; Una prospettiva italiana 1400–1700', in *Militari in età moderna: la centralità di un tema di confine*, ed. A. Dattero and S. Levati (Milan, 2006), 15–65; for firing instructions, ASPr, Governo Farnesiano, Milizie 33: Esercizio della militia a piedi, n.d. (*c.*1630). The official describing these tactics to Duke Odoardo claimed there was no need to spell everything out to the prince. '*Io non metto in carta tutti li modi di combattere per non tediare V.A.S., e presuponendo ancora che l'ufficiale che comanda sappia fare.*'

[115] ASPr, Governo Farnesiano, Milizie 33: Esercizio della militia a piedi; see also ASPr, Governo Farnesiano, Milizie 1: Istruzione per la fanteria di milizia.

[116] Mortimer, 'War by contract, credit and contribution', 101–17.

[117] Marcello Manacci, *Compendio d'Instruttioni per gli bombardieri* (Parma, 1640).

[118] Davide Maffi, 'Guerra ed economia: spese belliche e appaltatori militari nella Lombardia spagnola (1635–1660)', *Storia Economica*, 3 (2000): 489–527.

[119] Stefano Pronti, 'Produzione e diffusione delle armi nello stato di Piacenza in età Farnesiana: indicazioni per ricerche', in *I Farnese: Corti, guerra e nobiltà in Antico Regime*, ed. A. Bilotto, P. Del Negro, and C. Mozzarelli (Rome, 1997), 487–92.

visiting Prince de Condé admired the finished citadel of Parma, where he counted more than 100 artillery pieces of various dimensions, and inspected several storerooms stocked with modern weapons in abundance for both horse and foot, along with munitions of all kinds.[120] We have an inventory of these munitions for the sole citadel of Parma, compiled after the extinction of the dynasty in 1736, where it is clear that much of it was very old, and many of the 61 cannon (which were dated) on the ramparts or in storerooms were first acquired in the late sixteenth and early seventeenth century. The arsenal still contained 870 iron breastplates and 1,400 helmets, surely dating from the period of the Thirty Years' War, which had long gone out of use, and almost 7,000 muskets of various calibre, together with another 6,000 unmounted musket barrels, and almost 2,000 more modern rifles, 1,300 carbines, and 2,360 pistols in various states of repair. Those were just the firearms: there were also 1,800 pikes and 100 halberds, and 'many other pieces of firearms and blade weapons and other hardware'. There was a stock of close to 60,000 iron cannon balls and 12,000 stone balls, 1,300 chests full of musket balls and many tonnes of gunpowder.[121] Many of Odoardo's weapons purchases were still stored away a full century later.

What of the arrangements for provisioning and supply? The duke designated a number of sutlers or *vivandieri* in Piacenza who had permission to buy and transport all kinds of goods to sell to the soldiers, both inside the duchy and beyond its borders. He contracted with private-sector bakers, or *impresari*, to provide bread at subsidized prices to the soldiers, but troops actually also bought most of their other food and sundry other comforts from these entrepreneurs, who were expected to pay the usual taxes on the articles. One licence given to a consortium of six sutlers in May 1636 listed the articles they would furnish, which included every kind of foodstuff, wine and brandy, clothing and footwear. These traders, who received a licence to bear arms, were expected to shuttle back and forth between Piacenza and the camp, wherever it was. The risks they took of being plundered were somewhat offset by their ability to buy the soldiers' booty at advantageous prices, for the latter wished to convert their loot as quickly as possible for something they could consume right away as they did not have the means to hold onto any unnecessary item for very long.[122]

One novel piece of kit was the uniform tunic, which the chronicler Boselli saw for the first time in July 1635, as the city was filling up with contingents ready to take the field. The duke's own regiment of 1,000 men wore green tunics (*casache*), while later contingents of both horse and foot, numbering 1,000 men, wore similar yellow garments.[123] A year previously, similar tunics had been distributed to soldiers hired in Castro on the instructions of Francesco Serafini, who apparently laid great store by

---

[120] Giorgio Cusatelli and Fausto Razzetti. *Il Viaggio a Parma: Visitatori stranieri in età farnesiana e borbonica* (Parma, 1990), 55.
[121] BPPr, Ms Parmense 631, Stato dell'artiglieria, armi, munizioni e altre robbe in questo Real Castello di Parma, 31 January 1736.
[122] ASPr, Governo Farnesiano, Fabbriche Ducali e Fortezze 9, fasc.3, Vivandieri in Piacenza.
[123] BCPLPc Ms Pallastrelli 126, Croniche Boselli, 109.

them.[124] This supply of identical garments would have placed Odoardo's army among the very first to wear a uniform. Soldiers tended to wear sensible clothes, such as strong shoes, breeches, and linen shirts, but had traditionally been free to wear what they liked. Armies in Germany reportedly contained regiments that were known by their colours, but this might merely have referred to the standards they carried, six feet square, the common symbol of the unit, and not the garment itself.[125]

AUXILIARY FORCES

In addition to the mercenary soldiers who comprised the garrisons and the field army, Odoardo's forces included two other components worth mentioning here. The first was a group of gate guards for both cities, under the supervision of the commander of the respective citadels. Authorities ordered some gates to be bricked up during the conflict in order to prevent them from being surprised by enemy parties or else stormed by attackers who could wedge an explosive device called a petard underneath the great doors themselves and blow them apart. Odoardo assigned each gate a commanding captain, a sergeant, and a few corporals, along with a small number of professional soldiers of quite diverse origin, including Italian subjects of the King of Spain. They might not have been the men most apt for soldiering, for these gate guards were static forces. In peacetime, all five gates of Piacenza employed no more than 60 officers and soldiers. In addition to this skeleton force, gate captains received a couple of dozen militiamen from the countryside for guard duty.[126] The function of these soldiers was not merely to open the gates every morning to people who needed to enter from the countryside with their provisions, and to keep watch over them at night. Gates were very convenient places at which to inspect the arrival and departure of all kinds of merchandise, and tax collectors were on hand with their books of tariffs to collect the appropriate fees. Being a gate captain was a very lucrative function, as we learn from an estimate of the revenues of Parma's gatekeepers. Their annual salary was several times an artisan's income, at 864 lire, but, in addition to that, they received perquisites of grain, grapes, firewood, and various gifts of poultry, eggs, fresh produce, and other items, totalling between 4,000 and 6,000 lire, depending upon the gate. In wartime, the duke's pressing need for money would be abetted considerably by their diligence and honesty, and particularly their willingness to challenge rich and influential people, both lay and especially ecclesiastic, so presumably the generous perquisites would make their corruption less likely.[127]

Finally, the duke could count on his inexhaustible militias, both peasant and urban. Duke Ottavio founded the peasant militia in the sixteenth century, on the model of other states like Venice, Tuscany, Piedmont, and the Papal States. Ottavio

---

[124] ASPr, Governo Farnesiano Milizie 1, 7 June 1634.
[125] Geoffrey Parker et al., *The Thirty Years' War* (London, 1984), 191.
[126] ASPr, Collatereria Generale 529 and 530: Ruoli delle porte di Piacenza, 1634 and 1636.
[127] ASPr, Governo Farnesiano, Milizie 1: Capitani delle Porte di Parma, n.d.

first published the articles, privileges, and exemptions of this ducal militia in 1581, and periodical decrees modernized the institution. Rural populations were often armed to the teeth before the eighteenth century. Militiamen were able-bodied volunteer soldiers between the ages of 18 and 40 who mustered periodically in their village companies and their district regiments or *tercios* to be counted, inspected, and 'trained' by officers designated by the duke. This huge militia force mustered twice a year: the men practised shooting somewhat more frequently. Militiamen kept their weapons and armour (when they had any) at home. They could not expect the duke to pay them for this service, but they were personally exempt from the many service details imposed upon the peasant communities where they resided and they enjoyed judicial guarantees such as exemption from seizure or torture and especially generous payment terms for debts that made it worth their while. The criminal sentences meted out to them had to be reviewed by special military magistrates mindful of the duchy's military interests and the special status of such soldiers.[128] The ducal peasant militia under the Farnese included a staggeringly large number of men in its nine district *tercios*, estimated variously at 38,000 individuals. In the aftermath of the great plague, they would still likely number in the tens of thousands. Militia captains were not supposed to enlist more than a quarter of the adult men in any given community, but this article could be waived. The companies were proportional in size to the population of the districts where they served, so single village companies in the rich plain could number over 300 men. Farnese dukes with these militia bands under their command imposed themselves on rural feudatories. They also periodically mobilized militiamen to make demonstrations on the borders with Modena or the Landi princes.[129] Potentates in Italy and elsewhere in Europe mobilized militia in order to make visible demonstrations of their power and military potential, and to keep public order in times of crisis.

Reading the instructions to militia officers published in 1616, specifying the various ranks and describing their duties, one might confuse them with paid mercenaries.[130] But their very armament betrayed that these were not soldiers in the proper sense of that word. In the early seventeenth century, Farnese militiamen, like those of Medicean Tuscany, were overwhelmingly equipped with firearms.[131] The duke's principal military official, Count Girolamo Rho, and the agent responsible for recruiting, Collatore Generale Bartolomeo Cantelli, mustered the various *tercios* in the spring of 1633, verified the identity and age of each man in every *squadra* (corresponding to a hamlet), and noted the weapon they carried. The duke expected that militiamen would provide their own weapons, which were not entirely standardized even among professional soldiers of a single state. It is frequent to find helmets and pieces of armour in post-mortem inventories of rural

---

[128] ASPr, Gridario 11/55: Articoli, privilege ed esenzioni toccanti alla milizia ducale di Parma e Piacenza, 20 July 1581.
[129] Boscarelli, 'Appunti sulle istituzioni'.
[130] ASPr, Governo Farnesiano, Milizie 1: Istruzione per la fanteria di milizia.
[131] Pezzolo, 'La "Revoluzione militare"', 15–65.

dwellers. At least three-quarters of the men carried muskets and arquebuses (mostly the former), while a handful wielded a *partigiana* or poleaxe for close-in fighting rather than a pike. The absence of trained pikemen meant that these companies were useless for service in the field where they might encounter cavalry, but they would be more effective defending enclosures.[132] In addition to the rural companies, citizens of Parma and Piacenza comprised the guard of the ramparts of their cities and the respective citadels. Peasants rotated every month through the handful of ducal fortified towns and castles, and perhaps tens of thousands of men from the duchy stood watch over the Po, or escorted baggage along the highways; however, it would not have been feasible to mobilize all the militiamen simultaneously simply due to the difficulty of feeding them. The very large numbers of militiamen on both sides would soon tempt commanders into placing them in harm's way, where the result was usually disappointing, but they would also become a reserve of semi-trained manpower to replace regular soldiers.[133] Militia service was never very popular with peasants of either side, however, who were more than likely to curse their princes for submitting them to its rigours.[134]

The pace of everything quickened in the late spring and summer of 1635, immediately after the Duke of Rohan invaded the Valtellina and cut the direct route between Milan and the Austrian Habsburg lands. French troops assembled in Turin on 10 and 21 April 1635, where the count reached an impressive 21,702 soldiers on horse and foot, although this likely included the strong garrisons at Casale and Pinerolo. Odoardo was still expecting French reinforcements in early August to bring his own tally to 5,000 foot and 1,000 horse, which was more than he had promised, but he required substantial French subsidies to maintain them, such as the 20,000 scudi he received at the end of May from Richelieu.[135] Sieur Bellièvre arrived in Parma at mid-August to spur the duke into jumping into the fray without further hesitation.[136] Odoardo marshalled his troops in Piacenza in late August, as he learned of the deployment of the Franco-Piedmontese army around Casale Monferrato. The Comte de Saint-Paul, a French officer reporting to Richelieu, was not impressed. '*La cavalerie du Duc de Parme n'est guère bonne et je doubte bien de toute*

---

[132] The militia rosters are very numerous, although none dates from the war itself. I surveyed at random a handful of these rosters from 1633 and 1634; ASPr, Collatereria Generale 2557, 2a compagnia Bettola; Collatereria Generale 2675, Compagnia di Ponte; Collatereria Generale 2796, Compagnia di Borgonovo; Collatereria Generale 2930, Compagnia di Sarmato, all in the *tercio* of the Val di Nure west of Piacenza.

[133] Maffi, 'Le milizie dello Stato di Milano (1615–1700): un tentativo di controllo sociale', in *Las milicias del Rey de España (siglos XVI y XVII)*, ed. José Javier Ruiz Ibáñez (Madrid, 2009), 245–67; also Ribot Garcìa, 'El reclutamiento militar en España a mediados del siglo XVI', 63–89; also Mario Rizzo, 'Istituzioni militari e strutture socio-economiche in una città di antico regime. La milizia urbana a Pavia nell'età spagnola', in *Eserciti e carriere militari nell'Italia moderna*, ed. C. Donati (Milan, 1998), 63–89.

[134] Gualdo Priorato, *Il guerriero prudente e politico*, 81.

[135] For the French numbers, Archives des Affaires Etrangères (henceforth AAE) Paris and La Courneuve], Correspondance Politique Sardaigne 23, 10 and 21 April 1635; for Odoardo's contingent, AAE, Correspondance Politique Parme, 5 August 1635; the Spaniards were informed of the French subsidy, AGS Estado 3837, letter of 18 June 1635.

[136] Galeazzo Gualdo Priorato, *Historia delle guerre del Conte Galeazzo Gualdo Priorato*, 295.

l'infanterie italienne.' Odoardo had at least kept his promise to Richelieu with respect to the numbers he could commit to the alliance. While the record-keeping may be partially flawed, the tally for the first days of September gives 665 cavalrymen in seven companies, and 4,262 foot soldiers in 25 companies. In addition, there may have been some gentleman volunteers riding with the duke. Of the units mentioned by chroniclers, only the noble Cornetta Bianca guard company appears to be missing from our rosters. Perhaps an additional force of militiamen marched with the 400 baggage carts and four cannon, but it is doubtful that many of them followed the invasion force far into Lombardy. The army certainly looked well equipped and up to date, in their new green or yellow tunics. The prince who had the edge in war was the one with the most veterans with the greatest willingness to fight, however. Contemporaries were doubtful that the Duke of Parma's army comprised of such soldiers, but they noted that the force was well financed and appeared in fine mettle. Odoardo's rich little duchy had raised, trained, and adequately supplied an army that equalled roughly 2 per cent of the entire population of a quarter of a million inhabitants, which was double the European average of 1 per cent in the seventeenth century.[137] France's combined field armies in 1635 of about 75,000 men was about one soldier for every 240 inhabitants, roughly five times fewer.[138] However, in his unbounded confidence in Richelieu's ability and his own star, the young and eager duke did not perceive this.

---

[137] For some interesting gross calculations on the number of professional soldiers in Italy and elsewhere over the century, see the chapter by Yves-Marie Bercé, 'Les guerres dans l'Italie du XVIIe siècle', in *L'Italie au XVIIe siècle* (Paris, 1989), 324–5.

[138] David Parrott, 'French military organization in the 1630s: the failure of Richelieu's ministry', *Seventeenth Century French Studies*, 9 (1987): 151–67.

3

The Duke of Parma's Great Adventure

ODOARDO OVER THE BRINK

War began in northern Italy even before it was declared formally in Brussels, when the Duke of Rohan led an invasion down the Valtellina corridor with a mixed army of French and Swiss Grison troops. After occupying the valley in late April, the French general advanced towards Lake Como, where a body of Spanish and Italian troops under the Lombard general Serbelloni dug itself in near the foot of Fort Fuentes to block his advance. Rohan's force was too small to proceed any farther, and the mountainous Swiss cantons to his rear were unable to supply him adequately with provisions. Rohan's relations with the Swiss, who were Calvinists like himself, were often fragile, for he was operating very far from home and had neither the men nor the money to impose himself on them.[1] The Grison leaders were impatient for him to restore Calvinist institutions to the ethnically Italian population of the Valtellina, which had risen up and slaughtered the Protestant elite in 1620 and called Spanish troops to their aid. Rohan had strict secret orders from Cardinal Richelieu and Louis XIII to prevent a Protestant restoration that would turn the local Catholic majority against his army. He could never reconcile the German-speaking Swiss Protestants to his pro-Catholic position, however much he might sympathize with them.[2] In the meantime, his force blocked the most direct access to Spanish reinforcements from Germany. The emperor sent a small army into the passes to starve Rohan into withdrawing, but the troops in the Austrian Tirol were too far away to operate in conjunction with Serbelloni's force near Lake Como, and so the French Huguenot defeated them both in turn during the summer.

French troops began descending from the Alpine passes from Dauphiné into Piedmont in April too. The impending war against Catholic Spain was widely unpopular in France and the cardinal had to mount a sustained propaganda campaign in support of it.[3] Louis XIII held a *lit de justice* before the parlement of Paris, a ceremony whereby the king's presence compelled the magistrates to enact into law some 42 tax decrees they resisted, some of which created new venal offices

---

[1] Davide Maffi, 'Confesionalismo y Razòn de Estado en la edad moderna. El caso de la Valtellina (1637–1639)', *Hispania Sacra*, 57 (2005): 467–89; for the other side, Pierre Deyon and Solange Deyon, *Henri de Rohan, huguenot de plume et d'épée, 1579–1638* (Paris, 2000), 158–75.
[2] Yves-Marie Bercé, 'Rohan et la Valtelline', in *L'Europe des traites de Westphalie. Esprit de la diplomatie et diplomatie de l'esprit*, ed. Lucien Bély (Paris, 2000), 321–35.
[3] Michel Devèze, *L'Espagne de Philippe IV*, 2 vols. (Paris, 1970), vol. 1, 154.

detrimental to government efficiency.[4] Before the summer was out, French cities and towns in south-western France would rise in revolt against the new taxes, requiring the diversion of professional soldiers to restore order and levy the money by force. The solution, thought Richelieu and his Parman ally, was to proceed swiftly with the conquest of Spanish Lombardy.

This ignored the fundamental interests of Victor Amadeus, who was more concerned about not losing territory to France than with conquering Lombardy. Spanish diplomatic envoys to Turin did their utmost to change his mind about the French alliance during the spring and summer. Meanwhile, Spanish military officers feverishly improved the fortifications of the towns nearby, using militia manpower.[5] Victor Amadeus stalled the onset of the campaign for weeks, which had important consequences. The window for an early modern campaign was normally less than six months of the year, from the time the horses finished restoring themselves on fresh spring grass, until the onset of autumn rains that forced the men into shelter.[6] The specific pretext for stalling was a disagreement with his French co-commander over strategy. Créquy wished to advance down the Po valley and occupy the fortresses south of the Po. That would enable the French army to reach Piacenza and connect the chain of bases and bridgeheads, isolating Milan from its communications with Spain and the rest of Italy. Victor Amadeus argued for a more defensive posture, placing the army in the great plain opposite Novara to prevent Spanish penetration towards Turin. The result was that the confederates divided their forces, with Créquy's larger army at Casale being prodded to move by Richelieu. The French general finally crossed the Po on 14 August 1635, issuing the soldiers' pay just before departure in order to lift their spirits.[7] His army of 10,000 infantry and 1,500 cavalry first invested and besieged a small, undermanned Spanish fort at La Villetta just across the border, which surrendered on 21 August (Bernardino Stanchi, a well-informed observer in nearby Valenza, says the 19th) after a six-day operation.[8] In order to expedite the capture of the fort, Créquy allowed the garrison of several hundred Spaniards, Neapolitans, and Swiss to withdraw to the friendly fortress of Mortara. They marched out the gates with drums beating, banners unfurled, wicks lit, and musket balls in the soldiers' mouths, a symbolic posture meaning they were ready to fight if provoked. 'This is the funeral pomp for a fort which surrenders with its reputation intact', wrote Bernardino Stanchi. These first French conquests were made in the name of the Duke of Savoy, but the French invited the local nobility to pay homage to Louis XIII, in exchange

---

[4] A. Lloyd Moote, *Louis XIII the Just* (Berkeley and London, 1989), 252.

[5] Gualdo Priorato, like many contemporaries was certain that Victor Amadeus maintained secret relations with Spain, *Historia delle guerre del Conte Galeazzo Gualdo Priorato* (Venice, 1646), 290. Of these I have encountered no trace in the papers of the Consejo de Estado conserved in the Simancas archive, nor in the meagre correspondence available in Turin.

[6] Gabor Perjés, 'Army provisioning, logistics and strategy in the second half of the 17th century', *Acta Historica Academiae Scientiarum Hungaricae*, 16 (1970): 1–51.

[7] Bernardino Stanchi, *Narrazione dell'assedio di Valenza nel 1635, fatta da Bernardino Stanchi* (Milan, 1638), in *Memorie storiche Valenzane*, Francesco Gasparolo, vol. 3 (Bologna, 1986), 258–96.

[8] AGS Estado 3342 claims Créquy commanded 13,000 or 14,000 infantry; Souvigny, *Mémoires du Comte de Souvigny, lieutenant-général des armées du roi*.

for which the foraging parties would spare their estates.[9] Then Créquy's army recrossed the Po below Casale on 27 August, threatening the powerful fortress city of Alessandria.[10]

The governor of Milan, Cardinal Albornoz, and his senior military commander, Don Carlos Coloma, had spent the previous few months preparing for this moment. The auditor-general or chief financial officer, Don Juan Arias Maldonado, had moved great stocks of cereals into Milan and the other major fortresses as soon as they ripened, and had issued commands to fetch grain from Sicily and Naples by sea.[11] Engineers had laid out improvements to the fortifications at Novara, Alessandria, Valenza, and Mortara that were closest to the enemy, and to the citadel of Tortona, which guarded the line of communication with Genoa. Past governors of Milan had improved some of these after 1600 as money became available, but several of the places were fortresses in name only.[12] Coloma mustered the militiamen of those districts and hurriedly put them to work with spades and picks to shore up the earthworks. Valenza on the Po was his particular focus, not only because he thought it was the weakest fortress, but because he considered that its loss would be more severe than any other.[13] He put in place a bridge of boats connecting the north bank to the city on the heights across from it, with a bridgehead fort to protect its access. He also posted hundreds of militiamen from the Alessandria district there to aid the garrison. The entire Spanish field army (distinct from the garrisons) numbered 10,500 professional infantry, but they could not be concentrated in one place. Perhaps only 7,500 defended the entire border with the enemy Piedmont and Monferrato, backed by 8,000 mobilized militiamen who could not be placed in the line of fire. The Spanish cavalry was about equal to their adversaries in number, but much inferior to them in quality. Coloma could spare only about 4,000 paid soldiers to support Valenza, deployed on either side of the Po.[14] He spread smaller forces out along the Po opposite Parma and Piacenza, in order to gather provisions and to bolster the earthworks and increase the garrisons of the citadels of Cremona and Lodi. Cardinal Trivulzio's militia draftees aided that work considerably.[15]

With his army finally assembled, fully equipped, and ready to march, Odoardo watched the first weeks of campaigning with baited breath. Andrea Pugolotti recorded the last details of Odoardo's preparatory operations in the capital, Parma. Early in July Odoardo ordered the displacement of Parma's artillery to Piacenza,

---

[9] Giovanni Fossati, *Memoire historiche delle guerre d'Italia del secolo presente* (Bologna, 1641), 144.
[10] Girolamo Ghilini, *Annali di Alessandria*, ed. A. Bossola, 3 vols (Alessandria, 1903), 93–127.
[11] Fossati, *Memorie historiche delle guerre*, 140–3.
[12] Archivio Comunale Pavia (henceforth ACP), Ms II 59, Gabrio Busca, 'Descrizione delle fortezze di frontiera dello Stato di Milano' (*c.*1600). Busca's report, complete with illustrations, emphasized how the long peace had allowed even critical fortresses to deteriorate.
[13] Carlos Coloma, 'Discurso en que se representa quanto conviene a la Monarchia española la conservaciòn del Estado de Milan, y lo que necesita para su defensa y mayor seguridad (1626)', in *Lo Stato di Milano nel XVII secolo: Memoriali e relazioni*, ed. M. C. Giannini and G. Signorotto (Rome, 2006), 1–15.
[14] AGS Estado 3342/147, letter of 15 September 1635.
[15] AGS Estado 3837, letter of Cardinal Trivulzio, 22 July 1635.

four new demi-cannon, cast perhaps in the ducal foundry near the palace. These great tubes weighing over two tonnes were mounted on wheels with a heavy axle, and required a dozen horses to pull each one. They fired a 24 lb ball, no more than ten times an hour, to avoid overheating the barrels. The munitions, and sundry tools and barrels, filled up wagons that required additional horses.[16] On 17 July Odoardo issued a call-up of all available draft animals, and soon some 122 ox-drawn carts, laden with munitions, left for Piacenza. At the end of July, the French troops quartered in Parma and in the countryside were ordered to assemble at Piacenza, where the duke himself took up quarters on 28 July.[17] The entire field army mustered outside the city on 4 August, and for several more weeks the soldiery haunted the monastery barracks and taverns while Odoardo waited for dispatches from France.[18] Upon hearing of the fall of La Villetta, the Duke of Parma left Piacenza with his army for Castel San Giovanni, a small town on the border with the duchy of Milan, accompanied by four cannon and 400 supply wagons. Pressured by Rome and Florence not to embark on such a perilous warlike undertaking, he awaited at the border the arrival of the French envoy Bellièvre, who was bringing news.[19] Bellièvre and the French officers in Odoardo's own entourage convinced him that the conquest of Spanish Lombardy would be an easy thing. Our impatient duke's first hostile act was to send 800 horse and foot from Piacenza to the town of Codogno near Lodi on 29 August, with orders to punish the vassals of Cardinal Trivulzio, who were enticing Odoardo's soldiers into Spanish service. The Farnese soldiers made a special target of an apothecary who served as the recruiting agent in the Lombard border town.[20] The infantry helped themselves to a lot of booty, and spread panic among the townspeople, with the result that Duke Odoardo's own vassals, living in villages north of the Po, started streaming into Piacenza out of fear of reprisals by Milanese soldiers.

Screwing up his courage, Odoardo finally declared war, a formality accompanied by the publication of a letter detailing his reasons, and the striking of a medallion bearing a hand holding a naked sword, with the inscription '*J'ay bruslé le fourreau*' (I have burned the scabbard). Western European princes thought that they must declare a just war publically, according to accepted conventions. Louis XIII declared war against Spain the preceding 19 May by sending a herald to Brussels bearing the proclamation. Odoardo had already signalled his new allegiance on 29 May 1633 when he removed the effigies of the Golden Fleece from the equestrian statues in the Piacenza town square, and he returned the precious

---

[16] William Guthrie, *Battles of the Thirty Years War: From White Mountain to Nordlingen* (Westport, CT, and London, 2002), 7; Frank Tallett, *War and Society in Early Modern Europe, 1495–1715* (London, 1992), 33.

[17] Andrea Pugolotti, *Libro di memorie. Cronaca parmense del XVII secolo*, ed. Sergio Di Noto (Parma, 2005), 91–9.

[18] BCPLPc, Ms Pallastrelli 126, Croniche o diario del Rev.o Sgr Benedetto Boselli, rettore della chiesa di Santo Martino di Piacenza (1620–70), 110.

[19] Vittorio Siri, *Memorie recondite di Vittorio Siri dall'anno 1601 fino al 1640* 8 vols. (Lyons, 1677–9), 256.

[20] Giovanni Pietro Crescenzi Romani, *Corona della Nobiltà d'Italia, ovvero compendio dell'istorie delle famiglie illustri*, 2 vols. (Bologna, 1639–42), vol. 2, 285.

insignia to Madrid. The slight of the Milanese envoys years before was high on the list of provocations Odoardo cited, but contemporaries saw it as a flimsy pretext, for King Philip IV could easily invalidate the demands of envoys. Odoardo also cited the debts incurred by his house in Spanish service, dating back to the previous century, and the humiliation of his ancestors by previous governors of Milan, who deprived them of Novara and forced them to dismantle the new fortifications in Borgo San Donnino.[21] Saint Augustine, over 1,000 years earlier, established a list of good and legitimate reasons authorizing Christian princes to make war on each other.[22] War was justified if it established a better peace, or lifted a threat over the prince, or forced the recognition of a right, or brought aid to a victim. Odoardo's contemporaries also included vendetta as a valid reason for going to war, and they understood the prince's desire for personal glory and his quest to emulate his ancestors.[23] It was a Christian prince's prerogative to make war to satisfy reasons of state, or to expand his territory. Odoardo's published pretexts were, for the most part, old grudges against Spain, some of which were of negligible importance, such as the forcible seizure of some boats laden with grain on the Po, or the lengthy delay in replying to a waiting courier. Odoardo went farther in claiming that his gesture was for the public benefit of Italy, a well-worn claim of another pathological opportunist, Charles Emanuel I, Duke of Savoy.[24] The instrument of Odoardo's satisfaction was now King Louis XIII, 'entirely occupied with World Peace and with the Happiness of Italy'.[25]

When Odoardo marched out of Piacenza on 1 September, he rode at the head of his little army in all its component contingents. *'Bella gente!'* wrote Pugolotti, who nevertheless confessed in his diary that he feared greatly for the consequences. Contemporary historians like the Milanese priest Fossati, thought that the duke's army was more notable for its nobility and its well turned-out infantrymen, than for the military talent the units contained.[26] Nevertheless, the duke, alone of the confederates, had kept his promise and delivered to the alliance more than the 4,000 infantry and 500 cavalry that he promised. Assembling them at the border on 4 September, deploying this force with his own hand, unfurling the standards and the banners, he gave the order to march.

---

[21] ASPr, Biblioteca Manoscritti 36/2: Bolsi, 'Memorie storiche di Parma'. This manuscript contains the three-page declaration of war sent to the resident in Rome, Cav. Alfonso Carandini, for publication there. The manuscript also contains a four-page rebuttal by Spain, published in Milan and Cremona. A copy of the declaration of war is contained in the published account by Crescenzi Romani, *Corona della Nobiltà d'Italia*, vol. 2, 274–5.

[22] Daniel Séré, *La Paix des Pyrenées: Vingt-quatre ans de négociations entre la France et l'Espagne (1635–1659)* (Paris, 2007), 43.

[23] Galeazzo Gualdo Priorato, *Il guerriero prudente e politico (1640)* (Venezia and Bologna, 1641), ed. Angelo Tamborra (Naples, 2002), 13. This book was dedicated to both Louis XIII and to Cardinal Richelieu.

[24] Pietro Giovanni Capriata, *Dell'Historia delli movimenti d'armi successi in Italia* (Genova, 1649), 128.

[25] BPPr, MS Parmense 737, Hippolito Calandrini, L'Heroe d'Italia, overo Vita del Sereniss.o Odoardo Farnese, p. 409.

[26] Fossati, *Memorie historiche delle guerre*, 144.

Parman cavalry scouts chased away a mounted patrol of Spaniards monitoring Odoardo's advance, and removed the obstacles that the enemy had placed across the highway. Stradella was the first small town on Odoardo's route, and his Huguenot councillor, Nicart, advised him to make an example of it in order to strike terror into the hearts of those thinking of resisting. Odoardo declined, saying that he would wage a Christian war, and simply demanded 'refreshment' for his troops from the local worthies. Broni, the next town, only 2 kilometres distant, took the hint, offered similar provisions to the passing army, and was treated leniently for its pains. Farther down the road, the larger town of Voghera made some preparations for a siege, but, like the others, it was bereft of modern fortifications and professional troops capable of defending them. The duke was about to lay siege to the place on 7 September when two Capuchin fathers emerged bearing the offer to surrender. This last detail is rich with significance. Armies are almost never intent on killing everyone in their path. There are universal conventions, which probably existed before the appearance of humanity itself, signalling submission: these enable the conqueror to establish superiority without excessive bloodshed on either side, for, in the absence of the possibility of surrender, the underdog would be forced to fight to the death.[27] In seventeenth-century Italy, the classic non-combatant was a Catholic cleric, and, among those, the humble friars who had formally renounced the affairs of the world. Catholic clergy would appear time and again as mediators in this struggle, not completely neutral (most favoured Spain), but at least wielding sufficient authority to shelter other non-combatants from the worst excesses of the soldiery. In Voghera the few dozen members of the garrison retreated into a strong tower along the ramparts, and the town gave more refreshments to the troops in exchange for their lives and the security of their property. Odoardo placed a few pickets around the tower and marched his army westwards, much to the annoyance of those men in his army impatient to loot some large and rich town.[28]

Odoardo encountered the enemy at Pontecurone the following day, 8 September, only a few kilometres west of Voghera. As soon as he learned of the departure of the Parmans on campaign, Coloma designated an ad-hoc force under Don Gasparo d'Azevedo to advance and intercept it. The backbone of this contingent, which constituted half the available field army, consisted of two *tercios* recently arrived in Alessandria, Azevedo's Spanish one and a Neapolitan one under Filippo Spinola, son of the Genoese banker-general who acquired fame in Spanish Flanders. They had several hundred cavalry as their support, and an unspecified number of militiamen called up from Tortona. The total number of professional soldiers was probably not much greater than 2,000 men and it is unclear if they were veterans or hasty levies.[29] Azevedo wasted no time, however, and advanced with his

---

[27] Marco Costa, *Psicologia militare: elementi di psicologia per gli appartenenti alle forze armate* (Milan, 2003), 83.

[28] Crescenzi Romani, *Corona della Nobiltà d'Italia*, vol. 2, 286.

[29] Guill Ortega, 'L'Assedio di Valenza del 1635'. This text is drawn from the author's book, *Carlos Coloma 1566–1637: Espada y pluma de los tercios*, trans. Carlo Dabene and published in Italian in, *Valensa d'na vota*, 23 (2008): 25–52.

vanguard in what dispatches later described as a loose and bizarre order. Scouts reported back that the duke's cavalry was made up of militia levies, which was, to a large degree, accurate. Azevedo's eagerness to fight the invaders was probably not displaced: he knew that if he could force the inexperienced Farnese troops to disband here, deep in Milanese territory, he would eliminate Odoardo's threat definitively. An inquest six months later claimed that Coloma warned Azevedo not to be overconfident, but it appears that he took little trouble to reconnoitre the force he had in front of him.[30]

When Odoardo saw the first Spanish companies lined up behind the bridge outside the walled village on the opposite bank of the narrow stream, his lifelong wish finally came true. He deployed his troops himself, with the supposed veterans under Francesco Serafini in the vanguard, and his cavalry to the rear. Then he gave a rousing speech to his men, emphasizing the spoils they would strip from the defeated enemy, and promising them the plunder from the village too. The Lucchese colonel Serafini made another speech in the same vein while the duke circulated excitedly with unsheathed sword among the soldiery, and then Odoardo ordered them to advance. He had two of his four cannon loaded with musket balls, and discharged them at the waiting enemy just as Serafini's troops crossed the little stream separating the two forces. The Spanish commander, Azevedo, offered battle before his entire force had arrived, for the Neapolitans under Filippo Spinola were still advancing up the road, several kilometres to his rear. Spanish officers led from the front, standing in the first rows of their troops before receiving the assault. A musket ball to the head killed Azevedo in the first salvo of the Farnese army, and Serafini's troops then bore down on them obliquely. The Spanish array collapsed immediately and many soldiers retreated into the village, from where they could protect the approaching column behind them. A Farnese cavalry charge then bore down on the horse under the command of Don Alvaro de Quiñones, a hero of the great Battle of Nördlingen less than a year before. The Spanish broke under the charge and galloped back down the road in direction of Tortona. But they soon re-formed under their commander and drew up in order to protect the retreat of the infantry. The Parman troops gave no thought to pursuit anyway. Odoardo had finally promised them booty and so they stormed the little town, whose defenders resisted another half-hour before the survivors took flight. Odoardo placed his noble elite cavalry unit, the Cornetta Bianca, around a convent of nuns in order to place it off limits. Elsewhere, the soldiers grabbed what they could while the officers assembled around the duke to receive his congratulations, and Fabio Scotti praised and flattered the youngster, who was living his finest hour. Odoardo dined in the shattered town in the company of his officers, before spending the night outside with the troops. Casualty estimates from the period are inclined to be exaggerated and at best remain approximate. The most detailed account of the action claims that Odoardo lost no more than 40 men, and no officers, and that an unknown number of

---

[30] Estado 3345/5, report of the Marques de Leganés, 29 April 1636.

Spaniards died; their corpses carried away (it was claimed) by compatriots while the Parmans were engaged in looting. Two Piacenza noblemen were reportedly slightly wounded.[31]

Odoardo's army continued its march in high spirits the next morning, in the direction of Tortona, a small town like Voghera, whose weak walls and elongated configuration made the perimeter indefensible. A hilltop citadel of modern design, well garrisoned and supplied, overlooked it however. Rather than capture fortresses, Odoardo's principal concern was to effect a meeting with the French army, moving eastward in his direction. As the French troops advanced, they burned mills and caused damage in the nearby villages they looted, reputedly even destroying vineyards by cutting the roots.[32] Duke Odoardo, for his part, assembled the leading inhabitants of the villages he passed, and forced them to swear oaths of fealty to him. The intercessors between the victorious duke and the prostrate little towns on his route, like Castelnuovo Scrivia, were again Capuchin friars.[33] At Sale, the misguided peasants later refused to supply Spanish troopers on the grounds that they were now Odoardo's subjects, so Coloma punished them with exemplary severity.[34] The Spanish general hoped to hold the French back with militia forces drawn up along the Tanaro river, but they were too few in number and too green to be reliable, and so, wisely, they moved out of harm's way. The bulk of the French army wound its way along the south bank of the Po in the opposite direction, skirting Valenza and then, crossing the Tanaro river, advancing to meet Odoardo's force. On 10 September, the commanders finally met on the plain near Sale.

Créquy's first unpleasant surprise was that, despite the resounding triumph of Odoardo's march, some 90 kilometres, starting from Piacenza, the victorious Parman army was much diminished by desertion. The military governor of Piacenza had to call up the militia in the border districts and throw up earthen fortifications around the villages and towns in order to protect them from the marauding deserters who preyed upon traffic on the highways. The soldiers had beseeched the duke to let them plunder from the moment they crossed the border, for everyone considered it a perquisite of military life. Many of the Italian soldiers, content with their booty from the sack of Pontecurone, chose that moment to call it a campaign and disappeared. No doubt many of them joined the Spanish forces, but we do not have records to confirm it. Perhaps only 2,500 infantry, by now most of them French, and 700 cavalrymen joined the confederate forces.[35] In any case, the commanders conferred, and then decided to lay siege to Valenza on the Po.

---

[31] BPPr, Ms Parmense 737, Hippolito Calandrini, 'L'Heroe d'Italia, overo Vita del Sereniss.mo Odoardo Farnese il Grande, quinto duca di Parma e di Piacenza', 433–50.
[32] Stanchi, *Narrazione dell'assedio di Valenza nel 1635*, 262.
[33] Crescenzi Romani, *Corona della Nobiltà d'Italia*, vol. 2, 288.
[34] Ghilini, *Annali di Alessandria*, 96.
[35] Souvigny, *Mémoires du Comte de Souvigny*, 290.

THE SIEGE OF VALENZA

Valenza was a sensible objective for the allied army to seize. The principal Spanish fortress in this part of Lombardy was Alessandria, about 15 kilometres to the south, but that city boasted stout fortifications and a strong citadel, both well garrisoned and stocked with supplies. It commanded two important roads, one to Genoa and the other leading to the port of Finale Ligure, from which Spanish reinforcements arrived. Farther west lay Tortona, but it would have been risky for the confederates to lay siege even to a weak fortress with enemy strongpoints astride their lines of communication. The capture of Valenza would still impede the communication between Genoa and Milan, and it lay close to friendly Monferrato, from which reinforcements, supplies, and forage could be conveniently drawn. Casale Monferrato served as an impregnable magazine for the French army, and was only one long day's march away. Créquy would establish a shuttle service of wagons back and forth between the siege lines and his supply depot 23 kilometres distant.[36] Capturing fortified towns placed along lines of communication constituted the principal activity of armies in the seventeenth century, for they needed to receive supplies daily if they were not to disband in the field. Moreover, captured towns controlled the district around them and served to show if one side was 'making progress' in its war. They could either be kept or handed back to the adversary in a final peace, but in the meantime they would be precious supply depots for the army holding them and secure bases for controlling the surrounding area.[37]

A small town of 2,000 or 3,000 inhabitants, Valenza sat on a crest overlooking the Po river, enclosed with a simple medieval wall and protected by a couple of natural ditches on the east and west sides. Sixteenth-century engineers improved its fortifications with some small bastions and narrow ditches, but these had been allowed to crumble during the long peace, so Coloma considered the place hopelessly weak. The military governor of Valenza, Don Martino Galiano, ordered the engineer Pompeo Robutti of Alessandria to build some earthworks to keep the enemy away from the weak walls, and then Carlos Coloma had a series of earthen redoubts thrown up a couple of hundred metres before the gates, each with ramparts and double palisades, ditches, and sometimes demi-lunes too, which were triangular or semi-circular projections fortified only on the outer side, to enable the defenders burrowed there to deliver a crossfire onto the killing ground before the earthworks.[38] Soldiers, peasants, and townsmen under the direction of an engineer could erect earthen fortifications with wooden supports very quickly, and these were effective at stopping cannonballs, although these temporary shelters

---

[36] Perjés, 'Army provisioning, logistics and strategy'; the inhabitants saw the French army as protectors who shielded them from mistreatment at the hands of their traditional enemies, the Savoyards. See Bremio, GianDomenico, 'Annali Casalesi (1632–1661) di Gian Domenico Bremio, speciaro di Casale Monferrato', Giuseppe Giorcelli, ed., *Rivista Storica Alessandrina*, 18 (1909): 381–436.

[37] John Lynn, *Giant of the 'Grand Siècle': The French Army 1610–1715* (Cambridge, 1997), 189.

[38] Barghini, 'Una piazzaforte di livello Europeo', in *Valenza e le sue fortificazioni: Architettura e urbanistica dal medioevo all'età contemporanea*, (Alessandria, 1993): 47–123.

would become a shapeless mass after the rainy season.[39] The chief disadvantage of an earthwork perimeter far from the ramparts was that it would require many more men to defend it, and so Valenza required supplies in proportion to the total garrison. Coloma's bridge of boats to the town from the north bank of the Po enabled him to funnel reinforcements into it while the French army held the field to the south, but some of the Spanish officers still thought that the place could not resist for long.[40] Once it became clear to Coloma that the town would be the initial French target, he placed in it a large garrison of about 2,500 Spaniards, Neapolitans, and Germans, plus a detachment of 300 militiamen from the Alessandria district who would mount guard in the city centre and carry out much of the necessary manual labour.

We are fortunate to have multiple and remarkably concordant eyewitness accounts of the siege, from French soldiers and diplomats and the Spanish general Coloma himself, to the civilian official Bernardino Stanchi inside Valenza, who was entrusted with accounting for provisions, and from another well-informed notable inside nearby Alessandria, Giuseppe Ghilini. Moreover, the famous Flemish painter Pieter Snayers painted a large canvas synthesis of the major episodes of the siege not long after the event, which depicts the town, its fortifications, and the French camp in considerable detail. Duke Victor-Amadeus left his own account in a detailed report to king Louis XIII, which is conserved in Florence (for some unexplained reason) along with some of his other secret correspondence.[41] These multiple detailed sources offer us a glimpse of the minutia of military campaigns in the seventeenth century, and the logistical requirements underpinning them.

The confederate army backtracked over the Tanaro river to invest Valenza on 11 September, the first day of the siege. Then it quickly laid out three camps, two French ones to the west and south of the town along the road to Alessandria, and a Parman camp on the east side around a castle about a kilometre and a half from the Spanish lines. It was understood that the Duke of Savoy would occupy the north bank of the Po and cut the city off from all help, but until his arrival Coloma camped his small field force there and conveyed men and provisions across his bridge. He injected reinforcements and withdrew depleted units from the town almost unhindered until the arrival of Duke Victor Amadeus two weeks later. Coloma visited the senior officers in the place, and periodically inspected the forward trenches himself to keep up morale. By 12 September, Spanish forces had already sallied forth from the earthworks to skirmish with the Parmans, who, they judged, were the weak link in the confederate chain. The intention might have been to draw them out of their positions and engage them in the open field where they were most vulnerable, but they would not comply and, with French

---

[39] For a modern experiment recreating a field fortification under the conditions of the Thirty Years' War, see Vaclav Matoušek, 'Building a model of a field fortification of the Thirty Years' War near Olbramov (Czech Republic)', *Journal of Conflict Archaeology* (2005): 114–32.

[40] Fossati, *Memorie historiche delle guerre*, 146.

[41] ASFi, Miscellanea Medicea 183, Relatione data al Re per ordine del Duca di Savoia dell'assedio di Valenza, f.318–27.

Fig. 3.1. Snayers, siege of Valenza in 1635. The painting depicts multiple episodes of the siege, flattening the topography and removing much of the vegetation for clarity. Parman quarters were at the top right.

assistance, they held their posts.[42] Duke Odoardo's redoubts and batteries laid out under the direction of the ducal engineer Carlo Soldati were not ready until 15 September, and even then he put in place only two cannon. These began a desultory and largely ineffectual bombardment of the bridge of boats from long range. Even a lucky hit meant little, for the Spaniards would just provide new boats and cables and reassemble the bridge. The cannon did destroy the half-dozen grain mills floating on the Po, which might have crippled the garrison had Coloma not furnished the town with much less efficient hand-powered mills for grinding grain.[43] The French army did not bring enough artillery for an efficient siege, perhaps a dozen guns in all, a number about equal to that which the garrison possessed, although they were probably of larger calibre. Some cannon would have to be trained on the garrison dug into the earthen redoubts, leaving only a few to fire at the city wall.

---

[42] Souvigny, *Mémoires du Comte de Souvigny*, 292.
[43] Stanchi, *Narrazione dell'assedio di Valenza nel 1635*, 270; hand mills ground grain very coarsely and quickly broke down due to excessive usage. See Perjés, 'Army provisioning, logistics and strategy'.

Fig. 3.2. Snayers, siege of Valenza (detail). Note the labourers moving earth or collecting materials to make fascines, with soldiers' huts in the background.

Fig. 3.3. Snayers, detail, camp scenes at Valenza. Men excrete along the earthworks not far from the tents. It is doubtful European armies dug latrines.

The allies' lack of manpower became painfully apparent to the confederates. Odoardo deplored the insufficient number of peasants hired to move the earth before his lines, and it was too dangerous, and perhaps impossible, to bring more of them from Piacenza. These 'pioneers' probably came from nearby Monferrato, but sometimes armies employed peasant workers in enemy territory by threatening to burn their villages if they did not comply. Commanders put their soldiers to work simultaneously, and the Snayers painting depicts these men with their wooden wheelbarrows. Créquy gave Odoardo two French regiments to help him guard his segment of the line. The French line was also thinly held, and, during the night of 14/15 September, some Spanish reinforcements from Alessandria penetrated Créquy's sector. Although the French managed to finish their continuous entrenchment facing the city by mid-September, the siege was off to an inauspicious start.

Part of the problem of laying siege to a fortress stemmed from the requirements of food and fodder that constituted the fuel of early modern armies. On the move, they transported their biscuit, beverage, stocks of grain for the men, their tents, and other impedimenta in carts. If one were to calculate the confederate forces around Valenza at 20,000 soldiers, grooms, and sutlers, the army would require 15,000 kilograms of flour daily just for bread rations, a battery of ovens, and a mountain of firewood to produce the loaves. These were likely located in the nearby city of Casale, but the finished loaves required haulage teams to bring them to the army. Soldiers also expected a meat ration to accompany their bread, which would be seized on the hoof in the district farms and prodded into the camp. Historian Jean Chagniot claims that, from 1636 onward, French soldiers were no longer required to purchase their food in the field, and no document concerning Valenza clarifies this point.[44] Horses consumed several times more food than a man, and, in addition to the cavalry mounts, other horses drew wagons and cannon. They could not be paid with promises or made to wait like the soldiery, and had to be provided with oats and fodder every day, to the tune of 10 kilograms of dry fodder and 45 kilograms of fresh hay or green matter. This last commodity was too bulky to consign to supply wagons and had to be harvested from the territory crossed by the army. Créquy's 4,000 horses would have required pastures of 60 hectares every day, or 100 cartloads of bulk fodder.[45] Collecting these foodstuffs for man and beast was the special task of the cavalry, whose troopers were more active with scythes and pitchforks than they were with sabres and pistols. Perhaps as much as half the cavalry was away foraging at any one time.

The longer the army stayed immobile before the town, the farther afield the foragers would need to go in search of grass, hay, and livestock. This led to an increasing dispersion

---

[44] Jean Chagniot, *Guerre et société à l'époque moderne* (Paris, 2001), 112.
[45] Padraig Lenihan, 'Unhappy campers: Dundalk (1689) and after', *Journal of Conflict Archaeology* (2007): 196–216; the general estimates come from Gabor Perjés' article, 'Army provisioning, logistics and strategy'.

Fig. 3.4. Promiscuous culture in the Parmigiano. This lush landscape in north-central Italy made it difficult to spot troop movements from afar.

of the parties of horse who were already deep in enemy territory.[46] Mowing the standing crops in order to feed them to horses threatened the very survival of peasant communities caught in the theatre of operations. Mills were also a strategic asset for whichever army controlled the territory, and so constituted a special target for destruction. Moreover, French foragers often behaved cruelly towards the villagers in the district, as in Mugarone and Pecetto, where they set houses on fire. September was the season of the grape harvest that was crucial to the welfare of both town and countryside. Lombard militiamen formed small contingents escorting the harvesters to their vines, and ambushed and killed enemy foragers whenever they could. They were aided by the 'promiscuous' agriculture of the landscape, where the hedges, rows of trees, and other green barriers surrounding each field prevented anyone from seeing beyond a few dozen metres. Some of the foragers and even greater numbers of infantrymen used these occasions to surrender to Spanish forces. Significant numbers of Parman troops, both infantry and cavalry, arrived in Alessandria to give themselves up from 15 September onwards; these included a lieutenant of horse and 30 of his troopers on a single day.[47] Practically

---

[46] Raimondo Montecuccoli recommended foraging places distant from the siege lines first, gradually harvesting the fields closer to camp. But the confederate commanders did not imagine that Valenza would resist so long. *Memoires de Montecuculi, generalissime des troupes de l'Empereur, divisé en trois livres*, 110.

[47] Ghilini, *Annali di Alessandria*, 101–5.

Fig. 3.5. Parma: farmhouse with hayloft. Each of these numerous farms stocked precious supplies of fodder for horses and oxen.

as soon as he arrived at Valenza, Odoardo sought to make good his losses from desertion by hiring several companies of militiamen from the Monferrato.[48]

One ominous feature of the campaign was that the lines of authority in the confederate army were never clear. Each leader understood that this problem invited disaster, and so they made grudging compromises with each other from time to time.[49] Victor Amadeus first camped with his forces near Vercelli, where he argued the invasion should have taken place. Richelieu instructed Créquy to defer to the Duke of Savoy as his commanding officer, but the two men were rivals and justifiably mistrusted each other. The Duke of Savoy did not wish to see the French army occupy Lombardy without his assistance, though, so he paid a visit to the Franco-Parman camp before Valenza, inspected the siege works together with his senior advisor, Marshal Toiras, and predicted a negative outcome.[50] Duke Odoardo also felt free to inspect every part of the confederate trench works, where he expected to be given ceremonious demonstrations of reverence by Créquy, who was his political inferior.[51] Créquy was a grand seigneur, however, of illustrious lineage, celebrated military forbears, and boasted a large number of successful duels in defence of his prickly honour. '*Viveva alla grande*', wrote one anonymous

---

[48] Crescenzi Romani, *Corona della Nobiltà d'Italia*, 289–92.
[49] Costa, *Psicologia militare*, 458.
[50] BNF MS Fr 16929, Rélation de M. d'Esmery de ses négotiations en Piedmont en 1635 etc., fo.531r.
[51] BPPr Ms Parmense 737, Calandrini, 'L'Heroe d'Italia', 475; Capriata, *Dell'Historia*, 156–70.

biographer, meaning he was inclined to luxury and good living, even in camp.[52] In the seventeenth century, French officers had already acquired the reputation of placing great stress on the quantity and quality of their food in garrison and on campaign, '*fare buona cierà*' (*bonne chère*).[53] Senior officers like Créquy, and Odoardo too, tightened clientèle bonds by opening their purses and their table to underlings, for long sieges multiplied the occasions for sociability. Unlike the common soldiers, aristocratic officers were able to purchase food and other luxuries from Casale.[54] However, Odoardo, always impatient, never lost sight of the urgency of pressing forward as the summer drew to its close. The young prince thought the siege lacked vigour, so reproached the French marshal for going on hunting parties, and then lost his temper when the latter replied that he was waiting for the arrival of Victor Amadeus before accelerating the affair. Créquy lost his temper too, telling the duke that he had no experience of waging war, that he had come into the camp with many fewer troops than he had promised, and that many of those were unskilled and desertion-prone militiamen who could not defend their own quarters by themselves.[55]

The tensions among the high command were not all confined to the confederate army. Carlos Coloma was subject to the authority of Cardinal Albornoz, who was ignorant of military matters. Albornoz had already removed from Coloma's authority the contingent under Giovanni Serbelloni, which was facing the Duke of Rohan in the Valtellina. The Spanish cardinal undermined Coloma's credibility in Madrid by emphasizing the poor health and physical incapacity of the 69-year-old general, as he wished to replace him with one of his relatives, the highly regarded and experienced young Count of Celada who had recently arrived from Spain en route to Germany. Coloma keenly resented the meddling of the cardinal and his chief accountant Don Antonio de Porras, who held back funds in order to make the general more pliable. Coloma quickly arrived at a compromise with Celada, who was given command over the defence of the besieged town, where he effectively spurred the garrison on to stiff resistance. Coloma remained outside with his small but growing field force, waiting to take the initiative.[56]

On 20 September, fearing that the Savoyard army might finally move to assist the siege, Coloma risked a strong sally from the fortress, again in the direction of the Parman sector where the trenches were weakest. For two days previously, even common soldiers in the Frascarolo camp freely discussed the strategic scenario, and the need to act quickly to take Odoardo prisoner and to seize the great store of silver plate he kept in his tent. Pacifico da Cremona, an Italian cavalry trooper in the company of Don Federigo Enrique recalled later that they received the order to move from camp in the middle of the night. Soldiers covered the bridge planks with manure in order to deaden

---

[52] BEM, Ms Sorbelli 1410, Vite e morti di personnaggi illustri, 60–9; for camp sociability in the higher ranks, Brian Sandberg, *Warrior Pursuits: Noble Culture and Civil Conflict in Early Modern France* (Baltimore, 2010), 96 and 270.

[53] Gualdo Priorato, *Historia delle guerre*, 309.

[54] Edward J. Coss, *All for the King's Shilling: The British Soldier under Wellington 1808–1814* (Norman, OK, 2010), 131.

[55] Capriata, *Dell'Historia*, 181.

[56] Guill Ortega, 'L'Assedio di Valenza del 1635'.

the echo of the horses' hooves. At daybreak the force commanded by the Neapolitan cavalry general Gambacorta issued forth from Valenza towards the Parman trenches. It consisted of infantry a couple of thousand strong marching towards the trenches near the Po, including the *tercios* of Azevedo and Filippo Spinola set for a rematch after Pontecurone, and a cavalry force of 18 companies (perhaps 1,000 troopers) in three waves trotting due east in the direction of Castello Stanchi. The most influential Habsburg cavalry commander of his time, the Italo-Albanian Giorgio Basta recommended that the commander should always be visible to his troopers, riding two or three lengths out front, with the ensign just to his left, bugle at the ready.[57] At the head of the vanguard rode 'a Spanish captain who wore a red plume on his helmet', who might have been the nephew of Cardinal Albornoz. Riding at the front of the second wave was Troilo Rossi, Count of San Secondo and a feudatory of Duke Odoardo. A dozen testimonials from various individuals in both camps give us a compelling glimpse of what happened next. Cavalry trooper Giovanni Maria Magni was on guard with the company of Luca Clerici when he spotted the large force advancing towards their trench. Everyone shouted '*arma, arma*!', and there was barely time to warn the camp. Count Giovan Francesco Marazzani, who was attending the duke's person, noted that the enemy advanced slowly, 'almost pretending to be our men, especially because they were not wearing their red sashes' (customarily used to distinguish Habsburg forces from their adversaries). One of the civilian members of a train of bread-wagons was in the tent of Count Fabio Scotti in order to obtain a passport to return home when the alarm sounded in the camp. An attendant rushed in and shouted, 'Illustrissimo, to arms, red alert! (*arma calda*), the enemy's here!', such that the minister ceased his writing, sent for his horse, and donned his armour. 'I went to a vantage point on my horse', explained the witness Agnolo Chiodi, 'to watch two large squadrons of enemy horse slowly approach the chapel a musket's shot distant from the palazzo [Stanchi], and one of the squadrons had a lot of sheep in front of it [probably brought there to feed the army and pastured in front of the trench], and the other squadron caracoled two or three times…I also saw our Commissary-General [Clerici] taken prisoner by the enemy, and so I moved away to be safe, but then I came back and I saw them adjust their collars and their sashes [to prepare for close-action against the Parman cavalry where it would be difficult to distinguish friend from foe]. Out in front of the other squadron I saw Troilo Rossi, with his long nose, dark face and long black moustache, whom I had seen before other times, like at the wedding of His Highness.' Another feudatory, Galeazzo Peretti served as an aide on the night shift. Fabio Scotti sent him out to the advance post redoubt held by 50 men to verify the first alarm, and when he saw the dust rising from just outside Valenza, he rushed back to the sector of the battery which Cavalry General Avogadri commanded. 'He began to shout, saddle up, saddle up!…and then told me to alert captain Marino (Badoero), who told me that most of his soldiers were off foraging. I returned to the chapel [just ahead of the trenches] to see the general [Avogadri] go out, shouting "alon [allons?], alon soldati!" The general sallied forth so impetuously and bravely that some enemy fled and some fell from their horses dead and wounded, and I was on foot in the middle of it. I saw the general's horse go

---

[57] Giorgio Basta, *Le gouvernement de la cavallerie legere* (Rouen, 116), 68.

down and Count Fortunato Scotti got off his horse and gave it to him, while he obtained another. Then the general advanced with our men in file, so I could race back to our trench, just as the signor adjutant Maiocco moved up with his musketeers as more enemy cavalry approached.'

Cavalry surprised in its quarters was subject to great confusion, for troopers could not put on their armour, or saddle and ready their horse without assistance, which took time.[58] Avogadri decided to give the men in camp extra time to prepare themselves by sallying forth with a 'forlorn hope' of barely 30 troopers, who were quickly joined by a few other squadrons in order to break the momentum of the first wave of Spanish horse, which advanced at a regulation trot. Avogadri did not have the time to don a complete set of armour, just a breastplate and dorsal protection. One might wonder about the efficacy of sending cavalry against entrenched troops, but the first wave consisted of mounted arquebusiers who would probably dismount at close range and storm the lines on foot. Basta recommended that horsemen dismount and fight with firearms whenever possible.[59] At Valenza some of these, like Marchese Claudio Pallavicino, were wounded by musket balls, then stabbed or clubbed with musket butts, but survived to relate their misadventure. Reliable eyewitness descriptions of cavalry tactics are extremely rare, and much has been written about cavalry 'shock' tactics in this era that relies more on drill books than on close description.[60] The testimony of participants on both sides makes the Parman document especially precious, for it depicts two distinct manners of fighting on horseback. Avogadri's little band skirmished with this first wave in a short melee of swords and pistols. Captain Alessandro Scotti was unhorsed and lost his weapon in the skirmish. Avogadri himself was wounded in the face by a sword. The Parman nobleman Girolamo Garimberti was badly wounded in the fray. The enemy cavalry led by the nephew of Cardinal Albornoz then stormed a little redoubt placed perhaps 50 or 100 metres in front of the trench, 'distant the length of the town square of Piacenza'. Captain Luca Clerici had just been taken prisoner. Michele Morselli, a noble trooper in Clerici's company recounted, 'I understand that corporal Guerra in the company of Badoero shot the nephew of Cardinal Albornoz just as he was capturing Clerici, and so the latter got away, and I had my servant send him a horse, and so he returned to the fray with his carbine and sword, and the enemy withdrew.' The Parman force followed for some distance in order to bring relief to the advanced redoubt closer to Valenza. The respite was very brief. Avogadri ordered his companies to re-form, shouting '*a me, a me*!', for trotting towards them was Troilo Rossi's wave of horsemen. Initially, the two bodies of cavalry caracoled each other, that is, advancing within 15 yards of the enemy, wheeling about, and delivering fire with their carbine one line after another.[61]

---

[58] Basta, *Le gouvernement de la cavallerie legere*, 23.
[59] Basta, *Le gouvernement de la cavallerie legere*, 17.
[60] Gavin Robinson, 'Equine battering rams? A reassessment of cavalry charges in the English Civil War', *Journal of Military History*, 75 (2011): 719–31.
[61] For a description of cavalry tactics, see Jean-Michel Sallmann, 'Le cheval, la pique et le canon: le rôle tactique de la cavalerie du XIVe au XVIIe siècle', in *Le Cheval et la guerre du XVe au XXe siècle*, ed. D. Roche and D. Reytier (Paris, 2002), 253–67.

Cremona Visdomini was in the troop close to the general. 'As we fired at them—they were like a half-moon firing at us, I was hit with a ball on the helmet above the left eye', which must have been deflected by the steel. Some of the Parmans then closed to engage the enemy in a melee. 'Our general courageously charged the enemy's front, calling the men to follow him, and I saw him fall', recounted Galeazzo Peretti. Other voices shouted to caracole, 'wheel to the right! wheel to the right!' 'Then everyone was mixed and we struck with our swords', explained Visdomini, 'and the general was wounded there and shortly after fell to earth dead, and we advanced to his body as the enemy withdrew, where we halted to await orders to see who should command the cavalry. We made many prisoners.' Count Alovisio Scotti was one of the captains in the fray; his father Fabio sent Galeazzo Peretti out to verify if the rumour that he was wounded was true. News spread through the army that Troilo Rossi had singled out Avogadri personally, and had felled him with a shot from his carbine. Both bodies of cavalry separated and they stood facing each other in formation for a while, waiting for fresh orders. Back at the trenches, Odoardo leapt onto his horse and called his noble Cornetta Bianca guard to his side, then led a mass of infantry down towards the assailants. No account of the action speaks of hand-to-hand contact with pikes and swords between the two armies, so the Spanish infantry may have been content to exchange musket salvoes with the Parmans in the hope that they would recoil or break under the strain. Some of the Italian companies, sorely depleted in numbers by desertion, looked shaky, but the French companies showed resolve.[62] Some additional French troops began to arrive on Odoardo's flank to help. Before too long, the two Parman cannon began to find the range of the Spanish force, and so the latter withdrew. The bulk of the attacking force then withdrew from Valenza at night across the bridge of boats, to await the next engagement.

It is not easy to surmise the result that Coloma and Gambacorta expected from this great sortie. A cavalry charge against blocks of professional musketeers and pikemen was not often successful, and cavalrymen at close range were easy targets for musketeers firing at a rate of one ball every two minutes or better. But against shaky infantry who might drop their weapons and take to their heels, the tactic was a better bet. The traditional cavalry charge against infantry was the caracole, where the front row of troopers would close in on the foot at a trotting pace and then discharge their pistol on the great mass of men, whose heavy metal helmets and breastplates were often still effective in deflecting shot. Then the troopers would wheel their horses and ride off to the right, trotting to the rear of the formation to reload their firearms. The second rank would then gallop forward to repeat the operation, followed by the third, and so on. Once the infantry before them seemed to become unsteady, it was time to draw sabres and plunge into the spaces between the pikes to break up the hapless defenders.[63] The very physical mass of the horse and rider, each one 2.3 metres high and 3 metres across, approaching as a mass,

---

[62] Siri, *Memorie recondite di Vittorio Siri*, 291.
[63] William Guthrie, *The Later Thirty Years War: From the Battle of Wittstock to the Treaty of Westphalia* (Westport, CT, and London, 2003), 19.

160 metres across, like a 'wall of centaurs', was designed to strike terror in the hearts of untested infantry.[64] In this particular instance, however, the momentum of the charge was slowed and then broken by the 'forlorn hope' of several dozen troopers led in person by Odoardo's cavalry commander, Ricciardo Avogadri, who broke through the first wave of horsemen and then engaged the second, led by Rossi. There are hints in the accounts of witnesses that officers paired off against each other and fought duels while their troopers selected the lesser fry. The publicity of these encounters were certain to enhance officers' status in the army.[65] Rossi is widely credited with singling out Avogadri and felling him with a pistol or carbine shot at point-blank range (for, with their short barrels, these firearms were notoriously inaccurate even at 20 paces). Vittorio de Lanci, a Piacenza soldier serving in the French army, later recounted being inside Valenza to get his passport (probably having deserted) and seeing Count Troilo Rossi expressing to brother officers his admiration of the 'gran soldato' who charged him with merely 25 or 30 soldiers. Avogadri's courage and sacrifice elicited the admiration of witnesses, and chroniclers of both sides recorded the event in practically every account of the siege for centuries.[66]

After the action, soldiers escorted the prisoners into Odoardo's tent like trophies, and then placed them in a shed near Palazzo Stanchi. A trumpeter came out from Valenza with his eyes bandaged 'according to custom in war' to obtain news from Fabio Scotti on the fate of the nephew of Cardinal Albornoz. 'We unbandaged his eyes so he could visit the dead and wounded, and near the shed with the prisoners he saw the corpse and started to cry, saying that this was the nephew. Count Fabio promised to send the corpse back the next morning.' Galeazzo Peretti talked with the trumpeter that evening, 'who explained that the plan was to send the arquebusiers against the trench to the area near the Po while the cavalry charged the middle with the aim of capturing Odoardo and the rest of us'. The historian Gualdo Priorato, writing only a few years after the event, assessed the Parman losses at seven officers and two hundred men killed outright, alongside a comparable number of Spaniards, but there are no reliable figures in the papers closer to the event.[67]

The great skirmish of 20 September, although constituting a second personal success for Odoardo, only accelerated the desertion of men from his units. Almost

---

[64] Nicole de Blomac, 'Le cheval de guerre entre le dire et le faire: quelques variations sur le discours équestre adapté à la réalité militaire', in *Le Cheval et la guerre du XVe au XXe siècle*, ed. D. Roche and D. Reytier (Paris, 2002), 55–65.

[65] Sandberg, *Warrior Pursuits*, 152.

[66] The details of this engagement were recorded in a trial for rebellion against Count Rossi, where participants on both sides (including prisoners taken from the Spaniards) left 80 pages of testimony. ASPr, Ufficio delle Confische e congiure, 25, Processus Criminalis con.o Com. S.ti Secondi pro crimine felonie, 4 December 1635. For the logic of high-ranking officers 'duelling' in the midst of battle, see Hervé Drévillon, ' "Publier nos playes et valeurs". Le fait d'armes et sa notoriété pendant la guerre de Trente Ans (1635–1648)', in *La Noblesse de la fin du XVIe au début du XXe siècle, un modèle social?*, 2 vols., ed. Josette Pontet, Michel Figeac, and Marie Boisson-Gabarron (Anglet, 2002), vol. 1, 289–308.

[67] Gualdo Priorato, *Historia delle guerre*, 294.

as soon as he was encamped outside Valenza, the duke was forced to admit to Richelieu that a large number of his soldiers (the Italian infantry in particular) had disappeared en route. A chronicler inside nearby Alessandria reports that so many of the besiegers' infantry deserted that it was difficult to cope with the volume. Even Moralt's large Swiss company, which had not lost a single man to battle, saw about half its complement desert in the week after 17 September. They might have been deserting to other Swiss units in French or even Spanish pay, for we have no way of tracking them. As for the Italian soldiers recruited in Lombardy and the Papal States, most of them had already departed, reducing the Parman sector to a skeleton force continually replenished with French troops conceded by Créquy. The French field marshal berated the soldiers of the Duke of Parma as being rural militiamen unable to fight a battle. He also often addressed the Duke of Parma in imperious, rather than reverential, terms, something that Odoardo complained about in letters to Paris. Odoardo in turn blamed Créquy for prosecuting the siege at too leisurely a pace. Both accusations were true. The troops under Odoardo's command never permanently seized any of the earthworks in front of them, but they did discourage the garrison's sorties.[68]

Chroniclers and French army officials are completely concordant in their account of the undoing of the Duke of Parma's army. The ambassador Hémery reported to Richelieu on 27 September that only 1,800 foot and 500 cavalry remained, which proved that it was useless to raise Italian troops. He thought that, before long, the duke would be left with only French soldiers, who could not desert with the same ease. The company registers record the desertion of the soldiers day by day, and, more often, from pay to pay. Before the end of September, foragers gave themselves up, or signed on with the Spanish army, bringing their horses with them. Parman deserters reduced the size of the army by almost half by the first days of October, by which time it was necessary to dissolve several of the Italian companies and distribute the remaining members elsewhere. Not all the companies kept good records, but, nevertheless, there is a stark contrast between them, depending on the date it was put together and its ethnic composition. Three companies raised in 1633, those of Serafini, De la Guette, and Roquebrune, lost proportionately fewer of their complement relative to more recent creations. Serafini's mostly Italian company lost 38 per cent of its complement of 245 men to desertion, and only four died during the 1635 campaign. The largely French companies lost 15 per cent (De la Guette) and 32 per cent (Roquebrune) to desertion, and suffered 25 fatalities among the 402 men in both units. The 18 infantry companies established in 1635, whose records we can use, had widely divergent destinies. The ethnically diverse company of the French captain Jean de la Haye lost 50 per cent of its men to desertion (93/187) and another 13 died. That of André Aquin held up rather better, at 21 per cent desertion, and five fatalities out of a complement of 91. Rates of desertion were comparable among the other French companies, of Gaspard de Villiers (18 per cent of a complement of 153), François Nicart (21 per cent of 205), Louis Rossillon (19 per cent of 102),

[68] Capriata, *Dell'Historia*, 170.

Fig. 3.6. Callot: Cavalry skirmish, *c.*1633. Squadrons broke up on contact to permit close-quarter fighting until one or both sides disengaged to regroup.

Jean Frottier de la Roquette (31 per cent of 130), and Annibale Pallavicino (21 per cent of 128 men). The French also suffered more fatalities during the campaign, these same companies losing a total of 47 men to combat and illness. Among the recent Italian companies desertion rates were much higher, and fatalities were lower. Francesco Arcelli's little company of 70 men lost 56 per cent to desertion, and had a single fatality. Giovanni Innocenzo Ceva lost fully 81 per cent to desertion and had merely three fatalities in his large company of 252 men. Francesco Pepoli's desertion rate was 57 per cent; that of Cornelio Palmia, 57 per cent; Scotti-Pallavicino, 45 per cent of 78; Ferrante Portapuglia, 75 per cent of 162 men at the outset; Brasilio Marchi, 74 per cent of 180 men; Ercole Osnaghi, 43 per cent of 166 soldiers; Annibale Scotti, 37 per cent of 188; Fausto Melari, 53 per cent of 258; Giovanni Maria Coggia lost 76 per cent of 149. Such steep losses embarrassed the duke, who 're-formed' the companies of Melari and Coggia in early October and in November respectively, that is, he suppressed them and redistributed the remaining soldiers among the other companies. The fatalities among the same 11 predominantly Italian companies amounted to only 11 men, and two soldiers captured! These figures are more indicative than conclusive, in part because the destinies of the men belonging to two additional companies were rarely recorded, and I suspect that casualties were under-reported. Nevertheless, the numbers do coincide with the testimony of observers, and they bear out Bernard Masson's claim that companies thrown together hastily with disparate elements were those that came apart just as quickly in the field.[69] No source implies that provisions were in short supply, which was the usual reason for mass desertion. Rather, these officers were unable to establish trust and to motivate their men, through their words and their example, to follow them.[70]

---

[69] Bernard Masson, 'Un aspect de la discipline dans les armées de Louis XIII: la lutte contre la désertion du soldat 1635–1643', *Revue Historique des Armées*, 162 (1986): 12–23.

[70] Costa, *Psicologia militare*, 127.

Fig. 3.7. Callot: Collecting deserters, c.1633. Troops herd captured deserters back to camp. Few would suffer severe punishment.

The siege of Valenza was not especially dangerous for the attacking army, although peasants often ambushed soldiers in the densely planted landscape of northern Italy. Spanish cavalry patrols prowled about the French camp, looking to capture enemy scouts and sentries with the aim of extracting information from them, or *'prendre langue'*.[71] Of the five cavalry companies that noted down their attrition, scribes only reported seven troopers killed and six captured during the entire campaign. But 154 men deserted the ranks, mostly with their horses, and another 81 were struck from the rolls from sickness or for some other reason. Among the infantry, the French companies seemed to stand and fight more often. Eighty-six infantrymen appear as fatalities in the registers in the months following the triumphal march out of Piacenza, but 57 of them were French and four more were Piedmontese or Monferrini. The Swiss company of Moralt lost the majority of its complement in a single week near the beginning of the siege in mid-September, but only one man of more than 250 was reported killed. The flight of the subjects of the King of Spain, and soldiers originating in the Italian neutral states, was especially pronounced. The companies of Marchi, Pepoli, Osnaghi, and Melari came apart without a single man being killed or dying of disease, leading to the dismissal of the unlucky captains. New recruits arrived steadily, but they could not stanch the outflow. The company rosters from 1635 record the names and origins of 729 men who signed on between the Battle of Pontecurone and the onset of winter, of whom 191 were cavalry troopers. Many of Odoardo's Italian deserters had gone over to Spanish service, signing on with the new *tercio* raised by Cardinal Trivulzio. The deployment of this unit to the defence of Valenza demoralized Odoardo further, we are told.[72] Of the new cavalrymen, barely 10 per cent hailed from Farnese

---

[71] Paul Azan, *Un tacticien du XVIIe siècle* (Paris, 1904), 39.
[72] Girolamo Brusoni, *Dell'Historia d'Italia* (Venice, 1661), 110.

territory, while French subjects constituted almost three quarters. Of the infantry, Frenchmen constituted over half of the newcomers, men from Italian neutral states were less than a fifth, and Farnese subjects fewer than 10 per cent. Hémery's prediction, that Odoardo would eventually have only Frenchmen in his service, was coming true.

Victor Amadeus appeared with part of his army, perhaps 4,000 or 5,000 men on 25 September, two weeks after the beginning of the siege. Only six of these regiments were paid from the Savoyard treasury. There is no way to determine the ethnic make-up of his troops: Piedmontese and Savoyard volunteers were probably outnumbered by subjects of the King of France.[73] His arrival forced Coloma to withdraw eastwards to Pieve del Cairo, about 15 kilometres distant, finally cutting the town off from help. Créquy also received reinforcements from France of several thousand men, the debris of a much larger number recruited in southeastern France, most of whom had deserted while en route. The Duke of Mantua ordered 2,000 militiamen from the Monferrato to stand watch in the siege lines beside the professional soldiers. Many of them presented themselves at the gates of Alessandria to desert instead.[74] While the siege continued there was little concrete result, for the entire population of the town set to work building fascines and sharpening stakes to set in the ring of outlying forts, which became 'planets [whose alignment was] favourable to the besieged'.[75] The impatient field marshal threw French infantry at these forts on 26 September, and sometimes briefly overwhelmed one at a heavy cost in lives, only to lose it again in a spirited counter-attack. Count Souvigny described one of these skirmishes, a frontal assault of five regiments (about 1,500 or 2,000 men) on one of the Spanish outworks. Before long, the French units that were engaged became a large and immobile crowd, which he contrasted to the Spanish counter-attack of pikemen supported by 'sleeves' of musketeers who spread out on each flank and subjected their assailants to a fierce crossfire. Small cavalry contingents galloped back and forth to support them. The majority of the French infantry was too bunched up to return effective fire until Count Souvigny sorted them out, but then artillery fire from the town drove them back.[76]

The confederate artillery bombardment continued unabated, but few of the French bombardier officers had much experience of a long siege. Even Odoardo knew that it was pointless to lob cannonballs here and there against the city ramparts, and so complained that no one was directing fire to a single short segment of the wall to effect a breach.[77] The only significant progress occurred when rainy weather swelled the Po and carried away the Spanish bridge. Guido Villa, a talented Ferrarese nobleman in

---

[73] Salvatore Foa, *Vittorio Amedeo I (1587–1637)* (Turin, 1930), 261; Paola Bianchi deplores how scarce good sources are for this period, and that we must rely on the old assessments of Nicola Brancaccio. Bianchi, *Sotto diverse bandiere: L'internazionale militare nello Stato sabaudo d'antico regime*, (Milan, 2012) 124. The archives in Turin relevant to the Piedmontese army become abundant only in the last years of the seventeenth century.
[74] Ghilini, *Annali di Alessandria*, 105.
[75] Stanchi, *Narrazione dell'assedio di Valenza nel 1635*, 271.
[76] Souvigny, *Mémoires du Comte de Souvigny*, 294.
[77] Brusoni, *Dell'Historia dell'Italia*, 110–12.

Savoyard service pressed the attack on the north bank of the Po.[78] He led a bloody assault on the fort on the north bank, which was beaten back, but on the night of 28 September, the last Habsburg defenders withdrew by boat into the town. In that operation, they lost perhaps the largest number of men yet, when the impetuous current swept two boatloads of soldiers into the Parman lines, where they were captured. Others drowned when boats overturned. Weapons lost in the operation were retrieved from the mud a few days later when the river fell. It is very difficult to determine the rate of attrition for the garrison, which would have counted between 2,000 and 3,000 professional soldiers and a few hundred militiamen at this stage of the siege. The parish register for Valenza survives, but it indicates only 114 burials during the two months of the siege, and another 150 during the following two months, about half of whom were German and Swiss soldiers, the remainder being Spaniards, Walloons, Lombards, and Neapolitans. Peacetime burials during the 1630s numbered between 40 and 50 individuals annually. Many soldiers were, therefore, buried without parish clergy officiating, but it is not possible to know their number.[79]

Even in the absence of success, Odoardo remained faithful to the French cause. The papal vice-legate from Bologna arrived in camp on 25 September, after meeting with the Spanish high command, with the mission of ordering the duke, as a vassal of the neutral Pope, to quit the alliance. These 'extraordinary' nuncios entrusted with peace missions were very busy in the 1630s, and enjoyed the authority to cast papal censure upon Catholic princes who made war on their co-religionists.[80] Odoardo hid some French officers behind a screen, to their great amusement, before he ushered the papal diplomat into his quarters, and then roundly insulted him.[81] The nuncio proposed that the duke should sell his heavily mortgaged fiefs near Rome to the Barberini papal nephews, but the latter, outraged, dared the Pope to take them with cannon, since he would not have them by gold.[82] When the diplomat finally emerged from Valenza in his coach under a general ceasefire, the cannon from the Parman battery fired in his direction. Following a brief, insincere apology, Odoardo ordered the vice-legate to await his pleasure in Piacenza.[83] The King of France, in a letter to Pope Urban VIII, claimed that the Duke of Parma was not dependent upon the papacy for anything more than a simple payment for investiture in the fief at his accession. This claim was an important one, for Richelieu and the king argued that both German and Italian states could make wars and alliances as fully sovereign states, unhindered by imperial or papal jurisdiction. Odoardo was free to make alliances as he pleased as long as he did not make war on the Papal States directly.[84] Odoardo's firmness reassured Louis and Richelieu that this ally, at least, could be counted on.

---

[78] Guill Ortega, 'L'Assedio di Valenza del 1635', 42.

[79] Archivio parrocchiale Valenza (henceforth APV), Registro parrocchiale (unnumbered) 1631–9.

[80] Pierre Blet, 'La politique du Saint-Siège vis-à-vis des puissances catholiques', *Dix-septième siècle* (1990): 57–71.

[81] Siri, *Memorie recondite di Vittorio Siri*, 292.

[82] Giacinto Demaria, 'La Guerra di Castro e la spedizione de'presidii, 1639–1649', *Miscellanea di Storia Italiana*, ser. 3, 4 (1898): 197.

[83] Stanchi, *Narrazione dell'assedio di Valenza nel 1635*, 272.

[84] Siri, *Memorie recondite di Vittorio Siri*, 292; Sven Externbrink, '"Le coeur du monde" et la "Liberté d'Italie": aspects de la politique italienne de Richelieu, 1624–1642', *Revue d'histoire diplomatique*, 114 (2000): 181–208.

As the siege dragged on, Odoardo multiplied his meetings with the French ambassador to the Duke of Savoy, Michel Particelli d'Hémery, descendant of an Italian banking family in Lyons, an agent of Richelieu, like Créquy, and a key figure of the alliance. He had served as commissaire and intendant to the army of Italy in 1629, entrusted with organizing recruitment, finance, and supplies. In 1635 this task devolved to his brother-in-law, Antoine Le Camus, while Hémery dealt with the larger political picture and served as the eyes and ears of the cardinal in Italy. His reports on the state of the alliance and the condition of the army make compelling reading, for the ambassador often employed undiplomatic language. France initiated war with the Habsburgs in 1635, expecting to be able to launch multiple armies on all its frontiers that would sweep away the overextended Spaniards. The number of soldiers Richelieu raised, perhaps 80,000 men, appears to have been larger than any previous French effort, but it proved impossible to pay the men or even feed them in the field beyond their bread ration.[85] French kings and ministers did not wish to imitate the German model of making war, where colonels and generals raised their own units and fed them too, and then leased them to the warlord by the month or by the campaign. Nor were French commanders expected to impose crushing financial burdens on towns and villages in the path of the armies. France preferred to keep the management of its military assets firmly in the Crown's hands. Every royal army had an intendant after 1630, although Hémery appears to have filled both administrative and political roles in this army, which required close collaboration with the Duke of Savoy. Much routine army administration was in the hands of provincial intendants far to the rear, in Dauphiné and Provence. Both army and provincial intendants were wealthy magistrates whose families had entered royal service. A good army intendant, like a good general, could not live off the stipend accruing to the function, assuming it would be paid. Rather, they drew money from their own private purses to deal with an endless succession of emergency expenditures. Richelieu expected Hémery and Le Camus to deal with contingency issues like troop lodgings, the regular supply of bread for the men and fodder for the horses, and, above all, pay.[86]

Cardinal Richelieu never intended to pay the troops their full wages on campaign, and, at best, allotted them small sums that only covered what they would need to survive. He expected the army to live off the land, off the private money of the officers, or off the assistance of French allies until the short war was over.[87] As David Parrott has shown, this was policy, not mere coping with contingency. Richelieu had increased French taxes exponentially since 1630 to the point that whole provinces were in open revolt against tax collectors and their agents by the beginning of the war.[88] Generals

[85] David Parrott, 'French military organization in the 1630s: the failure of Richelieu's ministry', *Seventeenth Century French Studies*, 9 (1987): 151–67.

[86] Douglas Clark Baxter, *Servants of the Sword: French Intendants of the Army, 1630–1670* (Urbana, IL, 1976).

[87] David Parrott, *Richelieu's Army: War, Government and Society in France, 1624–1642* (Cambridge, 2001), 172–6, 346 and 517. For the logic of appointing rich men to command, see Hervé Drévillon, *L'Impôt de Sang: le métier des armes sous Louis XIV* (Paris, 2005), 138.

[88] Lloyd Moote provides some figures on French revenues, which stood at 43 million livres tournois in 1630, then 72 million in 1633, to settle at about 100 million livres thereafter. The army devoured a third of that, but payment of the interest on the royal debt made up most of the remainder. Lloyd Moote, *Louis XIII, the Just*, 231–9.

and intendants in the field might send urgent cries for help to the secretary for war, Servien, but he was just a secretary for the king. Whatever cash was available to the minister of finance served to pay the interest on the ballooning royal debt. The man with the power over the purse strings was the superintendent of finance, Claude de Bullion.[89] Since war on this scale surpassed by far the ability of the state to pay for it, and even threatened the patrimony of the officers appointed to prosecute it, it must be made to pay for itself.[90]

The obvious repercussion of the lack of proper financing of military operations was that the confederate army was never close to the size promised in Richelieu's treaties. It was too weak to besiege any large city, which had to be surrounded first, before active approaches were made against the ramparts. Both the king and the cardinal expected captains and colonels to spend their time and resources finding recruits in the areas of their estates, paying good bonuses to the men who signed on. But service abroad was very unpopular and the majority of the recruits never arrived at their destination. French officials estimated that over half the French recruits raised in Dauphiné or beyond deserted before they reached Piedmont. The men on the spot also had good motives for deserting once the opportunities for plunder fell off. Many of the men might desert in a single day, following a breakdown in their provisioning, or to avenge ill-treatment by an officer. In addition to men 'fleeing' from the camp, others received a short leave of absence from their officers, and then 'forgot' to return. Not all the deserters quit military service, however, for they might be happy to sign up with another unit nearby, preferably in a different army, to the delight of a captain wishing to replace his losses. Generals like Créquy never really knew how many men were under their command at any one moment, and the new arrivals were never numerous enough to stanch the flow of desertion. The inability of the army to maintain its numbers just exacerbated the arguments over operations in the camp of the confederates, between Victor Amadeus and Créquy.[91] Likewise, Spanish officials complained of the propensity of the Neapolitans and other Italians to desert while in the theatre of war, as it was relatively easy for them to do so.[92]

It was Hémery's delicate task to keep the three commanders on speaking terms with each other. But his own relationship with Paris was far from enviable. The finance minister Bullion was not one of Richelieu's clients, and he was a personal enemy of Hémery. The ambassador thought that Bullion did his utmost to block the proper funding of the Italian theatre of war, which was only one of several, and one of the most distant from Paris. By 2 October the French troops were rioting for their pay. Hémery, too, thought that Créquy had bungled the siege of Valenza, but since he was particularly good at finding recruits in nearby Dauphiné, he could not be replaced. The ambassador's rapport with Victor Amadeus was not good

---

[89] Parrott, 'French military organization in the 1630s', 161.
[90] Chagniot, *Guerre et Société à l'époque moderne*, 103–5.
[91] Gabriel de Mun, *Richelieu et la Maison de Savoie: l'ambassade de Particelli d'Hémery en Piémont* (Paris, 1907), 92.
[92] For desertion rates of different contingents from the Spanish army marching en route to Germany the previous year, see Luis Antonio Ribot Garcìa, 'Milano, piazza d'armi della monarchia spagnola', in *Millain the Great. Milano nelle brume del Seicento* (Milan, 1989), 41–61.

either, for, while he thought that the duke was a sincere party to the alliance (few people agreed with him), he could not bring the prince to cooperate seamlessly with the French contingent. Finally, Hémery's patience was tried by Odoardo Farnese, whom he saw as a large spoiled child, brutal, crude, quarrelsome, and vain, who might act from sheer spite if he thought himself neglected or scorned by his allies. Odoardo had little weight in the alliance, since his forces were no longer very numerous, and he could not supply them from Piacenza.

The situation was entirely different for the Spaniards, who began to draw upon emergency funds collected the previous winter when war looked inevitable. Milan's loyalty to the Habsburg dynasty made all the difference. Its elites preferred a distant king who respected the traditional institutions and local customs to the centralizing ambitions of a King of France or Duke of Savoy.[93] Davide Maffi calculates that Milan furnished 6 million scudi annually for the war, five times its annual tax revenue![94] The same author calculates that the state of Milan provided about 4,000 recruits for the Spanish army every year, on average, which is considerable for a state numbering only 800,000 inhabitants.[95] In addition to the professional troops, Spain mobilized large numbers of militiamen. An edict decreed that 8 per cent of the men of military age would be called up to serve in fortresses, with the best of those troops dispatched to the vicinity of the borders and to Alessandria in particular.[96] In addition to milking the duchy of Milan, Spain activated its defensive alliance with the Grand Duke of Tuscany, who promised to pay some 17,000 scudi every month to the war effort, as well as provide ships for the fleet and a contingent of soldiers for Lombardy. Tuscan levies probably only amounted to a fraction of the 4,000 men the Grand Duke promised, but every additional company helped tip the balance.[97]

The real pillar of Spanish resistance during the 1630s was the kingdom of Naples, despite the misgivings of Spanish commanders towards the troops from southern Italy. The kingdom served as the rear support zone for the entire Spanish Empire, reportedly sending to Milan 48,000 infantry, 5,500 cavalrymen, horses in proportion, and money amounting to three and a half million scudi just between 1631 and 1636.[98] These enormous sums, if they are accurate, would probably still only account for the resources sent from Naples, not those effectively received in Milan, but the Neapolitan participation in all the battles in the theatre of war is

[93] Antonio Alvarez-Ossorio Alvariño, 'The state of Milan and the Spanish monarchy', in *Spain in Italy: Politics, Society and Religion 1500–1700*, ed. T. J. Dandelet and J. A. Marino (Leiden and Boston, 2007), 100–32.

[94] Davide Maffi, *Il baluardo della corona: Guerra, esercito, finanze e società nella Lombardia seicentesca (1630–1660)* (Florence, 2007), 305–14.

[95] Maffi, *Il baluardo della corona*, 126.

[96] Sara Pedretti, 'Ai confini occidentali dello Stato di Milano: l'impiego delle milizie rurali nelle guerre del Seicento', in *Alle frontiere della Lombardia: Politica, guerra e religione nell'età moderna*, ed. C. Donati (Milan, 2006), 177–200; Gualdo Priorato writes that Albornoz had 18,000 militiamen at his disposal, but not all of them were mobilized simultaneously; *Historia delle guerre*, 269.

[97] Gualdo Priorato, *Historia delle guerre*, 300–2; Tuscany was also subsidizing the Imperial army in Germany with a contingent under Prince Matthias de'Medici. See Carla Sodini, *L'Ercole Tirreno: Guerra e dinastia medicea nella prima metà del '600* (Florence, 2001), 187–96.

[98] Angelantonio Spagnoletti, *Principi italiani e Spagna nell'età barocca* (Milan, 1996), 150; on the misgivings of Spanish commanders about Neapolitan troops and officers, 184–9.

undeniable. Naples sent infantry and horses to northern Italy, and warships too. The naval expedition sent from Naples under the Marques de Santa Cruz repaired the storm damage from the previous spring, and, early in September 1635, seized the Iles de Lérins off the Provençal coast, between Antibes and Cannes. These fortified but undermanned islands fell quickly to the Spaniards, who transformed them into bases for attacking ships and coastal towns. It all but stopped the transfer of French troops by sea to Piacenza, and it forced Louis XIII and Richelieu to assemble a fleet and still another army to dislodge them.[99] In the meantime Santa Cruz and the Marques de Villafranca at Finale were free to divert some of their Spanish and Neapolitan soldiers to reinforce Alessandria, and Coloma's field detachment at Pieve del Cairo. The besieging forces periodically had insufficient men to both man the trenches and blockade the town. Consequently, on 2 October, a Spanish detachment of 400 men and additional munitions pierced the confederate lines and reinforced the beleaguered garrison.[100]

It gradually began to dawn on Créquy that this ill-fortified town might not fall to his army. A great skirmish developed around the German redoubt to the west of the town on 1 October, where the defenders were briefly overwhelmed before a Neapolitan counter-attack recovered it, albeit at a reported cost of 100 casualties on each side. On 9 October, the French guns began to batter the town itself with 12 cannon, but still without concentrating on a single point. The defenders began to count the number of shots fired at them every day, which rose from about 100 at the start of the month, to double that by the second week. The heavy balls, weighing 65 lbs, began to do serious damage to the houses in the town, knocking down several walls with each shot.[101] Spaniards repulsed a French assault on the earthworks in front of the town on 12 October, purportedly costing the attackers hundreds of casualties and, similarly, 200 losses among the defenders. The swelling intensity of the fighting did not preclude acts of courtesy between enemy commanders. Hearing that the Count Celada was ill, Créquy called a truce and delivered a gift of ice (possibly sorbet) and fresh fruit from Genoa to his stricken opponent. The defenders spotted coaches arriving in the French camp and understood these to indicate the presence of ladies from Casale Monferrato coming to watch the siege, for the great guns began to fire more frequently than before for their entertainment. Inside the town, soldiers and populace collected the cannonballs and received a small sum for delivering them to the quartermaster, to be fired back at the French. A reputed miracle occurred on 18 October as much of the townsfolk and the garrison, numbering 300 people, assembled in the parish church to pray for the health of Celada, with the Holy Sacrament exposed on the altar. A cannonball smashed through the glass window above the entrance to the church and struck the corner of the altar displaying the relics of the Apostle James (Spain's patron saint), and then bounced back onto the floor without hurting

---

[99] Réné La Bruyère, *La Marine de Richelieu: Sourdis, archévêque et amiral (6 nov. 1594–18 juin 1645)* (Paris, 1948), 39.
[100] Ghilini, *Annali di Alessandria*, 105.
[101] Stanchi, *Narrazione dell'assedio di Valenza nel 1635*, 274.

anyone. The projectile is still exhibited in the church today as a sign of divine intervention. By this time, the confederates were battering the walls and the town itself with about 300 projectiles daily. After the loss of the floating mills in the Po, which were sunk by Parman guns, the quartermaster Stanchi set four-man teams to work at grinding grain at each of the four hand-powered mills, but these broke down often so that they were only able to produce five sacks of flour a day, enough for only 200 rations. Celada held the price of bread low by decree so that the soldiers and the townspeople could still afford to buy it. Thanks to the foresight of Coloma, the quartermasters were still able to distribute 4,300 rations of bread every day from the stocks of flour on hand.

At Pieve del Cairo, just out of reach of the confederate army, Carlos Coloma collected detachments of troops from various quarters, including at least one new *tercio* made up of deserters from Odoardo's army. These, and militia contingents supplied from nearby Pavia, erected a fortified camp large enough to shelter a small army. Other Spanish and Neapolitan contingents disembarked at Finale Liguria and marched by a circuitous route to join him.[102] Fresh cavalry forces at Coloma's disposal began to bite more deeply into the foraging patrols, and parties of infantry began to seize the towns and castles in the vicinity of the siege. On 15 October, Coloma mustered this force, which was composed of only 6,700 infantry and 1,800 cavalry, including the militia, and 8 pieces of artillery.[103] The general assembled his regimental commanders for a council of war, where they quickly settled on a plan to rescue the town.

Coloma first feigned to build a new bridge of boats across the Po just downstream from Bassignana, which was in the Parman sector. When allied forces converged there to prevent a crossing, he marched his army west, to the village of Frascarolo, only 4 kilometres upriver from Valenza, and set his soldiers and peasants to work building a fortified camp a kilometre west of the village on 20 October. The site was well chosen, with a stream protecting the flank closest to the siege, and the Po river nearby.[104] Its proximity to the siege made it necessary for the allies to dislodge Coloma's troops before they drove off the besiegers from the north bank. The next day, the bulk of the Franco-Parman-Savoyard army crossed the river in the Parman sector and advanced, attempting to drive off Coloma with a force numbering between 6,000 and 8,000 men. Créquy led the vanguard with his French forces, Victor Amadeus deployed just behind him with the main body, and Odoardo brought up the rear. Our 23-year-old duke used the occasion to issue a challenge of personal combat against the aged Coloma, who declined it.[105] The allies were advancing through closely planted hedgerows, to attack a force already dug in, whose size they could not determine. Neapolitan mounted infantry and parties of musketeers placed forward of the village peppered Créquy's column with

---

[102] Guill Ortega, 'L'Assedio di Valenza del 1635', 42.

[103] Anon., *Relatione veritiera di quanto è successo nell'assedio di Valenza del Pò* (Milan, 1636?).

[104] Alexandre de Saluces, *Histoire militaire du Piémont*, vol. 4 (Turin, 1818), 11; for the criteria on selecting a camp and its protection, see Montecuccoli, *Memoires de Montecuculi*, 108.

[105] BPPr Ms Parmense 737, Calandrini, 'L'Heroe d'Italia', 562; this ancient custom surfaced occasionally during the French Wars of Religion: see Sandberg, *Warrior Pursuits*, 191.

fire as it approached. The Spanish account describes a bitter firefight at close quarters, initiated first by the Neapolitans and Lombards, joined soon after by the veteran Spanish *tercios*, who closed in to use their musket butts as clubs. Before the allied troops were fully deployed, Créquy gave his troops the order to retreat, to the great disappointment of Victor Amadeus and Odoardo. After they withdrew to the Parman sector bridgehead to watch and wait, the three commanders bickered violently with each other over their respective shortcomings.[106] Meanwhile, another coordinated relief force of 600 Spanish and Italian troops under Ludovico Guasco sallied forth from Alessandria and crossed the siege trenches into Valenza from the south on the night of 23 October, almost unopposed. The Piedmontese pickets remained strangely inobservant and inactive, but, to be fair, the lines were very thinly held.[107] This relief force suffered a few dozen killed and wounded because they arrived unannounced crying 'Spagna, Spagna!' and the defenders in the forward redoubt, fearing a ruse, threw grenades at them.[108] There was now much apprehension in the air, for the city often received messengers from outside who brought letters written in cipher. One of these emissaries was a Dominican friar who swam naked across the Po in the middle of the night. The French were now in a hurry, and began to burrow towards one of the redoubts on the west side of town. The interim commander of the defenders, Filippo Spinola, had a countermine built to oppose it. When the defenders set it off on 24 October, the ensuing explosion threw dozens of French marksmen into the air, 'as high as a church steeple', and buried alive the men who were digging.[109]

The final episode of the siege followed the next day, on 25 October. Under cover of a thick morning fog, wagons bearing boats rolled out of the camp and down to the Po just upstream from the besiegers. Within a few hours the craft were in the water and loaded with men and provisions. Meanwhile, the bulk of Coloma's force formed up in battle order and threw itself against the earthen fort on the riverbank opposite the town, which was guarded by hardly more than 150 men. Spanish commanders first sent forth an emissary offering quarter to the little garrison if it surrendered, but a volley of musketry signified their refusal. Then the Italian and Albanian soldiery began the assault. Fighting for the control of an enclosed space often had a more bitter and prolonged character than that occurring in places without a well-defined boundary. The Neapolitan colonel Marchese di Terracuso, a veteran of Nördlingen who led from the front, was saved from a pike thrust by the missal devoted to the Virgin Mary he wore about his neck.[110] The French soldiers inside put up a stout resistance, but once the attackers had broken down the defensive palisades and mounted the earthworks the defenders began to cry out for mercy. In this case the frenzied attackers slaughtered scores of them and spared

---

[106] BNF Ms Fr 16929, *Relation de M. D'Esmery sur les negociations en Piemont*, fo. 535.
[107] Guill Ortega, 'L'Assedio di Valenza del 1635', 42.
[108] Stanchi, *Narrazione dell'assedio di Valenza nel 1635*, 289.
[109] Stanchi, *Narrazione dell'assedio di Valenza nel 1635*, 289.
[110] Raffaele Maria Filamondo, *Il Genio bellicoso di Napoli: Memorie istoriche d'alcuni capitani celebri napolitani che han militato per la fede, per lo re, per la patria nel secolo corrente*, 2 vols (Naples, 1694), vol. 1, 145.

only about 40.¹¹¹ Confederate troops quickly converged on the nearby bridgehead in the Parman sector to save the vital strongpoint, but most of the cavalry was off foraging and the three dukes could only watch helplessly as the enemy ruptured the siege perimeter. The boats laden with men and provisions then floated downstream past the entrenched besiegers west of the town, who inflicted few casualties upon them. The town received 400 fresh Spanish and 400 Neapolitan troops, plus the equivalent of 110 cartloads of precious food and ammunition.¹¹² Coloma and his officers then entered the town and there were mutual congratulations all around, though the Marques de Celada, heroic commander of the fortress, lay dying of the bloody flux, or e-coli contracted from fecally contaminated water, a common danger in camps and besieged towns.¹¹³

The allied leaders could only agree, in a climate of acrimony, that the siege would have to be lifted immediately, before the onset of rainy weather reduced their forces still further. The night after the successful relief, the French began to withdraw the heavy guns from their batteries while musketeers fired continually in order to mask the noise. On 27 October the allied wagons and their escorts began to trundle out of their encampments in the direction of the Monferrato, to the west. In his haste to leave the camp, Odoardo left a great deal of heavy equipment behind him in the trenches, and set fire to whatever would burn in his sector. At the end of long sieges or a typical campaign, many of the tents and the huts of soldiers would have been reduced to unserviceable scrap.¹¹⁴ The defenders later claimed to have recovered 4,000 muskets and hundreds of pieces of armour for infantry and cavalry, some of it engraved and gilt belonging to the duke's ceremonial guards, along with 200 bread caissons, 100 carts, planks, and saddles, all turned over to the inhabitants of Valenza as their share of the booty. Muskets sold for scarcely more than a loaf of bread, and a great store of hardware changed hands. The garrison and people then ventured out to examine the French earthworks south of town, and marvelled at the wide, deep ditches and the labyrinthine trenches leading to the redoubts facing those of the defenders. The besiegers likely stripped bare the district's forest cover, as fascines (sticks and branches tightly bound together as a bundle, used for protection against shot), huts, and support beams required great quantities of wood.¹¹⁵ As admirable as the works were in dry weather, they filled with water with the onset of the rains, and one can only speculate on hygienic conditions in their proximity. Snayers' great painting depicts French soldiers calmly defecating along the rear of the entrenchments.¹¹⁶

---

¹¹¹ John Keegan, *The Face of Battle* (Harmondsworth and New York, 1976), 165–7.
¹¹² Guill Ortega, 'L'Assedio di Valenza del 1635'.
¹¹³ Anon., *Relatione veritiera*, 8.
¹¹⁴ Marc Russon and Hervé Martin, *Vivre sous la tente au Moyen-Age (Ve-XVe siècle)* (Rennes, 2010), 195.
¹¹⁵ Russon and Martin, *Vivre sous la tente au Moyen-Age*, 197; also Matoušek, 'Building a model of a field fortification', 114–32.
¹¹⁶ Stanchi, *Narrazione dell'assedio di Valenza nel 1635*, 291–3; Guill Ortega, 'L'Assedio di Valenza del 1635'. Snayers' great painting impresses us by its apparent verisimilitude, but we must not forget that he never left his studio in Brussels. See the article by Joseph Cuvelier, 'Peeter Snayers, peintre de batailles (1592–1667): Notes et documents pour servir à sa biographie', *Bulletin de l'Institut Historique Belge de Rome*, 23 (1944–6): 37–9.

Coloma estimated that 2,500 coalition troops died during the siege, but there is no way of confirming that number, nor even of knowing how he came by it.

The allied army withdrew to winter quarters in the towns and villages not far from Casale Monferrato, and Odoardo himself retired to Candia on the opposite bank of the Po with 1,000 men. Many of his deserters began to congregate there to rejoin the colours for the quiet winter season. Odoardo spent most of his time in comfortable lodgings in Casale, but an epidemic that broke out there killed many officers and soldiers spared by the siege of Valenza.[117] Parman detachments scoured the nearby Lomellina district for scarce provisions, but in this they competed with Spanish forage patrols for the same resources. One November night, Odoardo's force crept out of Casale in an attempt to seize Valenza by surprise, but they were soon discovered and the enterprise called off.[118] When the Spaniards learned that the Duke of Rohan had made a breakthrough in the Valtellina, they dispatched 3,000 foot and 500 horse to stop his progress, under the direction of Troilo Rossi, who would die in battle a few days later. Almost simultaneously, the new governor of Milan the Marqués of Leganés arrived in Genoa with 4,000 Spanish troops and a million and a half ducats destined for the next campaign. Leganés, who was one of the heroes of the Battle of Nördlingen the previous year, would also replace Coloma as commander-in-chief. With his arrival, the whole duchy of Milan celebrated its deliverance.[119]

Richelieu's optimism for success in Italy was completely dashed; and initial French successes in other theatres of war were similarly followed by disappointments.[120] Even winter quarters brought their share of disillusionment. Victor Amadeus forbade the supply of fodder to French units from his Piedmontese stores. The Monferrato district had already been 'eaten' during the previous campaign, so the French had to draw their own supplies at considerable expense from over the Alps.[121] Due to lack of provisions, the war was beginning to take on a cruel aspect. On 20 November a French detachment intent on capturing the castle at Sartirana refused to accept the surrender of the militia defenders, and killed them all. This was followed by a counter-massacre of allied foragers by other militiamen at Mede in Lomellina on 25 November.[122] In an attempt to consolidate their hold on the slender portion of Spanish territory they held in western Lombardy, Créquy and Victor Amadeus agreed to build a strong pentagonal fortress around the village of Breme, which was close to the Po river. The Dutch-style earthen walls rose around the place in the short space of three months, and soldiers were lodged in the houses inside it, but money and supplies for the garrison there were cruelly lacking.[123] Soldiers often tore down houses in order to find

---

[117] Giorcelli, 'Annali Casalesi (1632–1661)'.
[118] BPPr Ms Parmense 737, Calandrini, 'L'Heroe d'Italia', 595–600.
[119] Stanchi, *Narrazione dell'assedio di Valenza nel 1635*, 295.
[120] Parrott, *Richelieu's Army*, 123–42.
[121] De Mun, *Richelieu et la Maison de Savoie*, 112.
[122] Ghilini, *Annali di Alessandria*, 112.
[123] Giovanni Cerino Badone, 'Le Seconde Guerre d'Italia (1588–1659): Storiografia, Temi, Fonti' (PhD thesis, Università degli Studi del Piemonte Orientale, 2011), 242.

firewood to burn, but this did not prevent widespread mortality among the troops in winter.[124] Odoardo gave his cannon to Créquy to help defend the new fort. The duke shared the short supplies with his allies and his little army became something of a burden to him while his faraway duchy remained unprotected.[125] Hémery would have liked to see the last of Odoardo, and proposed to give French troops to him to see him off home. Odoardo had other ideas: he wished that Louis XIII would place him at the head of a strong French army that he would lead to certain victory.[126]

As the French forces dwindled, and deserters left to visit Rome or Venice, or took up residence in Italian cities to exercise trades there, Spanish strength swelled steadily.[127] Just as Spanish contributions to the German Imperial war effort first stalled and then crushed the Swedes in 1633 and 1634, now it was the turn of the Emperor Ferdinand II to shift troops south and allow the Spaniards to recruit units in Germany for the Italian theatre of war. Italian officers frequently passed from Spanish service to Austrian service, and then back again, like Prince Borso d'Este, uncle of the Duke of Modena.[128] Money and men from Tuscany, Modena, and even tiny Lucca were also starting to arrive. New contingents from Naples, from Spain, and the Milanese itself were now at the disposal of Coloma's replacement, the Marqués de Leganés, a relative of the chief minister or *valido* Olivares. Even the naval flotilla in Liguria received additional ships, until it totalled 38 galleys and 12 sailing vessels, manned by thousands of soldiers and seamen.[129] Leganés received orders to lay siege to and capture the city of Parma, but governors of Milan often treated their instructions with a great deal of liberty. More than simple military commanders, they were statesmen sensitive to the delicate political equilibrium in Italy and Europe, and took care not to alienate worried neutral states. Leganés felt that although the seizure of Parma might be an easy thing, it would further antagonize Pope Urban VIII, whose policy had been far from Hispanophile, and who ceased subsidizing the Habsburg war in 1635 after it was no longer a confessional struggle against Protestants.[130] Better to press the French back into the Monferrato off Spanish territory, and try to break up the Savoyard alliance.[131] The breathing space would also allow Leganés to reform his companies so as to keep a proper ratio between the number of officers and the soldiers, demoting or sending home the officers who proved to be ineffectual.[132]

---

[124] Souvigny, *Mémoires du Comte de Souvigny*, 302.
[125] Crescenzi Romani, *Corona della Nobiltà d'Italia*, 298.
[126] Hémery, *Relation de M. d'Esmery*, fo. 551–2.
[127] Gualdo Priorato, *Historia delle guerre*, 301–2.
[128] Jean Bérenger, 'La collaboration militaire austro-espagnole aux XVIe–XVIIe siècles', in *L'Espagne et ses guerres. De la fin de la Reconquête aux guerres d'Indépendance*, ed. A. Molinié and A. Merle (Paris, 2004), 11–33.
[129] Roger Charles Anderson, 'The Thirty Years War in the Mediterranean', *Mariner's Mirror*, 15 (1969): 435–51.
[130] Jaitner, 'The popes and the struggle for power during the sixteenth and seventeenth centuries', in *1648: War and Peace in Europe*, ed. K. Bussmann and H. Schilling, 2 vols (Munster-Osnabruck, 1998), vol. 1, 61–7.
[131] Maffi, *Il baluardo della corona*, 18.
[132] AGS, Estado 3343/140, Consulta of 27 March 1636.

ODOARDO AND HIS ARMY PART WAYS

In these straitened circumstances, Odoardo decided to send his army home to Piacenza under Fabio Scotti and the Comte de Saint-Paul. In November he appointed Francesco Serafini to the key position of governor of the citadel of Piacenza, with orders to recruit new men by offering pardons to deserters, and to prepare the duchy to receive the army.[133] Créquy and Victor Amadeus gave Odoardo command over some French soldiers and, above all, over a force of 800 Savoyard horsemen led by Count Guido Villa, a Ferrarese nobleman in Savoyard service. Villa, who proved to be one of the most capable confederate officers at Valenza, had overall command of around 4,000 men. These troops were an assortment of French, Piedmontese, Monferrini, and about 800 'Lombards', meaning Parmans and sundry north Italians. Small detachments like this one had considerable mobility, and Villa expected to reach Piacenza in fewer than ten days. The force would have to scrounge some of its fodder and food from the villages it occupied en route. Villa's force left Breme on 19 December, crossed the Monferrato towards Alessandria, and then forded the Tanaro river a few kilometres upstream from the fortress. In order to inflict the maximum damage on the enemy, Villa's troops burned many of the mills on their march, although the inhabitants of some villages offered the usual 'refreshments' and so were spared.[134] Two more villages, San Giuliano and Caselli, were put to the torch in reprisal for the murder of a pair of French soldiers. The Alessandrian chronicler Ghilini claims that the force caught and killed 100 peasant militiamen en route to help Leganés, although this does not figure in other accounts and may simply constitute a rumour.

As usual, the Spanish were well informed of these movements, and so Leganés decided to move to block Villa's march with a composite force of professional soldiers and militiamen. The governor arrived at Tortona on the evening of 22 December, well ahead of the French, and sent his scouts to discern their path of advance. Villa's column advanced along the road towards the town, where they deployed into battle formation. They were almost directly opposite the town, whose cannon took aim at them while about 600 Spanish musketeers and some militia sprinkled them with lively fire from the opposite riverbank. After standing firm for two hours, Villa's little army began marching north, which convinced Leganés that Tortona itself was not the target. Leganés possessed about 2,000 infantry and 1,400 horsemen, along with some district militia. On the morning of 23 December he spread these forces out in small detachments along a 10-kilometre front behind the Scrivia river, skirmishing with Villa's cavalry patrols to prevent them from seizing the important fords. The Spanish force was forced to march parallel to the Franco-Savoyard one on the opposite bank of the river, leaving guards to defend the fords behind them, and so diminished as it proceeded downstream. Just above Castelnuovo Scrivia Villa's cavalry found a ford large enough for their purposes and the general drew his army up for battle. A few enemy musketeer companies arrayed just outside the town walls

---

[133] BCPLPc Ms Pallastrelli 126, Croniche Boselli, 113; Crescenzi Romani claims 1,200 'Parmans' and 2,000 Piedmontese; Leganés speaks of 3,000 infantry and 800 horse, sometimes with precise company sizes.

[134] Ghilini, *Annali di Alessandria*, 113.

prepared to block their crossing. Led by the officers in front, the Franco-Parman infantry lowered their pikes and forced their way through the water, which was up to their waist in the deepest spots. The vanguard chased their adversaries away from the bank and over a nearby ditch where they regrouped with the help of some cavalry. Villa pushed his cavalry to the fore and had them stand motionless in the face of musketry while reinforcements arrived from the second wave. Then the third wave crossed, and altogether they rushed the Spanish foot until the latter broke and took to their heels. The confederate cavalry chased them for about a kilometre, killing some and capturing others, until dusk induced them to fall back and regroup. An eyewitness to the action claimed that few of the confederate troops were killed outright, and even the defeated enemy lost fewer than 100 men captured, for many retreated into the walled town nearby.[135] Leganés' forces arrived later on and skirmished with the rearguard for several kilometres, before the allies disappeared into the darkness. The French left their wounded in a Franciscan monastery at Casei Gerola, and their dead by the side of the road. On Christmas Eve Leganés ordered the colonel, Marqués de Caracena (a future governor of Milan), to pursue the force and seize the laggards, and the local militia felled trees along the route to slow up the confederate march.[136] Lombard villagers murdered four of the soldiers, while they were in a drunken slumber, on Christmas night. The column waited a day to pick up stragglers at Broni, and then continued on to the first friendly town, Castel San Giovanni on Christmas Day.[137] In the aftermath, Leganés received detailed reports on the state of the Parman army, which identified the names of individual companies and their pitiful complement; he was certain that these forces were worn out and useless for combat in the short term.[138] The same report identified the lodging places of Villa's individual companies of horse and revealed French plans to reinforce these in the future.

Bereft of his army and merely killing time at Casale Monferrato, not trusting Victor Amadeus and having little faith in the abilities of Créquy, Odoardo decided to lay his case for command of the allied army with Louis XIII in person.[139] When

---

[135] Archivio di Stato di Modena (henceforth ASM), Ms della Biblioteca 188: Imprese militari; the witness appears to be a cavalry captain in Savoyard employ, Duke Savelli; The report to Duke Victor Amadeus claimed that 40 men in the confederate forces were killed in the action, and about a hundred wounded. ASFi, Miscellanea Medicea 183, f.328331.

[136] AGS Estado 3343/94 and 119, letter of 15 January 1636.

[137] For the Farnese account of this march see Crescenzi Romani, *Corona della Nobiltà d'Italia*, vol. 2, 298–302.

[138] AGS Estado 3343/119.

[139] Several contemporary or near-contemporary authors who were either eyewitnesses or working from official accounts of the visit have left us texts. The most detailed is the *Journal dressé par Mr de Chefdeville, gentilhomme servant de sa Majesté, de la Reception, Traitement et Cérémonies des visites faites à Edouard Duc et Prince de Parme, depuis le 7 février 1636 jusques au 20 mars qu'il partit de Fontainebleau pour son retour en Italie* (Paris, 1636). A manuscript version of this document is conserved in the ASPr, Casa e Corte Farnesiana ser. 2, 29, fasc. 2; Sieur de la Veletrie, *Harangue à Monseigneur le duc de Parme, sur les exercices militaires faictes par le Régiment des Gardes du Roy, en présence de sa Majesté et de son Altesse à Paris* (Paris, 1636); Montglat, *Mémoires de François de Paule de Clermont, Marquis de Montglat* (Amsterdam, 1727), t.1, 117–19; Vittorio Siri's account used an official relation of the visit drawn up by order of Cardinal Richelieu by the bishop of St Malo, Siri, *Memorie recondite di Vittorio Siri*, 389–95; Vicomte de Noailles, *Episodes de la guerre de Trente Ans: Le Cardinal de la Valette, lieutenant-général des armées du roi, 1635 à 1639* (Paris, 1906), 245–9.

Odoardo went off to Paris, Hémery warned Richelieu of the young duke's character, so that he would not be openly derided at the court. On 7 February, Louis dispatched several of his most important palace functionaries to Orléans together with a number of officials governing the royal table to make the necessary preparations. Odoardo arrived in Orléans on 16 February 1636, where he met the Gascon dignitaries Duke of Valette and the Duke of Duras, envoys of the king who would organize his reception. Like the layout of a palace where a visitor penetrates rooms of ascending importance before reaching the inner sanctum, the King of France and Cardinal Minister Richelieu used the entire district of Paris as a succession of antechambers to heighten the anticipation of the occasion. Richelieu instructed the mayor of Orléans to receive the duke as if he had been the king himself, although Odoardo did not merit a raised reception platform and streets lined with tapestries. He also ordered the city fathers and the chief dignitaries of the tribunals and religious establishments to attend, though they did not all obey. When Odoardo entered Orléans on 11 February, the bourgeois militia, 1,500 men strong, lined the streets on the way to the accommodations that had been set up for him. The duke descended from his coach dressed in the French style in a simple suit of scarlet adorned with silk lace, and accompanied by Fabio Scotti and his son, his personal secretary Jacques Gaufridy, and nine other noblemen from his states, along with some officers, his valets and waiters, about 15 other servants of his retinue, and his dwarf! After listening to speeches by the mayor and the king's emissaries, the duke climbed into the royal coach with his close collaborators to visit his lodgings, and the rest of his suite mounted the carriage behind. Once at his lodgings, the duke received visits from local dignitaries who presented him a large assortment of jams and jellies, pears (a French winter delicacy then in vogue), basins of green grapes, and bottles of wine from the district. At the banquet held in his honour, he was served like the king, with the king's maître d'hôtel conducting ceremonies with his baton, and all the sword-bearing gentlemen attendants with heads uncovered. All that was lacking was the royal *nef*, or the symbolic decorative royal tablepiece. Odoardo's retinue and the king's protocol master dined at a second table nearby. The next morning, Odoardo proceeded to hear a high mass (that is, with music and incense), where he met the rector of the university together with a dozen or so leading professors, who gave speeches in French in his honour, followed by a delegation of German students who speechified in Latin and French. In the church of Sainte Croix Odoardo sat near the altar, where the seated canons of the chapter greeted him ceremoniously.

A royal coach soon carried Odoardo to Toury, about 40 kilometres closer to Paris, where, by royal order, the chief officials of Orléans paid him their compliments as they had done once before for the Duke of Savoy. Workers decorated his chamber with tapestries, and surrounded the bed with curtains of crimson damask trimmed with gold and silver. The next day, the inhabitants of Étampes greeted the duke with a reception of chief dignitaries at the town gates, and streets lined with militiamen in arms. On these successive days, the distance travelled diminished gradually. At Chilly Odoardo met a royal delegation that joined his cortège with 25 coaches. The duke met other dignitaries soon after, led by the Duke of Mercoeur and the Duke of Beaufort, peers of the realm, at Bourg-la-Reine just outside Paris, who took him in royal coaches to his lodgings at the Louvre, accompanied by numerous gentlemen in another 55 six-horse coaches. Odoardo's entry into the city was marked by yet more pomp, and, in the courtyard of the Louvre, crack regiments of Swiss and French guards lined his path, as they did for the king, with the difference that their drums were silent. Then, in the great reception hall of the Louvre, Odoardo was met by the captain of the Gardes du Corps who led him to the waiting monarch.

Louis met Odoardo in his room, made several steps forward (an important courtesy) and embraced him 'tenderly', in front of a crowd of powerful people, like his brother and heir to the throne Prince Gaston d'Orléans, the archbishop of Reims, and Marshal Harcourt. After half an hour, the king led him to the queen in her apartment, where Odoardo made a deep bow and kissed the bottom of her robe, before a crowd of princesses and ladies of the highest rank. Louis then bid Odoardo to sit himself on a folding chair placed next to the king's armchair, 'but not on the same line.'[140] After half an hour of polite conversation, pages of the king's Grande Écurie led our duke to his chamber. Fabio Scotti was quartered nearby and the rest of his suite lodged in the Luxembourg palace belonging to the exiled Queen Mother, Maria de'Medici. The king conferred on the Duke of Parma a set of pages and lackeys for his service and a priest to say mass, but refused him the master of ceremonies with the baton, which, in a royal palace, was reserved for the king himself. The next day, 17 February, Odoardo was taken to the royal residence of Saint-Germain en Laye outside the western suburbs of the city, where he was greeted by the king and the queen, followed by visits to Monsieur (Gaston d'Orléans) and, finally, Cardinal Richelieu himself. These last two personages paid him complimentary return visits. This last appointment was an important one, for our Italian warlord and the bellicose cardinal retreated into the corner next to the duke's bed where they remained for half an hour, talking business in a very low voice. After this, Odoardo accompanied the cardinal to the door of his coach.

On these first days, everyone wished to see what the prince looked like, for credibility could be read in his face, his '*bonne mine*'. There was, in the meantime, a full programme of things to do and see in Paris. On 19 February Odoardo toured the corridors of the Louvre and the salon of antiquities, which, in the seventeenth century, was not open to the public. From there he visited, together with Fabio Scotti, the theatre that Cardinal Richelieu had built in his palace next to the Louvre, to watch a play and a ballet, in the company of the ambassador of Savoy and a secretary of state. The next day he visited the Sorbonne, where he was asked to listen to the defence of theses which had been dedicated to him. In Odoardo's honour, Louis staged a ballet and danced in it himself, on 22 February. On 23 February, the king invited Odoardo to the Tuileries palace where a horse ballet or carousel unfolded for his entertainment, after which he watched the Guards Regiment perform drill. The second week, Odoardo was invited to a banquet at Versailles, which was then a royal residence-cum-hunting lodge, not yet the massive palace erected by Louis's son and successor in the 1660s. Odoardo sat at a table

---

[140] Noailles, *Episodes de la guerre de Trente Ans*, 245–9.

near the king on a folding chair of red velvet: 12 serving gentleman presented successively as many platters of food to each ruler. He sat there first with bared head, but the king made him replace his hat (another important courtesy implying equality) before commencing. After the banquet, Odoardo rode with the king in his coach to the Saint-Germain palace, where he slept in the apartment of the Comte de Soissons, a prince of the blood. Over the next few days, Odoardo was able to have brief interviews with the major figures of the realm. On 28 February, at a dinner in the palace of the Cardinal Richelieu, Odoardo met another of his supporters, the papal nuncio to the French king, a low-born but very clever Roman priest, papal diplomat, and ex-army captain named Giulio Mazzarini, who, in a few years, would wield more power as first minister in France than Richelieu himself.

Odoardo's haughtiness and arrogance soon made themselves felt, however. As examples of *maladresse* quickly commented upon at the court, he neglected to accompany the dukes who escorted him beyond the door of his chamber, and omitted to offer his hand (to be kissed) to some of the noblemen in attendance. Soon the great lords of the realm were heard to grumble that they had to '*céder le pas*' (Odoardo not allowing them to walk on his right side) to the duke, whose ancestors were reigning princes only a brief hundred years. In silent protest they made themselves scarce, and few of those who remained observed Richelieu's prescriptions on protocol. The cardinal was keen on discussing policy with his young guest. On 5 March, Richelieu made a second visit to Odoardo, spending hours in conference with the duke, probably in the presence of Fabio Scotti and Gaufridy. One important request from Odoardo concerned the conferral upon him of the Royal Order of the Saint-Esprit, leaving it up to the king to decide which specific rank he might hold. Mazarin placed this idea in his head as some small compensation for having returned the collars of the Golden Fleece to Madrid. Louis did not respond quickly to the request, for every honour conferred on Odoardo made some other allied prince envious.[141]

On 7 March, another visitor arrived in Paris, Duke Bernhard of Weimar, junior brother of a German prince, who commanded a real army in Germany in French service. Bernhard's visit to the Duke of Parma was to have been reciprocated the following day, but Odoardo refused to give the German general his right hand, just as he had refused it to the other dukes who paid him courtesy calls, and so Bernhard called off the appointment. Instead, Odoardo received the Duke of La Force, the Cardinal of Valette and the Comte d'Harcourt, all field marshals in active service, who would be his brothers in arms, so to speak, but not his equals. Louis and Richelieu made much of Odoardo's status as a sovereign prince (a status he could not credibly claim in Italy itself) and denied the Duke of Weimar similar treatment on the basis of it. When the German heard that Louis bid Odoardo put his hat back on in the king's presence, he demanded the same treatment. Bernhard (accurately) protested that he was of a house that had sprung from emperors while the Duke of Parma was merely the descendant of a pope's bastard.[142]

---

[141] AAE Paris, Correspondance Politique Parme 1, fol. 151, 27 February 1636.
[142] Montglat, *Mémoires*, 119.

By the middle of March, it was time for Odoardo to return to Italy and wait for the army he had been promised. Reciprocal gift-giving marked this phase. Odoardo had already received half a dozen choice war horses from the cardinal, outfitted with velvet tack and saddles embroidered in gold and silver, as well as swords, and an assortment of French gallantries, like beaver felt hats from Canada, English ribbons and stockings, bottles of perfume, and gold watches. Odoardo gave the cardinal in return a gold chain worth almost 2,000 livres (a Paris artisan might earn 200 livres in a year), and bestowed other gifts on each of the nobles who were in attendance on him. The king was not to be outdone, presenting through an intermediary a diamond chain containing 58 large and 177 small stones, reportedly worth 150,000 livres, along with 12 gold watches enamelled in many colours, two dozen jewel boxes (*étuis*), scarves embroidered with gold and silver, English ribbon again, a dozen pairs of gloves similarly embroidered in gold and silver, and other beautiful trifles. Fabio Scotti was not forgotten either. He received a diamond worth almost 10,000 livres and a colonel's commission for the army of Italy. Just before leaving, our duke met again with Richelieu, but also with the powerful superintendent of finances, Bullion, entrusted with finding money for the enterprise. Then, on 18 March, he took the road home. At Fontainebleau he encountered a hunting team sent by the king to help him chase boar in the great woods there, where he killed five of the animals in the space of three hours. Then, presenting gifts to the officials who had escorted him throughout his time in France, he left on post horses and made rapid progress in the direction of Piedmont, where he arrived on 1 April. A new campaign awaited him, and this time he would be at the head of a proper army.

4

Parman Sideshow

THE SINEWS OF WAR

Odoardo Farnese, who was an archetypal 'roi de guerre', did not compel his subjects to go to war on his behalf. Nor were they numerous among the soldiers of the 1635 campaign. The duke did, however expect them to pay for his war. He could accurately claim that, compared to many other European states, his subjects had hitherto escaped lightly. If, in France or Spain, there were two or three years of war for every year of peace, in the lucky principalities of north-central Italy war clouds usually assembled quickly on foreign horizons, caused a brief flurry of turbulence, and then dispersed again. So princes spent the taxes from these rich lands on palaces and operas, on spectacles, church ceremonies, Jesuit colleges, and sometimes too on water control, and capital improvements on the land and livestock.

The tax machinery devised over many generations was fairly sophisticated by seventeenth-century standards. The Farnese system that the dukes inherited from Milan comprised of two separate tax regimes, one for persons of wealth and influence who lived in cities, but who owned land in the rural *contado* (the *civile*) and another for peasants who lived on the land they tilled (the *rurale*). City people drew revenues from the countryside but paid taxes in the city, whose exemptions were more numerous. They often enjoyed privileges, exemptions, and immunities in the villages where they spent much of their time, for example, not being subject to the magistrates dispensing justice in the name of the feudal lords. This privilege often extended to their employees and servants too. However, in contrast to countries like France, noble status was no impediment to paying taxes proportionate to a person's wealth, and even feudatories had to pay large sums to the treasury for both feudal dues they owed to the Farnese, and on the property (called allodial) they owned but which was not registered under their feudal title.[1] Both the *civile* and the *rurale* tax assessments were based on a great roster of property assessment (land, buildings, and livestock) called the Estimo or Compartito. When the Farnese acquired the duchies of Parma and Piacenza, they introduced some refinements to the tax machinery that aimed to harvest a greater share of the considerable wealth produced there. Duke Ottavio's revised Estimo of 1558 was quite sophisticated in the way it tabulated the possession of livestock of various kinds (only excepting fowl), and differentiated among the different kinds of farmlands by

---

[1] ASPr, Governo Farnesiano, Mastri Farnesiani 32, 547: Tassa sui feudatari per li beni feudali e allodiali.

location, access to irrigation water, and the kinds of crops grown. In 1596 Duke Ranuccio I inaugurated, no doubt on the model of Milan, a great mercantile Estimo that assessed all kinds of commercial and manufacturing capital. Like most taxes in early modern Europe, officials established the entries on the basis of self-reported holdings. While this might seriously under-report the wealth of subjects, the government encouraged people to make anonymous accusations of neighbours they believed were defrauding the tax collector, with the denouncer pocketing a third of any subsequent fines. Another reform of 1631 tried to close all the loopholes in order to make tax evasion more difficult.[2]

Despite the long era of peace, social elites in the early seventeenth century withdrew their money from commerce and manufacturing in Piacenza, the economic hub of western Emilia. With the onset of general war in northern Europe after 1620, the richest merchants were no longer just interested in commerce. Merchants and artisans sank their savings into farmland, whose availability on the market reflected, in part, the growing difficulties of peasants to make a living, for they did not sell their land unless there was no other choice. The richest merchants also turned increasingly to tax collection, where they could still make substantial profits of over 10 per cent per annum.[3]

No one suspected that the economic decline would last for a century, and I have never encountered in our young duke the slightest sensitivity towards economic issues. By April 1633, when he issued the first recruiting patents, Odoardo had been resolved to go to war at the first opportunity. From that moment onward, he multiplied the burdens on all his subjects, urban and rural, feudatory and peasant. The imposition of new taxes corresponded with increased garrisons in key places. In Piacenza authorities established a guard post in the city square, lodged soldiers on the ground floor of City Hall, and increased the number of guards and sentries at each city gate. They then hired workers to repair the walls of the citadel and the city. The brick walls and bastions were only the most visible feature of a seventeenth-century fortification system. Moats needed additional excavation, and crews proceeded to landscape the outer edge of the ditch in order to reduce the part of the wall visible from the outside. Along this edge (the counterscarp) they piled up earth to form a parapet or covered way. Additional triangular earthworks called ravelins, appended to the exterior of the ditch, served to keep the enemy farther away from the wall. Normal rainfall and settling over time tended to erase these efforts, which had to be renewed at great expense. The approach of war accelerated this spadework, and crews erected palisades around the exterior as an additional obstacle.

The presence of so many foreign soldiers in Piacenza was itself enormously disruptive. Francesco Serafini read out the rules of behaviour towards the citizenry to the troops assembled in the main square in April 1633. Concentrating hundreds, then

---

[2] Paolo Subacchi, 'L'imposizione fiscale in età Farnesiana: formazione degli estimi piacentini', *Archivio Storico per le Province Parmensi*, ser. 4, 44 (1992): 151–73.

[3] Paolo Subacchi, *La Ruota della Fortuna: Arricchimento e promozione sociale in una città padana in età moderna* (Milan, 1996), 115–22.

Fig. 4.1. Merchants' seat in Piacenza, *c.*1750. Merchants were among the principal victims of Odoardo's ambitions.

Fig. 4.2. Farnese palace in Piacenza, *c.*1750. The late 16th-century residence served as a refuge for the ducal couple, and their military advisors.

thousands, of foreign soldiers in the cities brought public order to the verge of collapse, as in April 1634 when the Barnabite fathers raised the alarm against soldiers found plundering ex-votos and other precious offerings from the tomb of St Brigida in their church. Citizens fetched their swords and the pole-arms they kept at home, when the soldiers went too far in their provocations.[4] It was not mentioned whether

---

[4] On the use and significance of private weaponry of townspeople, see B. Ann Tlusty, *The Martial Ethic in Early Modern Germany* (Basingstoke and New York, 2011).

the culprit soldiers were Protestants, but many of the foreign troops were unreconstructed Calvinists fresh from the wars of religion in France. Chief amongst them was Sergeant-Major Nicart, who declared to the merchants on 19 February 1634 that the city square was now military space, and that if they wanted to continue selling their wares from their stalls, then they would have to pay stiff fees to support his troops. His soldiers knocked over the tables of anyone who protested. The governor of Piacenza sided with the soldiers and banished the traders from the square.[5] By March 1635 there were so many contingents of soldiers in Piacenza, that it was necessary to dispatch 800 of them to the smaller towns of Borgo San Donnino, Fiorenzuola, and Cortemaggiore. But this just spread the disruption across a wider portion of the duchy. People voiced similar complaints against the soldiers in the Parma garrison too. Soldiers there almost rioted in July 1635, when they learned that the gate guards had priority over them for pay.[6]

As soon as work commenced on the fortifications of Piacenza, Odoardo and his ministers began seeking new ways to cover the substantial costs incurred. The Farnese states were relatively rich by European standards, and revenues in 1622 had amounted to about 750,000 scudi, or roughly between four and five million lire. This income collapsed in the aftermath of the plague of 1630, for much of the revenue relied on consumption taxes, but it was certainly on the mend after 1631. It was still not enough to pay for a great war, however, and so new taxes were necessary.[7] On 14 July 1633, the duke imposed a new tax of 10 lire each on chimneys, which, like most imposts, sought to make richer people pay. This was a substantial sum equal to more than a month's supply of grain for an adult, levied both on the city and the countryside. Officials did not usually raise taxes by increasing the percentage people would pay relative to their property assessment (or Estimo). Instead, the duke and his officials sought to lay the taxes on people who showed signs of well-being; chimneys were easy for officials to count and almost impossible to hide. There was a real danger, however, that preparations for war would reduce the tax base by disrupting normal business patterns. In February 1635 Odoardo summoned the bankers and merchants of Piacenza and demanded from them a large sum of money to help pay for the war, 'which made them confused and afraid'.[8] By the summer, the bankers, speaking on behalf of the majority of their colleagues who came from other parts of Italy, notified the duke that their fair would no longer be held in Piacenza.

Odoardo's own subjects were not all compliant. In Busseto, which was administered separately from Parma and Piacenza as the 'Pallavicino State', people refused to disburse all that ducal officials asked. The court expected the town government

---

[5] BCPLPc, Ms Pallastrelli 126, Croniche o diario del Rev. Sgr Benedetto Boselli, rettore della chiesa di San Martino di Piacenza, 1620–1670, 99–104.

[6] ASPr, Governo Farnesiano, Interno 383, 17 July 1635.

[7] Gian Luca Podestà, 'Dal delitto politico alla politica del delitto (Parma 1545–1611)', in *Complots et conjurations dans l'Europe moderne*, ed. Y-M. Bercé and E. Fasano Guarini (Rome, 1996), 679–720. The imprecision of the figure depends in part on the unspecified type of scudo; the silver scudo was worth only 5 lire, while the gold coin of the same designation was worth 7.25.

[8] Benedetto Boselli, *Croniche*, 104.

not only to feed the soldiers in winter quarters (in addition to the local militia), but also to buy more weapons, and to pay for the new earthwork fortifications. Fabio Scotti had to come to Busseto to exhort the population of this district to raise 20,000 ducatoni, or 210,000 lire, an enormous sum even for the prosperous district it was.[9] The chief complainants were ecclesiastics, who were extremely numerous, all highly literate, and recruited from among the chief families of the state. Priests could not legally be taxed without a prior agreement between the state and the Pope, and even then churchmen were not subject to the jurisdiction of state magistrates and tax collectors. The clergy proved to be more than a match for the King of Spain in nearby Milan, where the Catholic king first tried, in 1617, to have clerics participate in financing fortifications works in time of war against Savoy. The Pope did not refuse his cooperation outright, but even after proposing a sum that the clergy might pay (much inferior to the one demanded by the king), it was necessary to revise the existing clerical Estimo of 1558. Furthermore, even after the Pope conceded the principle of levying money on churchmen, the bishops of Lombardy and the other clergy stalled, and fussed, and appealed the imposition until Madrid gave up. Despite the onset of a much more dangerous war in 1635, the clergy would not willingly pay taxes, and while the king and his ministers threatened to lodge soldiers on farms owned by the Church (perhaps one-fifth of all the property in Lombardy), they would not take the fatal step.[10]

The Farnese bishops were not supine either. When Savoyard soldiers took up lodgings in farmhouses owned by the clergy around Busseto, or moved in with the priests themselves, the vicar-general of the diocese of Borgo San Donnino decreed that they had all incurred papal excommunication.[11] Duke Ranuccio I set great store on expressions of conspicuous piety, placing himself at the head of the devout. His propagandist secretary, the courtier Ranuccio Pico, developed the theme of the holy prince who renounced secular aims in the pursuit of loftier goals.[12] Warlike Odoardo considered that all his subjects, including ecclesiastics, should be liable to pay for soldiers' lodgings, should not be liable for exemptions, and should pay new taxes, but, on 3 August 1633, the bishop of Piacenza excommunicated his judicial officials and their servants for violating church immunity.[13] Despite holding his duchy as a fief of the Papal States, Odoardo was not afraid of the consequences of high-handed actions against priests. Some of the complaints of the clergy surface in the surviving records of the ducal administration, such as a cleric in the district around Piacenza complaining of the soldiers billeted in his house. The clergy complained that the duchy's Jews (a few hundred people at most, based largely in

---

[9] Marco Boscarelli, *Contributi alla storia degli Stati Pallavicino di Busseto e di Cortemaggiore (secc. XV–XVII)* (Parma, 1992), 96; there was a shift in the value of the ducatone between 1635 (9 lire) and 1636 (10.5 lire), an official devaluation meant to facilitate financing the war.

[10] Massimo Carlo Giannini, 'Risorse del principe e risorse dei sudditi: fisco, clero e comunità di fronte al problema della difesa commune nello stato di Milano (1618–1660)', *Annali di Storia moderna e contemporanea*, 6 (2000): 173–225.

[11] Boscarelli, *Contributi alla storia*, 89.

[12] Adriano Prosperi, 'Dall'investitura papale alla santificazione del potere', in *Le Corti farnesiane di Parma e Piacenza (1545–1622)*, ed. M. A. Romani (Rome, 1978), 161–88.

[13] Benedetto Boselli, *Croniche*, 99.

Cortemaggiore) had obtained a universal exemption from billeting in exchange for an annual payment of about 19,000 lire, which was true. Ducal officials allowed Jews to sue soldiers who owed them money, without delays or complications from the ducal administration, and to seize the soldiers' property as long as they did not touch the weapons or other military stores.[14] Odoardo and his spouse Duchess Margherita, who dealt with these recriminations after September 1635, both gave the Catholic clergy short shrift. The duchess, in a very harshly worded letter to the bishop, complained that obstruction from the priests came from a few rogues (*scelerati*) whose egotism imperiled the state in its hour of danger. She assured the bishop that, even without his support, she would take the necessary measures to silence the strident voices arguing in favour of church immunity: 'Since these matters are so important, the normal rules do not apply…' Her only compromise would be to provide the bishop with the names of seven or eight chief troublemakers; he could then have them arrested by ecclesiastical police. In the end, these priests were simply rounded up and cast into ducal dungeons. One letter from a ducal functionary suggested letting one of them off for good behaviour, for no one had yet formulated any charges against him after confining him to a cell for a month.[15] The duchess ordered the execution of two priests from Monticelli in the district of Piacenza on 25 March 1636, which was a very rare procedure in the seventeenth century.[16] Ironically, the clergy could have carried the tax burden without too much trouble. We have a list of the salt tax revenues from the Parma customs bureau, with the price paid by different social groups. The total exemptions granted to pious institutions during the war on this lucrative government monopoly amounted to merely 3 per cent of the total revenue of 764,732 lire.[17]

Despite the widespread hard feelings towards the soldiers, most people expected the problems to ease once they marched away, towards Milan. When a decree of July 1635 ordered everyone to bring their horses to Parma so that ducal functionaries might inspect them and select some for hauling military stores, subjects understood that the temporary loss of their animals would help rid the territory of the soldiers. Soon after the army's departure from Piacenza, the military governor of Parma announced the news of the great victory at Pontecurone, and held a celebratory *Te Deum* ceremony in the Farnese dynastic church of the Steccata. The governor himself walked barefoot in the procession to thank heaven for its providential aid to the duchy. Victory was surely at hand.[18] Likewise, in Piacenza, the people greeted with relief the disappearance of the army down the road and the first news of victory. In the interim, an unpaid army of 2,300 citizens, including a sprinkling of old soldiers with service in Flanders and Germany, guarded the city under the orders of

---

[14] ASPr, Governo Farnesiano, Carteggio Interno 383, 19 September 1635.
[15] ASPr, Governo Farnesiano, Carteggio Interno 384, 3 February 1636.
[16] Ettore Carra, *Le esecuzioni capitali a Piacenza e la Confraternità della Torricella dal XVI al XIX secolo* (Piacenza, 1991), 69.
[17] ASPr, Governo Farnesiano, Carteggio Interno 384, 11 October 1637.
[18] Andrea Pugolotti, *Libro di Memorie. Cronaca parmense del XVII secolo*, ed. Sergio Di Noto (Parma, 2005), 92.

those local noblemen who had not left town.[19] September saw the first large call-up of the peasant militia to clear the roads of deserters, to cover the borders, and to raise earthwork fortifications around towns like Borgonovo and Castel San Giovanni. The duchess and her advisers had the good sense not to launch raids against neighbouring towns under Spanish jurisdiction, in order not to invite reprisals.[20]

The nature of the war changed completely at the year's end, when the organized remnants of the ducal army returned to Piacenza under the strong escort of Piedmontese cavalry under Count Guido Villa. Now the troops and the reinforcements would have to be wintered and refreshed for a new campaign in the spring. Officials instructed the billeting committee in Piacenza to prepare lodgings for returning infantry in the city monasteries, where they might recover their strength from the dangerous forced march they had just undertaken. The cavalry was posted to the villages around the city where there was fodder and stabling for their mounts, but the requirements for so many troopers and animals (between 800 and 1,200 cavalrymen) meant that they would have to be spread across a large area. In the absence of French help, in the absence even of Duke Odoardo, the duchy would have to cope on its own. Large villages and small towns would now have to be garrisoned in order for the Farnese to hold on to their own territory, and to stockpile food and forage to keep it safe from enemy marauders. Odoardo's younger brother Francesco Maria, a mere teenager, accompanied some officers and engineers to determine what could be done in Colorno, a Farnese residence close to the Po and near the border with Modena. The experts decided to raise a parapet behind the castle wall and build some platforms for cannon. Work on that scale would employ 300 (militia) soldiers digging under the direction of an engineer for 10 or 12 days, while a company of cavalry patrolled the roads nearby to forestall a surprise attack. About 1,000 lire would suffice to cover the cost, over and above subsistence costs for the men. These works would not include defending the town itself, however, which would cost too much money and tie down too many precious soldiers.[21]

Citizens were forced to accept soldiers lodged on their properties in the city and in the rural hinterland, which led to daily litigation between politically influential landlords and the officers, whose first loyalty was to the men in their companies.[22] The newly hired soldiers in Parma were very numerous, so the city government responsible for their lodgings was reluctant to grant tax exemptions to anyone. The government was also on the lookout for straw, a precious commodity in wartime, for the needs of the cavalry. Troops in winter quarters did not receive their wages, but they still needed to be fed *like soldiers* if they were not to desert.[23] The records

---

[19] Giovanni Pietro Crescenzi Romani, *Corona della nobiltà d'Italia, ovvero compendio dell'Istorie delle famiglie illustri*, 2 vols. (Bologna, 1639–42), vol. 2, 283.

[20] Benedetto Boselli, *Croniche*, 112.

[21] ASPr, Governo Farnesiano, Fabbriche Ducali e Fortificazioni 9, fasc.1, Letter to Principe Francesco Maria Farnese, 16 April 1636.

[22] ASPr, Governatore e Comunità di Parma, 23–4, 13 March 1636.

[23] For a glimpse of soldiers' diets nearby, see Paul Delsalle, François Pernot, and Marie-France Romand, 'Peut-on connaître la vie quotidienne des soldats ?', in *Hommes d'armes et gens de guerre du Moyen Age au XVIIe siècle: Franche Comté de Bourgogne et comté de Montbéliard*, ed. Arnold Preneel and Paul Delsalle (Besançon, 2007), 183–200.

we have focus on the need to provide the soldiers with food and the horses with fodder, this last perhaps more difficult to come by. In the space of a couple of weeks the Savoyards cost the treasury over 18,000 bread rations, consisting of 24 ounces of bread per ration. Horses and mules devoured about 40 pounds of fodder each, every winter day, for 374.5 cartloads. Each *staro* of wheat (a *staro* fed one adult for about two months) cost the treasury about 23 lire, and mixed grains (*mestura*) 15 lire. The duke acquired most of this grain and flour from a handful of leading bakers and grain merchants, who, in Parma, seem to have produced the loaves in ducal ovens. The court majordomo, Count Cesare Sanvitale controlled the accounts for these indispensable transactions. The Parma garrison cost the treasury almost 600,000 lire over the duration of the war. The treasury disbursed money to the garrison perhaps four or five times a month, but in a very irregular manner. We have details about the winter quarters for French soldiers in the large village of Fornovo, normally inhabited by about 400 or 500 people, not counting those scattered across farms in the district. In March and April 1636 Fornovo was host to 178 French infantrymen, who occupied 31 houses, including the village hospital, the house of the parish priest, one belonging to a Jesuit father, and two more belonging to nobles. There were roughly six to eight soldiers per house, but 20 soldiers lodged in the villa of *casa* Garimberti. The soldiers consumed 300 to 400 bread rations daily, plus 450 lbs of meat every day(!), and generous provisions of wine as well. Even if the soldiers were sharing these rations with grooms, servants, women, and others, the army diet compared very favourably to that of the peasants in whose houses they stayed. This diet was more liberal than that which was mandated by French regulations.[24] The soldiers living in houses between Fornovo and Berceto in the mountains nearby needed beds and mattresses, bedding, tableware, and kitchenware, and required storerooms for their provisions of meat and wine. The ducal overseer or *commissario* for the mountain villages noted the provisions of straw, grain, beans, flour, wine, and various kinds of meat—some pork and salami, but notably salt beef, lamb, and goat—along with eggs, cheese, oil, lard, salt, pepper, and candles. There was even some rose oil (*olio rosato*) provided for treating wounds. The total cost of the lodgings, which included haulage fees, came to about 14,000 lire. The accounts for lodging fewer than 200 men for four weeks were only settled in 1641, about five years after the expenditure.[25] Complaints from Fiorenzuola following the arrival of the Savoyards emphasized the excessive expectations of the more than 150 soldiers, beyond the bread, soup, meat, and wine the town was expected to provide for them. The officers especially, various *marchesi*, counts, barons, and other *cavalieri*, had high standards.[26] In more genteel places, like Parma, the merchants and gentlemen took in the officers as their guests and then lodged the troopers around Parma in the hostelries and

---

[24] Brian Sandberg, *Warrior Pursuits: Noble Culture and Civil Conflict in Early Modern France* (Baltimore, 2010), 97 and 236.
[25] ASPr, Comune 1738, Truppe francesi 1636.
[26] ASPr, Governo Farnesiano, Carteggio Interno 384, 28 January 1636.

monasteries at the city's expense.[27] Cavalry were much more expensive to maintain; lodging four companies in Piacenza totalling just 200 troopers with their horses was expected to cost 816 lire every day, a sum which would have to be allocated to the *estimi* of both the city and its rural hinterland.[28]

It was clear that the expenses were going to be enormous. Since tax revenue would not be enough to cover the expenditures, the duke would have to borrow money too. Odoardo mortgaged his Lazio fiefs to the hilt, making an initial loan by using them as collateral for 915,000 scudi, then remortgaging them later to Roman bankers for another 700,000.[29] Punitive and emergency impositions helped to narrow the gulf between revenues and expenditures. Early in 1636, the duke and duchess decreed the confiscation of all the property and effects of the late Troilo Rossi, Count of San Secondo, to the ducal treasury. In a normal year, these assets (worth 5 million lire after deducting the debts) might have been auctioned off, but in wartime there were no takers.[30] The order then went out in January to raise another enormous sum of money as a special tax, on top of prior impositions, calculated pro rata on the *estimo civile* and *rurale* of Piacenza and Parma, for 120,000 and 80,000 ducatoni respectively, over 2 million lire, roughly half the normal tax revenues for a year. A committee of eight notables in each city sorted out appeals concerning land lost in erosion, land tied up in dowries, or land transferred to ecclesiastics in pious legacies, or still other lands involved in pending lawsuits, which were all cases where the nominal landlord did not control the incomes from those properties.[31] People of every status, whose political loyalties would be subject to ducal scrutiny, had to pay this enormous surtax. The feudatories undertook to provide a share of it, although the duchess allowed them to divide it up amongst themselves and pay their portion separately. The merchants of Parma were assigned 6,000 of the 80,000 ducatoni demanded from the entire territory.[32] Hundreds of shopkeepers had their assets assessed by their own guild officials, who served as intermediaries.[33] Once the duchy came under intense military pressure after the summer, ducal officials imposed a really crippling tax of 5 soldi on each window, levied monthly.[34] Raising these sums was made more difficult by the beginnings of raiding around the edges of the duchy by Spanish troops, although Parman and Savoyard troops did their share of damage too. The magistrates of towns like Soragna, which had already suffered from these, wished to deduct the money they were assigned from the unpaid corvées, and other lodging expenditures they had already spent money on.[35] People who could not or would

---

[27] Ms Parmense 737, L'Heroe d'Italia, overo Vita del Sereniss.o Odoardo Farnese il Grande, d'Ippolito Calandrini, 656.
[28] ASPr, Governo Farnesiano, Milizie 1: Istruzioni, Modo di tenere la cavalleria in Piacenza (1635).
[29] Giovanni Drei, *I Farnese: Grandezza e decadenza di una dinastia italiana* (Rome, 1954), 207.
[30] ASPr, Casa e Corte Farnesiana 48, Confisca del feudo di San Secondo dal 1636 al 1650.
[31] ASPr, Governatore e Comunità di Parma, 23–4, 4 February and 13 March 1636.
[32] ASPr, Governo Farnesiano, Carteggio Interno 384, 22 March 1636.
[33] ASPr, Archivio Comunale Parma 1763, Estimo commerciale 1636.
[34] ASPr, Archivio Comunale Parma 331, 8 October 1636.
[35] ASPr, Governatore e Comunità di Parma, 23–4, 28 March 1636.

not pay their assigned portion, town officials complained, were subject to visits by constables, who seized property from them and inflicted legal costs too, which they wanted suspended at least until the end of the war. Given the enormous sums demanded in a time of economic crisis, the money did not materialize immediately, but was collected in small installments.

'The prince who has rich vassals still has the wherewithal to fight a war.'[36] But in addition to money, the duchy was going to have to mobilize all the resources of the population and sweep aside any claims of privilege or exemption in the process. On 17 February, the duchess proclaimed that all the citizens (that is, the notables) were eligible for military service, which meant that all must remain at home so that the local captains could enlist them, regardless of their rank.[37] Neighbourhood officials had just finished establishing a census of mouths to feed in Parma, in case of siege. Powerful people, or those who worked for the court, sometimes told the census takers to go away, but, by the summer, even feudatories had to provide exact lists of everyone dwelling in their houses. After 2 June, the gentlemen and artisans of Parma and Piacenza, issued weapons from the ducal magazines, stood sentry on the ramparts.[38] By August, when the Spanish forces began to attack in earnest, the duchess added the feudatories to the persons conscripted for duty, with nobles taking responsibility for guarding gates and ramparts with district militiamen. The gates were particularly important, not only because they could be surprised by the enemy and the city sacked as a consequence, but because tax collectors levied tolls and tariffs there on goods entering or leaving the city. The state needed subjects of wealth and influence to challenge rich and well-born people who were tempted to commit tax fraud, but it was not a task the nobles relished. Odoardo threatened powerful people of the duchy with confinement to a fortress if they lacked diligence in carrying out their functions. Feudatories and members of the ducal staff were, at least, exempt from labour corvées on the city earthworks. Not so mere citizens, who were drafted by neighbourhood officials for unpaid guard and labour services. On 1 June, the court ordered all the priests and friars of Parma to take up arms to defend the city, under their own officers. After being issued weapons, they took up positions along the city wall. People noted with bemusement how the Benedictine monks of San Giovanni Evangelista, whose city monastery was one of the richest in all Italy, worked at the fortifications with digging tools in hand. The same clerics tended their city garden (which still exists) with their own hands by virtue of the monastic rule.[39] On 24 August, everyone was ordered to present their horses, whether saddle, carriage, or pack animals, for inspection and possible requisition. Early in September, officials ordered peasants taking refuge in the city to report to work on the fortifications too, on pain of expulsion and confiscation of their goods.

As the enemy forces attacked both duchies in the summer of 1636 the available manpower, labour, and money were clearly inadequate. Full pay for the soldiers was

---

[36] BPPr, Ms Parmense 737, Calandrini, 'L'Heroe d'Italia', 793.
[37] ASPr, Gridario 32/46, 17 February 1636.
[38] Pugolotti, *Libro di Memorie*, 96.
[39] BPPr, Ms Parmense 737, Calandrini, 'L'Heroe d'Italia', 692.

a thing of the past, which disappointed French troops in particular. As noted earlier in this chapter, Richelieu just allotted the men the bare minimum they needed to survive. Their captains reached into their own pockets to recruit the men and outfit both men and horses.[40] In Parma and Piacenza the captains hoped to receive some *good* money from time to time to keep their soldiers happy. Early modern money was based on coins consisting of some quantity of precious metal. Foreign coins were happily accepted as currency if they contained the desired consistency, and both bankers and merchants were wise to the relative merits of specific denominations, both domestic and foreign. The basic money of account was the lire of 20 soldi, but there were no coins in that specific amount; rather, mints struck coins consisting of odd multiples or fractions of lire. The most common business coins were the scudo (7.25 lire), and the ducatone (10.5 lire). The ability to demand payment in good coin was an expression of power, and foreign soldiery accepted no less, but the little duchy's resources could no longer cope with the demands for it. The court evaluated its incompressible expenditures in Parma at 80,000 lire per month, for the needs of the ducal family, the court officials, the garrisons of the citadel, and some outlying castles defended by professional soldiers. The combined members of the ducal family and their immediate staff required 17,000 lire, as much as the requirements of the citadel, the guards at the gates, and three infantry companies combined, but it was less than the operating expenses of two cavalry companies (19,000 lire). There was only 40,000 lire left in the treasury, and the state could only hope to raise 35,000 more from local revenues. Expedients were necessary to cover the shortfall. In December the ducal treasurer, Dr Pietro Rossi, borrowed silver plate weighing 78 lbs, then had the objects melted down and recast as coins to pay the foreign soldiers. The same month, an unnamed Jew from Mantua paid 17,600 lire in good coin for 'useless' objects from the ducal wardrobe sold to him.[41] These efforts were bedeviled by the appearance of counterfeit coins in Parma. The treasurer Rossi pinpointed a likely culprit in May, a French soldier who lodged in an inn by the central bridge, who passed off counterfeit large-denomination Genoese coins to grocers to buy eggs and cheese, and received proper coins as his change.[42]

A common expedient was to invent new monetary signs, that is, strike coins made of copper or bronze that bore values much higher than the metallic worth of the piece. The French field marshal, Toiras, besieged at Casale Monferrato in 1630 with no other means to pay his soldiers, melted a bronze cannon into coins and derived over 100,000 livres from it. The soldiers then used these coins in their daily purchases from local merchants, who were obliged to accept them at face value.[43] At Parma, late in 1636, the treasurer Rossi put the mint to work striking a tonne of these copper coins, stamped with denominations from half a lira to two lire.[44] This was like a forced loan imposed on the entire population. The artisan Pugolotti

---

[40] Jean Chagniot, *Guerre et société à l'époque moderne* (Paris, 2001), 103–5.
[41] ASPr, Governo Farnesiano, Mastri Farnesiani 32, 690.
[42] ASPr, Governo Farnesiano, Carteggio Interno 384, 2 May 1636.
[43] Chagniot, *Guerre et société*, 128.
[44] ASPr, Governo Farnesiano, Mastri Farnesiani 32, 670.

complained that he had over 800 lire worth of these 'red' coins in 1637. The duke promised that they would all be taken back and exchanged for proper coins eventually, but our chronicler was not optimistic that this would happen soon. In the meantime, such coins circulated at a discount, that is, merchants would no longer accept them at face value, but assigned to them some lesser worth.[45] Debased coinage was a fairly common method of extracting more resources from the population by cash-strapped governments who needed good coins to pay foreigners.

Lest it is thought that these predicaments were particular to the unfortunate Parmans, we have a vivid chronicle from Casalmaggiore, an active town on the Po river in Spanish Lombardy, on the border with the Farnese duchy. The chronicler Ettore Lodi, a town notable, described Casalmaggiore as an idyllic place before the plague of 1630 and the wars that followed, 'before they put gabelles (value-added taxes) on everything'. Military operations against Mantua in 1629–30 meant that, from lodging Imperial troops, the town was bled dry. Casalmaggiore was also on the march path of the troops collected by Spain for operations in Germany in 1633 and 1634, and so it paid for troop lodgings again. The town government had to pay for the subsistence costs of the soldiers, but also for boats and troop transport, for haulage, for teams of workers building bridges, for the erection of earthen fortifications and the escort of munitions, besides sundry other expenses for the army. Odoardo's war required new impositions in 1635 and 1636, not only for professional troops garrisoning the town, but also to pay for the transit of soldiers between Spanish Lombardy and the duchy of Modena. The war with Parma entailed multiple disruptions, beginning with obligatory militia service for hundreds of inhabitants, who erected redoubts along the river and patrolled the district to dissuade the Parmans from crossing on raiding forays. The war interrupted the town's flourishing wine trade with the Farnese duchy (for, at that time, wine did not keep for much more than a year). A good portion of the money the town used to pay the soldiers was derived from taxes raised from grain mills floating on the Po (the *macinato* tax on flour was a crucial gabelle because it was easy to collect and everyone needed to grind their grain), but in 1635 ice destroyed these. When the town was unable to meet its tax payments to Milan, soldiers and constables from Cremona appeared to seize oxen. When the Spanish troops, dispersed amongst them in winter quarters, made outrageous demands, the officers just told local officials to carry their criticism to the regimental sergeant majors. The little hamlets were particularly hard-pressed by these soldiers, and many families fled to other states, leaving their houses empty and the fields untilled.[46]

THE DUCHY STRANDED

Duchess Margherita de'Medici administered Parma and Piacenza as regent in the absence of her husband Odoardo. Vital messages passed back and forth between them through Genoese territory, but the everyday business of managing a beleaguered

---

[45] Pugolotti, *Libro di Memorie*, 98.
[46] Ettore Lodi, *Memorie istoriche di Casalmaggiore*, ed. E. Cirani (Cremona, 1992), 108–21.

statelet fell to her, and to a council made up of key advisors from the principal feudatories of the duchy (Camillo Anguissola, Alessandro, and Cesare Sanvitale) on the one hand, and the highest-ranking French officers (the Comte de Saint-Paul, Claude Vernatel, François Nicart) on the other. As always, the key to Farnese independence was the control of the citadel of Piacenza, which Odoardo confided to the indispensable colonel, Francesco Serafini, and a garrison of Italian soldiers. The duchess herself was about six months pregnant at the end of 1635, but she had already filled the principal requirement of a ducal consort, that of providing a male heir to the duchy. Aged 16 when she arrived in Parma, the duchess was soon stripped of most of her protective Tuscan personnel. Her young husband was, by nature, mistrustful, and not inclined to show gratitude to those around him. However, he quickly established an enduring harmony with his bride, whose nemesis would be her mother-in-law.[47] Margherita has not left us her opinion of Odoardo's great adventure, but she appears to have been supportive. In contrast, the Duchess of Mantua opposed the French alliance of her husband Charles and actively fed information to Madrid.[48]

The most urgent task at hand was rebuilding a professional army. Odoardo had succeeded in convincing Créquy, Victor Amadeus, and Hémery to give him two French regiments and a heavy cavalry escort of Piedmontese in order to escort home the debris of the original Farnese army of 1635. In total, counting generously, these amounted to about 1,500 horse and 3,000 infantry, a force that was large enough to shunt aside the Spanish contingent of cavalry and militia that opposed them en route. But the men who arrived in Piacenza just after Christmas were completely exhausted and needed rest.[49] No more troops could be expected from the west, for Victor Amadeus refused to allow French horses to winter in Piedmontese territory, and the Monferrato was too small to compensate for this. French garrisons in northern Italy probably numbered no more than 6,000 men during that winter.[50] A report on the French army in the winter of 1636 claimed the presence of 2,900 French soldiers and 200 cavalry divided between Parma and Piacenza. The Savoyard cavalry was estimated at 800 troopers, and no figure was given for the Italians, either horse or foot.

We are not nearly as well informed about the army of 1636 as that of the previous year. Most of the few new *patenti* appointed castle commanders or *commissari* entrusted with organizing winter quarters for the troops and horses. Of the 46 surviving company rosters from 1636, 39 concern infantry units, totalling about 4,000 men. Not all of them would have been serving simultaneously, for six of the French companies were not formed until August. The companies were much

---

[47] Lucia Mascalchi, 'Margherita dei Medici Farnese: Strategie politiche e dinamiche familiari alla corte di Parma e Piacenza', in *Le donne Medici nel sistema europeo delle corti: XVI–XVIII secolo*, ed. Giulia Calvi and Riccardo Spinelli (Florence, 2008), vol. 1, 283–312.

[48] AGS, Estado, Legajo 3838, Consulta of 25 June 1636.

[49] AAE, Paris, Correspondance Politique Sardaigne, vol. 24, f.25: Estat de l'armée qui sera en Italie depuis le 1er janvier jusqu'au dernier mars.

[50] Jacques Humbert, *Le Maréchal de Créquy, gendre de Lesdiguières (1573–1638)* (Paris, 1962), 233.

smaller than those of the previous year, and the losses from battle were much greater. In addition to the surviving rosters, however, I have encountered 38 other companies mentioned in the records, of which only a small number could have been militia units. The rosters of 1636 do not designate the geographical origin of the rank and file with nearly the same consistency as before, but one can still make a few generalizations. The cavalry companies were predominantly Italian (seven of ten), formed of troopers hailing from the capital cities, the leading small towns, and from some of the lush parishes of the low-lying districts near the Po, alongside troopers from the Veneto and other districts of northern Italy. We have one roster for the company of Antoine Maillard, from Fribourg in Switzerland, almost all of whose troopers were French.

Infantry companies in 1636 may have been predominantly French. Of the 28 surviving company rosters, 19 were French, sometimes almost uniformly so. If we assume that all of the French captains named in several records possessed companies, the tally is 38 infantry units out of 74, or about half. Only two companies hailed from the German-speaking world, and Moralt's Swiss company was diluted, by about half, with Italians from both Farnese territory and other north Italians. The eight Italian companies for which we have complete rosters threw together Duke Odoardo's subjects in considerable numbers, alongside strong contingents of Corsicans and Ligurians, and other north Italians. They still included substantial numbers of deserters from Spanish territories in Italy and an assortment of Germans and Belgians. We can know nothing about the other units, for which we have only the name of the captain, gleaned from the rosters, from the patents, and even from the records of the Piacenza hospital. Of the 34 captains whom we can identify as Italians, 24 were subjects of the Duke of Parma. The companies themselves were always leaky containers that had to be continually replenished with whatever elements became available. Occasional references to troop concentrations give the impression that, at any one time, there might have been about 4,000 professional infantry in ducal pay. This number looks very much like a kind of ceiling: the maximum number the little duchy could support on its own resources. The French troops were precious and had to be hoarded and concentrated; the Italians might have been comparable in number, but they were packed into companies without much concern for homogeneity or cohesiveness.

One of the most interesting features of the war in 1636 was the generous use commanders made of the immense pool of militiamen, who sometimes served under commissioned officers, and sometimes followed men who just emerged as raiding leaders. During the central decades of the seventeenth century whole regions of Europe were given over to ongoing combats between militia bands, articulated around the defence of their villages and medieval castle strongpoints. Apart from Germany where anarchy reigned in contested zones, Spanish-ruled Franche-Comté, adjacent to French Burgundy, was too isolated to be defended by regular troops and was left to its own devices.[51] After the kingdom of Portugal seceded from Spain in 1640, a long war of desultory raiding festered in the border

---

[51] Gérard Louis, *La guerre de Dix Ans 1634–1644* (Besançon, 1998).

zone for over 20 years.[52] Wars such as these, without recourse to hungry professional soldiers, could become eternal.

Spain long hesitated before creating a classic peasant militia in the duchy of Milan, but the governor did put one together during the crisis of 1625. Cities had always armed their citizens for the defence of the walls and gates but the countryside was devoid of similar protection. The new militia did not seek to arm a large portion of the male population, as was the case in the Farnese duchies. Rather, the government came up with a useful number of auxiliary soldiers—8,000 men—and then proceeded to levy them by village lotteries when there were insufficient volunteers. These formed local companies under captains chosen by the governor of Milan from a list of eligible notables proposed by local authorities. Combined companies formed *tercios* under colonels on the model of the regular army, with the governor of Milan having final approval over all the officers. The first peasant militia organizations disbanded shortly after the crisis passed, but Madrid resurrected them in 1635 along the same lines as before. Leganés formalized this still further in a decree of 30 May 1637. The principal function of the militia was to replace the garrisons of fortified places and thereby liberate professional soldiers for operations in the field. Militiamen received weapons from government magazines, and Madrid intended that they should receive the same pay as regular soldiers during their operations. In the meantime, they should enjoy tax and judicial privileges and immunities.[53] In addition to the formal militia, some feudal lords created armed bands levied from estates they owned in the border districts, like Cardinal Trivulzio, who was the principal landowner in the lower Po districts near Piacenza.[54] Spain's ability to mobilize such large numbers of militiamen attests at least to the durable loyalty of social elites to the House of Austria, who recognized the value of the monarchy in maintaining order at home and promoting their interests in the empire.[55] Commanders did not intend to throw militia units into operations against enemy troops, but they cast those reservations aside almost immediately. Militia contingents from the Alessandria district served in garrison during the siege of Valenza, while others patrolled the countryside in order to ambush enemy forage parties. Leganés used militiamen to hinder the passage of Odoardo's army back home, where French troops reputedly massacred isolated detachments of them.[56]

Even before Odoardo's army returned to Piacenza, during Christmas 1635, Duchess Margherita and her councillors threatened to unleash a horde of militiamen on Bobbio, the nearest enemy town in the Trebbia valley, upstream from

---

[52] Lorraine White, 'Spain's early modern soldiers: origins, motivation and loyalty', *War and Society*, 19 (2001): 19–46.

[53] Sara Pedretti, 'Ai confini occidentali dello Stato di Milano: l'impiego delle milizie rurali nelle guerre del Seicento', in *Alle frontiere della Lombardia: Politica, guerra e religione nell'età moderna*, ed. C. Donati (Milan, 2006), 177–200.

[54] Mario Rizzo, 'I cespiti di un maggiorente lombardo del Seicento: Ercole Teodoro Trivulzio e la milizia forese', *Archivio Storico Lombardo*, 120 (1990): 463–77.

[55] Giovanni Muto, 'Noble presence and stratification in the territories of Spanish Italy', in *Spain in Italy: Politics, Society and Religion 1500–1700*, ed. T. J. Dandelet and J. A. Marino (Leiden, 2007), 251–97.

[56] Girolamo Ghilini, *Annali di Alessandria*, ed. A. Bossola, 3 vols.(Alessandria, 1903), 113.

Piacenza. The military officers recommended devastating the mountainous district around the town if it did not surrender, but the duchess and her chief advisors hesitated to give them the order. 'Contact with the enemy was judged inopportune,' wrote Crescenzi Romani, with a fine sense of understatement.[57] A period of mutual grimacing was not followed by any serious action, but the respite was short-lived. By late December or early January 1636, the Lombard marchese Pozzolo, commander of militia in the Tortona district, led men against Piacenza border villages and castles in search of livestock and other plunder. Farnese sources describe these troops as bandits, and it is possible that they were at least in part rag-tag collections of armed men and outlaws pardoned in exchange for military service. Of course, these raids triggered reprisals from Farnese territories almost immediately. Typically these operations consisted of a few score professional soldiers, backed by hundreds of well-armed district and city militiamen hoping to intercept the enemy on the road, or else to seize the hillside hamlets and their castles just across the border. The soldiers sometimes set fire to hamlets or castles to teach the rascals a lesson. Occasionally skirmishes erupted, resulting in dead and wounded on both sides, but the number of victims rarely numbered more than a dozen or a score. Farnese troops disarmed and undressed the prisoners, then marched them, two by two, to Piacenza, where a tribunal sentenced them to (non-existent) galley service. This was a classic 'little war' between neighbours who, in normal times, would cooperate in smuggling.[58] In a larger operation on 14 January, some Savoyard cavalry companies under Guido Villa, 100 French musketeers and 150 militiamen from Piacenza, marched on the border town of Stradella, seeking to establish troop lodgings there. After being politely rebuffed by the authorities, they blew open both gates simultaneously, and stormed the place at the substantial loss of 30 men, both dead and injured. The militia defenders, led by a local priest, put up a spirited fight until French officers threatened to turn the churches, houses, and women over to '*la discrétion des soldats*'; this was enough to induce the garrison in the castle to surrender.[59]

The arrival of several thousand professional soldiers and a strong corps of Savoyard cavalry put new strain on the region's resources. Fodder was a scarce and precious commodity in a part of Europe so densely populated, and where a flourishing new butter and cheese industry concentrated large numbers of cows. Fodder was also a bulky commodity whose importation from neutral areas would be very costly. A lack of fodder forced peasants to slaughter the oxen with which they worked the land.[60] Normally, armies sought to pasture their horses on districts belonging to the enemy, but the presence of Spanish professional troops in the plain just across the border precluded collecting it from the duchy of Milan.

[57] Crescenzi Romani, *Corona della nobiltà d'Italia*, vol. 2, 296.
[58] Crescenzi Romani, *Corona della nobiltà d'Italia*, vol. 2, 297; BPPr, Ms Parmense 737, Calandrini, 'L'Heroe d'Italia', 613–25.
[59] AAE, Paris, Correspondance Politique Sardaigne, vol. 24: Relation de la prise de Stradella, fo. 52; also the account in the *Gazette de France 1636* (Paris, 1636), n. 27.
[60] Vittorio Siri, *Memorie recondite di Vittorio Siri dall'anno 1601 fino al 1640*, 8 vols. (Lyons, 1677–9), vol. 7, 399.

The solution to feeding a thousand cavalry over winter in our little duchy was to take them to some neutral state judged too weak to defend itself; in this case, the duchy of Modena. In the aftermath of the war it was plain that this was a significant blunder, so the paternity of the idea is unclear. A letter from Odoardo to Duke Victor Amadeus of 11 January 1636 proposed to forage the Savoyard horse in the district of Reggio Emilia, quite clearly to punish Duke Francesco d'Este for not joining the French alliance.[61] It seems that the Duke of Savoy and the Marchese Villa did not offer much resistance to the scheme, for the Piedmontese cavalry *required* forage, and widening the war was one way of preventing the French victory they feared.[62] In a report penned after Parma had withdrawn from the war, the French ambassador to Turin Hémery claimed that the idea was typical of Odoardo's spite and myopia. He claims that he pleaded with the duke to see reason and emphasized the negative impact this would have on his own states, for Parma drew resources from the duchy of Modena and transported grain from more distant places across it. War with the Este dynasty next door would only serve to isolate Parma more. The ambassador claimed that Victor Amadeus resisted Odoardo's suggestion, and that this added further to the tension between the dukes. Relations were already strained by the reciprocal refusal to accede to the other's desire for more high-sounding titles.[63] Parman apologists after the war claimed that the whole idea was the Duke of Savoy's.[64] The project did not seem to be shrouded in secrecy, either. Andrea Pugolotti recorded in his diary on 31 January that the 800 Savoyard cavalry left Parma, accompanied by 500 Parman militiamen who had volunteered to help, 'and they say that it is to inflict damage to the duke of Modena'. 'Please God, may this assistance [of the militia] be a good thing, but…'[65] The Duchess Margherita tried to soften the blow the next day by sending an emissary to Duke Francesco (her brother-in-law) requesting permission to forage peacefully and explaining that anything taken would be repaid in full after the war, but Villa did not wait for a response before marking out his forage areas not far from the Po.[66] Militia soldiers escorted wagons, then seized stocks of grain from wealthy landowners, before trundling the carts back to the palace in Parma to fill the storehouses. 'This war was the true mother of thievery', lamented the court historian Calandrini.[67] Accountants documented the arrival of cartloads of grain plundered from leading landowners in the Reggiano, whose wheat, enough for

---

[61] AAE, Paris, Correspondance Politique Sardaigne, vol. 24: letter from the Comte de Verrua to Cardinal Richelieu, 11 January 1636.

[62] Gabriel de Mun, *Richelieu et la Maison de Savoie: L'ambassade de Particelli d'Hémery en Piémont* (Paris, 1907), 127; for a contemporary view by an historian with access to French papers, see Galeazzo Gualdo Priorato, *Historia universale del Conte Galeazzo Gualdo Priorato, delle guerre successe nell'Europa dall'anno 1630 sino all'anno 1640* (Genoa, 1642), 306–7.

[63] BNF, Ms Fr 16929: Relation de M. d'Esmery de ses negotiations en Piedmont en 1635 etc., fo. 551.

[64] BPPr, Ms Parmense 737, Calandrini, 'L'Heroe d'Italia', 656.

[65] Pugolotti, *Libro di Memorie*, 93.

[66] Odoardo Rombaldi, *Il duca Francesco I d'Este (1629–1658)* (Modena, 1992), 23.

[67] BPPr, Ms Parmense 737, Calandrini, 'L'Heroe d'Italia', 673.

50,000 rations, was stocked in the Pilotta palace in Parma.[68] Villa remained only a week, for he lacked infantry and artillery to oppose the growing opposition.[69]

Duke Francesco d'Este immediately mobilized his own militia, about 7,000 foot and 600 horse, to repel the invader, but he was not about to throw them headlong at veteran cavalry forces like Villa's. Instead, he asked Leganés for help, and then waited for Spanish reinforcements who arrived a few days later, about 1,500 foot and 1,300 horse, under the command of the Spanish military governor of nearby Cremona, Don Juan Vasquez de Coronado.[70] These crossed the Po at the Modenese border fortress of Brescello (held by a few hundred professional soldiers), and were then further supplied and reinforced by the tiny duchy of Guastalla, a staunch Spanish ally. Additional Spanish forces and a body of militia converged on Casalmaggiore on the north bank of the Po across from Parman territory in order to draw off Farnese troops. Villa's foraging expedition was soon over, and by 10 February he withdrew back to the Enza river border with Modena to await developments and to collect militia detachments with which he hoped to stem the enemy counter-attack. Alone, Modenese forces advanced cautiously to Ponte d'Enza on the border, where Farnese militia units waited behind some hastily raised sconces. On 13 February, four companies of Savoyard cavalry joined the latter in repulsing the green Modenese militia, many of whom waded back across the shallow stream to escape the onslaught. However, the Modenese rallied, after which they killed four Parmans and captured 180 more.

Vasquez de Coronado used the Modenese as a holding force, and surprised several hundred Parman militiamen with his cavalry a few kilometres downstream at Ponte di Sorbolo. There the untested 'soldiers' threw down their arms and disbanded merely at the sound of the horses trotting in their direction.[71] Spanish troops skirmished with more Parman militia a few kilometres farther south near the castle of Montechiarugolo, whose garrison remained uncowed.[72] Still farther upstream in the hills, the commander of the Farnese castle of Rossena opened the gates to enemy forces in exchange for a large sum of money. After these inconclusive skirmishes Villa withdrew his men to Colorno where they refreshed themselves for several days before withdrawing towards Parma. Spanish and Modenese forces then advanced resolutely along the Via Emilia in the direction of the Farnese capital on 17 February. Some panic assailed the citizens, but Prince Francesco Maria made himself visible in his armour in order to set an example to the population, which drew weapons from the ample stocks of the citadel.[73] Villa concentrated his troops a few kilometres back from the border along the Via Emilia, just outside the lazaretto (a quarantine pen for plague victims close to large urban centres) and within sight of the city church steeples. He placed several hundred militiamen and

---

[68] ASPr, Governo Farnesiano, Milizie 36: Viveri alla Cavalleria Savoiarda.
[69] Archivio di Stato Torino (henceforth ASTo), Materie militari, 1, n. 30.
[70] AGS, Estado, Legajo 3343/147; letter of 4 February 1636; also Pietro Giovanni Capriata, *Dell'Historia delli movimenti d'armi successi in Italia*, 2 vols. (Genoa, 1649), vol. 2, 200–3.
[71] BPPr, Ms Parmense 737, Calandrini, 'L'Heroe d'Italia', 666.
[72] Pugolotti, *Libro di Memorie*, 93.
[73] BPPr, Ms Parmense 737, Calandrini, 'L'Heroe d'Italia', 673–80.

professional soldiers drawn from the city in the hedges and vineyards to the left (north) of the road in order to direct a crossfire on the advancing enemy cavalry.

We have several accounts of the 'action' that unfolded at San Lazzaro from French and Savoyard viewpoints but, like many battlefield sources, there are numerous discrepancies among them and enough imprecision to make it difficult to reconcile them.[74] Both sides deployed a combination of cavalry and infantry facing each other along the axis of the highway, which was blocked with an 'abbatis', or piled debris, defended by musketeers. Spanish musketeers advanced through the fields and vineyards against Villa's dismounted carabiniers and some Monferrato foot, who withdrew after expending their ammunition. The advancing force must have removed the abbatis, for the Spanish horse, with the Modenese cavalry in support, advanced confidently along the straight highway until they faced the Savoyard horse. Both sides then fought a long caracole action in the narrow space, which was roughly 30 paces (20 metres) wide. The medieval tactic of headlong charges with lances was a distant memory, for the French cavalry abandoned the lance in the late sixteenth century, and the Habsburg horse in northern Italy employed only a single lancer company. A cavalry 'charge' entailed a deliberate but relatively slow advance of about 7 kilometres an hour, in order to keep the formation intact. It was on the tightness of the formation that the attackers relied for victory. Since troopers fought with pistols and carbines primarily, a faster pace, even a trot, would prevent them from firing accurately from their saddles. Even a charge at a trot only allowed the horse a speed of about 10 kilometres an hour.[75] The defending Savoyard cavalry drawn up across the road responded to the attack with a caracole charge of its own, with company after company being committed to the fray until the its ammunition was exhausted. Meanwhile, the battle raged in the fields on both sides of the highway between the Habsburg and confederate forces, who each numbered about 3,000 men in total. A non-identified regiment of Spanish foot pushed hard in order to squeeze the cavalry back up the Via Emilia. The supporting Neapolitan infantry of Lucio Boccapianola was caught by surprise by Villa's musketeers, hiding behind the trees, and the latter inflicted heavy casualties on them.[76] Habsburg troops were prevented from advancing by fresh waves of Piedmontese cavalry.[77] The Piedmontese regiment of Prince Maurice reportedly took heavy losses while stemming the Spanish charge. French and Parman musketeers on the flank kept up their fire for two hours, after which the Spanish withdrew

---

[74] Savoyard accounts exist in ASTo, Materie militari, 1, n. 30; Alexandre de Saluces, *Histoire militaire de Piémont*, vol. 4 (Turin, 1818), 15; French accounts are contained in the dispatches to Paris, elements of which were published in the *Gazette de France 1636*, n. 38, 12 March.

[75] Frédéric Chauviré, 'Le problème de l'allure dans les charges de cavalerie du XVIe siècle au XVIIIe siècle', *Revue Historique des Armées*, 249 (2007): 16–27.

[76] Raffaele Maria Filamondo, *Il Genio bellicoso di Napoli: Memorie istoriche d'alcuni capitani celebri napolitani c'han militato per la fede, per lo re, per la patria nel secolo corrente*, 2 vols. (Naples, 1694), vol. 1, 418.

[77] Much of the Piedmontese cavalry might have been comprised of French subjects, large numbers of whom enlisted after 1620; see Claudio De Consoli, *Al soldo del duca: L'amministrazione delle armate sabaude (1560–1630)* (Turin, 1999), 149–54.

in good order, pressed by Villa's horse. It had been a close call, and while Spanish sources estimated that Villa had taken 150 casualties, they lost 100 prisoners of their own in addition to 200 or 300 men killed and wounded. Villa only admitted to seven or eight dead and four or five taken prisoner among his cavalry, with the Spanish suffering the death of 15 or 20 cavalry troopers. These low numbers probably reflect the fact that these soldiers were still heavily armoured and sometimes referred to as 'lobsters'.[78] Parma celebrated victory that evening and feted the Piedmontese and Savoyard officers, but would not admit the rank and file into the city.[79] The French ambassador Hémery relayed the news back to Cardinal Richelieu in a letter dated 27 February, but stressed that the tension was building: 'It was our good luck that the Marquis Villa [in Parma] and Monsieur de Saint-Paul [in Piacenza] found themselves in this country where commanders and experienced troops are so few, and where the people are afraid and bear little love for their prince.'[80]

Another Spanish force marched into Farnese territory near Piacenza in order to prevent the transfer eastward of confederate reinforcements.[81] A small Spanish army under the Neapolitan commander Carlo della Gatta advanced on the western frontier from Voghera, with the intention of drawing Villa's forces away from Parma or at least seizing nearby Farnese territory to suck resources from it and thereby husband the finite resources of the duchy of Milan. By now Spanish forces were reaching unprecedented numbers, perhaps 30,000 men and nearly as many horses, billeted on a state with fewer than a million inhabitants. Lombards were quartering five or six times as many soldiers relative to the population as wartime France, and so strategy demanded that enemy territories be seized and 'eaten' whenever possible. A couple of Farnese towns on the north bank of the Po, Guardamiglio and Fombio, could not really be defended; officials withdrew their munitions into Piacenza, and their militia garrisons surrendered without a struggle as soon as a large Spanish force appeared before the gates.[82]

Della Gatta's little army lay siege to Castel San Giovanni on 12 February, with 400 horse, 2,000 foot, and a pair of cannon, plus a couple of thousand militia infantry tagging along to watch. The town's capture would put an end to Farnese raids into Milanese territory, but also demonstrate, 'that the enemy could suffer too, and would find no safety'.[83] The French commander in Piacenza, the Comte de Saint-Paul, sent a cavalry force of several hundred troopers from the city to

[78] David Blackmore, *Arms and Armour of the English Civil Wars* (London, 1990) 7–12.
[79] Capriata, *Dell'Historia*, vol. 2, 203; the best description of the action was penned by Guido Villa in a letter to the Duke of Savoy, which was passed on to Paris, AAE, Paris, Correspondance Politique Sardaigne, vol. 24, 27 February 1636.
[80] AAE, Paris, Correspondance Politique Sardaigne, vol. 24: letter from Hémery to Cardinal Richelieu.
[81] For these events from the contemporary Hispano-Lombard perspective see Giovanni Fossati, *Memorie historiche delle guerre d'Italia del secolo presente* (Bologna, 1640), 158; from a local historian with access to French documents, Siri, *Memorie recondite di Vittorio Siri*, vol. 8, 396.
[82] Davide Maffi, 'Un bastione incerto? L'esercito di Lombardia tra Filippo V e Carlo II (1630–1700)', in *Guerra y Sociedad en la Monarquia Hispanica*, ed. E. Garcia Hernan and D. Maffi, 2 vols.(Madrid, 2006), vol. 1, 501–22.
[83] AGS, Estado, Legajo 3343/150: letter from Leganés, 17 February 1636.

impede Spanish progress. After a furious cavalry skirmish the Spaniards chased their attackers to a hamlet near Rottofreno where 500 musketeers lay in wait for them. The Franco-Parmans then counter-attacked after a terrible volley on the Spanish horse, and a fierce melee developed between the contingents on both sides. Here again, the French and confederate cavalry bested their Spanish counterparts in close fighting. The French and their Farnese allies prevailed in this 'action' at the cost of only 15 men, but the Spaniards withdrew in good order, while the bulk of their army laid siege to Castel San Giovanni.[84] The town had few regular troops to defend it, and, like most other fortified villages, its medieval wall without an earth rampart behind it was barely 'improved' by a few earthworks and palisades guarding the approaches. The little garrison of a few dozen soldiers and militiamen withdrew into the castle after a day's defence of the perimeter, so Della Gatta bombarded it for two days without much result. Losing patience, the Neapolitan general ordered soldiers to pull down the damaged houses, and promised to demolish every building in the town if the castle did not capitulate. This had the desired result.[85] Spanish troops immediately set to fortifying the little town in earnest with more extensive earthworks and palisades, turning the place into an advance base held by 60 ethnic Spaniards in the castle and 600 soldiers in the town, perhaps not much inferior in number to the remaining civilian population.[86]

Then, with the aid of a newly arrived German cavalry regiment, the Marqués de Caracena advanced on the next town en route to Piacenza, Rottofreno. It fell too, by an old ruse, after a brief siege. Caracena called out the inexperienced castle commander, Cristoforo Ferrari, to parley and then seized him. This treachery completely demoralized the officers of the largely militia garrison, who surrendered soon after.[87] Caracena placed a large garrison of 800 men in the town and transformed it into a base from which to plunder the district. The army under Caracena was beginning to swell with fresh troops, and, with its militia contingent, numbered close to 7,000 men.[88] Rottofreno was merely 10 kilometres down the highway from Piacenza and, as a result, feelings were running very high in the city—against the French! The Piacenza chronicle of the parish priest Benedetto Boselli reflects the ambient sense of impending doom, especially after the first Spanish raids around the city in mid-January. The municipal council, fearing a siege, ordered a census taken of the population so that it could plan for rationing. But the large French garrison under the Comte de Saint-Paul was a thorn in their side. 'In this month (January) the overbearing pride of the French in this city has grown to a point that the very citizens are not allowed to open their mouths, and many see themselves harmed in their goods, in their honour, in their lives. They were bold enough to demand from the Serene Duchess that they should

---

[84] AAE, Paris, Correspondance Politique Sardaigne, vol. 24, 13 February 1636.
[85] AGS, Estado, Legajo 3343/150.
[86] AAE, Paris, Correspondance Politique Sardaigne, vol. 24: letter in cipher from the Comte de Saint-Paul, 6 March 1636.
[87] BPPr, Ms Parmense 737, Calandrini, 'L'Heroe d'Italia', 655.
[88] AGS, Estado, Legajo 3343/150; Capriata, *Dell'Historia*, vol. 2, 204–10.

control the guards in the city square, which was in the care of the citizens. They [the French] were justly mortified when she took from their hands the keys to the gates, which she gave them when they first arrived.' The disasters of February west and east of the city heightened the drama. 'On February 15 the entire city rose up against the demands of the French soldiers and prevented them from occupying the city square. They say that day they wanted to have in Piacenza another Sicilian Vespers, such was the mood on each side, and while three French soldiers were killed, only two or three Piacentini were wounded.' A week later, the city council decreed the compulsory mobilization of all men between 15 and 60 years of age.[89] The Duchess Margherita remained faithful to her husband's war policy, hoping for the best, and, consequently, she arrested important people she suspected of fomenting trouble, beginning with the baron Francesco Marazzani (a former colonel in Wallenstein's Imperial army), along with one of his brothers, and the Venetian captain Antonio Maria Sarego, and confined them to the dungeons of the Rocchetta prison in Parma. (Marazzani would only emerge from it after Odoardo's death more than ten years later.)[90] Before the end of the month, Saint-Paul and Marchese Annibale Scotti marched forth with 6,000 militiamen and a pair of cannon to chase the Lombard Marchese Pozzolo away from the mountain villages upstream that he was terrorizing with his armed raiders. Any action was better than none.[91]

The Spanish strategy of hitting one side of the duchy, then another side, was coordinated from the centre; it kept Saint-Paul and Villa off balance and unable to take initiatives of their own or come to each other's assistance. Having drawn attention to the Piacentino, Spanish and Modenese forces under Coronado then advanced into the Parmigiano on 25 February, occupying the town and castle of Colorno near the Po almost without a fight. Its commander was a decrepit Parman nobleman, Guido Ceredoli, who was unsuitable for active service. Colorno's capture closed off shipments of grain to the duchy of Parma from the Papal States and Mantua.[92] Duke Francesco of Modena was quite content to call off the war once he was in possession of the town, and opened peace talks via the papal nuncio, but Coronado intended to press on and overrun the whole district, looting the farms and removing the large livestock. This process was completely typical of warfare in the seventeenth century. Their forays only episodically entailed large bodies of troops moving on a military target, but, rather, the men divided into small groups to plunder what they could, making them difficult to monitor. Hoping for some easy booty, Lombard militiamen from north of the Po crossed the river too and occupied some of the redoubts abandoned by the Parman militia.[93] The pickings

---

[89] BCPLPc, Ms Pallastrelli 126, Croniche Boselli, 117–19; the Sicilian Vespers (1282) were a major event in Italian history, wherein the population of Palermo rose up spontaneously and massacred the French population established there by the (French) King of Naples, and called in the (Spanish) Aragonese to help them repel the survivors.

[90] Pugolotti, *Libro di Memorie*, 94.

[91] BCPLPc, Ms Pallastrelli 126, Croniche Boselli, 17 February 1636.

[92] AAE, Paris, Correspondance Politique Sardaigne, vol. 24: letter from Hémery to Richelieu, 23 March 1636.

[93] Crescenzi Romani, *Corona della nobiltà d'Italia*, vol. 2, 303–5; see also BPPr, Ms Parmense 1261, Storia di Parma, dell'abbate Gozzi, 1114.

were worthwhile, and in Colorno the troops remained for 13 days in order to loot it meticulously. Soldiers wanted money first and foremost, either taken directly from the houses of the inhabitants, or obtained through some other arrangement. For example, the objects from the Monte di Pietà were worth 25,000 lire, but rather than march away burdened with household objects with a low unit value, the commissioner of the Spanish horse offered to sell it back to the inhabitants for that price; the latter could borrow the money from somewhere.[94] The town clock and the local bells were more interesting plunder, with the latter destined to be melted down and made into ammunition.

Large contingents of troops towing cannon behind them appeared before the gates of the fortified towns, but these raids were selective. San Secondo, which was the seat of the late Troilo Rossi, the Spanish cavalry commander killed in battle against the Duke de Rohan the previous November, was spared entirely. Indeed it became something of a refuge for the peasants in the vicinity. In Soragna a large detachment arrived on 5 March, and after taking the town they led away livestock and whatever else was there.[95] The people of Parma sent an expedition to the town of Fontanellato to retrieve there the image of the Madonna, and brought it back to the city where an anxious population had favours to ask of it.[96] In Parma ducal officials conscripted the entire male population for service on 17 February, following the compilation of a house-by-house census undertaken in preparation for a siege. Parties of enemy cavalry advanced close to the city walls and burned the ducal gunpowder mill located outside them. It is difficult to know how much death and destruction they inflicted but often they were content to 'refresh themselves after the German fashion', which meant extorting money and food from the inhabitants on the threat of burning buildings. By the unwritten rules of seventeenth-century warfare, everyone understood that places that surrendered without a fight deserved clemency, for it would be unwise for soldiers to provoke the population into defending itself more vigourously.[97] Leganés was ever mindful of the political ramifications of military action; only a few short years before, the destruction of Magdeburg in Saxony galvanized German Protestant princes to join the King of Sweden against the Habsburgs. Similarly in Italy, Pope Urban VIII might be driven into the French alliance if the duchy of Parma were devastated by Spanish troops. The Pope sent an envoy to Piacenza to discuss ending the dispute with Modena, but neither the Duchess Margherita nor the French ambassador Hémery could make an impact on Odoardo in this matter.[98] Parman troops sheltered in the

---

[94] D. Costantino Canicetti, *Memoria di Colorno (1618–1674)*, 24 February to 7 March 1636; Ulbricht, 'The experience of violence during the Thirty Years' War: A look at the civilian victims', 97–129.

[95] BPPr Ms Parmense 963, *Estratto di memorie attinenti alla generalità dello stato di Parma, da un libro di memorie di un certo Pietro Belino della Villa del Carzero di Soragna*; see also Boselli, 'Cenni storici di letteratura dialettale parmense', 43–57.

[96] BPPr, Ms Parmense 737, Calandrini, 'L'Heroe d'Italia', 692.

[97] Barbara Donagan, *War in England, 1642–1649*, 130–7; Porter, *Destruction in the English Civil Wars*, 31–2.

[98] De Mun, *Richelieu et la Maison de Savoie*, 115; also BNF, Ms Fr 16929: Relation de M. d'Esmery, fo. 559.

principal castles and fortresses of the duchy, leaving the Spaniards a free hand in the countryside, but patrols sallied forth nevertheless. Calandrini reports that every night troops of cavalry left Parma, accompanied by 40 young noble volunteers, to carry aid to the peasants and to surprise enemy raiding parties.[99] In Parma the military governor issued a commission to Francesco Ferrari to levy a cavalry unit of 50 'adventurers', whose purpose was to harass enemy forces and seize the plunder back from them.

It would get much worse. Around Christmas 1635 the Genoese Prince Gian Andrea Doria and the Spanish resident in Genoa hatched a plan to invade the Farnese duchy from the south. The prince was the rightful heir to the town of Borgo Taro usurped from the Landi feudatories by the Farnese in 1578. He was still feudal lord of Compiano and other fiefs in the upper Taro valley, of Bardi farther north (both defended by strong castles), and of San Stefano d'Aveto and other places in adjacent Genoese territory. Like many eminent Genoese aristocrats, Doria belonged to the group of Italian '*potentados*' devoted to the Spanish interest. The original plan was just to recover his birthright and cut off Farnese communications to the sea, for nobody wished to provoke the Pope by advancing farther.[100] On 11 March 1636 a small army comprised of Spanish and German troops, vassals of the prince and other mountain peasants from the nearby Lunigiana, commanded by the Neapolitan colonel Tuttavilla and Federigo Imperiale, a Genoese colonel in Spanish service, crossed the mountain passes and invested Borgo Taro, defended by only 70 peasant militiamen, without canoneers or professional infantry to help them. The fortifications of the town were by no means negligible but the townspeople had always collaborated with the Spaniards and Genoese in the past, and they had little desire to resist. The Dominican monks in the town first offered to serve as emissaries between the population and the garrison, and next between the garrison and the Spaniards to cease hostilities. As we have seen in other instances, priests and friars formed an articulate pressure group in favour of peace with Spain and by virtue of their vocation nobody considered them to be combatants. The town council sent messengers to Piacenza to plead for reinforcements, but the governor surrendered the place on March 19 before the 400 French musketeers could arrive.[101] The soldiers and any inhabitants of the town who wished were allowed to march away to a friendly post, and those who remained were given the promise that their lives, honour (an allusion to rape), and property would be safe.[102] Imperiale placed a German garrison in the town, where they further improved the fortifications with additional earthworks. Borgo Taro became a base for plundering operations in the mountainous valley of the upper Taro, fairly densely populated with hillside hamlets. Bitterly fought encounters between the

---

[99] BPPr, Ms Parmense 737, Calandrini, 'L'Heroe d'Italia', 841; Crescenzi Romani, *Corona della nobiltà d'Italia*, vol. 2, 329–30.

[100] AGS, Estado, Legajo 3343/75: letter from the Count of Monterrey, 22 December 1635.

[101] BCPLPc, Ms Pallastrelli 126, Croniche Boselli, 15 March 1636; see also Crescenzi Romani, *Corona della nobiltà d'Italia*, vol. 2, 309.

[102] ASPr, Casa e Corte Farnesiana, ser. II, 29, f.101: Capitulationi fra la Terra del Borgo Val di Taro, 19 March 1636.

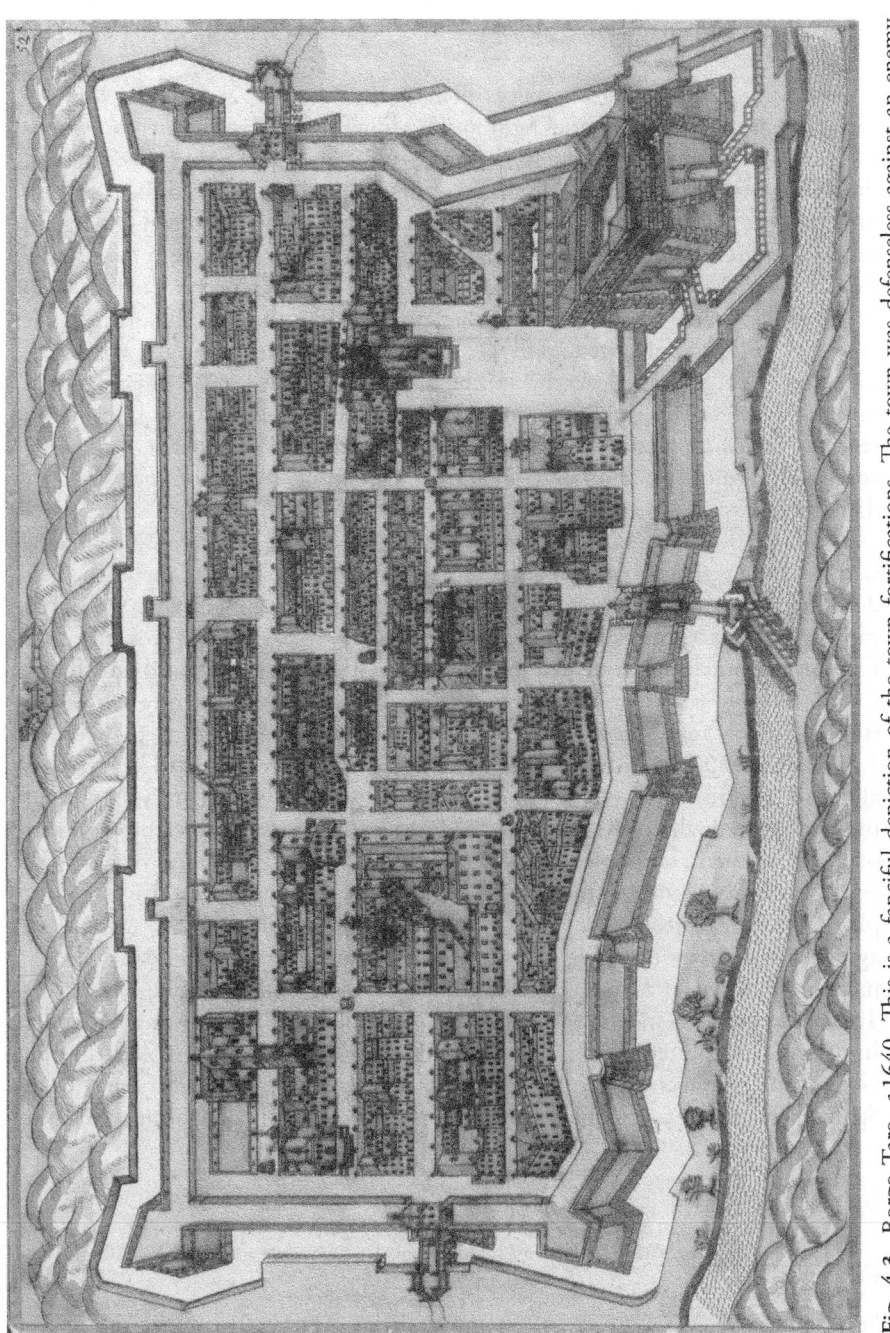

Fig. 4.3. Borgo Taro, c.1640. This is a fanciful depiction of the town fortifications. The town was defenseless against an enemy with large cannon.

German soldiers and peasant militiamen and professional soldiers ensued in the following weeks, during one of which scores of invaders were reported killed and their bodies cremated in lime pits, while the victors purportedly cried 'Viva casa Farnese!'[103]

Prince Doria and his accomplices then descended the Val di Nure, hitherto spared by invaders. After a brief fight in the Monte Penna pass, where the Farnese militia took to its heels into the fog before about 200 invaders, the latter captured the mining town of Ferriere and burned or destroyed the forges and the tools that provided the Farnese with arms and ammunition.[104] Further down the valley, Imperiale seized the town of Bettolle, an important commercial hub connecting the Po valley with the Mediterranean. Here some vital reinforcements arrived at the critical moment and a swirling action unfolded, until the militiamen finally bolted.[105] Imperiale advanced no farther into the plain behind Piacenza, for significant French forces lurked nearby and he had no intelligence. A Parman column under Francesco Arcelli then advanced into the mountains in April, burning, in revenge, the Doria mountain town of San Stefano d'Aveto, another active trading community, whose warehouses, containing oil and other bulky commodities, soldiers set alight.

Habsburg forces swelled with each passing week. Spain's defensive alliance with Tuscany yielded a contingent totalling roughly a *tercio* of infantry. The first detachments to arrive were conspicuous by their lack of combativity. When the castles they garrisoned came under attack by the Franco-Savoyards, the Florentines quickly established pacts by which both sides would fire blank rounds so they could make a show of defence before surrendering.[106] By the spring, Tuscan reinforcements brought their expeditionary force to between 1,500 and 2,000 foot and several hundred horse, who were dispersed in garrisons alongside Spanish infantry.[107] Before Villa foraged the Este territories adjacent to Parma, the duchy of Modena had only provided Spain with a tiny regiment of undermanned companies, kept far away from an active theatre of war. The confederate invasion transformed Duke Francesco into a more active ally, supplying another contingent of foot, but by April Spain and Modena reached an agreement whereby the little duchy provided money instead of untrustworthy men. Seven more *tercios* arrived from the kingdom of Naples, principally by sea. These disembarked in the port of Finale, and then marched through friendly Imperial fiefs located along the Bormida river, culminating at Alessandria. Genoa remained technically neutral, but in ways this was more advantageous to Spain than to France. Spanish control of the district west of Piacenza made it

---

[103] BPPr, Ms Parmense 737, Calandrini, 'L'Heroe d'Italia', 703.

[104] Crescenzi Romani, *Corona della nobiltà d'Italia*, vol. 2, 311–15.

[105] Crescenzi Romani, *Corona della nobiltà d'Italia*, vol. 2, 311–15; see also Capriata, *Dell'Historia*, vol. 2, 210–13.

[106] ASTo, Materie militari, 1, n. 30; report on the Savoyard capture of the castles of Confienza and Robbio.

[107] Francesco Martelli and Cristina Galasso, *Istruzioni agli ambasciatori e inviati medicei in Spagna e nell' 'Italia Spagnola' (1536–1648)* (Rome, 2007), vol. 2, 58–63.

safe to convey Spanish and Neapolitan troops, grain, and military supplies unimpeded from Genoa to Milan.

More reinforcements arrived from Germany. Carlos Coloma mistrusted his Neapolitan and Lombard cavalry, too lightly mounted and unskilled relative to the French and Savoyards. This defect made it necessary to avoid field engagements where they would be most vulnerable.[108] In 1635, Spain began to hire standing German Imperial regiments under prestigious officers for both the Flanders and the Italian theatre of war; these would enjoy some autonomy relative to the Hispano-Italians.[109] In Lombardy these began to arrive in some numbers over the winter and, at the end of January, several thousand of them became available for operations. German troops were notable for the number of women and children who followed them, unflatteringly labelled '*garses*' or sluts. Contemporaries felt that these camp followers pushed the soldiery to plunder friend and foe alike.[110] Some certainly acquired a sinister reputation, like the regiment of foot under the Walloon military enterpriser Gil de Haes, a baker's assistant and the barely literate son of an Ypres bricklayer who rose to prominence under Count Wallenstein.[111] Swiss troops fought for Spain as well as for France and Parma.[112] There was considerable fear at Spanish headquarters that most of these reinforcements might desert while in winter quarters, due to the lack of resources to maintain so many men and horses. Commanders recognized that steady pay dissuaded soldiers from deserting, and, given that it was impossible to pay them in full, they were happy at least that there was a steady supply of bread rations for everyone. Officials handed out army clothing to the most needy. The captains and junior officers were exhorted to be good to their men and not to drive them away.[113]

The disappointments of the first campaign and the obvious increase in Spanish strength led the Duke of Mantua and Victor Amadeus to consider leaving the war. The former continued to trade with Spanish Lombardy through Mantua as if he were still at peace.[114] The situation of the Farnese by the middle of March looked desperate, for it seemed impossible to bring large quantities of supplies from any direction. Hémery sent a large sum of money to Piacenza to buy grain, for he estimated that the place had stocks for only about six weeks. Reinforcements could still be sent in little unarmed packets across Genoese territory, along with vital dispatches. The duchy recruited Italian troops around Ferrara (despite a papal

---

[108] Carlos Coloma, 'Discurso en que se representa quanto conviene a la Monarchìa española la conservaciòn del Estado de Milan, y lo que necesita para su defensa y mayor seguridad (1626)', in *Lo Stato di Milano nel XVII secolo: Memoriali e relazioni*, ed. M. C. Giannini and G. Signorotto (Rome, 2006), 1–15.

[109] Fernando Gonzalez de Leon, *The Road to Rocroi: Class, Culture and Command in the Spanish Army of Flanders 1567–1659* (Boston and Leiden, 2009), 24 and 232.

[110] *Gazette de France 1636*, n. 30, 9 February.

[111] Peter H. Wilson, *Europe's Tragedy: A History of the Thirty Years' War* (London, 2009), 397.

[112] Gualdo Priorato, *Historia universale*, 300–1.

[113] AGS, Estado, Legajo 3343/140: letter from the Marques de Leganés, 6 December 1635.

[114] AAE, Paris, Correspondance Politique Sardaigne, vol. 24: letter from Hémery to Cardinal Richelieu, 28 February 1636; see also BNF, Ms Fr 16929: Relation de M. d'Esmery, fo. 560; on Milan's resilience, Stefano D'Amico, 'Rebirth of a city: immigration and trade in Milan, 1630–1659', *Sixteenth Century Journal*, 32 (2001), 697–722.

prohibition to enlist in Farnese service). The supply of militiamen inside the little duchy seemed to be inexhaustible, and although they could not be relied on to face enemy troops in the field, their encounters with the enemy were becoming more frequent and bloody. Rumours abounded that the German troops lodged around Rottofreno had committed brutalities against the local peasants, killing them and hanging their corpses from trees.[115] To help relieve the pressure, Créquy and Victor Amadeus decided to create a diversion of their own at the end of February, by advancing across the Sesia river boundary between Piedmont and Lombardy in the direction of weakly fortified Vigevano, south of Novara. Leganés called together some scattered contingents and the two armies met in the rice paddy district between the two cities. After some skirmishing, in which the Spanish had the upper hand, the confederates withdrew back across the frontier. Neither side could keep an army in the field in midwinter for very long.[116]

In March Bishop Scappi of Piacenza organized public prayers for the return of the duke from France. Counter-Reformation piety was expressed in lavish ceremony pacts made between people and collectivities in need and the heavenly potentates whose help they sought. On this occasion the Farnese offered a cloak of silken brocade trimmed in gold and rich embroidery to ornament the statue of the Madonna in the state's principal shrine, Piacenza's Madonna di Campagna church. The cloak would complement the crown of solid gold bedecked with gemstones and diamonds, and the majestic baldaquin canopy of gold brocade placed over the statue. On this occasion, the shrine was decked out with scarlet damask tapestries, to which attendants attached verses drawn from hymns, and quotations of prophets and doctors of the church in praise of Jesus' mother. Religious paintings by famous artists hung throughout the sanctuary to heighten the solemnity of the occasion. All of these treasures had been donated to the shrine by pious individuals and groups over time, to be brought out on solemn occasions. The ceremony entailed carrying the precious statue under its baldaquin from its pedestal in the shrine to the cathedral of Piacenza over a kilometre away, at the other extremity of the city, during which musicians accompanied the procession's march. The duchess, who had just recovered from giving birth to Orazio walked with little Prince Ranuccio, the heir.[117] Observers counted more than 4,000 lighted torches carried by the attendants, led by a great cortège of nobles—with the Savoyard captains in prominent places and the ducal functionaries in their robes of office—followed by the court ladies on foot (which was not customary for them). In the cathedral the statue was greeted by the cries and tears of individual supplicants, each with an important message for the Virgin Mary. Attendants placed the statue on the high altar during the solemn high mass, after which the procession marched it through the streets back to its niche in the shrine. Along the route, homeowners suspended rich drapery and fine fabrics from their windows, while church altars, bedecked

---

[115] *Gazette de France 1636*, n. 69, dispatch of 20 April.
[116] Biblioteca Nacional Madrid (hereafter BNM), Ms 2367, Italia 1636, 32–6.
[117] Crescenzi Romani, *Corona della nobiltà d'Italia*, 316.

with gold and silver treasures drawn from the sacristies, echoed the finery of the statue through open doors.[118]

The Virgin Mary seemed to be listening to the duchess, for in April most of the Spanish forces withdrew in a northerly direction to block the progress of the Duke of Rohan. French troops reoccupied Colorno and beefed up the castle's fortifications for a new garrison. Parma and Piacenza were no longer in any immediate danger, now that the enemy garrisons in Rottofreno and Castel San Giovanni had been reduced to about 500 men each.[119] Piacenza itself had a sizeable garrison of 2,000 foot and 1,000 horse, which just included the professional troops.[120] In the absence of strong Spanish forces, the Marchese Villa set out to recapture Rottofreno, but was twice driven off by Neapolitan horse under the cavalry general Gambacorta. Villa had concentrated his cavalry, professional infantry, and some important militia levies—in all about 4,000 men and four cannon—to recover Castel San Giovanni in mid-May. The garrison of professional soldiers put up a fight for four days, while the Parman guns fired 80 heavy projectiles of 30 lbs and 130 light projectiles of 10 lbs against the fortifications, until a breach was opened. The Spanish garrison accepted the conditions of surrender offered, and marched out with their arms and baggage to the nearest friendly post. Villa then marched west, 'to refresh his men, acquire fodder and gain reputation', storming for a third time the town of Stradella and subjecting Broni and its vulnerable district to contributions.[121] The army backtracked to Rottofreno to lay similar siege, but on 11 June a force led by Gambacorta appeared once more and put them to flight.

The conflict at Parma was never more than a sideshow, an irritant in a dangerous position behind the Spanish centre of gravity. Early in 1636, the predicament of his duchy did not seem to worry Duke Odoardo overmuch, but when he returned to Italy from Paris at the beginning of April, he was panicked by the evolving situation and tried to browbeat his allies into helping him return home. Reports from the Comte de Saint-Paul in February had already made it clear that Odoardo's subjects were hostile to the war and 'peu affectionnés' towards the duke himself.[122] Hémery wished to have Odoardo out of the way, and offered him 2,000 French soldiers if only he would go home with them. The French and Piedmontese concocted a plan in February whereby a confederate force would march on Oleggio, north of Novara in the direction of Milan, while the Duke of Rohan would strike west from the Valtellina to join up with them. Odoardo would then take his troops in the Monferrato and force his way across the southern portion of the duchy of Milan in direction of Piacenza.[123]

---

[118] Fra Bernardino Contino, *La Celebre processione della Madonna di Campagna, in sollevamento del Popolo piacentino* (Piacenza, 1636).

[119] Siri, *Memorie recondite di Vittorio Siri*, vol. 8, 400.

[120] AAE, Paris and La Courneuve, Correspondance Politique Sardaigne, vol. 24: letter in cipher from St-Paul to Hémery, 5 May 1636.

[121] Crescenzi Romani, *Corona della nobiltà d'Italia*, vol. 2, 317; For the motivations of Villa, Gualdo Priorato, *Historia universale*, 324.

[122] AAE, Paris and La Courneuve, Correspondance Politique Sardaigne, vol. 24. n. 128, 16 February 1636, letter from Hémery to Gaston d'Orléans; also letter in cipher from Saint-Paul to Hémery, 10 March 1636.

[123] De Mun, *Richelieu et la Maison de Savoie*, 124–7.

Odoardo refused to cooperate. What he wanted above all, was command of a large French army so that he might give orders to a French field marshal who would help him become a modern Alexander. This ambition motivated his trip to Paris to see King Louis XIII in late February. His secretary Gaufridy and Count Fabio Scotti assured him that French resistance to his projects would melt before his personal entreaties. Odoardo held some good cards, in fact. His defection from the alliance would have ended French influence in Rome, Venice, and elsewhere.[124] In Paris he did indeed project the impression that he sincerely promoted French interests, which was a great improvement over the Duke of Savoy. The entreaties worked, for by a letter of 18 March, Louis XIII ordered Créquy and Victor Amadeus to prepare a substantial army for the Duke of Parma to command. As for a talented subordinate field marshal, the name of Toiras was proposed, but he was not completely trusted by the king or his cardinal minister. Toiras had no desire to serve under Odoardo either, for the duke was known for rejecting good advice.[125] Meanwhile, it appeared ever less likely that the promised second army for the Italian theatre would materialize. Richelieu raised 20,000 more troops for the new campaign in Italy, but only 10,000 of them ever reached their destination, and even many of those soon deserted.[126] The Spanish were, as usual, well informed of the dissensions in the alliance and made Odoardo some secret peace overtures, which he spurned. Meanwhile, Italian and Spanish engineers intuited the allied plan to march to the relief of Piacenza, and began erecting some very strong earthworks along the right bank of the Scrivia river, making it very difficult for any army to force through them.[127] As soon as the allies discussed loading 3,000 men and provisions into barges to float them down the Po, the Spaniards erected a set of barriers across the river at Valenza. Once more, French ministers suspected the Duke of Savoy of undermining the success of the coming campaign.[128]

Odoardo's relations with the French ambassador and with the Duke of Savoy continued to worsen. The contention between the dukes turned on the titles and salutations they demanded of each other. Odoardo insisted on a title upgrade for himself, *Osser.mo* (sic), which Turin had never unilaterally conceded to any Italian prince, not even to the Grand Duke of Tuscany.[129] It had been conceded to the Duke of Modena, but only once he recognized the new royal title the House of Savoy craved.[130] 'Tous ces peuples sont extremement Espagnols…' lamented the French ambassador.[131] Odoardo complained to Hémery of the timetable of relief

---

[124] Humbert, *Le Maréchal de Crequy*, 234.

[125] AAE, Paris, Correspondance Politique, Parme 1; Mémoire envoyé à Mons. Emery, 18 March 1636, fo.158.

[126] Gualdo Priorato, *Historia universale*, 312.

[127] AGS, Estado, Legajo 3344/45: letter from Leganés, 26 May 1636.

[128] BNF, Ms Fr 16929: Relation de M. d'Esmery, fo. 562 v.

[129] The exact title has never been spelled out. Does it mean 'Osservantissimo', a reference to the Farnese position of hereditary standard-bearer (Gonfaloniere) of the Holy Church? I owe this suggestion to Mario Zannoni and to Toby Osborne.

[130] ASPr, Casa e Corte Farnese e Borbona: Carteggio estero 400 (Savoia), Letter from the Sieur Thomas to Monsieur (Gaufridy ?), 1 February 1636.

[131] AAE, Paris, Correspondance Politique Sardaigne, vol. 24: letter from Hémery to Cardinal Richelieu, 1 February 1636.

efforts, and would not consider problems of supply or forage to be valid excuses. He could not be made to understand that armies could not move until at least the month of May when the grass was tall enough to feed, purge, and restore the horses after their winter fast.[132] Odoardo would also not allow French troops into the fortress he held at Sabbioneta, as he would then lose control over it. Worst of all, Hémery could not extract a promise from Odoardo that the army he commanded would not be used against Modena instead of Spain. The duke obsessed over the duplicity of his brother-in-law and schemed to get even at any cost, despite the fact that making peace with Modena would enable him to acquire grain from the Papal States.[133] 'Sa passion estoit au-dessus de tous ses interests!', concluded Hémery.[134] Vittorio Siri added to the chorus of voices claiming that Odoardo was his own worst enemy. 'A most courageous prince, very attached to France, and stubborn in his intentions, but without any real experience, suspicious and avaricious perhaps because of the small revenues that he squeezes from his states, and for the excessive commitments that he took on in order to carry on this war he entered out of ill-judgment, and so his vain hopes were dashed, his considerable lands in the kingdom of Naples were confiscated, and his states in Lombardy surrounded.'[135]

By June, however, the French campaign army in Italy numbered about 15,000 foot and 1,300 horse, while Savoy could field, in addition to its fortress garrisons, an army of 6,000 foot and 2,300 horse, and also provide an artillery train of 10 pieces.[136] Spanish forces were just as numerous, but since the Franco-Savoyards held the initiative, about half of the former would be tied down in fortresses. The allies returned to the old Oleggio plan, whereby the majority of the army would make a bold movement north of Novara in order to effect a junction with the Duke of Rohan, while Odoardo's smaller army would try to crash through the more thinly held lines along the Scrivia. The Marchese Villa would march westward simultaneously from Piacenza in order to assist Odoardo's passage from the other side. Odoardo's little army of only 4,000 foot and a few hundred horse assembled at Nizza della Paglia in the Monferrato, but the French soldiers who comprised it did their utmost to scuttle the venture.[137] Everyone thought that by following Odoardo they would never see another pay muster, and the officers protested that there were not enough provisions for the trip. This crisis was the second crucial test of Odoardo's martial mettle, and he panicked. He decided to abandon his army and sneak away incognito in the company with a handful of his subjects. He rode hard to the coast at Voltri, near Genoa, where he embarked on a boat that bore him further east along the coast to Lerici. Disembarking there, he rode north

---

[132] The best description of this necessity is by G. Perjés, 'Army provisioning, logistics and strategy in the second half of the seventeenth century', *Acta Historica Academiae Scientiarum Hungaricae*, 16 (1970), 1–51.

[133] AAE, Paris, Correspondance Politique, Parme 1: Mémoire du duc de Parme donné à vive voix à M. d'Hémery, 10 May 1636.

[134] BNF, Ms Fr 16929: Relation de M. d'Esmery, fo. 562–3.

[135] Siri, *Memorie recondite di Vittorio Siri*, vol. 8, 400.

[136] Siri, *Memorie recondite di Vittorio Siri*, vol. 8, 402.

[137] *Gazette de France 1636*, n. 93.

into the duchy of Parma, arriving on 24 June.[138] As soon as Marchese Guido Villa learned that Odoardo had returned home, and finding the road in front of him free, he took his cavalry into Piedmont, his mission accomplished.

The Franco-Savoyard army under Créquy and Victor Amadeus deceived Leganés of their intentions for a time. The Spaniards assembled near Valenza on the Po just as the allies marched north to Oleggio and Fontaneto, undermanned forts of no significance. The imprudent marshal, Toiras, was killed while monitoring too closely the bombardment of the latter. The Ticino river was not a substantial barrier and once Créquy crossed it on 14 June, there were no obstacles of any kind between him and Milan. Forty kilometres east of the great city the little army of the Duke of Rohan, hungry and unpaid, reached Lecco and the Adda river bridge ten days earlier, but he was obliged to retreat back towards the Valtellina in search of provisions. Créquy and Victor Amadeus disagreed on their immediate objective. Victor Amadeus wanted to wait for Rohan to join him by a circuitous march through the Alpine lake district. Créquy wanted to push on, and so built a bridge across the Ticino river and established his camp on the other shore, which he strengthened with entrenchments. The location, a hamlet called Tornavento, was a strategic one, for it was the starting point of an important navigation and irrigation canal that flowed towards Milan. By blocking the canal's water intake, Créquy was threatening the great city with hardship, if not famine. French troops quickly sacked the hitherto untouched district and triggered a flow of frightened refugees towards Milan. It would not have been possible for an army as small as the Franco-Savoyard force and its mediocre artillery train to have laid formal siege to a city the size of Milan, even if they were joined by Rohan, for the number of cannon inside the city would have been far greater than those of the besiegers. However, while there was considerable fear inside Milan, there was no thought among the nobles there of embracing the French cause.[139]

The Franco-Savoyard engineers soon became dissatisfied with the army's position, which they considered difficult to fortify and too close to possible interception from Novara, and recommended finding a better one closer to Lake Maggiore. They dismantled the bridge before marching north on 20 June to seek a better crossing. Créquy, with about 6,000 foot and 1,500 horse, moved parallel to the eastern bank of the Ticino, while Victor Amadeus marched along the other side. Leganés, who watched this carefully from his entrenched camp at Abbiategrasso to the south, judged the moment opportune to offer battle to the enemy. If he struck quickly, he could annihilate Créquy's force before Victor Amadeus could come to his aid. Battles were infrequent events because they were risky and not often decisive. An average commander was usually able to elude a large-scale confrontation with an enemy army dragging artillery along with it, but Créquy could not

---

[138] De Mun, *Richelieu et la Maison de Savoie*, 140.
[139] Davide Maffi, *Il baluardo della corona: Guerra, esercito, finanze e società nella Lombardia seicentesca (1630–1660)* (Florence, 2007), 18; for the solidarity of the Lombard feudatories see Mario Rizzo, '"Ottima gente da guerra": Cremonesi al servizio della strategia imperiale', in *Storia di Cremona: L'Età degli Asburgo di Spagna (1535–1707)*, ed. G. Politi (Cremona, 2006), 126–45.

withdraw to safety without building a bridge first. Leganés called together most of his scattered contingents to meet him near Tornavento, just south of the modern airport of Malpensa. Most of the army arrived on 21 June, but many of the contingents were tired from their march and so there was only light skirmishing with the French horse while they waited for Gerardo Gambacorta to arrive with his Neapolitan cavalry.[140] As soon as they learned of the Spanish advance, Créquy and Victor Amadeus reversed direction and raced to reoccupy their old positions. Victor Amadeus set the engineers to work to restore the boat bridge across the river during the night, so that by the morning of 22 June he could send his troops across to help his French ally. Créquy's men for their part, after a long day's march, spent the night improving the earthworks around their positions.

The position was not very extensive, extending perhaps 2 kilometres in a rectangle with each flank anchored on the Ticino river. Much of the French cavalry was placed outside the entrenchments to the north, where it could manoeuvre. Leganés formed up his first line of German, Spanish, and Neapolitan troops into nine large fighting formations, and at eight in the morning advanced resolutely on the French entrenchments, while Gambacorta's dragoons charged the French cavalry on the Spanish right flank. The Spanish infantry marched up to the entrenchments on the north side and stormed them, with the support of deadly artillery crossfire from the battery on the south flank. For a while, this succeeded: the French fell back further towards the crest and lost a second line of entrenchments. Then, from the thick smoke, the French horse suddenly emerged and drove the surprised attackers back to the edge of the entrenchment. While the infantry regrouped out of harm's way, Gambacorta tried to repair the situation by storming the second-line entrenchments anew with the German foot and other cavalry in support. Just as he reached the foot of the earthworks, musketry felled the cavalry general in full view of his troops. By dint of their numerical superiority, the Habsburg formations pressed the French down the ridge, where they found a third line of entrenchments along the Panperduto canal. A long exchange of musketry ensued, during which the Spaniards found themselves exposed to a pair of cannon firing grapeshot.

Leganés tried his luck then with a strong column of infantry on the south flank: two French infantry battalions took heavy casualties and then broke in the direction of the bridge, which stood completed. Spanish troops would have pressed on had another desperate cavalry charge not broken their ranks. Créquy's troops were hard pressed, but eventually stood their ground. After four hours of desperate fighting, the French infantry halfway down the ridge was beginning to tire. By noon, however, Victor Amadeus personally led the first formations of his troops across the bridge and into position, allowing the original troops to withdraw and regroup. They deployed first towards the south at the valley bottom, and then spread out on their left as new units arrived. Before long, the Franco-Savoyard infantry outnumbered their opponents. Leganés would not retreat, however. Fresh units of his just

---

[140] AGS, Estado, Legajo 3344, letter in cipher from Léganes, 25 June 1636; also Fossati, *Memoire historiche delle guerre d'Italia*, 167; Hanlon, Gregory. *Italy 1636: Cemetery of Armies* (Oxford, 2016).

arriving from their night march, like the Tuscans, stepped in to relieve the infantry in the front line. Most of Leganés' cavalry remained posted to the rear where they could prevent stragglers from running away. The most dangerous moment in a battle came not from the face-to-face encounter with the enemy at close quarters. Rather, it was the perception that the defeated army was trying to depart the field that triggered the instinct of pursuit in the victors and gave them fresh energy to add to their bloodlust. This is what had happened at the great Battle of Nördlingen two years before, at which Leganés, Gambacorta, and a good many other senior Habsburg officers had been present. This was the outcome that Leganés sought to avoid, and so he continued to commit his tired foot to the battle until nightfall. Then, under cover of darkness, he withdrew his guns and his wagons and marched his infantry south towards his entrenched camp at Abbiategrasso, about 20 kilometres away. He had muskets with their glowing wicks placed along the first trenches, to give the impression that his line was strongly held, while his dragoons paced back and forth all night, firing blindly into the French positions.

Casualties on both sides were reportedly very heavy, especially among the officers, who stood at the front of their unit and personally led them close to the enemy. Multiple accounts of the Battle of Tornavento all confirm that it was a hard-fought engagement lasting an entire day. We can therefore credit Gualdo Priorato's claim that about 3,000 men on both sides died in the action. This figure would probably have been higher for the Spaniards, who were attacking troops behind entrenchments, who would have been partially protected by their parapet. Hémery estimated that French dead and wounded were in the range of 1,300 men, of which over 100 were officers. If Gualdo Priorato's estimate is approximately correct, the battle would have killed about 10 per cent of the men participating in it, which was high by early modern standards, but these losses would have been incurred at the rate of only 100 every hour for each side, or three men a minute. We should not imagine that the tempest of musket balls at short range mowed down men like grass.[141] Perhaps the low *frequency* of casualties made it possible for men to stand in close formations for long periods within range of the enemy. The function of the officers was to reduce the fear of the rank and file and bring them closer to the enemy, at considerable risk to themselves. The aim was not so much to inflict greater casualties on the enemy as it was to frighten them into withdrawing, or even better, turning tail and fleeing, which tended to occur from the rear of the formation. It was generally at this moment that the mechanisms inhibiting killing evaporated and the losses among the vanquished quickly escalated.[142] In any case, the 'will to combat' of the participants was a more powerful factor in achieving victory than tactics or weapons, which tended to be fairly evenly matched. Leganés'

---

[141] For the effectiveness of musketry in battle in a later era using similar weapons, see Rory Muir, *Tactics and the Experience of Battle in the Age of Napoleon* (New Haven and London, 1998), 7 and 49; for the rate of shot to casualties, 83; also George Raudzens, 'Firepower limitations in modern military history', *Journal of the Society for Army Historical Research*, 67 (1989), 130–53.

[142] John Keegan, *The Face of Battle* (Harmondsworth and New York, 1976), 165–72; for a critique of Marshall's fieldwork, see Robert Engen, 'Tuer pour son pays: Nouveau regard sur l'homicidologie', *Revue Militaire Canadienne*, 9 (2009): 120–8.

troops marched into the Battle of Tornavento with high spirits, and they withdrew in good order with most of their cavalry intact and able to provide a screen for the retreating infantry. In an army accustomed to success like the Spanish one, many of the soldiers who drifted away from their companies during the fighting would appear in camp soon after.

Tornavento was a setback for the Spanish army, but not a serious defeat, for it relinquished little territory in the aftermath, and they continued to remove into fortresses the forage and ripe grain close to the enemy.[143] The French and Swiss Protestant army of the Duke of Rohan was in no position to move away from its Valtellina base to join Créquy. Every muster of troops Rohan held revealed a force that was smaller than he thought, and by the spring of 1636 his field army probably numbered only 4,500 men. He had no supply from Paris to speak of, and his relations with his Swiss allies were near breaking point. The soldiers had not been paid in over a year and many of his men were dressed in rags. By the time of the Battle of Tornavento some of his French regiments had mutinied, and the dissension spread to the Swiss regiments too.[144] The Franco-Savoyard army held its position at Tornavento for several weeks more, anticipating a new battle as Spanish reinforcements arrived, but losses from the heat, from the disastrous hygienic situation (corpses of soldiers and horses lay strewn about for days after the battle), and from men ambushed while looting enemy farms, continued to mount. By the end of July, Spanish patrols operating from Novara threatened to cut off supply convoys from Piedmont, and so the confederate army withdrew back behind the Sesia frontier. For all intents, the campaign of 1636 was over and Leganés' army was stronger than before. This meant he could deal with Odoardo and his battered duchy without hindrance.

[143] Gualdo Priorato, *Historia universale*, 335–9.
[144] Pierre Deyon and Solange Deyon, *Henri de Rohan, huguenot de plume et d'épée, 1579–1638* (Paris, 2000), 171–5.

5

The Deluge

THE DELUGE

Jubilation greeted Odoardo's return to Parma on 26 June, recorded by an exultant Andrea Pugolotti, who had been sceptical about the war from the beginning.

> Thursday at one hour after sundown arrived in Parma his Serene Lord Duke Odoardo, may God keep and save him, who came from his army by route of the mountains of Genoa and of Rigosso... The entire city went out to meet him and for most to kiss his hand, and some an arm, some a leg and some a foot, everyone crying, 'Viva! Viva!' because most people suspected that he would have been assassinated by the French ministers. And during this joyous arrival, all the bells of the city rang continuously until he had dismounted, and he could not dismount from his horse for the great throng of people around him, who carried him to the top of the stairs of the palace, where there was the Serene Madama his mother and his sisters. For the above-mentioned allegrezza, for three continous evenings, in the Great Square, and in the square at the end of the bridge there were beautiful bonfires and various fireworks, and very copious alms given out to mark his arrival. The Illustrissima Comunità [city officials] had a Te Deum mass sung in the church of the Steccata, and for the next three days there were solemn ceremonies throughout the city and joyous festivities every evening.[1]

Odoardo soon galloped off incognito to Piacenza with a small escort, in order to confer with his wife and ministers about continuing the war. The duke's surprise departure from the Monferrato district caught everyone off guard. Hémery was not impressed and called him a coward. 'Fear took hold of him and Count Fabio [Scotti] too, who is spineless [*lâche*] and thinks only of himself and cares not about his master, and for a long time now I have thought we would not see anything good come out of these people...'[2]

With the few thousand professional soldiers he had at his disposal, Odoardo formed several detachments and launched them in different directions simultaneously to recapture lost towns, or to avenge the torment of his duchy with retaliatory raids of his own in the Cremonese and the Lodigiano. His French officers were by no means overjoyed at his return, as is clear by the fact that they gathered to deliberate

---

[1] Andrea Pugolotti, *Libro di memorie. Cronaca parmense del XVII secolo*, ed. Sergio Di Noto (Parma, 2005), 95.
[2] AAE Paris and La Courneuve, Correspondance Politique Sardaigne, vol. 24: letter from Hémery to Gaston d'Orléans, 26 June 1636.

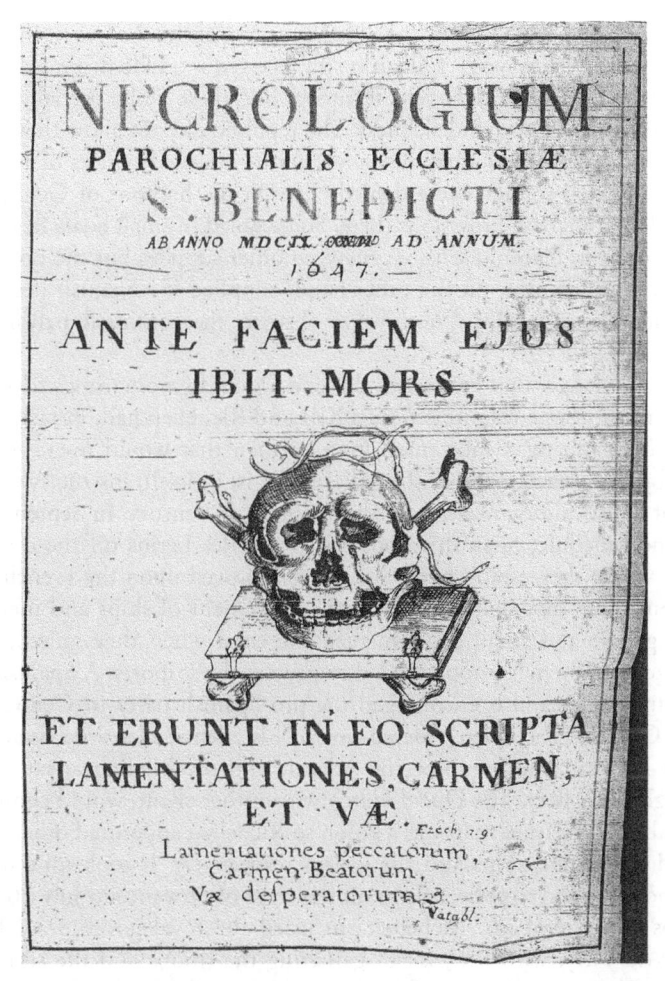

Fig. 5.1. Cover page, mortuary register. This pen-and-ink title-page to the parish burial register reveals war's human toll.

whether or not they should return home.[3] On 13 July Odoardo wrote to the French resident in Genoa, Sabran, to complain that Saint-Paul had told his officers to expect no help from France, and that they must draw all their sustenance from Parma. Odoardo warned Sabran that the reinforcements Richelieu promised him had better bring a lot of money and their own provisions with them, otherwise he did not want them. Hémery claimed that troops in the duchy had received more pay than those camped on the Ticino river, but Odoardo denied it.[4] He complained

---

[3] Ms Parmense 737, L'Heroe d'Italia, overo Vita del Sereniss.o Odoardo Farnese il Grande, d'Ippolito Calandrini, 784–6.
[4] AAE, Paris, Correspondance Politique Sardaigne, vol. 24: letter from Hémery to Cardinal Richelieu, 15 July 1636.

that Hémery had sent no money for a long time, proof that he was trying to undermine the duke in every way.[5] Odoardo still received a trickle of French reinforcements overland through Genoese territory, but these only partially offset the numbers lost to desertion and sickness. The republic did not allow them to march in large groups with their weapons, and bandits attacked parties of them in the mountains. French soldiers were denied entry in the harbour of Genoa itself, so were unable to purchase provisions there. Some sailed in small boats from Voltri to Rapallo and on to Piacenza with virtually no other supplies but the bread in their knapsacks. The Genoese, on the other hand, supplied the Spanish fleet at Finale Liguria with biscuit, and did nothing to obstruct the continual arrival by sea of Spanish troops.[6]

There was a danger that France would send Odoardo more troops than he could support on his meagre resources. Louis XIII and Richelieu had, in fact, kept their promise of organizing a substantial force of men that would rescue Parma and Piacenza by sea. The episode of this relief effort is, in itself, instructive of the difficulties of logistical organization in the seventeenth century. In September 1635, well behind schedule, Spanish troops seized the Îles Lérins off the east coast of Provence, where they established a base and improved upon the French fortifications. From there they could intercept the movement of ships and men towards Italy (for galleys and small boats hugged the coast when they sailed), and they immobilized the French troops needed to protect the seaports. A Spanish military presence in that area also encouraged the pro-Spanish party in Genoa and tiny Monaco. Cardinal Richelieu ordered one of his clients, Henri de Sourdis, archbishop of Bordeaux, to combine the Atlantic and the Mediterranean squadrons into a single great fleet. The Duc d'Harcourt, another client, would command the troops on board. Neither man was a sailor, so Richelieu appointed other officers to command the sailing ships and the galleys respectively. It took nine months to prepare the ships and to collect them off the coast of Provence in July 1636, where the troops would embark. Richelieu entrusted the royal governor of Provence, Monsieur de Vitry, with the task of gathering the troops and the stores for the expedition. The mere existence of this fleet, which was larger than any English fleet of the first half of the seventeenth century, would intimidate the Italian states like Genoa or Tuscany into neutrality or better. But in order to salve the feelings of his various clients, the cardinal neglected to designate one officer among them who would have the ultimate command over the expedition. He gave Sourdis a letter telling him that he would be the de facto chief, but he was to keep this secret from Harcourt and Vitry. The result was continual infighting over precedence, authority, and general command, which kept the ships in harbour and the troops ashore, awaiting provisions.[7]

---

[5] AAE, Paris, Correspondance Politique Parme, vol. 1: letter to M. de Sabran, 13 July 1636.

[6] Raffaele Ciasca, ed., *Istruzioni e relazioni degli Ambasciatori Genovesi*, vol. 3: *Spagna (1636–1655)* (Rome, 1955), 4–6.

[7] E. Delahaye, 'Une campagne de l'armée navale sous Louis XIII: la reprise des iles de Lérins et le secours de Parme (1636–1637)', *Revue Maritime* (1929): 13–37.

The fleet anchored near Toulon on 2 August, where the three co-commanders bickered over strategy. The fleet numbered several dozen armed sailing vessels in contrast to the Spanish 12 (most of which were lightly armed). However, the commanders possessed only 12 galleys to the Spanish 40 (including a few Tuscan craft). Galleys were troop- and artillery-conveyance vessels that could operate close to shore. Spanish superiority in that arm meant that the French would be unable to land troops on the islands without great peril. There were two galley actions on 8 and 10 August, engaging roughly equal numbers of ships on each side. Although the French claimed victory, the Spanish continued to convey supplies and reinforcements to the island without interruption, with the help of several French pilots.[8] Richelieu's fleet then moored in the Piedmontese harbour of Villefranche for two months to no effect, and the troops began to disband on their own. Despite an appeal from Louis XIII for the fleet to do something, it returned to Toulon on 11 December. Fabio Scotti in Paris warned that, without reinforcements, Odoardo's withdrawal from the war was imminent, and so Richelieu announced plans to send a new force of 4,000 foot and 200 horse by sea, a portion of which embarked at the end of January 1637. It was finally ready to weigh anchor on 3 February, when Fabio Scotti arrived with news of Parma's treaty with Spain. The real existence of this substantial relief force guided Odoardo's decisions in this last segment of his war and underlay the public relations he employed to continue it.[9]

Rather than consolidate his forces, Odoardo desired only to take revenge on his many adversaries. The betrayal of his brother-in-law, Duke Francesco of Modena would have to wait; Odoardo would not listen to a peace project promoted by his mother (in Parma) and his sister (in Modena). Both thought he was being unreasonable and peevish, and predicted that Francesco would dismiss his excessive demands out of hand.[10] More strategically sound was Odoardo's plan to punish Prince Doria for seizing Borgo Taro and the mountain fiefs that the latter claimed as his patrimony. Both sides viewed this conflict as an ongoing vendetta between the Landi and the Farnese usurpers. For generations after the assassination of the first Duke of Parma and Piacenza, the Landi and the Farnese remained mortal enemies. Philip III's award of the Golden Fleece to Federico Landi in 1612 effectively rendered him untouchable. In an act of spite, Ranuccio Farnese used another false plot against his life in 1617 as a pretext to seize all the remaining lands of the leading branch of the Landi still in Farnese jurisdiction. Federico Landi bounced back by becoming the Holy Roman Emperor's emissary to all the Imperial fiefs in Italy from 1619 to 1621. The Landi prince lacked a son onto whom he could pass his patrimony, but King Philip III of Spain blessed his project to marry his daughter to a powerful Genoese dynasty under Spanish protection. Prince Giovanni Andrea Doria was already the lord of the mountain fiefs Santo Stefano d'Aveto and Varese

---

[8] Archives du Service Historique de la Défense (hereafter ASHD), A33, n. 166; the entire microfilm consists of an account of this affair.

[9] In addition to the article by Delahaye, see Réné La Bruyère, *La Marine de Richelieu: Sourdis, archévêque et amiral (6 novembre 1594–18 juin 1645)* (Paris, 1948), 39–53; also Roger Charles Anderson, 'The Thirty Years War in the Mediterranean', *Mariner's Mirror*, 15 (1969): 435–51.

[10] ASMo, Ambasciatori Parma 6, dispatches of 18 August 1636.

Ligure, contiguous to the Landi fiefs of the upper Taro and Ceno river valleys. The marriage created a mountain 'state' of adjacent fiefs more extensive than before. Not to be outdone, the Farnese turned to a junior branch of the Landi under the Piacenza count Ippolito, who swore fealty to the Farnese rather than to the emperor. Ippolito Landi remained a solid Farnese client, holding the strategic fief of Rivalta near Piacenza. Odoardo later appointed him garrison commander at Sabbioneta.[11]

To avenge himself on Doria, Odoardo dispatched the Chevalier de la Haie with four companies of French soldiers, supported by a company of mounted arquebusiers under Antonio Rota and several hundred choice militiamen, up the Val di Nure to attack Santo Stefano. The little garrison of Corsican soldiers surrendered the castle after three days and signed on with Farnese forces, which is the only example I have found in Italy of a practice widespread in the German Thirty Years' War. Then this little army descended into the upper Taro valley to sack and burn the hamlets there in reprisal and to offer some compensation to the unpaid soldiery. The militiamen defending these settlements withdrew to the strong castle of Compiano, which could not be taken without artillery.[12] Borgo Taro could not be recovered without siege equipment either. Nevertheless, the seizure of Santo Stefano opened a shorter and safer route to the Mediterranean coast through which the expected French reinforcements could pass.

Keen to accomplish something decisive, Odoardo massed several thousand of his troops and militia and ordered them to transform the blockade of Rottofreno into a proper siege, whose success would liberate Piacenza from imminent danger. Due to the inexperience of the officers and the soldiers and the small numbers of men and cannon available, they made little headway for several weeks. The infantry commander Comte de Saint-Paul was on bad terms with the head of the cavalry, Fulvio Clerici, and there were deep antipathies between the Italian and the French officers generally.[13] Thanks to the relative inactivity of the Duke of Savoy after Tornavento, Leganés dispatched Don Martin d'Aragon with a force of about 1,500 cavalry and 3,000 professional infantry, and several thousand militiamen from the defensive lines along the Scrivia, with the aim of lifting the siege. Odoardo in Piacenza was unhappy about the discord among his officers, and, despite the rumours that the enemy numbered 10,000 men, he was of a mind to ride out to Rottofreno and lead his army into battle personally. Fearing the worst, Serafini, the citadel commander, talked him out of putting himself in harm's way. Farnese cavalry scouts spotted Don Martin's little army at Castel San Giovanni in the afternoon of 15 August. The Spanish force advanced so quickly that Saint-Paul did

---

[11] For the century-long Farnese-Landi feud see Riccardo De Rosa, 'La congiura di Claudio Landi contro i Farnese e i suoi riflessi sulla questione di Borgo Val di Taro', *Bollettino Storico Piacentino*, 97 (2002): 131–50; and, by the same author, 'Per la storia dello Stato Landi tra Cinque e Seicento: la controversia tra Ippolito e Federico Landi per Borgo Taro', *Bollettino Storico Piacentino*, 96 (2001): 95–114.

[12] Ms Parmense 737, L'Heroe d'Italia, 791; Giovanni Pietro Crescenzi Romani, *Corona della nobiltà d'Italia, ovvero compendio dell'Istorie delle famiglie illustri*, 2 vols. (Bologna, 1639–42), vol. 2, 315.

[13] Ms Parmense 737, L'Heroe d'Italia, 812.

not have time to deploy his besiegers into battle formation. Odoardo's badly outnumbered cavalry broke and fled in disorder, leaving the infantry behind. These latter began to exchange salvos with the enemy in front of them, when the gates of Rottofreno opened and the garrison attacked them from the rear. Panic set in immediately. Trying to stem the flight of the troops, Marchese Ranuccio Pallavicino was killed and his body stripped. Saint-Paul's son was taken prisoner, and a number of other French and Italian infantry officers paid for their bravery with their lives. The Farnese army fled towards the Trebbia, stopped near the river bank and re-formed on the open ground without orders, but the Spaniards did not pursue them farther. The estimates of men killed and captured vary from 150 to 900, although according to the French and Farnese sources I am inclined to accept the lower figure. There were few battles where both sides agreed on the tally of dead and wounded, and military administrations kept no proper accountancy of battle casualties. When commanders tallied losses, they usually did not specify between the number of dead, wounded, and prisoners. Even then, these one-day losses were much inferior to the wastage of armies through desertion and disease.[14] Rottofreno was an 'action', in the parlance of the seventeenth century, like the encounter at Pontecurone the year before, and the one at San Lazzaro outside Parma. It did not deploy an entire army in formal battle array, and the event was partly improvised by Don Martin d'Aragon. The results of the brief fight proved that the motley army of the Duke of Parma was still no match for the Spaniards in the open field, and the dispirited survivors began to think of their individual salvation.[15]

Leganés was still receiving reinforcements from Germany, from Naples, and from his allies in Florence and Modena too, even if not in the numbers the dukes had promised.[16] A strategic stalemate was in the Spanish interest, and there were voices suggesting that this was what the Duke of Savoy wanted too.[17] It was still possible to undo Richelieu's Italian alliance by knocking Parma out of the war. Many of Odoardo's companies, by early August, were only shadows of their former selves, and so the duchy became an inviting target in the aftermath of the Battle of Tornavento.[18] One of the weapons Leganés used to undermine Parma was hunger.

---

[14] Alain Guéry, 'Les comptes de la mort vague après la guerre. Pertes de guerre et conjoncture du phenomène guerre', *Histoire et Mesure*, 6 (1991), 289–312; George Raudzens, 'In search of better quantification for war history: numerical superiority and casualty rates in early modern Europe', *War and Society*, 15 (1997): 1–30. Raudzens's figures are based on published figures of dubious origin, alas!, although he admits as much in his text.

[15] AAE, Paris, Cartes Politiques Parme, vol. 1: Relation of the Battle of Rottofreno for Cardinal Richelieu, f. 214–16; Ms Parmense 737, L'Heroe d'Italia, 184; excessively high figures appear in the booklet of the notorious libertine author Ferrante Pallavicino, *Successi del mondo dell'anno MDCXXXVI* (Venice, 1638), 76, who writes of 600 Franco-Farnese troops killed (including 11 captains) and another 300 captured; Crescenzi Romani, *Corona della nobiltà d'Italia*, gives a figure of 'perhaps' 200 killed.

[16] Carla Sodini, 'L'Italie et la guerre de Trente Ans', in *Nouveaux regards sur la Guerre de Trente Ans: Centre d'Etudes d'Histoire de la Défense*, ed. Philippe Bonnichon (Vincennes, 1998), 37–56.

[17] Galeazzo Gualdo Priorato, *Il guerriero prudente e politico (1640)* (Venezia and Bologna, 1641), ed. Angelo Tamborra (Naples, 2002), 37.

[18] ASPr, Governo Farnesiano, Carteggio Farnesiano Interno 384, Rolo delle compagnie dei reggimenti Marchese Cana... (illegible) and of the Marchese Poma, 2 August 1636. Five companies of the first regiment totalled 247 men. Eight companies of the second regiment amounted to a mere 157 men. The document is in very poor condition.

A regiment of German cavalry under Gil de Haes, consisting of about 900 troopers, patrolled the district west of Piacenza, with the aim of preventing peasants from bringing in the harvest. Other Spanish horse based in Rottofreno similarly harried the peasantry. This classic 'petite guerre' often degenerated into wholesale looting, for the troopers could keep much of what they seized. Even inside Rottofreno, hunger was a powerful weapon, for the local population could be induced to help the Spaniards fortify the place by releasing food stocks for them.[19]

Leganés would gladly have seized Piacenza and Parma by surprise or storm, but the Spanish general had a high opinion of the strength of the fortifications of both cities, and expected that the enemy would be more resolute in the defence of the city walls. He could, on the other hand, asphyxiate the cities by occupying their rural hinterlands, and this became feasible in the aftermath of the fight. The Spanish general's method resembles nothing so much as the art of war prescribed in a textbook by Raimondo Montecuccoli, a Modenese adventurer in Imperial service who penned a hugely influential text while a prisoner of the Swedes around 1640. Offensive war entailed sowing division and fear among enemy leaders, and striking terror in the hearts of enemy subjects such that they do not think of resisting. This could be done by setting fire to the countryside, or brandishing the threat of fire to obtain compliance. Keep communications open with the rear by bridging rivers, and plant garrisons throughout conquered territory, Montecuccoli wrote.[20] Cruel practices such as these were time-honoured means of making war on enemy princes and, for most soldiers, this activity was much more common than battle, which they might never experience.[21] Habsburg troops first ravaged the countryside beyond the Trebbia from 16 to 18 August; the terrorized inhabitants fled to Piacenza with their possessions.[22] Then, on 19 August, Cardinal Trivulzio led his forces across the Po from the Cremonese, intent on occupying the rich plain and imposing 'contributions' on it. For the cardinal, who had his own *tercio* and additional troops of foot and horse under his command, this war was also a personal vendetta against Duke Odoardo.[23] His forces chased Farnese troops from the isolated outposts north of the Po and took the war across the river. This time the Spaniards had come not merely to pressure Odoardo, but to exact retribution, '*giusta vendetta*' for his trespasses against them. Over the next month, the combined Spanish forces invaded the duchy from three directions, with the design of sucking from it all means of waging war. This manner of making war against civilians was not unlike the medieval 'chevauchée', which entailed deliberate devastation on a

---

[19] Sandrine Picaud, 'La "guerre de partis" au XVIIe siècle en Europe', *Stratégique*, 88 (2007): 101–46; see also AAE, Paris, Correspondance Politique Sardaigne, vol. 24, letters of St Paul to Héméry, 29 April and 20 May 1636.

[20] Montecuccoli's aphorisms are reproduced in Marco Costa, *Psicologia militare: elementi di psicologia per gli appartenenti alle forze armate* (Milan, 2003), 116–22.

[21] Simon Pepper, 'Aspects of operational art: communications, cannon and small war', in *European Warfare 1350–1750*, ed. F. Tallett and D. J. B. Trim (Cambridge and New York, 2010), 181–202.

[22] BCPLPc, Ms Pallastrelli 126, Croniche Boselli, 20 August 1636, 124.

[23] Gianvittorio Signorotto, *Milano Spagnola: Guerra, istituzioni, uomini di governo (1635–1660)* (2nd edn, Milan, 2001), 127.

large scale.[24] The Comte de Saint-Paul understood the implications of this invasion. We must fear for the revenues of the duke, he wrote, '...and yet we see the duke as pro-French as he ever was, and unshaken by any of these tragic events or contrary fortune...' Odoardo was reduced to trying to hold his duchy with 2,000 or 3,000 professional soldiers, at least half of whom he concentrated around Piacenza.[25] Two understrength regiments of French and Italian infantry, totalling 1,000 men, slipped into Parma from Mantuan territory in late August.[26] To 'encourage' his subjects to make a greater effort, Odoardo made examples of commanders who had failed in their duties. At least two captains were executed for having abandoned their posts, after two priests were hanged for unspecified crimes connected to the war.

The Piacenza aristocrat Crescenzi Romani provides the most detail concerning the Spanish occupation of the duchy. In the district beyond the Taro, and occasionally elsewhere, soldiers set the villages ablaze after their capture and plunder. Fire was a powerful psychological lesson, punishing those who resisted or merely afflicting those who witnessed it with a sense of powerlessness.[27] A closer reading of the sources provides a much more nuanced picture. When soldiers came to stay, there was always a threat of violence, but it was more profitable for the officers who were concerned for the survival of their soldiers to squeeze resources from the inhabitants over a longer period of time. The soldiers *might* torch buildings, but the military code of the seventeenth century encouraged them to levy 'contributions' instead, that is, extort resources on the threat of burning the houses and barns of those who refused to comply, and confine the burning to those who fled to escape payment.[28] Outlying hamlets suffered the worst because small parties of uncontrolled raiders could generally do whatever they wished on the spur of the moment, and there was no record-keeping of the nature that accompanied more orderly requisitions. Burning the dwellings would have been counterproductive in many cases, for the soldiers preferred to lodge in the houses, not destroy them. In larger communities, local authorities were anxious to collaborate with the invaders in order to keep the destruction to a minimum. The war between the King of Spain and the Duke of Parma was conceived by both sides as a kind of personal feud, wherein the subjects of each enjoyed no rights that soldiers had to respect. It was, nevertheless, a maxim that it was good policy to treat the vassals of one's enemies courteously so as not to incite them to desperate resistance.[29] Finally, the see-saw nature of success in war over the longer duration gave rise to a sense of

---

[24] Brian Sandberg, *Warrior Pursuits: Noble Culture and Civil Conflict in Early Modern France* (Baltimore, 2010), 255.
[25] BCPLPc, Ms Pallastrelli 126, Croniche Boselli, 20 August 1636.
[26] Crescenzi Romani, *Corona della nobiltà d'Italia*, vol. 2, 322.
[27] Fritz Redlich, *De Praeda militari: Looting and Booty 1500–1815* (Wiesbaden, 1956), 44.
[28] Stephen Porter, *Destruction in the English Civil Wars* (Dover, NH, 1994), 33; for Germany see Otto Ulbricht, 'The experience of violence during the Thirty Years War: a look at the civilian victims', in *Power, Violence and Mass Death in Pre-modern and Modern times*, ed. J. Canning, H. Lehmann and J. Winter (Aldershot, 2004), 97–129.
[29] Gualdo Priorato, *Il guerriero prudente*, 59; for war as large-scale feud justifying the spoliation of subjects, Redlich, *De Praeda Militari*, 2–4.

Fig. 5.2. Callot: soldiers burning a village, c.1633. Armed villagers dug in around the church, dare the soldiers to come closer.

reciprocity, positive as well as negative. Odoardo's subjects were being punished for his trespass against the King of Spain, but the confederate armies were liable to reply in kind at the first opportunity if the soldiery got out of hand.[30]

In Busseto, which was typical of towns with a wall and a corporate identity, the Spaniards arrived in some force, pulling four cannon behind them, on 25 August. They would have occupied the town immediately but for a rainstorm. When the town opened its gates without resistance on 28 August, Don Martin d'Aragon met the town assembly and demanded that they pay 1000 doble or around 31,000 lire. This was a huge sum, impossible to pay immediately, so the general accepted a compromise. First, he wanted the grain that had been stockpiled there after being removed from the vulnerable farms in the district. Busseto also agreed to supply 200 rations of bread for the garrison daily and to provide firewood too. It was more efficient for Don Martin to leave the mechanics of this supply to the local worthies, who forced the ecclesiastics to pay a share.[31] The soldiers allowed the inhabitants of the district to finish the harvest and plant the fields for the following year. In nearby Soragna, occupied by Spanish troops on 29 August, there was a similar disparity of fate between the town and the country. In the countryside the soldiers led away the livestock and all they could carry, killing men, burning houses, and generally doing their worst, according to a local inhabitant, who did not specify exactly where or when these incidents occurred. As for the town, Marchese Gian Paolo Meli Lupi, who was a relative of Cardinal Trivulzio, rushed to Cremona to obtain special treatment for his fief. The inhabitants did not escape entirely, for our scribe records that in two occupations the soldiers took away 8 oxen and 7 cows, a mare, a vat of wine, and burned 326 bundles

---

[30] Parker, Geoffrey, 'The etiquette of atrocity: the more things change, the more they stay the same', *MHQ: Quarterly Journal of Military History* (1993); reprinted in *Empire, War and Faith in Early Modern Europe* (London, 2002), 143–68.

[31] Marco Boscarelli, *Contributi alla storia degli Stati Pallavicino (secc. XV–XVII)* (Parma, 1992), 97–105.

of firewood all belonging to (the chronicler) personally. He also paid a special 'contribution', amounting to 503 lire, during the five months of the troops' presence.[32] These were large sums for rural Italy, two or three times the annual income of a peasant nuclear family. Despite this hardship, people remained in their homes and planted the winter beans as usual.

Spanish forces similarly took up lodgings in Colorno, Sissa, Sala, Felino, and Torrechiara at the foot of the Apennines, all of them walled towns: none put up a fight. We have a detailed account of the capitulation of Cortemaggiore, an agricultural centre of considerable importance not far from Piacenza, because the duke opened an inquest following what he considered its premature surrender. Cristoforo Arcelli, a Piacenza noble, commanded three militia companies there, and the castle was described as having very strong walls, a wet moat, and a drawbridge. The transcript of the trial against Arcelli reveals that most of the infantry was away patrolling the Po when the Spanish arrived from the opposite direction. News spread that the Spaniards had set Fiorenzuola on fire, and people could see smoke on the horizon. The town council had just assembled and sought the advice of a nobleman who had some experience of military matters. Arcelli sent out a drummer to raise as many peasant militiamen as he could to defend the town, but only a few dozen presented themselves, and most of them retreated into the castle. The handful of militiamen remaining in the town exchanged fire with the first enemy scouts, but they were too few in number to hold the barricades against the main body of enemy, who probably numbered several hundred. Attacking infantry exchanged musket fire with the defenders around the gate, while the cavalry circled the town looking for a convenient place to storm the shabby ramparts. Enemy cavalrymen dismounted and stormed the weak point with sword in hand, killing one of the defenders and chasing the others back towards the castle. Other inhabitants streamed into the church to take sanctuary there. From the castle ramparts the militiamen watched the Spaniards sack the town and took pot shots at them from their vantage point. Soon a Spanish officer presented himself at the foot of the castle with a local priest at his side and asked to speak to Arcelli. The Spaniard claimed that his force consisted of a large number of men with six pieces of artillery directly under Don Martin d'Aragon. If the castle surrendered, he promised that the people inside would be safe, but otherwise all would perish by fire and sword. Discussions continued, with an exchange of hostages at the level of captain, but these were soon broken off and the hostages returned. The defenders wanted to ascertain that the enemy force was indeed as powerful as it pretended to be. Then the Spaniards set up a pair of cannon, probably eight-pounders, which fired half a dozen times without doing serious damage to the castle. This was merely a prelude to a new summons to surrender from an enemy officer, who threatened this time to inflict harm on those inhabitants taking shelter in the church. Arcelli considered the mood of his principal staff and decided to hold out for a while longer.

---

[32] Antonio Boselli, 'Cenni Storici di letteratura dialettale parmense', *Archivio Storico per le Province Parmensi*, 5 (1905): 1–127 Cronaca di Pietro Belino, 29 August 1636.

The leisurely cannonade continued for several hours, and the effect of a couple of dozen shots was to knock down part of a curtain wall, seriously unsettling many of the women taking shelter in the castle. A third summons to surrender that evening was embroidered by several priests and a town notable who complained that enemy dragoons had already carried off sacred objects, and killed and wounded people. This exhortation brought an agreement to discuss terms again the following morning. During the night the Spaniards brought several more cannon into the town and set them up in battery. This unnerved everyone inside even more, who began to reason that surrender under these conditions would be perfectly honourable. That evening the hostage left with Don Martin d'Aragon returned with the terms of capitulation for study. These provided that the soldiers would be allowed to leave the castle with their personal effects, their weapons, and their standard unfurled, to be escorted anywhere they wanted in Farnese territory. The inhabitants (*paesani*) would be safe on their property even outside the town. Arcelli's junior officers later denied they had any part in the decision to surrender, but they willingly obeyed the order to file from the castle to the church, where the Spaniards disarmed them. After spending the night in the church, a priest escorted these men to Piacenza. The entire garrison was said to number 25 or 30 persons, short on weapons but not on supplies. One witness remembered that a lieutenant involved in the discussions dined with the enemy and drank the health of the King of Spain, while Arcelli spent the entire day in the company of the enemy officers. Tongues began to wag that he had placed himself at their service. Arcelli sent a letter to the duke explaining his reasons for surrendering, but was careful not to go to Piacenza himself, mindful of the fate of the commander the castle of Val di Moccia, hanged in July for having abandoned his post. Witnesses reported that he went to Cremona and Milan soon after.[33]

Having lost most of the minor centres, Odoardo was concerned now to husband his professional soldiers in the two principal cities and in a handful of 'improved' castles guarding important passages into the duchy. Officers were instructed *not* to defend the scores of feudal castles adjacent to the villages. These were built or reinforced in the fourteenth and fifteenth centuries as the seat of power for the great feudal families. The arrival of the Farnese put an end to the dreams of autonomy of these little statelets, and the lords residing in the cities wielded considerable power.[34] A few of these complexes retained some defensive value, so desperate peasants, sometimes under the direction of their lords, decided to move their belongings inside the enclosures and to put up a fight to retain them, as in centuries past.[35] Europe's ancient castles still served as bases from which troops could patrol the countryside, surprise raiding parties, and recover their booty.[36] In this capacity they were as useful to the invaders as they were to the inhabitants. Now, in the

---

[33] BCPLPc, Ms Comunale 546, Processo contro Cristoforo Arcelli (1636).
[34] Roberto Greci, 'Il castello signorile nei piccoli stati autonomi del contado parmense', in *Corti del Rinascimento nella provincia di Parma* (Turin, 1981), 9–40.
[35] This kind of warfare had a long past; see William Caferro, *Mercenary Companies and the Decline of Siena* (Baltimore, 1998), 67–77.
[36] Sandberg, *Warrior Pursuits*, 209.

Fig. 5.3. Cortemaggiore castle, *c.*1780. Castles like these would resist for days if the assailants lacked heavy artillery.

autumn of 1636, the war turned into a series of short sieges as the Spanish forces saw each unconquered castle as a treasure chest waiting to be unlocked. If Crescenzi Romani's account is accurate, these sieges followed a set protocol. At Riva in the Piacentino, the militia major Cerati held his peasant garrison in hand for eight days, until the enemy cannon arrived. After the attackers ruined the village he then held out in the castle for 30 cannon shots before giving up. Muradello was defended by its lord, Alberto Nicelli, with some French soldiers and the local militia. They too withstood bombardment from cannon before they capitulated. In the plain, these castles generally only resisted until the cannon arrived.[37]

In the hills and the mountains, however, the resistance was more stubborn. At Rocca d'Algesi, both the noblemen and peasants brought their valuables into the castle, commanded by its lord, Count Federico del Verme, who paid the Spaniards (as did many other feudatories) not to burn the outlying houses. There and at Reggiano, similarly held by a handful of noblemen and peasants, the garrison barricaded the gates with heavy beams and peasant carts, which tied down hundreds of attackers for several days. At Reggiano the besiegers allowed non-combatant nobles and the women to be evacuated to Piacenza as a prelude to giving up the castle. Its surrender netted the Spanish 150 large head of livestock and 1,000 *stara* of wheat (enough to feed Don Martin's entire army for two weeks). A lieutenant Camia, held out for several days in the castle at Ferriere, the mining town in the high Apennines. When the same Spanish force reached the large commercial village

---

[37] Crescenzi Romani, *Corona della nobiltà d'Italia*, 322–5.

of Bettolle a few kilometres downstream from it, the local notables and militiamen withdrew into the town hall and its tower and put up a stiff fight. However, German troops forced their way into the rear of the building and massacred all those inside, including priests, nobles, and the district judge. Its fall induced most other nearby places to pay contributions without resistance, but the invaders were disinclined to penetrate more remote mountain districts.[38] Thus, from mid-August to mid-December, enemy parties overran much of the duchy and planted garrisons in several dozen castles.[39] These served as permanent bases for patrols imposing contributions on the inhabitants, and places where they could collect livestock and fodder for their army. The immediate districts around Parma and Piacenza remained under Farnese control, for strong columns of troops could sally forth during the day and do damage to the enemy patrols. But every night they would retreat back to the safety of the fortress city.[40] Most of the mountain districts similarly remained in Farnese hands, for providing provisions to isolated Habsburg detachments in snowbound strongpoints would be more trouble than it was worth.[41]

From September 1636 onward panic became general in the duchy. Everywhere people were trying to guess which way the invaders would march next, and every rumour triggered waves of departures towards the cities. 'At least wait until they march in your direction before retiring!', Odoardo ordered the garrison commander of the duchy's third-largest town, Borgo San Donnino, whose walls had been dismantled decades earlier.[42] The unpredictability of this defensive war induced an enormous amount of stress among the soldiers and civilians, with an attendant sense of helplessness, which was similar to depression.[43] Odoardo retreated into his palace at Piacenza, while tongues wagged that he sought to escape the rage of his subjects who had been dragged into a disastrous war by his caprice.[44] We can only deplore the condition of the surviving internal correspondence, whose pages are damp from water damage and are gradually decomposing into fragments. Those pages still legible never discuss the suffering of the population, which was not something that interested Odoardo. Concern for present and future tax revenue loomed much larger in his mind. At the end of October the Spaniards destroyed the costly machinery, tools, and firewood piles at the Salsomaggiore salt springs, and carried away the two great pans for evaporating water. Functionaries had written months previously that it would have been a wise precaution to transport these bronze pans inside Parma for safety, but each one weighed over six tonnes and would require a week's haulage on specially designed vehicles. The Spaniards also

---

[38] Crescenzi Romani, *Corona della nobiltà d'Italia*, 325–30.

[39] AGS Estado, Legajo 3839; Nota de los castillos y puestos que sean ocupado...desde 15 de Agosto hasta 17 de Diciembre 1636.

[40] Ms Parmense 737, L'Heroe d'Italia, 826.

[41] Biblioteca Universitaria Bologna (hereafter BUB), Ms vol. 9E 27, letter by D. Ventura, a monk in the service of Don Vincenzo (Gonzaga?) to Don Martin d'Aragon, 29 November 1636.

[42] ASPr, Governo Farnesiano, Carteggio Farnesiano Interno 384, letter from Ottavio Cerati to the duchess, 20 August 1636.

[43] Costa, *Psicologia militare*, 219; also Edward J. Coss, *All for the King's Shilling: The British Soldier under Wellington 1808–1814* (Norman, OK, 2010), 16.

[44] Pallavicino, *Successi dell'anno MDCXXXVI*, 77.

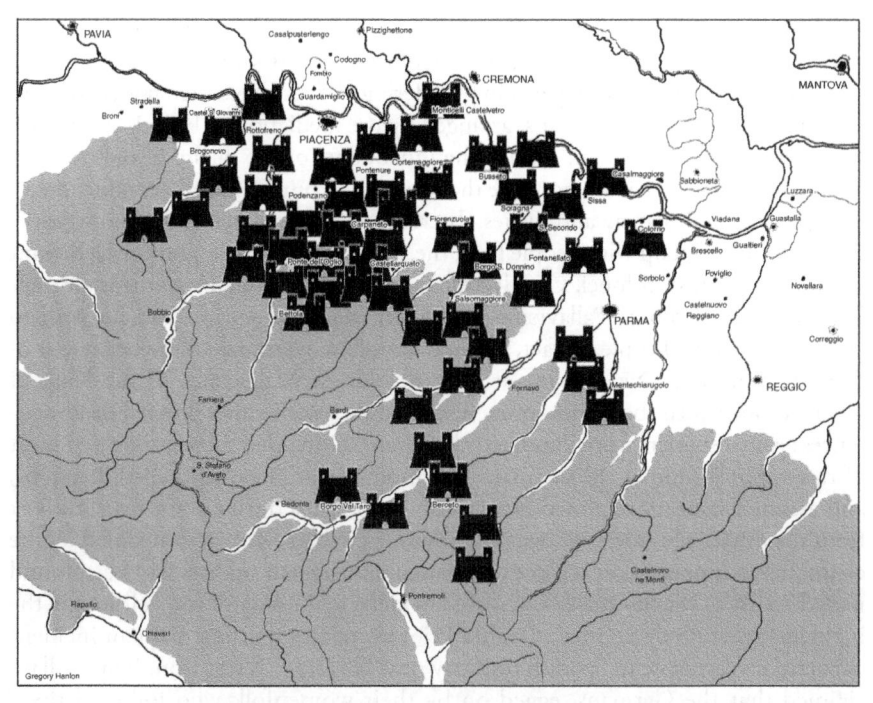

Map 5.1. Castles occupied by Spanish troops

presumably seized or destroyed the stock of 41 tonnes of salt placed in the warehouse. The ducal salt monopoly derived from the springs provided a significant part of Farnese revenues.[45] Ferrante Pallavicino reports that the sack of towns in the Piacentino after the 'battle' of Rottofreno netted the Spanish soldiers over a million lire in booty.[46] A commonly cited estimate of damages inflicted just on the Piacentino through fire and theft amounted to 8,530,000 scudi. Even wealthy people were ruined when enemy soldiers occupied their castles and villas, or looted the houses in rich towns like Borgo San Donnino, Busseto, Fiorenzuola, and Cortemaggiore.[47] It is difficult to verify figures like these, but if they are fairly accurate, the 60 million lire in losses would amount to 480 lire per capita, the income of a year or two for most families. More reliably, a steward sent an itemized list of losses accruing to the Farnese patrimony in various estates throughout the Parmigiano, amounting to almost half a million lire in damage of every kind.[48]

In the countryside or in small towns garrisoned by the enemy, the inhabitants were entirely at the mercy of the soldiery. With the breakdown of public order,

---

[45] Pugolotti, *Libro di memorie*, 98; for the correspondance around this salt see ASPr, Governo Farnesiano, Carteggio Interno 384, letter, 22 March 1636.
[46] Pallavicino, *Successi dell'anno MDCXXXVI*, 76.
[47] Crescenzi Romani, *Corona della nobiltà d'Italia*, vol. 2, 329.
[48] ASPr, Casa e Corte Farnesiana, ser. 2, 29, f. 128.

even enemy civilians arrived to help loot Odoardo's subjects. A surprise cavalry raid by the Marchese of Soragna near Colorno netted scores of inhabitants of Casalmaggiore, who were engaged in plundering.[49] These were then marched off to Parma and held for stiff ransoms, arranged by the mediation of Franciscan friars.[50] Enemy soldiers stopped and robbed the inhabitants of the duchy of their money and their horses, if they did not have the foresight to purchase a safe conduct document from Spanish army authorities. There were some refuges in the countryside; San Secondo filled up with people from the surrounding district, for the late count had been a Spanish colonel. Castell'Arquato was a fief belonging to the important Roman cardinal Sforza Pallavicino, and Don Martin d'Aragon had no wish to antagonize Rome. People, in fact, did not complain overmuch of the behaviour of Spanish, Lombard, Neapolitan, or Tuscan soldiers. Magistrates of the King of Spain accompanied the troops in the field, and they sometimes ordered death sentences against soldiers who plundered churches.[51] Odoardo's subjects directed most of their opprobrium at the Germans, the mounted arquebusiers called dragoons, and assorted infantry recruited from north of the Alps during the winter. Almost from the outset the stories of brutality towards civilians were accompanied by the claim, never supported by a place or a date, that German soldiers had been found nailed to trees. Such stories circulated widely in Germany too, although the incidents were rarely verified. Gualdo Priorato relates that just such an incident occurred at Vespolate in Spanish territory near Novara.[52] A text from Fontanellato claimed that the Germans, egged on by their womenfolk who followed them on campaign, were ferocious barbarians who killed people for no reason and destroyed houses like demons.[53] Certainly they laid claim to the contents of houses in their path, like chests full of finery, shoes, and boots when they could find them, bedding and linens, seed grain and oxen.[54] The Germans, people complained, did not respect contribution agreements or safe conduct documents, sold by the officers.[55] They cut off ears and noses of peasants to avenge

---

[49] Costantino Canicetti, *Memoria di Colorno (1618–1674)*, ed. A. Aliano (Colorno, 1997), 26 August 1636.

[50] ASPr, Governo Farnesiano, Mastri Farnesiani 32, 620, 10 September 1636; the captives were ransomed for 600 lire each.

[51] Crescenzi Romani, *Corona della nobiltà d'Italia*, vol. 2, 332; the Alessandria chronicle by Girolamo Ghilini identifies one of these Spanish military magistrates, Francesco Anolfi, and describes his functions in the field, *Annali di Alessandria*, ed. A. Bossola, 3 vols. (Alessandria, 1903), 120.

[52] Pallavicino, *Successi dell'anno MDCXXXVI*, 24; for similar but unverified stories current in Germany, see Geoffrey Mortimer, 'Individual experience and perception of the Thirty Years War in eyewitness personal accounts', *German History*, 20 (2002): 141–60; Gualdo Priorato, *Historia delle guerre del Conte Galeazzo Gualdo Priorato* (Venice, 1646), 311.

[53] BPPr, Ms Parmense 462, Miscellanea di Storia Parmense (copy by abb. Affò), Da libri della chiesa di Corticelle, 314.

[54] Ruth Mohrmann, 'Everyday life in war and peace', in *1648: War and Peace in Europe*, ed. K. Bussmann and H. Schilling (Munster-Osnabruck, 1998), 319–28; also Kroener, '"The soldiers are very poor, bare, naked, exhausted": the living conditions and organizational structure of military society during the Thirty Years' War', in *1648: War and Peace in Europe*, ed. K. Bussmann and H. Schilling (Munster-Osnabruck, 1998), 285–91.

[55] Redlich, *De Praeda Militari*, 44–7.

themselves for ambushes and other indignities.[56] It was reportedly the custom of Germans to remove the bells from the churches (to make ammunition), to dress up in priestly vestments, and to steal from the altars.[57] At Colecchio they reportedly attached five men to a beam and enclosed another eight in a room to die of hunger in order to induce them to reveal their hidden treasures; one victim was said to have chewed on his shoe leather to live longer. Although most of the stories of atrocities were unfounded or exaggerated, historians of the Thirty Years' War in Germany often conclude that Spanish and Dutch troops behaved better in comparison to Germans.[58] During the first two years of the war in Italy, only one wholesale slaughter of the inhabitants of a village occurred with certainty, at Montegrosso near Asti in Piedmont, attributed in large part to the German soldiers under the command of Prince Borso d'Este of Modena.[59] The Spaniards shared this fear of the Germans in their employ. Authorities supplying the Germans in Farnese territory feared, with good reason, the consequences of withdrawing them to winter quarters in the state of Milan once peace was implemented.[60]

As the situation went from bad to worse, the cement that held society together began to dissolve. A decree published in Parma on 24 August complained that Farnese troops were also robbing peasants on the roads and in their hamlets on pretext of collecting forage, and authorities threatened summary execution of the malefactors. Some of these might have been deserters or men struck off the rolls for some other purpose, who became 'marauders', a term that dates from this period.[61] Peasants streamed into Parma and Piacenza with their carts and their animals, with bags of grain and precious supplies, but there was no place to put them, and unscrupulous people, often the foreign soldiers not bound by ties of long-term coexistence and kinship, soon devised ways to separate them from their belongings. The governor of Parma threatened that soldiers who exploited refugees in that manner would be subject to the military penalty of hanging suspended by the arms for an hour in the city square.[62] Francesco Serafini, governor of the Piacenza citadel, did his utmost to prevent the fortress from becoming a cache for stolen goods. He was also preoccupied by the multiple ways that firearms left the magazines to

---

[56] Crescenzi Romani, *Corona della nobiltà d'Italia*, 332.

[57] Ms Parmense 737, L'Heroe d'Italia, 834.

[58] Ronald G. Asch, '"Wo der soldat hinkombt, da ist alles sein": military violence and atrocities in the Thirty Years War re-examined', *German History*, 18 (2000): 291–309; Réné Pillorget, 'Populations civiles et troupes dans le Saint-Empire au cours de la guerre de Trente ans', in *Guerre et pouvoir en Europe au XVIIe siècle*, ed. V. Barrie-Curien (Paris, 1991), 151–74.

[59] AGS Estado, Legajo 3344/205, Relacion de lo sucedido a las armas de Su Majd. en Italia desde ultimos de Agosto hasta 20 Septembre.

[60] AGS Estado, Legajo 3839, Consulta of 17 January 1637; for a depiction of German mercenaries as victims, see Bernhard R. Kroener, 'Conditions de vie et origine sociale du personnel militaire subalterne au cours de la Guerre de Trente Ans', *Francia*, 15 (1987): 321–50.

[61] Kroener, 'Le Maraudeur: A propos des groupes marginaux de la société militaire au début de l'époque moderne', in *Nouveaux regards sur la guerre de Trente Ans*, Centre d'Etudes d'Histoire de la Défense (Vincennes, 1998), 167–79.

[62] Archivio di Stato di Piacenza (hereafter ASPr), Gridario 32, 24 August and 22 September 1636.

circulate in the city.[63] Repetitive decrees also tried to prevent the sale of firearms and other military stores to unauthorized persons, for soldiers habitually gambled and drank using their weapons as collateral.[64] The French soldiers especially enjoyed impunity in Parma and Piacenza and so the inhabitants felt more comfortable having weapons of their own.[65]

As the enemy unfurled over his prostrate duchy, Odoardo was reduced to husbanding his remaining professional troops to defend the cities. French letters from Parma and Piacenza reiterated how unpopular the prince had become among his subjects. He had given up trying to transform his militiamen into a fighting force, 'realizing the fear that these men had, being drawn away from fieldwork and not accustomed to seeing a sword unsheathed, and fearing no less that these subjects would rise against him, more likely to make some arrangement with the Spaniards than to follow French caprices'.[66] The surviving rosters for 1636 and the fragmentary hospital records give us some idea of the attrition his units suffered over the course of the year. Farnese cavalry rosters indicated that 15 troopers had died during the year, half of whom were Odoardo's subjects. Although cavalrymen were continually committed to patrol duty in the open countryside, they were more expert foragers than the foot soldiers, and their mounts were able to bear them to safety in a tight situation. The rosters bear the names of 212 infantry fatalities over the year; we know the origins for 92 per cent. This time, Italians bore the brunt of the fatalities at 119 of those for whom we have a sure origin, and, of those, the subjects of the duke only numbered 33. French losses constituted about a quarter of the whole (49). These figures are surely only a fraction of the entire number, for the rosters only survive for a third of the companies we know existed, and some of them, especially the French, did not record the destiny of the soldiers. Even when we have the rosters, scribes did not always record the deaths of members of the unit. About 60 per cent of the soldiers dying in hospital who should figure in the company rosters are not found there. The date of death of those who do figure in the company books varied from the hospital records by a week or so. So how many soldiers died in the war? By advancing tentatively from what we know to what we do not know, we should multiply the 227 fatalities several times. We know nothing about militia fatalities, for none of their wartime rosters survives. Of course, only a portion of the fatalities were battlefield deaths, which we can surmise from the indications of the dates people were reported to have died. The worst single day was 15 August, the action at Rottofreno, where we have the reported deaths of 13 men. Even if we had all the rosters, and the militia rosters too, the toll of men killed in the battle would not likely surpass two or three score. Eleven more men figure as fatalities on 10 December, victims of the fighting around Piacenza.

---

[63] ASPr, Carteggio Farnesiano, Fabbriche ducali e fortificazioni, n. 4, Ordini da Osservarsi dalli soldati del Castel di Piacenza, 4 November 1635.

[64] Barbara Donagan, *War in England, 1642–1649* (Oxford and New York, 2008), 83.

[65] ASPr, Gridario 32, decrees focusing on public order multiply in August 1636, numbers 66, 67, 68, 70, 78, 82; Andrea Pugolotti recounts his encounter with a French soldier enjoying impunity in Parma, *Libro di memorie*, 97.

[66] Gualdo Priorato, *Historia delle guerre*, 340.

The actions around Rottofreno of 15 to 17 May resulted in 18 deaths in the register. For every soldier killed, we should assume that one or two more were seriously wounded, removing them from active service. Then there were the prisoners, who are no better tabulated. Sometimes the register indicates a day of capture, so in addition to the dozen men killed at Rottofreno on 15 August we find 144 prisoners. Captives could be held in some secure place like a castle or a tower, but, due to the trouble and expense of minding them, the rank and file could not be locked up for the duration of the war. The Italian soldiers taken prisoner by the Spaniards were soon given back to the Duke of Parma, sometimes within weeks of their capture, where they re-enlisted in their old companies. No French or Swiss soldiers were handed over, however, but they would have been exchanged for 'Spanish' prisoners elsewhere. Conventions between Spain and France for the fairly speedy exchange of prisoners existed elsewhere.[67] An unknown portion of the Italians and Swiss might have signed on to fight with Spanish forces after their capture, just as a handful of subjects of the King of Spain continued to enter Farnese service throughout the war.

There were three times as many desertions in the ranks of the army as there were recorded fatalities. The surviving rosters indicate 635 desertions, most of which gave a specific date of departure. Soldiers continued to prefer a warm billet in the cold season, and so there were only 24 desertions during the three months of winter in 1636. Double that number deserted in each of the following two months, but the losses might have been offset by enlistments and reinforcements. Fighting around Stradella and Rottofreno probably motivated the departure of another 60 in June, but the month of July opened the floodgates, with about 250 departures—for those registers recording the destiny of the men. Desertion dropped off in the successive months to about three or four dozen every few weeks. Again, we would need to have some kind of coefficient for the missing registers in order to arrive at a rough total. French troops could not desert with the same facility as the Italians, nor were they as likely to change sides. Cardinal-General Trivulzio welcomed French deserters, however, and gave each of them a passport and a scudo for their trouble. If we adopt a coefficient of 2 to represent the missing portion, the desertions would constitute about a third of the professional army of 4,000 men.

Spain's control of village castles aimed to isolate Parma from Piacenza. The erection of earthen fortifications around Fiorenzuola cut across the Via Emilia highway connecting the two cities. A nearby fortified bridgehead at Monticelli d'Ongina enabled the quick passage of reinforcements from Cremona and Milan, and blocked the Po simultaneously.[68] Contesting control over the countryside and resisting the enemy onslaught gradually passed into the hands of Odoardo's subjects and the remaining French soldiers. We have only one commission conceded to an officer designated as a 'partisan', Francesco Ferrari, called a '*huomo del popolo*' by the aristocrat Crescenzi Romani. He raised a company at his own expense to patrol the countryside and to take prisoners he could ransom. Other officers created

---

[67] Parker, 'The etiquette of atrocity', 143–68.
[68] *Gazette de France 1636* (Paris, 1636), n. 151; BNM, Ms 2367, 52.

similar companies of mounted arquebusiers, who would support themselves on the resources they captured from the enemy. 'These youths often lost all by trusting their boldness, seeking the status of brave men, but they acquired the status of fools,' intoned Crescenzi Romani.[69] In Parma, the government decided to create a company of 120 *tagliatesta*, '*gente scavestrata*' (reckless fellows?) who patrolled the roads every day. 'These people are the kind you had better respect, otherwise bad things will happen to you!'[70] Some accounts indicate that these companies consisted of an outlaw nucleus that attracted peasants to them. Both sought booty and prisoners, but since they did not know or observe the rules of war, they often killed their captives. Enemy soldiers on unfamiliar territory hired local boys and other servants as guides, who sometimes led them into fatal ambushes.[71] These skirmishes signalled that the war was becoming more implacable as the winter set in. In January 1637 something like a pitched battle occurred at Medesano, where two German companies, reportedly totalling 140 men, were caught and annihilated by *tagliateste* under the command of Marchese Ottaviano Mulazzano and a crowd of peasant auxiliaries. The force slaughtered most of the invaders but spared one captain and 15 men, whom they escorted to the Santa Croce gate at Parma. There they butchered the prisoners one after another before a great crowd, and then placed the recovered booty on a table in a corner of the city square, where they auctioned it off. Other groups of *tagliateste* hovered around Spanish forces laying siege to the castle of Montechiarugolo. One force crossed the Po and plundered Torricella Cremonese on 3 February, the eve of the peace ending Odoardo's war. The same day, an incautious detachment of Germans marched into the very shadow of the ramparts of Parma, aiming to make off with the livestock there. A large force of soldiers and militiamen sallied forth and chased them for six kilometres to the Taro river, killing a number of them and recovering their plunder.[72] Calandrini credits the *tagliateste* with killing 4,000 enemy soldiers, which is completely implausible. But the multiplication of bloody encounters points to a harshening of the war as it endured and the Spaniards were having ever greater difficulties obtaining fodder.

Odoardo's much-touted relief force never materialized. The Milanese general Paolo Sormani and his Lombard levies kept the Duke of Rohan penned in near Lecco and the exit from the Alps. After Tornavento and the removal of the allies to winter quarters in Piedmont, this small French army retreated back into its Valtelline mountain base, out of money and short of supplies.[73] Of far greater consequence was the surrender to Spain of the little fortress of Corbie on the Somme river in northern France on 15 August, the same day as the action at Rottofreno. Spain's largest professional army numbered 70,000 men in the spring of 1636. Cardinal Archduke Ferdinand considered the Dutch to be the principal enemy,

---

[69] Crescenzi Romani, *Corona della nobiltà d'Italia*, 330.
[70] Pugolotti, *Libro di memorie*, 97.
[71] Crescenzi Romani, *Corona della nobiltà d'Italia*, 332; Ms Parmense 737, L'Heroe d'Italia, 841–51; on the importance of local guides, Giorgio Basta, *Le gouvernement de la cavallerie legere* (Rouen, 1616), 44.
[72] Ms Parmense 737, L'Heroe d'Italia, 851–60.
[73] Davide Maffi, 'Confesionalismo y Razòn de Estado en la edad moderna. El caso de la Valtellina (1637–1639)', *Hispania Sacra*, 57 (2005): 467–89; title notwithstanding, the article is in Italian.

but, after encountering stubborn resistance there, the Habsburg army unexpectedly turned south and pressed the French instead. In the second half of August, Spanish troops surged across the Somme and marched on Paris. Their victorious army was not prepared for a long march and so it could not advance for long, but the cavalry patrols plundered a rich and untouched land, where town councils paid Habsburg commanders handsomely for sparing them the worst. Richelieu and Louis XIII were forced to take desperate measures to find the money and the men to recover the lost ground and to place back the bolt behind the door. Meanwhile, an Imperial army marched to rescue the Franche-Comté from French conquest, and penetrated the duchy of Burgundy, which they put to the sack. Under the weight of these heavy blows to the French heartland, the resources for the Italian theatre dried up entirely.[74] Louis XIII thought that by ending his subsidies to his Swedish and Dutch allies and by intervening in the war directly, he would save money. But French expenditures soared from 58 million livres in 1633 to 208 million in 1635, while revenues and new taxes could not hope to match the increase.[75] Meanwhile, much of western France had risen in revolt to prevent their collection, necessitating new troop levies to deal with internal security.[76] The mobilization of the kingdom to stem and repel the invasion of 1636 was accomplished largely on credit. Subsidies to the beleaguered Duke Odoardo of Parma were now out of the question.

Spain then launched a multipronged peace offensive in the direction of Savoy, Mantua, and Parma, while talks with France on a general settlement sputtered in Cologne and in Rome.[77] Victor Amadeus could not be persuaded to leave the French alliance, for Richelieu would annex Savoy in revenge. But if he was indeed trying to prevent a French victory in Italy, Spain concluded that he had succeeded.[78] Odoardo was a more willing ally who could not be brought to the peace table merely by blockading him in Piacenza. There was fear that bread was getting scarce in September, but there were plenty of provisions in the citadel, and peasants had brought a great deal of food with them. Large livestock crowded the stalls and courtyards throughout the city, and during daylight hours the treeless zone just outside the walls would have resembled an immense feedlot.[79]

Leganés was unable to lay proper siege at this late season; moreover, he only committed about 3,000 cavalry and 5,000 infantry to deal with the Farnese threat.[80] The Spanish blockade of Piacenza began to tighten at the end of October, provoking a shortage of firewood and of wine. Soldiers solved the former problem by dismantling

---

[74] Jonathan Israel, 'Olivares, the cardinal-infante and Spain's strategy in the Low Countries (1635–1643): the road to Rocroi', in *Spain, Europe and the Atlantic World: Essays in Honour of John H Elliott*, ed. R. Kagan and G. Parker (Cambridge, 1995), 267–95.
[75] Jean Chagniot, *Guerre et Société à l'époque moderne* (Paris, 2001), 128.
[76] ASHD, A 28, n. 150.
[77] Daniel Séré, *La Paix des Pyrenées: Vingt-quatre ans de négociations entre la France et l'Espagne (1635–1659)* (Paris, 2007), 70.
[78] AGS Estado, Legajo 3344/223, letter from Spain's ambassador to Rome, Don Francisco de Melo, 29 September 1636.
[79] BCPLPc, Ms Pallastrelli 126, Croniche Boselli, 15 September 1636.
[80] AAE, Paris, Correspondance Politique, Parme vol. 1, September 1636.

Fig. 5.4. Callot, peasants ambushing soldiers, c.1633; Troops relied on local guides to lead them to hidden treasures, with predictable consequences.

houses in the city.[81] Spanish forces, which included the Tuscan regiment, roamed unopposed right up to the edge of the city's cannon range, but the encirclement was not complete. At the end of November a great convoy of 50 wagons exited from the city and followed the Po downstream for 8 kilometres, collecting wood and straw and whatever fowl they managed to find before retiring under heavy escort.[82] In December, Leganés tightened the noose again. Trivulzio's musketeers crossed the Po and attacked the floating mills on the Po outside the city, most of which were captured and towed downstream to Cremona, and the remainder sunk. This crippled the ability of the city to grind its grain provisions into flour for bread. Spanish and German troops then resolved to capture the castle of Rivalta on the Trebbia, which was strongly held in order to ease the arrival of a French rescue force, if it ever came. The garrison of 150 French troops and 400 local militia put up a stiff fight and launched sorties against the attackers during the first days. A Spanish battery of four pieces opened a breach in the village wall on the fifth day with 248 shots, but still the defenders would not retire. Habsburg troops, reportedly thousands strong, assembled to storm the breach, and launched a night assault on a ravelin that was repulsed with many casualties. The governor then withdrew his men into the castle and negotiated a surrender. French troops finally marched off, carrying booty they had seized from the village![83]

With Rivalta in Spanish hands, Leganés put new pressure on Piacenza by blocking the canal that conveyed water from the Trebbia to power mills in the city and to flush away detritus. This worsened the sanitary situation considerably and increased the spread of disease. The garrison was well stocked with grain, but they would now have to grind it into flour with the aid of animals and men, a laborious and expensive task. Saint-Paul considered that his garrison of 1,400 professional

---

[81] AAE, Paris, Correspondance Politique, Parme vol. 1, letter from Fabio Scotti to Cardinal Richelieu, 22 October 1636.

[82] Archivio di Stato Firenze (hereafter ASF), Mediceo Principato 3182, letter from Domenico Pandolfini to Cioli, 29 November 1636.

[83] Crescenzi Romani, *Corona della nobiltà d'Italia*, 325.

Fig. 5.5. Spanish blockade of Piacenza, late 1636. Spanish batteries on the island in the Po bombard the city, 24 Dec. 1636.

troops was enough to hold the ramparts, but that the principal danger consisted in the sullenness of the population and the crowding of refugee women and children. The soldiers themselves committed '*mille insolenze*' towards civilians, with their customary impunity. Consequently, the people had turned against Odoardo and had no desire to see him.[84] On 20 December, Trivulzio launched his troops in boats to seize an island on the Po across from the city, where they threw up earthworks under cover of night and prepared positions for cannon. Several days later the bombardment of the city from this battery, which was well situated to fire at the palace, began. Spanish guns fired several hundred cannon balls at the ducal residence and other important houses nearby, although they did not fire at churches or convents.[85] Leganés and Trivulzio intended to unsettle Odoardo enough to make him think of peace.

Parma was cut off from reliable communication with the duke. Spanish forces around the city were too weak to threaten it directly, so they focused their efforts on capturing the castle of Montechiarugolo on the Enza river border with Modena. Parma was still technically at war with its neighbour, but, as a goodwill gesture, Duke Francesco allowed Parma to transport grain supplies through his territory. The fall of the castle would have ended that relief. Several hundred Spanish troops stormed it on 11 December, but the place was stoutly defended by French and Italian troops. The bombardment of the castle resumed a few days later, but on

---

[84] ASHD, A 30, n. 20, letters from Piacenza, 5 and 8 December 1636.
[85] Crescenzi Romani, *Corona della nobiltà d'Italia*, 329.

21 December the garrison made a strong sortie, and there were skirmishes every night afterwards. One such action resulted in the evacuation of four cartloads of Spanish wounded to Modenese territory, we are told. The castle held out against 377 cannon shots until commanders negotiated a ceasefire on 15 January. Resistance in isolated strongpoints did nothing to change the dismal situation of the duchy as a whole, however. Berceto, which guarded the easiest pass over the Apennines, fell to the Habsburgs at the end of November, after Spanish troops dug a mine under the castle ramparts. Its loss removed another avenue for reinforcements coming by sea.[86] In Parma itself, the price of grain rose to the alarming level of 40 lire a *staio*, despite fairly ample stocks of it. Refugees gathered around bonfires set in the palace courtyard, where rumours of all kinds were rife.[87] One held that the city governor Cerati had murdered Duke Odoardo's bastard sibling Ottavio in the palace dungeon. People no doubt thought it a sign that Odoardo's very status as the Duke of Parma was in jeopardy. Adding to Odoardo's '*mauvaise fortune*', Pope Urban VIII Barberini threatened the duke with excommunication if he did not withdraw from the war. This would free all his subjects of the oath they had made to obey him as their lord, while, in the meantime, normal religious ceremonies could not take place throughout his lands. Popes had much used and misused excommunications since the Middle Ages, until even Italian states lost their fear of them. This threat had no impact on Odoardo's attitude, although people began to suspect there was now a secret agreement between the pope and the King of Spain to eject the Farnese from the duchies.[88]

Odoardo, in everybody's opinion, had made rather a mess of it. He was by nature stubborn and inflexible, consumed by passions to the point that he was difficult to reason with. If the first function of a legitimate government was to safeguard the lives and property of the people living under it—and this is the principal justification for government everywhere—then the young duke had failed utterly. The vainglorious ruler's misadventure was beginning to remove the underpinnings of the seventeenth-century support for this dynasty among both the elites and the people, who had paid dearly to help him chase his dreams of glory. Absolute princes spent much treasure on lavish spectacles, which showcased them surrounded by their rich vassals in supporting roles. Cultural historians have sometimes been taken in by these triumphant representations of majesty to conclude that such emphatic declarations of loyalty were mirror images of elite attitudes. This oversimplifies the psychology of subjects of every status, whose capacity for ambivalence was identical to our own. *Somebody* had to be the prince, and there were good reasons for establishing a prestigious dynasty from outside as overlord. Hereditary rule removed the turbulent interregnum that punctuated the reigns of princes without well-defined rules of succession. Common sense compelled the nobility in particular to participate in artistic programmes that celebrated the ruling house, whatever their personal feelings about the man at the

---

[86] ASHD, A 31, n. 20, report from Saint-Paul, 5 December 1636.
[87] Pugolotti, *Libro di memorie*, 98.
[88] Vittorio Siri, *Delle memorie reconditi di Vittorio Siri dall'anno 1601 fino al 1640*, 8 vols. (Lyons, 1677–9), vol. 8, 417; Gabriel de Mun, *Richelieu et la Maison de Savoie: l'ambassade de Particelli d'Hémery en Piemont* (Paris, 1907), 152.

top.[89] Until Odoardo, the Farnese tenure in Parma and Piacenza was not worse than that of most other princely dynasties in Italy or beyond, and one could argue that these Italian principalities were well governed by the standards of the seventeenth century. But in 1636, would most subjects have objected if Spain and the Papacy simply carved up the duchy between them, along with the fiefs in Lazio and the kingdom of Naples? This time, Odoardo correctly read the alignment of the planets. Paris long thought that he was considering Spanish offers, and so Louis XIII and Richelieu no longer took his protestations of loyalty at face value.[90] However, voices murmured that this time the Spanish were plotting with the Barberini papal nephews to remove the Farnese from their lands. Throughout 1636, the Council of Italy and the Council of State in Madrid collected documents pertaining to the rights of the Catholic king in Italy, for they wished to make an example of Odoardo as a lesson for other Italian princes.[91] Spain would annex Piacenza and its crucial citadel, while the pope would recover Parma and probably concede it in fief to a Barberini nephew.

This menace spurred the offer of friendly arbitration from the Grand Duke Ferdinando II of Tuscany, who wished to preserve the status of his sister Margherita. Although Ferdinando was a Spanish ally, he was unwilling to see the power of Spain expand still further in Italy. So Florence sent the diplomat *cavaliere* Domenico Pandolfini to Milan and to Piacenza in order to initiate discussions. The Barberini too suspected that Spain might yield nothing to the papal family, and simply amputate the Papal States of its important dependencies. Rome dispatched the envoy Count Carpegna to represent to Odoardo the unpopularity of such a needless war. Odoardo would still not hear of peace until close to Christmas 1636, hoping that the French fleet would put to sea with his rescue force, despite the fact that the citizens of Piacenza beseeched the duke to do nothing to scuttle these talks, once they had begun. To smooth the discussions, Leganés supplied a calf every week to the ducal table. Odoardo had some legitimate worries. He feared for his control of the citadel of Piacenza, first of all. Philip II had restored it to Ottavio Farnese only in 1585, after he had made countless gestures to reassure Madrid that Parma was a loyal ally. Subsequent governors of the citadel appointed by the duke had to swear allegiance to Spain before the governor of Milan. The fortress was a prize coveted by the French as well.[92] As the discussions continued in a monastery outside Milan into the new year, hostilities gradually fell off, except

---

[89] Sandberg, *Warrior Pursuits*, 118.

[90] De Mun, *Richelieu et la Maison de Savoie*, 170.

[91] Antonio Alvarez-Ossorio Alvariño, 'The state of Milan and the Spanish monarchy', in *Spain in Italy: Politics, Society and Religion 1500–1700*, ed. T. J. Dandelet and J. A. Marino (Leiden and Boston, 2007), 100–32.

[92] On the danger of being reduced to satellite status when foreign troops occupy the citadel see David Parrott, 'The utility of fortifications in early modern Europe: Italian princes and their citadels', *War in History*, 7/2 (2007): 127–53; also David Parrott, 'The role of fortifications in the defense of states: the Farnese and the security of Parma and Piacenza', in *I Farnese: Corti, guerra e nobiltà in Antico Regime*, ed. A. Bilotto, P. del Negro, and C. Mozzarelli. (Rome, 1997), 509–60; on Odoardo's fear that the citadel of Piacenza would pass to Spanish troops see Gualdo Priorato, *Historia delle guerre*, 350; Siri, *Delle memorie recondite*, vol. 8, 417–24.

for the *tagliateste* raids.[93] The conclusions were not broadcast widely but the general terms became known early on and the public discussed them.[94] Odoardo would have to relinquish his control of Sabbioneta to Spain, who would pay him an indemnity for expenses incurred in keeping it out of French hands. French troops from Parma and Piacenza would be allowed to march undisturbed to Piedmont. Odoardo would also have to settle his dispute with Duke Francesco of Modena with Spanish arbitration. Peace there was established in May 1637, each duchy promising not to adhere to an agreement to the detriment of the other.[95]

A sure sign of Odoardo's discomfiture was the urgency by which the minor princes despoiled by the dukes of Parma stepped forth to recover their patrimony. At Busseto, capital of the old Pallavicino state, the Marchese Alessandro Pallavicino arrived to press his claim for lordship. He wanted the town council to pay him the tax on flour (*macinato*) and the hearth tax, but the community rejected this on the excuse of poverty, since it was still paying a huge contribution to the occupying Spanish troops. The marchese then tried to manipulate the annual election of councillors to the town assembly, which provoked a serious backlash. He appeared at Cortemaggiore soon afterwards, but the councillors there would not consent to any ceremonies expressing their subjection to him.[96] All the projects of Pallavicino to recover his duchies (which had finally been purchased before the war by the Farnese) came to naught. The Prince Doria, meanwhile, had materially aided the Spanish cause with the levy of professional soldiers and his militiamen, in order to recover Borgo Taro. Odoardo's army inflicted heavy damage on his mountain fiefs following his intervention in the war. In the interest of achieving a rapid settlement, Spain ignored the Doria claims to Borgo Taro, and returned the town to Farnese rule, but King Philip soon compensated the prince with the viceroyalty of Sardinia. Odoardo also recovered the fiefs in the kingdom of Naples confiscated when he entered the war.

With these better conditions, Odoardo's emissary signed the peace in Milan on 2 February 1637, to enter into effect two days later.[97] On 4 February, the French soldiers marched out of the Porta San Lazzaro in Piacenza on the pretext of a pay muster, and the gates closed behind them. Similarly, Count Cerati did the same with the French and Mantuan troops in Parma, who complained loudly of the cruel trick played on them, and then marched away towards Mantua.[98] All the Italian princes were delighted at the outcome, and Odoardo himself felt that he had played his role well. The King of France and Richelieu were relieved too, for they

---

[93] Alessandro Giulini, 'Un diario secentesco inedito d'un notaio milanese', *Archivio Storico Lombardo*, 57 (1930), 466–82, entry for 7 February 1637.
[94] Pietro Giovanni Capriata, *Dell'Historia delli movimenti d'armi successi in Italia* 2 vols. (Genoa, 1649), vol. 2, 247–50.
[95] ASMo, Ambasciatori Parma 6, Dispatch from Francesco Montecuccoli in Parma, 8 May 1637.
[96] Boscarelli, *Contributi alla storia degli Stati Pallavicino*, 130–1.
[97] AAE, Paris, Correspondance Politique, Parme vol. 1, 2 February 1637, Capitulation entre le duc de Parme et le Marquis de Leganés (in Spanish).
[98] BCPLPc, Ms Pallastrelli 126, Croniche Boselli, 4 February 1637, 129; Pugolotti, *Libro di memorie*, 99; ASPr, Governo Farnesiano, Collaterería Generale 3202; Odoardo retained at least one French cavalry company, that of Antoine Maillard, for we have a muster of the unit from April 1637.

could not protect the duchy effectively and were just throwing away good resources to keep French troops there. In the course of February, Spanish troops began a gradual withdrawal from the duchy. An edict enjoined the population not to contest anything already in the possession of the Spanish troops in order to accelerate their departure.[99] Early in January it had been necessary for Leganés to send supplies to the troops based in the duchy, due to the widespread devastation they inflicted and the subsequent flight of the population. Neapolitan infantry and German cavalry evacuated San Secondo and Fontanellato on 23 February, to the great joy of the inhabitants.[100] The soldiers withdrew from Colorno on 25 February, leaving houses ruined without their doors, windows, chimneys, and so on. The soldiers would knock down a wall to get a piece of iron, deplored the priest Canivetti when he finally returned from his Parma refuge. They plundered the church and the altar of St Margarita too. They were as bad as Turks![101]

Two large companies of German dragoons withdrawn from Parma settled into winter quarters at Casalmaggiore, just across the Po. These men were 'veteran soldiery, used to robbery', who took up lodgings in the town and in the villas of the landowners. 'They asked one day for one thing, and then the next day for something else: they had to be contented with drink and a bonus (*straordinario*).' Two or three months of their presence reduced Casalmaggiore to desperate straits, and peasants were afraid of bringing their crops or livestock to market for fear of being robbed by the soldiers. The Germans, anticipating a backlash by local government, moved into the houses of the town councillors in order to intimidate them better, threatening to kidnap their children if their demands were not met. The soldiery milled about threateningly in the street during council meetings. Town authorities secretly decided to concentrate the peasant militia in the town to intimidate the soldiers, and threw up barricades across the streets. On the strength of this show of force, the town councillors told the Germans that they would provide only what was instructed, and no more. The threat of armed conflict finally forced the Spanish military governor in Cremona to intervene and work out a compromise, and the townspeople had good reason to be proud of themselves thereafter. For them, the crisis was not over until the Germans left. Peace meant that the nobles and landowner merchants could move with their families and furniture back into their villas. Young married and unmarried women could go to church every morning and evening as before, and take their fresh air without harassment.[102] People could walk in the streets with their families unafraid, which they could not do before, due to the insolence and the violence of the soldiers. The chronicler Ettore Lodi waxed poetic with pastoral images of a town freed of soldiers. The men could congregate in their little groups, while women could play and sing with their children before their houses. The shops could open their shutters and craftsmen could exercise

---

[99] ASPr, Gridario 32, n. 44, 11 February 1636 (sic), refers in reality to 1637; other Farnese troops simply disbanded. ASPr, Carteggio Farnesiano 384, unsigned letter of 5 February 1637.
[100] BPPr, Ms Parmense 462, Miscellanea di Storia Parmense, 314.
[101] Canicetti, *Memoria di Colorno*, 25 February 1637.
[102] On the threat of rape, see Ulbricht, 'The experience of violence', 97–129.

their trade contentedly. Men could walk the lanes of the town and countryside, leaving their swords at home. Children could return to the schools that had been closed, and the market squares would fill again with vendors and goods that merchants were able to collect across the district. All this in a district spared the rigours of open war and enemy occupation.[103]

HOW BRUTAL WAS THE THIRTY YEARS' WAR IN ITALY?

The Thirty Years' War conjures up images of prolonged disasters during which soldiers preyed on civilians and not only killed many of them, but destroyed the survivors' will to live. Many of these images emerged from the time of the war itself, in the famous engravings by Jacques Callot, or in sensational accounts of atrocities soldiers committed in Germany. The postwar success of Grimmelshausen's picaresque novel *Simplicissimus* embellished the picture still further. Earlier work from administrative archives that attempted to quantify the scale of the disaster only confirmed the artistic and literary impression. A generation of work by more careful scholars has corrected some of the most vivid caricatures, but, by the most recent estimation, the intermittent wars in Germany between 1618 and 1648 resulted in a decline of population by about 40 per cent overall, with some regions experiencing a population loss of over two-thirds.[104] Other territories adjacent to Germany did not escape either. Gerard Louis' diligent examination of the region of Spanish Burgundy, or the Franche-Comté, concludes that the population declined by over half (55 to 60 per cent) in the space of just eight years (1635–43). It would require a full century for the region to attain the numbers of 1635.[105] Both German and French historians agree that the wholesale slaughter of the civilian population by soldiers was quite rare, a figment of the literary imagination. While the Franche-Comté lost 200,000 inhabitants, the burning of the town of Pontarlier with about 300 fatalities probably ranks as the worst single incident. Exposure, sickness, and hunger killed the majority of victims. The first was very often the result of soldiers burning the villages and towns, which, in the case of the county of Burgundy, was carried out by the French and the Imperials, the Swedes and the Lorrainers. Bubonic plague then culled a population weakened by hunger. A demographic collapse triggered a social collapse manifested by wholesale looting, and the kidnapping and ransoming of inhabitants. Without professional soldiers to protect them, local militias rallied around village notables and waged a war of parties against the invaders.[106] Population decline was not the outcome of 'an extravaganza of killing and maiming', as Steven Pinker's caricatural image of the Thirty Years' War would have it. Much of the drop in population was made up of

---

[103] Ettore Lodi, *Memorie istoriche di Casalmaggiore*, ed. Enrico Cirani (Cremona, 1992), 120–1.
[104] Asch, '"Wo des soldat hinkombt"', 291; on the historiography of the impact of the war, see Quentin Outram, 'The socio-economic relations of warfare and the military mortality crises of the Thirty Years War', *Medical History*, 45 (2001): 151–84.
[105] Gérard Louis, *La guerre de Dix Ans 1634–1644* (Besançon, 1998), 287.
[106] Louis, *La guerre de Dix Ans*, 31 and 181.

refugees, who fled to peaceful regions in nearby Switzerland or in France. In the Franche-Comté, as in Germany, hunger and sickness followed the collapse of commerce and agriculture, and a weakened population was more vulnerable to infectious diseases like the plague. In nearby Lorraine, a region contested almost continuously over three decades, both rural and urban zones experienced a '*cataclysme démographique*'.[107] The region lost about 60 per cent of its population between 1600 and 1660, comparable to the worst-hit regions of Germany.[108] Even regions that escaped prolonged fighting, but which were repeatedly crossed by troops saw a comparable collapse. In northern Champagne, Michel Stevenin calculates that 50 per cent of the villages were totally or partially destroyed between 1626 and 1660, inflicting a population decline of 60 per cent for the region overall and up to 80 per cent for the small cities. The confiscation of food and animals by the troops and a relentless wartime fiscality pushed people to leave in large numbers, although not very far and not for very long.[109] Civil conflict was no gentler; when French royal troops took up lodgings in parishes close to Bordeaux during the Fronde of 1649–51, the death toll in those villages immediately shot upwards to between three and eight times the normal annual mortality, inflicting losses equal to or superior to the plague of 1631. There was no single cause for this; Laurent Coste identifies fighting between civilians and soldiers, the confiscation of food, the interruption of agricultural work, the diffusion of disease that struck infants particularly hard, and drought.[110]

Wreaking devastation on the enemy was part and parcel of warfare long before the late seventeenth century. War-related hunger continued to be a European experience until the end of the century.[111] Even in England during the Civil War, where relations between the English soldiers and civilians were rather better, the former often removed doors and window shutters to make houses uninhabitable, they destroyed ploughs, farm vehicles, looms, and other tools, or else burned fodder and crops to deny them to the enemy.[112] But in England, unlike in Germany after 1630, campaigns designed to lay waste to enemy territory seemed to have been the exception. The reconstruction of mortality in Britain from precious parish registers has not yet begun in earnest, although those that have been consulted reveal a dramatic increase in burials wherever soldiers set up garrisons.[113] One estimate claims that the war led to the death of a quarter of a million persons in England

---

[107] Marie-Josée Laperche-Fournel, whose unpublished dissertation is cited by Stéphane Gaber, *La Lorraine meurtrie* (2nd edn, Nancy, 1991), 4.

[108] Philippe Martin, *Une Guerre de Trente Ans en Lorraine 1631–1661* (Metz, 2002), 227.

[109] Michel Stevenin, 'Une fatalité: les devastations des gens de guerre dans l'Est de la France (1620–1660): L'exemple de la Champagne', in *Les Malheurs de la guerre*, vol.1: *De la guerre à l'ancienne à la guerre reglée*, ed. A. Corvisier and J. Jacquart (Paris, 1996), 161–79.

[110] Laurent Coste, 'Les malheurs de la Fronde en Entre-Deux-Mers', in *Les Malheurs de la Guerre: de la guerre à l'ancienne à la guerre réglée*, ed. A. Corvisier and J. Jacquart (Paris, 1996), 131–45.

[111] Redlich, *De Praeda Militari*, 2–36; for a detailed study, see Myron Gutmann, 'Putting crises in perspective: the impact of war on civilian populations in the 17th century', *Annales de Démographie Historique* (1977), 101–28.

[112] Porter, *Destruction in the English Civil Wars*, 30–3.

[113] Martyn Bennett, *The Civil Wars Experienced: Britain and Ireland 1638–1661* (London, 2000), 96–105.

and Wales, equal to 4 per cent of the population. Most of the kingdom was spared prolonged fighting. Ireland, on the other hand, experienced the same '*cataclysme démographique*' as Central Europe.[114]

Quentin Outram places more emphasis on war-induced famine on a large scale, which occurred not only because the soldiers seized food stocks from helpless rural populations, but because the war interrupted the crucial tasks of ploughing, sowing, and reaping. After 1631 Germany was the theatre of campaigning for huge numbers of foreign soldiers who did not identify with the local population and would not have to live with their victims in the aftermath of the fighting. Croats and Swedes in particular acquired terrifying reputations. The absence of this 'imagined community' made relations between soldiers and civilians much more conflictual than in England, for much of their destruction was punitive and not simply redistributive. Village-burning on a vast scale created waves of refugees who overwhelmed the resources of nearby cities. Harvest shortages due to natural and manmade causes introduced hunger on a large scale, but the refugees also brought overcrowding in unhygienic attics and stables, making them vulnerable to typhus or e-coli infections.[115]

The soldiers' sinister reputation of brutality against civilians in Italy appears to be founded, although this has not been studied much until now.[116] Certainly they stole food from peasants when their own provisioning became inadequate and the oxen were a welcome ingredient to army soup. A decree at the beginning of October 1636 ordered all the peasants living near Parma to bring their ploughs, carts, forage, and large livestock into the city.[117] Officers often forced their soldiers to live below subsistence level. Cardinal Richelieu elevated this constriction of resources to an art, but he was not alone in his tendency to consider the soldiers' welfare only as an afterthought.[118] Much ink has been spilled about the ways in which officers cheated the men under their command of their pay, but we are beginning to also learn how much these officers were spending their own money and going into debt to keep their units up to strength.[119] These men with weapons, who enjoyed the connivance of their officers, could only survive by squeezing the population of its

---

[114] Eric Gruber von Arni, *Justice to the Maimed Soldier: Nursing, Medical Care and Welfare for Sick and Wounded Soldiers and their Families during the English Civil Wars and Interregnum, 1642–1660* (Aldershot and Burlington, VT, 2001), 9.

[115] Outram, 'The socioeconomic relations of warfare', 151–84; for a comparison of England and Germany, see also Quentin Outram, 'Demographic impact of early modern warfare', *Social Science History*, 26 (2002): 245–72; for the effect of typhus and e-coli, or the 'bloody flux', see the suggestive article by Padraig Lenihan, 'Unhappy campers: Dundalk (1689) and after', *Journal of Conflict Archaeology* (2007): 196–216.

[116] The most extensive research on this phenomenon, although not based on parish records, can be found in the doctoral dissertation of Giovanni Cerino Badone, 'Le Seconde Guerre d'Italia (1589–1659): Storiografia, Temi, Fonti' (PhD thesis, Università degli Studi del Piemonte Orientale, 2011), especially 249–65.

[117] ASPr, Gridario 32, no. 81, 2 October 1636.

[118] Kroener, 'Conditions de vie', 321–50; Kroener, '"The soldiers are very poor, bare, naked, exhausted"', 285–91.

[119] Hervé Drévillon, *L'Impôt de sang: le métier des armes sous Louis XIV* (Paris, 2005), 100–41. While Drévillon's important and original research deals with the subsequent generation, it is entirely pertinent to the Thirty Years' War.

resources. Armed men did not hesitate to scrounge open villages for food and whatever else they wanted, perhaps in the form of little expeditions of messmates who shared the proceeds.[120] Civilians had good reason to fear the soldiers, who used violence (including rape) or the threat of violence in order to render them more compliant. They occasionally killed civilians who could offer nothing or were unwilling to cooperate. Peasant resistance to the soldiers would also result in a spiral of retaliation and revenge that served to multiply the number of victims. The longer the war endured, the greater the number of people, including soldiers, who were pushed to the margins of survival. Consequently, soldiers certainly robbed civilians and they might kill them too, even with little provocation. As in Germany, their rootlessness helped ensure their impunity.[121]

People died in battle too, but we must be wary of the dubious figures offered in reports, which are usually round numbers, not specifying how many people were wounded. Soldiers were not typically buried in consecrated ground by parish priests, but rather they were dumped into shallow pits without any kind of record-keeping—when indeed they were buried at all. The numbers of people killed in the company rosters are certainly an understatement, but even by multiplying them through coefficients plucked out of the air, they are unlikely to represent more than a small fraction of the total fatalities, and they would only be valid for the Farnese side, leaving Spanish losses entirely in the dark. By arbitrarily picking a coefficient of three to determine the number of fatalities in Odoardo's army of 1636 and adding it to the 100 fatalities or so for 1635, the number of professional soldiers who died would not likely be superior to 700 men, perhaps only 100 of whom were ducal subjects. Throw in the militia defenders of towns and castles and the toll is still unlikely to surpass 1,000 victims.

Determining the total demographic cost of the war in Italy has never even been attempted. In part, this reflects the extreme dispersion of the most important documents, the parish registers of baptism, marriage, and burials, and the *status animarum* censuses. In other European countries, the ongoing campaign of Mormon missionaries to microfilm these makes it possible for researchers to consult these records at the nearest temple. In Italy, however, the Catholic Church halted the process part-way through, for it objected to the religious use of this information by non-Catholics. Only a few lucky dioceses have had their entire collection of parish registers microfilmed by the Mormons and made available to the public. Parma is one of these. For the diocese of Piacenza, only the city parishes and those of some towns and large villages in its hinterland are available. Most of the other registers sit on the shelves of the cabinets of parish rectories and cannot easily be consulted, even when the clergy permits it.

I have examined the mortuary registers of the dioceses of Parma and Piacenza during the whole of the 1630s, in order to weigh the impact of the war during the

---

[120] Coss, *All for the King's Shilling*, 106–11.
[121] Ulbricht, 'The experience of violence', 97–109; more impressionistic is the chapter by Tryntje Helfferich and Paul Sonnino, 'Civilians in the Thirty Years War', in *Daily Lives of Civilians in Wartime Europe, 1618–1900*, ed. L. S. Frey and M. L. Frey (Westport, CT, and London, 2007), 23–58.

years 1636 and 1637, when it involved peasants and townspeople. Whoever has worked on parish registers from the early seventeenth century will realize how frustrating they often are. The Council of Trent stipulated that the priests must keep careful records either in Latin or in Italian of every baptism, marriage, and burial in separate registers, in chronological order. While parish priests were all literate by this time, they often kept the registers in their own particular way, such as recording burials in alphabetical order (by the given name!), or neglecting to note down the names of the persons who were not important to their parishioners, such as small infants or children reputed to be stillborn, or else by forgetting to include people just passing through the parish when they were surprised by the grim reaper. Fortunately, other priests, particularly in the larger parishes or towns where higher standards prevailed, gave precise ages of the people they buried, and speculated on the cause of death. There is no uniformity, even in a single locality, for the registers usually cover long periods of time, and so were kept by different priests. There are frequently chronological gaps in the same register, so not all the extant documents for our period are usable. For the diocese of Piacenza, 41 mortuary registers survive for our period (26 for the city, and a mere 15 for the remainder of the diocese) out of 383 parishes.[122] Only 35 of them were continuously kept throughout the majority of the decade of the 1630s. We are better served for the dioceses of Parma and Fidenza, and for those parishes of the diocese of Piacenza now situated in the modern province of Parma, for archivists there completed the microfilming work begun by the Mormons. There, fully 140 parishes have mortuary registers dating from the period. Once those containing gaps are removed, however, only 99 can be retained, 19 for the city of Parma (about half the urban parishes), and 80 for the remaining diocese (substantially less than half). Even when the documents are continuous enough to be worthwhile examining, they still contain gaps (in 15 instances), particularly during the period the enemy soldiers were present, for priests sometimes fled their parishes along with their parishioners. Let us not dwell overmuch on the limitations of the sources, for by studying registers of mortality we are avoiding the common error of assuming that population decline was exclusively the result of mortality and ignoring the refugees. Examining the flow of burials during the 1630s (after the great plague) will teach us more about the impact of the war than any other source. But we can still only expect to arrive at imperfect, approximate results.

The statistical significance of the numbers is subject to caution, for parishes could be large or small. Given the small size of most of the rural, and even some of the urban, parishes (fewer than five burials annually in peacetime), it would be unwise to generalize upon either the high or low incidence of mortality for individual parishes. Only the cumulative numbers matter for small parishes, of course. Not all the burial registers reveal the existence of the war raging around them, either for reasons of statistical insignificance, or because the soldiers never reached those communities. Nevertheless, of 134 parishes retained, only 28 of them

---

[122] BCPLPc, Ms Pallastrelli 162: Compendio storico di Piacenza di D. Giulio Gandini, a chronicle dating from the second half of the eighteenth century.

(including 4 urban parishes) leave no telltale blip in the frequency of burials, and only in a single case was the mortality of the war years lower than the mean for the remainder of the decade. The absence of war does not necessarily signify the absence of dramatic mortality; there was an unspecified epidemic raging in the mountains such that for 17 parishes, 1638 was the worst year of all. I have omitted the year 1630 as the year of the plague, and, in some localities, the plague lasted until 1631. Even omitting the years of plague mortality, there are problems in the data, for the mortality in the immediate aftermath of the epidemic was bound to be lower than normal if only because most of the vulnerable people had already died. I have omitted the year 1631 because its mortality appears significantly lower than the subsequent several years. Inversely, the massing of troops and the collection of supplies to feed them pushed up the mortality in 1635, before the war reached our territory. I hope that some of the anomalies will cancel each other out and that the increase of mortality in 1636 and 1637 will give us an approximation of the hardship caused by the conflict.

Let's examine the two urban centres first, for if enemy soldiers plundered up to their very walls, they never gained entry. City parishes were not more uniform than the ones outside. In Piacenza, which withstood the brunt of the danger, we can use 24 parishes and compare the divergence between wartime and peacetime. Predictably, peasants and other people living in vulnerable places fled to the city to find safety. Piacenza was already home to at least 1,000 professional soldiers recruited from elsewhere, living in public buildings, in the citadel, in 22 monasteries, and in an unknown number of houses standing abandoned in the aftermath of the plague. Soldiers' hygiene was very approximate at the best of times, for they washed little and wore only one suit of clothes. The rigours of campaigning and living in the rough without privacy meant they were covered in dirt and lice.[123] These last were agents of typhus, an infectious disease that was tied to the standard of living of its hosts. Peasants taking refuge in Piacenza were protected against famine at least, for most brought their animals and their foodstuffs too, but chroniclers remarked that many of them had suffered greatly prior to their arrival.[124] Country people would usually have left their bedding behind them in their houses, and they lived in conditions of squalor far worse than the soldiers, exposed to lice and to flies in fetid stalls, then forced to huddle together in the cold. In November Leganés interrupted the gravity-fed canal running from the Trebbia river that flushed human and animal excrement into the Po. The registers reflect the consequences of this hygienic disaster. Counting the total number of burials during the years of peace in each parish and making a mean, we arrive at an annual number of 19.9 burials, averaging the 24 usable city parishes together (from 0.65 burials annually in the parish of S. Apollonia Appolonia, to 182.4 in S. Giuseppe, where the main hospital was located). The years 1636 and 1637 were traumatic for long-time citizens as well as the newcomers, for the mean annual number of burials for the same parishes was

---

[123] Richard Holmes, *Acts of War* (2nd edn, London, 2003), 111.
[124] Crescenzi Romani, *Corona della nobiltà d'Italia*, 331.

52.6, an increase of over 250 per cent. City priests sometimes added notes in the little paragraph recording each interment. In some cases, they simply noted that the deceased was not a parishioner and they did not know who they were. Sometimes the priest buried soldiers who had been killed by the enemy outside the walls, or otherwise '*morto di morte violenta*' (S. Niccolo Cattanei). Six people died every week, on average, in the principal hospital of S. Giuseppe over the two years of war. Many of them were soldiers, not all of them direct casualties, and a great many of the remainder were foundlings. In the parish of S. Alessandro, 7 of the first 13 burials of 1636 were soldiers, 6 of them Frenchmen. In that single parish, 20 French soldiers died that year, 6 of them violently. Some of those buried had probably been mortally wounded in battles outside the walls, like Giovanni Rebecchi, *ab Hispanis vulneratus*, on 21 August 1636, almost a week after the Battle of Rottofreno. In Piacenza, if about 900 people died during peacetime in an average year, the annual number between July 1635 and June 1637 is probably close to 2,500, which would result in a wartime excess of 3,000 people over two years.

While Parma suffered too, it was farther removed from the most intense fighting. Habsburg troops invaded the Parman countryside twice, first in March 1636, and then in the period after late August, until the following February, 1637. Of the 16 usable parishes we can compare inside the city (about 40 per cent of the total) the annual average number of burials in peacetime was 6.7 per parish, but this does not include the parish of the great hospital or many of the more populous neighbourhoods. There, the number of burials almost tripled to 18.6 annually during the war years. The parish priest of S. Nicolo identified 7 of the 18 people he buried in 1636 and 1637 as refugees from the countryside. It is more difficult to calculate the wartime excess mortality, although I doubt it was inferior to 1,000 people over the two years.

The countryside, including a score of walled towns, was far more vulnerable than the city. What of the places the Spanish commanders wished to spare? The registers from San Secondo are very badly faded, but are still legible and record a high number of burials, many of whom were indeed of refugees who took shelter there '*in tempo di guerra*'. For the small town at the centre of the fief, friendly terms with Spain brought little relief, although only one person, Matteo Pilastrelli, was ostensibly killed by soldiers. The annual average of just over 70 burials in peacetime gave way to 200 burials annually during the war, and 117 just in the two months of January and February 1637, *after* the fighting stopped. In this town, we can estimate the excess war mortality at about 150 individuals. Outlying parishes in the fief had burial rates only marginally higher than in peacetime, but I expect that many of the peasants fled their homes to the protection of the town, or indeed to Parma. The *parroco* of Corticelli outside the town noted that on 7 October 1636 Colonel Lucio Boccapianola of Naples came to take up quarters with five companies of Neapolitan infantry. When the last three companies left on 23 February 1637, the surviving villagers celebrated. The rural parishes in the Meli Lupi fief of Soragna did not enjoy much protection; at Carzeto the death toll increased by 50 per cent over its normal rate, especially in the first months of 1637, a time of war-induced famine. At Castellina, not far away, four people died in an average year, but over 30 during the war years, and an additional number were buried in the first three months of 1637 alone. These were the *protected* spaces.

What of the towns that offered contributions to the invading army in exchange for good treatment? For the most part these kept better records than small rural parishes. In the small city of Borgo San Donnino (today's Fidenza), the parish priests of three of the four parishes absented themselves during the turbulence; in the principal parish it was noted that the rector was absent in Parma '*per invasion milites*'. The rector of the parish of Parola, who in normal years buried only four or five of his parishioners, noted the enemy's arrival in the pages of his register.[125]

> On Thursday, 21 August 1636 the soldiers of the King of Spain began to arrive at Borgo San Donnino and its district, putting everything to sack with so much destruction that it appears that the world was upside down, where the principal inhabitants were reduced to saving their life and their honour [a probable allusion to rape] by fleeing to Parma, and partly by fleeing into churches and monasteries, leaving everything abandoned and exposed, which lasted until the end of February 1637. Between the Germans, the dragoons and the Spaniards, not only did they steal the contents of the houses, but they turned the inhabitants out of their dwellings and took their money without any compensation, from every sort of person, both ecclesiastics and laypersons. And with various unbearable torments they made poor people die after forcing them to reveal where they hid their goods, or made them reveal if other people had hidden goods. And in addition to the people they killed by torment, they caused the deaths of many others. And during this time, the parishioners of Santa Caterina of La Parola suffered 43 deaths, occurring in Borgo San Donnino, Parma and elsewhere, such that many of those who died are not registered here.

In the other two parishes we are certain that there was an upswing of fatalities because losses were already rising at the moment the priests fled, and they were above normal for a while after they returned. In the remaining parish of S. Pietro Apostolo, the deaths multiplied from September 1636 to February 1637, when the enemy soldiers were present, and priests indicated that many victims, including anonymous children, were people from outside. In this single parish where the records were continuous, wartime losses were *seven times* as high as those years of peace. This extreme upswing probably includes burials of people who belonged to the parishes from which priests fled. The soldiers did not operate with complete impunity, for among the victims was a young Milanese soldier shot by firing squad.

In the small town of Zibello on the Po river, where about 25 people died in a normal year, the rector listed the names of 47 people he buried in January and February 1637, only 17 of whom were men, 3 of whom were listed as military casualties. I suspect the death toll to be higher, for this priest recorded very few infant deaths. Priests were also upset by the misbehaviour of the soldiers, even when they did not cause people to die. Not far away, at Spigarolo in the jurisdiction of Busseto,

---

[125] Parish register of Parola, diocese of Fidenza, Mormon reel number 783272, Libro delle sepolture, 21 August 1636.

the rector left a copy of a letter to the diocesan vicar on events in his parish. 'Many people fled into the church... the rector was punched and mishandled, tied up and then dragged away for half a mile before he was untied and let go.' There the soldiers stole two chalices, the monstrance, the ecclesiastical vestments, and the valuable baldachin that served as a ceremonial canopy to the consecrated host and relics during religious processions. In the parish of Monticelli d'Ongina, where the Spanish built a fort, the courageous local priest was not frightened away by violence, for he had stayed in his large village during the worst of the plague to console his parishioners. Unlike other parishes, this one revealed signs of fighting, with 11 men, mostly Neapolitans (including two captains) buried after dying of their wounds. Soldiers shot one villager in his own house. One Milanese cavalryman was condemned by a military judge for a homicide, and died by firing squad.

The closer we move to Piacenza, the rarer the records become, but the Mormons have photographed registers for four of the principal communities, beginning with the towns of Fiorenzuola and Cortemaggiore. In peacetime, Fiorenzuola buried about 70 parishioners annually, but the invasion tripled those figures during each of the two years of the conflict. Apparently only one man died when the German cavalrymen raided the town on 21 August 1636. The excess mortality for that single parish would still be in the range of 300 people. At Cortemaggiore, where much of the population fled into the church and the castle when the Spaniards arrived, Don Martin d'Aragon promised good treatment if people cooperated. The parish rector buried several soldiers from the invading army on 22 and 23 August, along with one local man. There was a ten-day gap in the records following the town's surrender and its sack by the invaders. The rector tried to keep track of the fate of some of the people who fled elsewhere. From the moment the enemy arrived, the number of deaths began to shoot upwards; in a town where the peacetime burials numbered about 70 annually, 40 people died in January 1637 and almost 60 the following month, for a total excess mortality of about 250 individuals. At Cortemaggiore, the war killed almost as many people as the plague, which was responsible for most of the 311 burials in 1630 and 1631.

The most extreme case of a martyred community in our records would be Castel San Giovanni, on the border with the duchy of Milan, along the highway connecting Piacenza and Turin. In normal years, the priests there buried about 70 people, but this figure more than doubled in 1635 for reasons that are unclear. The town was the jumping-off point for the invasion of Spanish Lombardy in 1635, and a number of the deceased were soldiers. This higher-than-normal mortality continued into January 1636, with 25 burials, including four Savoyard soldiers from Guido Villa's army who were left in the hospital, and another man who had accidentally shot himself with his musket. The Spanish army attacked Castel San Giovanni on 15 February, which led to a brief siege in which four parishioners died, although the soldiers who were killed may not be included in our tally. The death toll began to rise almost immediately after the occupation, although only one man was reported killed by soldiers, and most of the other victims were small children. How violent were the soldiers? One of the men buried was a cavalryman from Novara, hanged for an unspecified offence on 11 April. Davide Maffi claims that Spanish military justice was active and severe during the war, and our casual discovery of at least three soldiers executed by army judges tends to bear this out, although the priests never record the precise nature of their transgression.[126] Returning to the unfortunate inhabitants of Castel San Giovanni, in March the death toll doubled to 51 victims, only one of whom was a battle casualty, and most of the others were either children, or elderly men and women. Although the weather improved in April, the number of victims shot upwards, with 67 dying in that month, at the rate of three people every day by the end of the month, then four every day in the first weeks of May, and seven victims daily by the end of the month when Guido Villa's troops liberated the town. The death toll of 144 in the single month of May was double the *annual* average in peacetime. In the liberated town, people continued to die in numbers not much inferior than before, with six victims daily in early June as the crops ripened, four victims daily in mid-month, and six burials every day at the end of the month when the crops were ready to harvest. With food now available, the death toll began to diminish, to about three daily burials in July. In the last weeks of the town's newfound liberty during the first weeks of August, about two people died every day. Don Martin d'Aragon's troops swept into the town on 15 August, the day of the brief battle at nearby Rottofreno, and they remained for the rest of the war. The death toll increased again, to about two and a half fatalities every day, but then collapsed to merely three or four per week when the weather started to cool. There were only six fatalities for the entire month of December. In many communities, 1637 was a more dramatic year, for the invasion had resulted in the massive spoliation of local crops and livestock. The fatalities at Castel San Giovanni were fewer in number, but death harvested more mature adults, with nine fatalities in January, twelve in February, and only three in March, after the soldiers left. There were only five or six burials monthly for the rest of the year, although this was still a heavy toll for a population that was a mere shadow of the pre-war number. In conclusion, the death toll during each of the two years of war (that is, including the winter of 1637) was about five times that of peacetime. The occupation of Castel San Giovanni by the Spanish army killed about twice as many people as the great plague of 1630, which carried off just over 300 victims or a quarter of the population. The proportion of one-half population decline for this single town is still an understatement, for still other inhabitants of the town died in Piacenza or on the battlefield. I suspect that Rottofreno, a town of similar size that suffered an enemy garrison for an even longer time, endured much the same fate. The priests present probably softened the soldiers' worst excesses. The leading ecclesiastic of Castel S. Giovanni was accused afterwards of being partial to the Spanish. Guido Villa reported to the duchess in his defense that his tact and ability (*destrezza*) probably saved the lives, honour, and goods of many of his parishioners.[127]

Hunger was the terrible weapon used against Castel San Giovanni but the arsenal contained others too. Wars have always spread disease by lowering the already precarious

---

[126] Davide Maffi, *Il Baluardo della corona: Guerra, esercito, finanze e societa nella Lombardia seicentesca (1630–1660)* (Florence, 2007), 268.

[127] ASPr, Governo Farnesiano, Carteggio Farnesiano Interno, 4 June 1636.

Fig. 5.6. Birds'-eye view of Castel San Giovanni, c.1900; Scene of a forgotten tragedy.

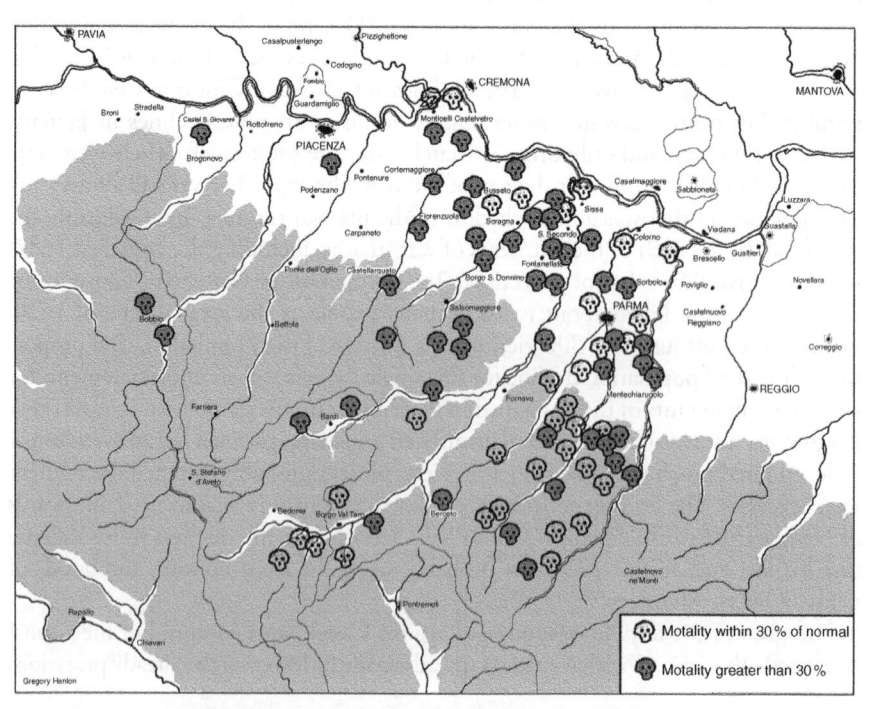

Map 5.2. Rural mortality in the Farnese duchies

standards of sanitation, and filling up protected places with refugees. The diseases the latter spread resembled the epidemics that were part of normal life before the nineteenth century. In the walled town of Castellarquato in the duchy of Piacenza, a fief of the church not visited by Spanish troops, the war triggered the outbreak of an epidemic that looks like smallpox. Refugees fleeing there most likely brought the disease with them. In this town, which buried about 20 people every year, small children began to die in early September 1636, just weeks after the Spanish invasion. Over the next four months, the register records the burials of children aged 1 to 6, with four or five infants dying every day at its peak. Through the monotonous list, we can intuit the terror of the parents. Almost 300 people died between September 1636 and March 1637.

Finally, there was another more diffuse and occult mortality little studied to date: the selective killing of newborns by married parents.[128] Unbaptized newborns were never recorded in the mortuary registers, for they bore no name or other social identity. But we can infer from the sex disparities of newborns figuring in the baptismal registers that this kind of infanticide was common in Emilia and elsewhere during the seventeenth century, and I suspect that it might have been a pan-European practice surviving into the nineteenth century, if not beyond. The death of an infant in the first days of life was no surprise to anyone. Parents likely decided at the moment of its birth whether or not to keep the infant, based on its sex, first of all, but probably also on whether or not they already had other children whose survival in hard times would have been compromised by the newcomer's demands on the mother. Newborn child murder should be seen, as Sarah Blaffer Hrdy says, as an act of love towards a toddler.[129] In rural districts, before the advent of widespread proto-industry, it made good sense for the parents to keep the boy and sacrifice the girl, who would need to be dowered, and who would leave home to live with another lineage. In Parma, on the other hand, where Laura Hynes has studied the phenomenon during this period, there was a stark contrast between the interests of the peasants outside the wall (who preferred boys) and the urban population, which kept the girls, particularly in the neighbourhoods where the textile industry held sway. Indeed, in this crisis year of 1636, the sex ratio of boys to girls among *baptized* infants was only 91 males for 100 females, instead of the universal 105. A number close to 15 per cent of the newborn boys were probably killed by their mothers before the onset of nursing, which represents about 60 individuals. This practice flourished to an as yet unknown extent in the countryside. In Cortemaggiore, a states of souls census for the town and its rural district undertaken nine years later suggests a dramatic imbalance for the children aged between 8 and 10, giving 38 boys and only 25 girls for the town and

---

[128] Gregory Hanlon, 'Infanticidio dei coppie sposati nella Toscana moderna, secoli XVI–XVIII', *Quaderni Storici*, 38/113 (2003): 453–98. A more condensed version of this research is found in my book, *Human Nature in Rural Tuscany: An Early Modern History* (Basingstoke and New York, 2007); for Parma, see the research by Laura Hynes, 'Routine infanticide by married couples? An assessment of baptismal records from seventeenth-century Parma', *Journal of Early Modern History*, 15 (2011): 507–30. Research on Aquitaine, which I am presently conducting with the aid of graduate students, on Agen, on Layrac, Caudecoste, Nerac, Tonneins, Villeneuve-sur-Lot, Caudecoste, and Astaffort has, to varying degrees, uncovered similar disparities. This research is ongoing.

[129] Sarah Blaffer Hrdy, *Mother Nature: A History of Mothers, Infants and Natural Selection* (New York, 1999).

Table 5.1. Mortality by parish in the 1630s

Mortality in the 1630s	1631	1632	1633	1634	1635	1636	1637	1638	1639	comments
Province of Parma										
Colorno	5	9	8	5	5	5	20	13	9	
Corticelli	4	1	7	5	8	5	22	8	7	
Diolo (Soragna)	5	0	0	10	7	3	14	9	8	
Baganzola	2	2	3	1	8	2	13	3	5	
Basilicagoiano	6	5	5	7	4	6	15	7	13	
Berceto	2	5	11	18	13	23	gap	gap	gap	
Carzeto	8	17	7	13	28	17	31	20	10	
Castellina	3	3	1	4	4	9	52	9	3	
Castione Baratti	4	5	1	2	2	2	4	1	1	
Ghiara (Fontanellato)	28	12	13	27	26	29+	40	27	9	
Malandriano	1	0	1	1	2	0	4	4	1	
Marano	2	0	1	1	5	5	8	4	7	
Madregolo	5	1	10	5	10	6	19	8	9	
Paradigno	0	0	1	0	3	8	3	2	3	
Priorato	16	12	13	16	20	gap	25+	14	15	
Montechiarugolo	4	4	6	6	2	9	8	4	7	
Monticelli Terme	gap	2+	2	2	6	1	7	2	2	
Ronchetti	gap	gap	3+	2	6	7	3	4	5	
Pizzo	5	6	1	13	10	9	12	4	5	
San Secondo	77	74	50	59	118	192	208	50	67	
Fidenza S. Pietro	2	4	4	9	4	45	55	2	19	
Bastelli	4	13	0	3	6	6	14	7	9	
Monticelli Ongina	52+	30	21	35	43	61	71	58	35	
Parola (Fidenza)	13	4	3	3	5	6+	8+	5	10	
Zibello	31	12	17	26	26	18+	64	16	10	few infants
Cignano	10	3	4	3	2	1	5	0	0	
Sant'Andrea Busseto	4	0	1	6	9	20+	35+	17	12	

Guardasone	4	2	5	6	14	2+	11	5
Varano de'Melegari	2	1	2	2	7	1	9	4
San Pietro Vigato	13	9	15	17	10	20	25	11
Lesignano Bagni	7	2	1	3	6	gap	gap	gap
Mulazzano	1	4	5	3	gap	7	2	1
Agna (Corniglio)	gap	gap	5+	4	10	7	9	5
Cazzola	13	3	4	3	6	6	0	1
San Rocco Busseto	35	18	11	16	61	77	8	10
Banzola Salsomagg.	0	2	1	3	3	1	0	3
S. Vittore Salsomagg.	gap	gap	gap	7	14	12	6	6
Tabiano Salsomagg.	1	5	1	3	5	10	5	5
Manzano	6	2	3	6	12	2	3	1
Sant'Ilario Baganza	gap	2	5	0	4	1	3	1
Orzale	8	0	1	0	2	3	0	1
Zibano	59	0	2	5	9	3	4	3	plague 1631
Chiesabianca	31	2	2	1	7	3	1	gap	plague 1631
Costageminiano	gap	3	0	3	9	6	3	2
Vianino	85	140	13	10	23	8	12	13	plague 1631/32
Iggio	3	6	7	6	12	2+	gap	gap
Specchio	3	7	14	7	22	11	17	10
Bellena	2	2	1	7	0	3	0	1
Corcagnano	0	1	0	9	1	1	1	1
Ronco Casa Canneto	gap	3	5	7	5	4	2	2
Coenzo	4	1	7	3	1	2	0	3
Cattabiano	1+	3	0	4	1	1	4	3
Gramignazzo	4	5	16	6	7	7	14	5
Porporano	2	0	2	1	3	0	3	1
Rivalta Lesignano	gap	gap	0	10	4	3	3	6	infants 1635
Roncopascolo	1	3	4	0	0	2	5	3

(*continued*)

Table 5.1. (Continued)

Mortality in the 1630s	1631	1632	1633	1634	1635	1636	1637	1638	1639	comments
Sala Baganza	8	5	8	5	14	6	9	14	7	
San Donato	2	2	4	2	3	1	2	2	2	
San Michele Gatti	0	0	1	1	1	0	0	1	2	
Castelvetro	gap	11	18	8	19	10	10	15	11	
Olza	11	9	gap	4	23	13	13	12	9	
Mediano	gap	2	1	2	0	0	0	1	0	
Strognano	0	1	1	0	2	2	2	1	3	
Musiara Inferiore	1	1	1	0	0	0	0	4	0	
Cozzano	11	4	1	5	4	2	2	15	4	
Cella	3	1	0	4	0	3	2	1	2	
Lupazzano	1	0	2	3	3	1	3	13	3	
Graiana	5	14	0	4	5	3	6	6	3	
Ruzzano	gap	gap	gap	1	2	0	1	7	0	
Mattaleto	84	5	7	5	10	8	8	4	12	plague 1631
Vestana	0	0	4	1	4	3	2	3	4	
Codogno	2	2	3	1	3	1	3	2	3	
Campi Albareto	gap	gap	1	5	3	1	0	0	1	
S. Vincenzo Borgo T.	gap	gap	4	0	1	3	1	2	2	
Porcigatone Borgo T.	1	5	12	0	0	1	10	5		
Pieve di Campi	13	2	0	0	3	1	5	3	3	
Parma Cattedrale	gap	3	4	5	6	22	6	2	5	
Parma S. Alessandro	1+	5	2	3	2	7	1	5	6	
Parma S. Benedetto	1+	1	3	4	7	13	18	11	21	
Parma S. Maria Maddal.	5+	6	4	4	8	8	10	7	9	
Parma S. Uldarico	2+	1	4	8	8	28	41	24	28	
Parma S. Barnaba	6+	3	6	10	11	23	10	3	9	
Parma S. Giovanni Evan.	gap	gap	gap	2+	2	7	6	1	2	

Parma SS Trinita	4	12	8	13	29	74	56	11	25
Parma S. Marco	3	0	3	4	5	3	4	3	4
Parma S. Stefano	1+	0	3	1	4	1	1	3	1
Parma S. Nicolo	gap	gap	gap	gap	6	5	8	3	2
Parma SS Mich. & Ant.	2	1	3	2	2	10	5	2	4
Parma S. Michele Canal	2	6	2	5	15	8	15	15	10
Parma S. Marcellino	gap	1+	6	6	7	19	13	6	2
Parma Sta. Maria	5	11	16	3	2	21	15	7	3
Parma S. Michele Arco	12	6	2	7	10	42	10	6	12
Parma S. Paolo	13	25	13	14	27	64	33	11	15
Parma S. Tommaso	5	3	2	3	9	10	9	4	3
Province of Piacenza									
Castellarquato	21	14	14	18	10	237	115	35	44
Cortemaggiore	114	74	36	79	96	199	171	23	67
Castel San Giovanni	57	64	68	72	159	678	67	76	32
Mucinasso	1	3	2	4	1	5	16	5	7
Fiorenzuola d'Arda	668	57	43	69	97	207	245	72	70	plague in 1631
Menconico	gap	gap	5+	8	2	17	3	gap	17
Valverde (Bobbio)	0	2	1	1	4	12	4	5	3
Bobbio	gap	10+	5	10	26	45	25	11	24
Piacenza SS Giac & Filip	4	3	2	0	3	6	7	4	1
Piacenza S. Appolonia	6+	1	1	2	0	10	6	0	0
Piacenza S. Maria Ass.	6	12	12	6	21	19+	13+	10	6
Piacenza S. Niccolo Catt	15	7	17	21	37	96	57	19	11
Piacenza S. Martino Foro	gap	gap	gap	3+	16	17	7	3	2
Piacenza S. Giuseppe	189	144	214	248+	gap	323	117	28+	gap	city hospital

many infants 1636/7

(*continued*)

Table 5.1. (Continued)

Mortality in the 1630s	1631	1632	1633	1634	1635	1636	1637	1638	1639	comments
Piacenza S. Maria Borg.	4	9	3	3	9	21	10	4	2	
Piacenza S. Stefano Pr.	10	11	8	19	16	52	23	10	11	
Piacenza S. Antonino	5	7	18	16	31	88	55	29	19	
Piacenza S. Giorgio	4	8	3	7	11	8	9	5	8	
Piacenza S. Andrea Borg.	6	4	2	0	10	34	23	5	11	
Piacenza S. Giacomo M.	9	1	9	14	28	82	23	14	14	
Piacenza S. Sepolcro	gap	17	16	16	26	102	47	10	18	
Piacenza S. Brigida	gap	9+	8	12	32	47	21	13	18	
Piacenza S. Alessandro	31	41	23	44	69	101	50	26	19	
Piacenza S. Salvatore	3	6	16	13	39	64	51	10	7	
Piacenza S. Ulderico	5	2	2	3	3	9	9	4	5	
Piacenza S. Maria Gariv.	6	30	15	48	69	144	84	36	29	
Piacenza S. Maria Zero.	0	3	6	2	8	9	5	4	5	
Piacenza Sant'Ilario	1	5	8	9	5	13	9	3	2	
Piacenza S. Gervaso	4	0	1	3	6	10	3	1	2	
Piacenza San Dalmazio	1	0	2	0	3	9	4	4	1	
Piacenza S. Giov. Canal	14	16	19	25	22	62	50	20	27	
Piacenza San Lazaro	11	18	11	6	15	19+	12+	18	10	
Piacenza San Savino	21	33	44	50	97	198	120	33	37	
Piacenza S. Fran. & Prot.	4	9	5	5	6	7	8	6	4	

24 boys and 16 girls for the rural district around it, implying that some 20 girls' lives were snuffed out just after birth. If we can generalize from Cortemaggiore, which contained somewhat under 1 per cent of the duchy's population, we might imagine a tally of infant murders in the vicinity of 2,000 people.[130] How many subjects died to satisfy Duke Odoardo's dreams of glory? We can evaluate the victims certainly in the thousands, probably at least 10,000 people, or 4 per cent of the total population, of whom military losses made up only a small proportion. This war was relatively short, and the dreaded bubonic plague did not make another appearance. People probably compared the war losses to those of the great plague of 1630, when 300 persons are reported to have died *every day* in Piacenza for months on end. A recent estimate of plague losses there estimates that the famine and plague of 1629–30 killed close to half the population.[131] Mortality from the war would have quickly been forgotten in relation to the great epidemic.

We can only hope that someone will photograph the parish registers for the villages of the rural hinterland of Piacenza, and nearby Milanese territory which Odoardo's soldiers and militiamen visited often, only after which we can make firmer generalizations on the brutality of the soldiers towards civilians. Soldiers certainly frightened civilians and sometimes killed them too. But clearly people died either of epidemics caused by misery, or of the famine accompanying and following the war. The death toll dropped off when warmer weather returned in April and May 1637. For decades thereafter, people had a legitimate new fear even in the more densely populated plain near the Po: wolves. The parish priest of Ghiara by the Taro river near Fontanellato noted their multiplication in the aftermath of the war, as he buried the remains of a five-year-old girl devoured by a pack of these animals in October 1637.[132]

Even in Germany, abandoned farms and villages saw their inhabitants return after several weeks or months.[133] In the duchy of Parma the depressed and angry survivors returned to their wrecked and burned farms late in the winter of 1637. Many head of livestock had been moved into city fortresses, and much money was spent on finding fodder to feed them over the winter and spring.[134] Many more head had been smuggled out of the duchy to neighbouring Mantuan territory to be fed there in safety.[135] The duke suspended the common practice of seizing oxen as pawns of indebted people in February 1637. Odoardo turned over many of his own horses and mules to pull the ploughs, and made arrangements to restore the

---

[130] Cortemaggiore, Piacenza, Microfilm reel 2272523, Status animarum 1640–1645.

[131] BCPLPc, Tesi di Laurea n. 243: Marco Tanzi, 'La dinamica della popolazione di Piacenza dalla metà del '500 alla peste del 1630' (thesis, Università degli Studi di Parma, 1983–4); on the severity of this plague pandemic, Guido Alfani, 'Plague in seventeenth-century Europe and the decline of Italy: an epidemiological analysis', *European Review of Economic History*, 17 (2013): 1–23; and for the diocese of Parma in particular, Matteo Manfredini, Sergio Di Iasio and Enzo Lucchetti, 'The Plague of 1630 in the territory of Parma: Outbreak and effects of a crisis', *International Journal of Anthropology*, 17 (2002): 41–57.

[132] ASPr, microfilm mortuary register 782 720 Ghiara (Fontanellato), 11 October 1637.

[133] Jean-Michel Boehler, 'La guerre au quotidien dans les villages du Saint-Empire au XVIIe siècle', in *Les Villageois face à la guerre, XIVe–XVIIIe siècle*, ed. C. Desplat (Toulouse, 2002), 65–88.

[134] Crescenzi Romani, *Corona della nobiltà d'Italia*, vol. 2, 330–1.

[135] ASPr, Governo Farnesiano, Mastri Farnesiani 32, 694.

depleted stock of oxen.[136] In Germany and France Bernhard Kroener suggests that the flight of the rustics to the cities with their large livestock would have seen the ownership of these animals pass into the hands of city notables. The same wealthy bourgeois would have lent money at usurious rates of interest to the peasants to restart the rural economy once peace arrived, but the peasants would have quickly lost their land to the lenders given the gradual decline of grain prices. Jean-Michel Boehler, who has studied the post-war period in Alsace, arrives at the substantially opposite conclusion: that peasant property flourished in a context of low grain prices and the lack of manpower.[137] Nobody has yet undertaken this work in Italy, but there are reasons for thinking that the passage of rural property to wealthy city-dwellers had been well under way for a generation before the onset of the war.[138]

It took years to restore the ducal revenues and properties to full production. Pietro Rossi encouraged the introduction of Modenese and Bolognese coins, making careful assays of their metallic value in order to displace a few of the 'red' coins produced during the war, and awaiting the resumption of proper Farnese coinage as resources came available. The same functionary oversaw the reconstruction of the salt refinery at Salsomaggiore. The principal obstacle lay in the rarity of haulage animals that made it difficult to supply the place with firewood. This would have to be done using new taxes in the form of work details or corvées.[139] The ironworks at Carmiano had to be restored before the duke could finish reconstituting the great pans for evaporating salt water. Workers were so scarce that the expert recommended paying people to cut the wood and conduct the haulage teams, in addition to the convict and corvée labour he normally employed.[140]

Duke Odoardo owed his subjects a great deal of sympathy and forgiveness after the end of the famine in 1637. The *suppliche* or petitions addressed to the duke after the end of the war teach us that murderers and other criminals received pardons in exchange for serving as soldiers. They confirm too that militiamen and other soldiers were forced to serve for long months with no pay.[141] The 153 petitions submitted by 'soldiers' living in Parma and its territory in 1637 reflect an ongoing rendering of accounts. It is interesting that not a single petition comes from a French soldier, signifying that they marched away free of pursuit by the duke for any crimes they committed. Regular professional soldiers constituted only 16 petitioners, (only one of whom reported a wife living with him) and almost

---

[136] ASPr, Governatore e Comunità di Piacenza 3, 25 February 1637; ASPr, Governo Farnesiano, Carteggio Farnesiano Interno 385, 7 July 1638.

[137] Jean-Michel Boehler, 'Les conséquences à long terme des guerres du XVIIe siècle en Alsace: pour l'élaboration d'un 'modèle rhénan', in *Les Malheurs de la Guerre: de la guerre à l'ancienne à la guerre réglée*, ed. A. Corvisier and J. Jacquart (Paris, 1996), 201–17.

[138] Kroener, 'Conditions de vie', 321–50; for the alienation of peasant property to urban dwellers in the hinterland of nearby Modena, the best study remains that of Marco Cattini, *I Contadini di San Felice: Metamorfosi di un mondo rurale nell'Emilia dell'età moderna* (Turin, 1984), 38.

[139] ASPr, Carteggio Farnesiano 384, letters of 15 March 1637.

[140] ASPr, Carteggio Farnesiano 384, letter from Giulio Cesare Trompelli, 3 August 1637.

[141] The petitions to the duke processed late in the war, and in the years immediately thereafter number in the hundreds just from Parma. I have perused a number of them contained in the series ASPr, Consiglio della Dettatura: Suppliche 43, 1636–7. These and a sample of later petitions were the object of an MA thesis by Colin Rose at Dalhousie University in 2010.

all the others were militiamen. Of these professional soldiers, three-quarters claimed to be natives of a city, and only one claimed a village origin, which coincides with the evidence contained in the company rosters. Homicide accounted for nine of the offences the duke pardoned, only one of which was accidental. Military offences were only a small portion of the whole (only 12), including four cases of desertion or shirking, and three cases involving the violation of curfew while bearing weapons. One man cheated soldiers of their pay, and another plundered an aristocratic villa. Two more men sought pardon for having guided enemy soldiers around the duchy. A decree of 14 November 1637 promised safe conduct documents to former *tagliateste* who were to present themselves within two weeks to judicial officials to answer for their pre-war crimes.[142] Pardon was a routine part of the judicial system, for by overturning a ruling by a tribunal, the duke granted a special favour to the guilty party and so sought the latter's gratitude. Odoardo had done much for his subjects to forgive.

[142] ASPr, Gridario 32, n. 109, 14 November 1637.

Conclusion

Spain tried to inaugurate talks for peace in Europe early in 1636, and various emissaries in Rome and Cologne assembled for some half-hearted negotiations. The stumbling block again was the intransigence of Cardinal Richelieu and Louis XIII, who were not overly dismayed at the results of the first military campaigns.[1] Spain's desire for peace guided the policy of successive military governors of Milan not to exploit the weakness of hostile Italian princes so as to avoid antagonizing neutral spectators.[2] Leganés scored a considerable success early in 1637 by reaching an agreement with the Grison League, which withdrew its support from the Duke of Rohan in the Valtellina.[3] With the death of Duke Charles of Mantua in September of the same year, the Duchess Maria acting as regent for the child-duke Charles II immediately withdrew that duchy from the French alliance.

In crushing the young Duke of Parma's vaulting ambitions, the King of Spain taught all the Italian princes a lesson. But he had no illusion about Odoardo himself, who had a selective memory. The historian Capriata, writing shortly after Odoardo's death, echoed the duke's vision of himself: 'Many people praised the lofty spirit of the duke of Parma, as a singular example of the forthright soul worthy of a free prince, who taught the Spaniards that they had to take Italian princes into account, and to show to them proper respect. However, others blamed the actions of the duke who was as a youth drunk with lofty ideals and ambitions greater than his rank, and that he did not have good and sufficient reasons to break with Spain.'[4] Pessimistically, the Spanish ambassador Francisco de Melo confided to Madrid that 'He will keep Italy in a perpetual anxiety as long as he lives... He will never be a good Spaniard, nor will he ever follow a policy of tranquillity... He confides to

---

[1] Daniel Séré, *La Paix des Pyrénées: Vingt-quatre ans de négociations entre la France et l'Espagne (1635–1659)* (Paris, 2007), 43–70; and Miguel Angel Ochoa Brun, 'La diplomatie espagnole dans la première moitié du XVIIe siècle', in *L'Europe des traités de Westphalie: Esprit de la diplomatie et diplomatie de l'esprit*, ed. L. Bély (Paris, 2000), 537–54.

[2] Davide Maffi, *Il baluardo della corona: Guerra, esercito, finanze e società nella Lombardia seicentesca (1630–1660)* (Florence, 2007), 46–9.

[3] Sandro Massera, 'La spedizione del Duca Henri de Rohan in Valtellina (1635–1637)', in *La Spedizione del Duca di Rohan in Valtellina: Storia e memorie nell'età della Guerra dei Trent'Anni* (Milan, 1999), 81.

[4] Pietro Giovanni Capriata, *Dell'Historia delli movimenti d'armi successi in Italia*, 2 vols. (Genoa, 1649), vol. 2, 254.

nobody save Scotti and his French secretary [Gaufridy]'.[5] The judgement on Odoardo was prophetic, for it was not long before he contracted new enmities.

Odoardo paid little attention to the concerns of accountants, until it was too late. The war had ravaged the duchy's finances and crippled its economy, from its pool of livestock to the discontinued banking fairs of Piacenza. Even worse, Odoardo could no longer obtain credit, now that all the bills from the war were due.[6] The Farnese estates in central Italy had been mortgaged twice, once by Duke Alessandro for the military expedition to the Netherlands, and again by Odoardo. Roman bankers Siri and Sacchetti, who were understood to be in secret relations with the papal nephew Taddeo Barberini, advanced the money and managed the revenues of these combined fiefs, which were largely derived from the sale of grain. The European price of grain began to decline during the 1630s, a consequence of the widespread impoverishment due to war. In 1638 the bankers demanded that Odoardo revisit the contracts and, in the meantime, refused to send him money. Odoardo made things more difficult for himself by refusing to purchase licences from the Pope to export grain from those territories that the Pope considered subject to his sovereignty. An official visit by Odoardo's ambassador, Marchese Pallavicino, to Taddeo Barberini soured when the papal relative made him wait, and then received him in his dressing gown, which was taken as a calculated affront.[7]

The impasse compelled the duke to visit his Roman palace to seek a settlement with his creditors.[8] Once in Rome, late in 1639, he refused at first to pay his respects to the Pope, his sovereign, feigning an impediment. After some negotiation, he consented to pay a visit to Urban VIII alone, but on condition that he would not have to encounter the papal nephew Don Taddeo Barberini, who, he suspected, was behind the intransigence of his bankers. At first the nephew consented to absent himself from Rome during the papal visit, and so Odoardo made a low-key visit where he was received with demonstrations of affection and admiration as one of the leading lights of his age. The duke was led to believe that the problem of his mortgages and of his grain licences was already resolved, but Cardinal Francesco Barberini raised some objections to it. The Barberini Pope also changed his mind about offering the cardinal's hat to the duke's brother, Francesco Maria. Odoardo paid a visit to Cardinal Antonio Barberini too, who snubbed him by refusing to accompany him to his coach as he was leaving. Two months of acrimonious discussions ended when Don Taddeo returned to Rome and deliberately placed himself in Odoardo's view. Pope Urban VIII and his nephews no doubt hatched a scheme whereby they would force Odoardo to sell his ancestral patrimony to them in order to satisfy his creditors. He responded to this proposal entirely in character: he lost his temper. He returned to Parma in March 1640 after a stormy interview at the papal palace, complaining that the pontiff didn't

---

[5] AGS, Estado, Legajo 3345/43; letter in cipher from Francisco de Melo, 5 March 1637. '*El duca de Parma nunca sera buen Espanol ni seguira el camino de la quietud...*'

[6] Geoffrey Mortimer, 'War by contract, credit and contribution: the Thirty Years' War', in *Early Modern Military History* (Basingstoke, 2004), 101–17.

[7] Gregorio Leti, *Il Cerimoniale historico e politico* (Waesberge, 1685), 148.

[8] Demaria, 'La Guerra di Castro e la pedizione de' presidii, 1639–1649', *Miscellanea di Storia Italiana*, ser. 3, 4 (1898), 191–256.

understand the resolve of princes of his stature, who were not to be meddled with, and warned that he would defend his prerogatives with his sword.[9] Pope Urban soon returned the compliment, calling the duke an excitable nitwit (*cervellino troppo vivo*), a presumptuous and ungrateful idiot, all smoke and thunder like his mother's Aldobrandini relatives. Cardinal Antonio forbade grain exports from the Farnese fiefs in March 1641, and for good measure caused the postal highway to detour away from the same towns, which reduced the volume of commercial transit. Such measures dried up the revenues Odoardo needed to pay the interest on his mortgages.

However, Odoardo had never disarmed completely. In 1640 there were still nine companies of 100 soldiers on the payroll, with numerous noblemen serving as troopers in the cavalry.[10] The duke soon began to hire additional military specialists without fixed attributions at the court. Castro he fortified as elaborately as he could in the spring of 1641, and hired on a few hundred soldiers as a garrison for it, who would not have been much fewer than the inhabitants of the town. Given Odoardo's chequered military career, the Barberini were not inclined to back down, and so Taddeo Barberini raised an army of about 6,000 men and moved on the little fortress, which surrendered after a two-week siege in October 1641.

This was Odoardo's pretext to fashion a confederation of Italian states to force the papacy to be more compliant to their demands, and, in August 1642, a formal alliance united Parma with the Republic of Venice, the duchy of Modena, and the Grand Duchy of Tuscany in a war against the papacy. Even before his allies were ready, Odoardo raised an army of about 4,000 cavalry and a small number of infantry and marched off to recover Castro in September. Hasty papal levies melted away from his force (which largely consisted, once again, of French troops) and Odoardo marched triumphantly into central Italy, to within a couple of days' march from Rome. The papal city was seized by panic at the easy progress of this force, which, however, was not equipped with materials necessary to recover Castro by siege. By late October, Odoardo returned home as a conquering hero, and collected another army that he would field in concert with his allies. But he was not ready to take a subalternate position, and so marched on Bondeno, a small and almost defenceless little town near the Po in Romagna, which was an important navigation hub near Ferrara and Modena. This he quickly fortified and garrisoned, and his forces did not budge from it for the entire campaign of 1643, although Venetian and Modenese armies operated nearby. However, the imminent death of Urban VIII early in 1644 convinced all parties to end the war and Odoardo recovered Castro as part of the peace.

Fortunately for Italy, the duke died on 11 September 1646, at only 34 years of age, leaving his adolescent son Ranuccio II to deal with the financial crisis. 'A prince with shining talents... His subjects loved him and served him out of duty. Among his faults was the lofty opinion he had of himself, and the immoderate desire he had to increase his dominion, a fault he shares with all Great Men

---

[9] Leti, *Il Cerimoniale historico e politico*, 418.
[10] ASPr, Governo Farnesiano, Milizie 35, Ruoli delle truppe 1640.

(Grandi).'[11] Almost immediately after his father's death, Duke Ranuccio II of Parma took a subsidy from the King of Spain to help pay for his citadel garrisons.[12] He also wished to stay clear of a recrudescence of French interest in the region after 1646, once Cardinal Mazarin was firmly in power in Paris. Ranuccio retained Jacques Gaufridy as his principal minister, but in 1649 someone ordered the assassination of the new bishop of Castro appointed by Pope Innocent X Pamphili, despite the objection of the Farnese duke. The Pope used this cold-blooded murder as a pretext for war and seized Castro again, this time demolishing every trace of the town. A hastily raised army marched from Parma to the papal border with Gaufridy at its head, where it met a similar opposing force on 18 August 1649. In the sharp exchange lasting several hours, the Parmans had the worst of it and retreated hastily. The Pope would not consent to any kind of negotiation until Ranuccio had Gaufridy decapitated at Piacenza the following year, and he still refused to restitute any of the ancestral Farnese territories in Latium. This misadventure cured Ranuccio II of all military adventurism for the remainder of his reign.

Even in the final stages of the Thirty Years' War, one is struck by the facility with which all the belligerents hired large numbers of professional soldiers of varied provenance. Geoffrey Mortimer holds that this facility stemmed from a gradual deskilling of the soldiering trade that occurred during the sixteenth century. 'Only moderate skill and strength were necessary to manage a pike, but firearms were dead easy to learn, the rudiments acquired within a week...For cavalry, anyone who could sit on a horse and fire a pistol at the same time was a match for a knight. So just being able-bodied was enough to become a soldier.' The only limit to hiring an army was the amount of money available, in cash or in credit.[13] But for most of these men, and for the Italians in particular, soldiering was a pause from their normal routine in a way that had changed little since the fifteenth century. Many of the men would desert to move on or else to change armies when it suited their interest. The wars themselves did not implicate most Italian states for very long, and so relatively few recruits passed from being a civilian to a professional soldier and a veteran whose skills and loyalty princes cherished.[14]

Parman noblemen who had acquired a taste for war now sought other venues, and for the most part followed careers in the French army for the remainder of the seventeenth century—but these were a mere handful.[15] Odoardo's treaty with Spain expressly prohibited Parman officers, like Fabio Scotti, to hold commissions

---

[11] BCPLPc, Ms Pallastrelli n. 62; D. Giulio Gandini, Compendio Storico di Piacenza, 207.

[12] Gianvittorio Signorotto, *Milano Spagnola: Guerra, istituzioni, uomini di governo (1635–1660)* (2nd edn, Milan, 2001), 40–1.

[13] Mortimer, 'War by contract, credit and contribution', 101–17.

[14] For a vision of the transformation of soldiers over the long duration, see Luciano Pezzolo, 'Professione militare e famiglia in Italia tra tardo medioevo e prima età moderna', in *La Justice des familles: Autour de la transmission des biens, des savoirs et des pouvoirs*, ed. A. Bellavitis and I. Chabot (Rome, 2011), 341–66. I thank Prof. Pezzolo for his generosity in allowing me to use an unpublished version.

[15] Biblioteca Palatina Parma, Mss Parmense 656; Padre Andrea di Parma, cappuccino: Opere diverse di storia parmense (secolo XVIII), 46 and 140, Antonio Cantelli and Giovan Battista Baiardi.

in the French army or to recruit soldiers from the duchy for French service.[16] Two of Ranuccio's four younger brothers cultivated military careers of their own in the 1650s. Orazio Farnese went to Venetian Crete leading a small Parman contingent to help defend the island from a Turkish invasion, but he died almost immediately from typhus or malaria. Another brother, Alessandro Farnese, spent most of his career in Spanish service where he attained the rank of governor-general of the Spanish Netherlands, being awarded the Golden Fleece before his death in 1690.

The mantle of military adventurism passed from Odoardo to his brother-in-law Francesco I d'Este of Modena, whose first experience of war followed the foraging expedition of Guido Villa. That success induced him to present himself at the court of Madrid, seeking command of a large Spanish army. King Philip IV awarded him the title of 'Highness', allowed him to stand godfather to the Infanta, and bestowed on him the Golden Fleece. However, these honours were insufficient to satisfy his ambitions.[17] Duke Francesco had hoped to recover the former family seat of Ferrara from the Pope during the Castro War in 1643. Since that military adventure was not a disaster, Francesco was willing to be seduced by Cardinal Mazarin in 1647, who was seeking to create a new Italian alliance to overthrow Spain in Italy. Francesco hired a largely French army that took the field against Cremona in 1647, but it proved too small to capture the place. With a new French army he attempted the siege of Cremona again in 1648, but failed for the same reasons, and this time the Spanish troops devastated the district of Reggio Emilia. He withdrew from the French alliance in the winter of 1649 while France descended into civil war. Unchastened, Francesco d'Este entered the French alliance again in 1654, after Spain had neglected to give him an army of his own, and in the following campaigns he led combined armies no larger than those of Créquy or the Duke of Savoy. The war between France and Spain was on the point of ceasing from mutual exhaustion when Francesco died in the field in October 1658. Francesco, like Odoardo before him, believed that their little states could still influence the outcome of the great struggle between the Bourbons and the Habsburgs, and that by siding with the victor, they could obtain more complete sovereignty and territorial gain.[18] But there was no victor, at least not in Italy, which still deserved the reputation of being 'the tomb of French armies'.[19]

William Caferro, studying the overall impact of war on the Italian early Renaissance, concluded that the contest of each against all benefited the territorial states like Florence, Milan, and Venice against their smaller neighbours. The large states expanded both territory and population, and thereby increased their tax revenues; they also acquired a more rational administration and greater integration

---

[16] David Parrott, 'Italian soldiers in French service 1500–1700: the collapse of a military tradition', in *Italiani al servizio straniero in età moderna*, ed. P. Bianchi, D. Maffi, and E. Stumpo (Milan, 2008), 15–40.

[17] Angelantonio Spagnoletti, *Le dinastie italiane nella prima età moderna* (Bologna, 2003), 63.

[18] Yves-Marie Bercé, 'Les guerres dans l'Italie du XVIIe siècle', in *L'Italie au XVIIe siècle*, ed. Y.-M. Bercé, J.-C. Waquet, J.-M. Sallmann, and G. Delille (Paris, 1989), 311–31.

[19] Gualdo Priorato, *Historia delle guerre del Conte Galeazzo Gualdo Priorato* (Venice, 1646), 305.

of their markets.[20] Jan Glete would say that these large states had a comparative advantage in violence, enabling them to protect their territory with lower transaction costs relative to small ones, which were easily overrun.[21] In the sixteenth century, the Sienese Republic disappeared from the map, along with the independent duchy of Milan and kingdom of Naples. The seventeenth-century wars just continued the same process, this time encompassing all of Europe. The competitive Italian principalities of the early seventeenth century almost all subscribed to a political vision that discouraged initiative and enterprise, safe as the princes were in the Spanish system. Richelieu's great design to establish French ascendancy in Europe found a willing tool only in Odoardo Farnese, and then Francesco d'Este during Mazarin's time, when Spanish exhaustion was increasingly manifest.[22] The Mantuan Succession War and the twenty years of fighting in northern Italy after 1635 gradually stripped away the illusion that these states mattered militarily.

These indebted little duchies had no stomach for war after 1660, the years in which Piedmont and north European states began to raise permanent standing armies as part of their sovereign attributes. The next generation of princes would seek nothing more than to maintain the status quo, or, at most, consent to outfit a battalion of soldiers for service to fight the Turks in the distant Mediterranean. In the age of standing armies, states like Parma, Mantua, Modena, and Tuscany, the Republic of Genoa, and the papacy ceased to count for very much.[23] Ranuccio II built up a treasure to buy Castro back from the papacy in the 1660s, and when that failed, purchased the last Landi fiefs north of the Apennines and sank his disposable revenue into music and theatre, the illusory 'soft power' whose many monuments are still tangible today. For the next 150 years, when foreign armies descended into northern Italy to continue the contest for ascendancy, these little Italian states did their best to stay out of the way, unable to influence the outcome in any realistic fashion.

---

[20] William Caferro, 'Warfare and economy in Renaissance Italy 1350–1450', *Journal of Interdisciplinary History*, 39 (2008), 167–209.

[21] Jan Glete, 'Warfare, entrepreneurship and the fiscal-military state', in *European Warfare 1350–1750*, ed. F. Tallett and D. J. B. Trim (Cambridge and New York, 2010), 300–21.

[22] Jean-Claude Waquet, 'Politique, institutions et société dans l'Italie du "Seicento"', in *L'Italie au XVIIe siècle*, ed. Y.-M. Bercé, J.-C. Waquet, J.-M. Sallmann, and G. Delille (Paris, 1989), 32–4; also Frigo, '"Small states" and diplomacy: Mantua and Modena', in *Politics and Diplomacy in Early Modern Italy: The Structure of Diplomatic Practice 1450–1800*, ed. Daniela Frigo (Cambridge, 2000), 147–75.

[23] Spagnoletti, *Le dinastie italiane nella prima età moderna*, 71.

Sources and Bibliography

ARCHIVAL SOURCES

Paris
Bibliothèque Nationale de France
Ms fr 16929: Relation d'Esmery sur les negociations en Piemont, fo. 528–604

Archives des Affaires Etrangères, Paris and La Courneuve
Correspondance Politique Sardaigne, vols. 23, 24
Correspondance Politique Parme, vol. 1, supplément vol. 1

Archives du Service Historique de la Défense, Vincennes
Série A, 27, 28, 30, 31, 33

Madrid
Biblioteca Nacional Madrid
Ms 2367 Italia 1636

Simancas
Archivo General de Simancas
Estado, 3673, 3816, 3832, 3833, 3834, 3837, 3838, 3839, 3841, 3843, 3842, 3843, 3844, 3845

Turin
Archivio di Stato di Torino
Materie militari, mazza 1, n. 30: Giornaliere della guerra fatta da SAR

Bologna
Biblioteca Universitaria Bologna
Collezione manoscritti, vol. 9E 27: Lettera a Don Martin d'Aragona

Florence
Archivio di Stato di Firenze
Mediceo Principato 3182, lettere di stato
Miscellanea Medicea 183, Guerra nel Monferrato nel 1636, f.318-47

Pavia
Archivio Comunale Pavia
Ms II 59: Gabrio Busca, 'Descrizione delle fortezze di frontiera dello stato di Milano', *c.*1600

Valenza
Archivio parrocchiale
Registro di sepolture Valenza, 1631–9

Modena
Archivio di Stato di Modena
Ambasciatori Parma n. 6
Ms della Biblioteca n. 188: Imprese militari

Biblioteca Estense Modena
Ms Sorbelli 1410: Vite e morti di personnaggi illustri, sec. XVII
Miscellanea Estense Ital. 635: Avvertimenti militari del colonello Bartolomeo Pelliciari di Modena, *c.*1641

Piacenza
Archivio di Stato di Piacenza
Gridario vols. 2 and 4
Lettere ducali alle comunità, filze 5, fasc. 2, supplica

Biblioteca Comunale Passerini-Landi di Piacenza
Ms Comunale 546: Processo contro Cristoforo Arcelli (1636)
Ms Pallastrelli 126: Croniche o diario del Rev. Sgr Benedetto Boselli, rettore della chiesa di San Martino di Piacenza, 1620–1670
Ms Pallastrelli 162: Compendio Storico di Piacenza da D. Giulio Gandini, 1768
Ms Pallastrelli 313: Relatione delle allegrezze fatte... nel discoperte la Statua di bronzo da essa città (1620)

Parma
Archivio di Stato di Parma
Comune 1738, Truppe francesi 1636
Comune 1934, Censimento di Parma 1636
Casa e Corte Farnesiana ser. 2, 29: Scritture diverse Odoardo Farnese
Casa e Corte Farnesiana, Carteggio Estero 400 (Savoia)
Governo Farnesiano, Fabbriche Ducali e Fortificazioni 4 and 9
Governo Farnesiano, Milizie 1, 2 (Svizzeri), 3, 4, 33, 35, 36 (Cavalleria Savoiarda)
Governo Farnesiano, Carteggio interno, 383, 384, 385
Governo Farnesiano, Computisteria Generale, 36
Governo Farnesiano, Computisteria Generale, Mastri Farnesiani, 32
Governo Farnesiano, Nobiltà e cittadinanza, 4390, 4391, 4392
Consiglio della Dettatura, Suppliche 43
Governatore e Comunità di Parma, 23, 24
Governatore e Comunità di Piacenza, 3
Catasti e Estimi Farnesiani e Borbonici 1548, Censimento del 1596
Gridario, vols. 11, 27, 32 (esp.)
Ufficio delle Confische e congiure, 25 (Processo contro San Secondo, 1635)
Patenti, vol. 7, 28, 41 bis
Collatereria Generale, n.229, 230, 231, 232, 262, 263, 264, 265, 266, 317, 318, 319, 337, 338, 340, 343–390, 529, 530, 599–604, 2557, 2581–82, 2606–07, 2675, 2796, 2797, 2930, 3202
Manoscritti della Biblioteca, 36.2 Bolsi: 'Memorie storiche di Parma'
Manscritti della Biblioteca, 59, Arte militare, n.d. (17th century)
Mappe e disegni 313, vol. 66
Parish Registers Diocese of Parma: Baganzola, Basilicagoiano, Bellena Fontevivo, Berceto, Bergotto, Carzeto, Casalbarbato, Casale Mezzani, Casatico, Castelguelfo, Castellina

Soragna, Castelnuovo Parma, Castione Baratti, Cattabiano, Coenzo, Colorno, Corcagnano, Corchia, Corticelli, Cozzano, Diolo, Fontevivo, Fornovo Taro, Fugazzolo, Ghiara Fontanellato, Giarola Collecchio, Gramignazzo, Madregolo, Maiatico, Malandriano, Marano, Medesano, Montechiarugolo, Monticelli Terme, Ozzano Taro, Paradigna, Pizzo, Porporano, Priorato, Quinzano, Rivalta, Ronchetti, Ronco C. Caneto, Roncopascolo, Sala Baganza, San Donato, Sanguigna, S. Michele Gatti, San Secondo, Santa Lucia, Soragna, Sorbolo, Valera, Parma Cattedrale, Parma S. Alessandro, Parma S. Andrea, Parma S. Barnaba, Parma S. Benedetto, Parma SS Gervaso e Protaso, Parma S. Giovanni Evangelista, Parma S. Marcellino, Parma S. Marco, Parma S. Maria in Borgo, Parma Sta. Maria Maddalena, Parma SS Michele & Antonio, Parma S. Michele dell'Arco, Parma S. Michele del Canale, Parma S. Nicolo, Parma S. Paolo, Parma S. Stefano in S. Antonio Abbate, Parma S. Tommaso, Parma SS Trinità, Parma Sant'Uldarico.

Parish Registers Diocese of Fidenza: Fidenza, Fidenza Sta. Maria Annunziata, Fidenza S. Pietro Apostolo, Bastelli, Castelvetro Piacentino, Chiusa Ferranda, Cignano, Croce S. Spirito, Fogarole, Monticelli d'Ongina, Olza, Parola, Sant'Andrea, Spigarolo, Villanova d'Arda, Zibello.

Parish Registers Diocese of Piacenza: Piacenza SS Giacomo and Filippo, Piacenza S. Tommaso, Piacenza S. Apollonia, Piacenza S. Maria Assunta, Piacenza Vaccarezza, Piacenza S. Nicolo Cattanei, Piacenza S. Martino Foro, Piacenza S. Agata, Piacenza S. Antonio Trebbia, Piacenza SS Faustina and Giovita, Piacenza S. Giuseppe (Hospital), Piacenza Sta. Maria Borghetto, Piacenza S. Stefano Protomartire, Piacenza S. Antonino, Piacenza S. Giorgio, Piacenza S. Andrea in Borgo, Piacenza S. Giacomo Maggiore, Piacenza S. Sepolcro, Piacenza S. Brigida, Piacenza S. Alessandro, Piacenza S. Salvatore, Piacenza S. Ulderico, Piacenza Sta. Maria in Gariverto, Piacenza St. Maria Zeroagli, Piacenza S. Ilario, Piacenza S. Gervaso, Piacenza S. Dalmazo, Piacenza S. Giovanni in Canale, Piacenza S. Lazaro, Piacenza S. Savino, Piacenza SS. Francesco and Protaso, Castellarquato, Cortemaggiore, Castel San Giovanni, Mucinasso, Fiorenzuola d'Arda, Borgonovo Val Tidone, S. Savino di Quarto, Menconico, Valverde, Bobbio.

Biblioteca Palatina Parma
Mss Parmense 437–439, Cronaca ossia Memorie delle cose accadute in Borgo S. Donnino da Alfonso Trecasali, cittadino di borgo, Prima notaio pubblico, e poi canonico
Ms Parmense 460, Cronaca anonima di Parma dell'anno 1684
Ms Parmense 461, Diario di Andrea Pugolotti, scritte per mia satisfazione e anco per curiosita di chi havesse gusto di leggerle
Ms Parmense 462, Miscellanea di Storia Parmense (copia Affò)
Ms Parmense 488, Brani di Cronache per la Storia di Piacenza
Ms Parmense 552, Memoire Parmigiane
Ms Parmense 570, Istoria di Casa Rossi, dal Cav.re Francesco Stella
Ms Parmense 582, Zibaldone di notizie e documenti di Storia Piacentini
Ms Parmense 631, Stato dell'artiglieria, armi, munizioni e altre robbe in questo Real Castello di Parma, 31 gennaio 1736
Ms Parmense 656, Padre Andrea da Parma, Cappuccino; Opere diverse di Storia parmense
Ms Parmense 737, L'Heroe d'Italia, overo Vita del Sereniss.o Odoardo Farnese il Grande, d'Ippolito Calandrini
Ms Parmense 825, Hippolito Calandrini, Specchio di Nobilta, overo Abbreviato compendio delle invicte glorie del Ser.mo Odoardo Farnese il Grande
Ms Parmense 843, Miscellanea di Storia, no. 12

Ms Parmense 963, Estratto di memorie attinenti alla generalita dello stato di Parma
Ms Parmense 1054, Cronaca di Parma e storia della famiglia Colombini
Ms Parmense 1083, Nomenclatura de feudi nello Stato di Parma e Piacenza (1761)
Ms Parmense 1181, Chronici Parmensi Fragmenta
Ms Parmense 1261–1263, Storia di Parma, dell'abbate Gozzi
Ms Parmense 1321, Cenni biografici di padri Cappuccini
Ms Parmense 1340, Note Storiche Parmigiane da Maurizio Tesini
Ms Parmense 1558, Memorie antiche della città di Parma (sino a 1650)
Ms Parmense 1673, Ettore Lodi, Istoria di Casalmaggiore
Ms Parmense 3711: Piante di alcune città d'Italia

PRINTED SOURCES

Anon. *La Mercuriale de Parme contre le Lutheranisme, ou raisonnement d'Ulric Groinsberg Alleman, soldat en l'armee de Parme, avec le Pere Girolamo, de Plaisance, confesseur et Predicateur des Recoltets* (n.p., c.1643).

Anon. *Relatione veritiera di quanto è successo nell'assedio di Valenza del Pò* (Milan, 1636 ?).

Araldi, Carlo. 'Giardino dilettevole dei piu vaghi fiori che adornarono la citta di Viadana', in *Benedetto Viani (1597–1678) sacerdote, speziale e notaio nel quarto centenario della nascita*, ed. G. Flisi (Viadana, 1997), 111–56.

Barozzi, Niccolo and Guglielmo Berchet. *Relazioni degli Stati Europei lette al Senato dagli Ambasciatori Veneti nel secolo XVII*, 10 vols. (Venice, 1856–78).

Basta, Giorgio. *Le gouvernement de la cavallerie legere* (Rouen, 1616).

Boselli, Antonio. 'Cenni storici di letteratura dialettale parmense', *Archivio Storico per le Province Parmensi*, 5 (1905): 1–127 (cronaca (1601–1650) da Pietro Belino da Carzeto.

Boselli, Giovanni Vincenzo. *Delle storie piacentine*, vol. 3 (Piacenza, 1805).

Bremio, GianDomenico. 'Annali Casalesi (1632–1661) di GianDomenico Bremio speciaro di Casale Monferrato', ed. Dott. Giuseppe Giorcelli, *Rivista Storica Alessandrina*, 18 (1909): 381–436.

Brusoni, Girolamo. *Della historia d'Italia* (Venice, 1661).

Canicetti, Costantino. *Memoria di Colorno (1618–1674)*, ed. A. Aliano (Colorno, 1997).

Capriata, Pietro Giovanni. *Dell'Historia delli movimenti d'armi successi in Italia*, 2 vols. (Genoa, 1649).

Carandini, Alfonso. *Risposta intercetta del cavalier Carandini residente, al Manifesto del sig. duca di Parma* (Milan, 1635).

Chefdeville, Monsieur de. *Journal dresse par M. de Chefdeville, ... de la reception, traitement et ceremonies des visites faites a Edouard, duc et prince de Parme, depuis le 7 fevrier 1636 jusques au 20 mars qu'il partit de Fontainebleau pour son retour en Italie* (Paris, 1656).

Ciasca, Raffaele, ed. *Istruzioni e relazioni degli ambasciatori genovesi*, vol. 3, *Spagna (1636–1655)* (Rome, 1955).

Coloma, Carlos. 'Discurso en que se representa quanto conviene a la Monarchìa espanola la conservaciòn del Estado de Milàn, y lo que necesita para su defensa y mayor seguridad (1626)', in *Lo Stato di Milano nel XVII secolo: Memoriali e relazioni*, ed. M. C. Giannini and G. Signorotto (Rome, 2006), 3–15.

Contino, Fra Bernardino. *La Celebre processione della Madonna di Campagna, in sollevamento del popolo piacentino* (Piacenza, 1636).

Crescenzi Romani, Giovanni Pietro. *Corona della nobiltà d'Italia, ovvero compendio dell'Istorie delle famiglie illustri*, 2 vols. (Bologna, 1639–42).
Du Plessis Praslin, César. *Memoires du maréchal Du Plessis: Memoires pour servir à l'histoire de France depuis le XIIIe siècle jusqu'à la fin du XVIIIe siècle*, vol. 7, ed. J. Michaud and J. Poujoulat (Paris, 1838).
Filamondo, Raffaele Maria. *Il Genio bellicoso di Napoli: Memorie istoriche d'alcuni capitani celebri napolitani c'han militato per la fede, per lo re, per la patria nel secolo corrente*, 2 vols. (Naples, 1694).
Fontenay-Mareuil, Marquis. *Memoires de Messire Francois Duval, marquis de Fontenay-Mareuil*, coll. Michaud-Poujoulat, vol. 19 (Paris, 1854).
Fossati, Giovanni. *Memorie historiche delle guerre d'Italia del secolo presente descritte dall'abbate Fossati* (Bologna, 1641).
Gazette de France 1636 (Paris, 1636).
Ghilini, Girolamo. *Annali di Alessandria*, ed. A. Bossola, 3 vols. (Alessandria, 1903).
Giulini, Alessandro. 'Un diario secentesco inedito d'un notaio milanese', *Archivio Storico Lombardo*, 57 (1930): 466–82.
Gualdo Priorato, Galeazzo. *Historia delle guerre del Conte Galeazzo Gualdo Priorato* (Venice, 1646).
Gualdo Priorato, Galeazzo. *Successe dall'anno 1630 sino all'anno 1636* (Venice, 1646).
Gualdo Priorato, Galeazzo. *Scena d'huomini illustri d'Italia* (Venice, 1659).
Gualdo Priorato, Galeazzo. *Il guerriero prudente, e politico* (Venice and Bologna, 1641), ed. Angelo Tamborra (Naples, 2002).
La Veletrie, Sieur de. *Harangue a Mgr le duc de Parme, sur les exercices militaires faictes par le regiment des gardes du Roy* (Paris, 1636).
Leti, Gregorio. *L'Italia regnante, o overo nova descritione dello stato presente di tutti prencipati e republiche d'Italia*, 4 vols. (Genoa, 1675–6).
Leti, Gregorio. *Il Cerimoniale historico e politico* (Waesberge, 1685).
Lodi, Ettore. *Memorie istoriche di Casalmaggiore*, ed. E. Cirani (Cremona, 1992).
Manacci, Marcello. *Compendio d'Instruttioni per gli bombardieri* (Parma, 1640).
Montecuccoli, Raimondo. *Memoires de Montecuculi, generalissime des troupes de l'Empereur, divisé en trois livres* (Amsterdam, 1752).
Montglat, Marquis de. *Memoires de François de Paule de Clermont, marquis de Montglat*, 4 vols. (Amsterdam, 1727).
Pallavicino, Ferrante. *Successi del mondo dell'anno MDCXXXVI* (Venice, 1638).
Pugolotti, Andrea. *Libro di Memorie. Cronaca parmense del XVII secolo*, ed. Sergio Di Noto (Parma, 2005).
Richelieu, Armand Du Plessis, Cardinal. *Memoires du Cardinal de Richelieu* (Paris, 1838).
Saluces, Alexandre de. *Histoire militaire du Piémont*, vol. 4 (Turin, 1818).
Siri, Vittorio. *Memorie recondite di Vittorio Siri dall'anno 1601 fino al 1640*, 8 vols. (Lyons, 1677–9).
Souvigny, Jean de Gangnieres, Comte de. *Vie, memoires et histoire de messire Jean de Gangnieres*, 2 vols. (Paris, 1906).
Stanchi, Bernardino. *Narrazione dell'assedio di Valenza nel 1635, fatta da Bernardino Stanchi* (Milan, 1638), in *Memorie storiche Valenzane*, Francesco Gasparolo (Bologna, 1986), vol. 3, 258–96.
Viani, Benedetto. *Benedetto Viani (1597–1678), Sacerdote, speziale e notaio, nel quarto centenario della nascita*, ed. G. Flisi (Viadana, 1997).

STUDIES

Adorni, Bruno. 'Interferenze spagnole nelle fortificazioni di Piacenza e di Borgo San Donnino sotto i primi Farnese', in *La difesa della Lombardia Spagnola*, ed. G. C. Zanella and L. Roncai (Milan, 2004), 237–48.

Albi de la Cuesta, Julio. *De Pavia a Rocroi. Los tercios de infanteria española en los siglos XVI y XVII* (Madrid, 1999).

Alvarez-Ossorio Alvariño, Antonio. 'The state of Milan and the Spanish Monarchy', in *Spain in Italy: Politics, Society and Religion 1500–1700*, ed. T. J. Dandelet and J. A. Marino (Leiden and Boston, 2007), 100–32.

Amoretti, Guido. *Il Ducato di Savoia dal 1559 al 1713, vol. II, dal 1610 al 1659* (Turin, 1985).

Anderson, Roger Charles. 'The Thirty Years War in the Mediterranean', *Mariner's Mirror*, 15 (1969): 435–51, and 16 (1970): 41–57.

Arcangeli, Letizia. 'Feudatari e duca negli stati farnesiani (1545–1587)', in *Il Rinascimento nelle corti padane: Società e cultura*, ed, P. Rossi (Bari, 1977), 77–96.

Arcangeli, Letizia. 'Giurisdizioni feudali e organizzazione territoriale nel Ducato di Parma (1545–1587)', *Le Corti farnesiane di Parma e Piacenza (1545–1622)*, ed. M. A. Romani, vol. 1 (Rome, 1978), 91–148.

Asch, Ronald G. ' "Wo der soldat hinkoembt, da ist alles sein": military violence and atrocities in the Thirty Years War re-examined', *German History*, 18 (2000): 291–309.

Azan, Paul. *Un tacticien du XVIIe siècle* (Paris, 1904).

Banzola, Vincenzo. 'Le antiche misure parmigiane e l'introduzione del sistema metrico decimale negli stati Parmensi', *Archivio Storico per le Province Parmensi*, ser. 4, vol. 18 (1966), 139–78.

Barghini, Andrea. *Valenza e le sue fortificazioni: architettura e urbanistica dal medioevo all'età contemporanea* (Alessandria, 1993).

Barilli, Arnaldo. 'La candidatura di un duca di Parma al trono d'Albania', *Aurea Parma*, 3 (1915): 11–24.

Barilli, Arnaldo. 'La congiura di Parma del 1611 e le confessioni dei congiurati', *Archivio Storico per le Province Parmensi*, ser. 3, vol. 1 (1936), 105–50.

Baumann, Reinhard. *I Lanzichenecchi: la loro storia e cultura dal tardo medioevo alla Guerra dei Trent'anni* (Turin, 1996).

Baxter, Douglas Clark. *Servants of the Sword: French Intendants of the Army, 1630–1670* (Urbana, IL, 1976).

Bazy, Jean-Pierre-Antoine. *Etat militaire de la monarchie espagnole sous Philippe IV* (Poitiers, 1864).

Beik, William. *Absolutism and Society in Seventeenth-century France : State Power and Provincial Aristocracy in Languedoc* (Cambridge and New York, 1989).

Beik, William. 'The absolutism of Louis XIV as social collaboration', *Past and Present*, 188 (2005): 195–224.

Bély, Lucien, Jean Bérenger, and André Corvisier. *Guerre et paix dans l'Europe du XVIIe siècle*, 2 vols. (Paris, 1991).

Benassi, Ugo. *Storia di Parma*, vol. 6: *Da Pier Luigi Farnese a Vittorio Emanuele II (1545–1860)* (Parma, 1907).

Benassi, Ugo. 'I Natali e l'educazione del duca Odoardo Farnese', *Archivio Storico per le province Parmensi*, 9 (1909): 99–227.

Benassi, Ugo. 'Governo assoluto e città suddita nel primo Seicento', *Bollettino Storico Piacentino*, 12 (1917): 193–203, and 13 (1918): 30–8.

Benigno, Roberto. 'Ripensare la crisi del "600"', *Storica*, 5 (1996): 7–52.
Bennett, Martyn. *The Civil Wars Experienced: Britain and Ireland 1638–1661* (London, 2000).
Bercé, Yves-Marie. 'Les guerres dans l'Italie', in *L'Italie au XVIIe siècle* ed. Y.-M. Bercé, G. Delille, J.-C. Waquet and J.-M. Sallmann (Paris, 1989), 311–31.
Bercé, Yves-Marie. 'Rohan et la Valtelline', in *L'Europe des traités de Westphalie. Esprit de la diplomatie et diplomatie de l'esprit*, ed. Lucien Bély (Paris, 2000), 321–35.
Bérenger, Jean. 'Le conflit Franco-Espagnol et la guerre du Nord', in *Guerre et Paix dans l'Europe du XVIIe siècle*, ed. J. Bérenger, L. Bély, and A. Corvisier (Paris, 1991), 309–40.
Bérenger, Jean. 'La collaboration militaire austro-espagnol au XVIe–XVIIe siècles', in *L'Espagne et ses guerres. De la fin de la Reconquête aux guerres d'Indépendance*, ed. A. Molinié and A. Merle (Paris, 2004), 11–33.
Bertini, Giuseppe. 'Il Farnese e il Toson d'Oro: L'ideale cavalleresco dei duchi di Parma', in *I Farnese: corti, guerra e nobiltà in Antico regime*, ed. A. Bilotto, P. Del Negro, and C. Mozzarelli (Rome, 1997), 267–88.
Bianchi, Paola. *Sotto diverse bandiere: L'internazionale militare nello Stato sabaudo d'antico regime* (Milan, 2012).
Black, Jeremy. *European Warfare 1494–1660* (London, 2002).
Black, Jeremy. *Rethinking Military History* (London, 2004).
Black, Jeremy. 'Civilians in warfare 1500–1789', *History Today*, May (2006): 10–17.
Black, Jeremy. *War in European History 1494–1660* (Washington, DC, 2006).
Black, Jeremy. *War: A Short History* (London and New York, 2009).
Blaffer Hrdy, Sarah. *Mother Nature: A History of Mothers, Infants and Natural Selection* (New York, 1999).
Blet, Pierre. 'La politique du Saint-Siège vis-à-vis des puissances catholiques', *Dix-septième siècle* (1990): 57–71.
Blomac, Nicole de. 'Le cheval de guerre entre le dire et le faire: quelques variations sur le discours équestre adapté à la réalité militaire', in *Le Cheval et la guerre du XVe au XXe siècle*, ed. D. Roche and D. Reytier (Paris, 2002), 55–65.
Boehler, Jean-Michel. 'Les conséquences à long terme des guerres du XVIIe siècle en Alsace: pour l'élaboration d'un 'modèle rhénan', in *Les Malheurs de la Guerre: de la guerre à l'ancienne à la guerre réglée*, ed. A. Corvisier and J. Jacquart (Paris, 1996), 201–17.
Boehler, Jean-Michel. 'La guerre au quotidien dans les villages du Saint-Empire au XVIIe siècle', in *Les Villageois face à la guerre, XIVe–XVIIIe siècle*, ed. C. Desplat (Toulouse, 2002), 65–88.
Boscarelli, Marco. 'Intorno alla nobiltà semplice piacentino nei secoli XVII e XVIII', *Bollettino Storico Piacentino*, 81 (1986): 1–33.
Boscarelli, Marco. *Contributi alla storia degli Stati Pallavicino di Busseto e di Cortemaggiore (secc. XV–XVII)* (Parma, 1992).
Boscarelli, Marco. 'Occupazione militare spagnola e chimerica restaurazione pallaviciniana nello stato di Busseto (1636–1637)', in *Contributi alla storia degli Stati Pallavicino di Busseto e Cortemaggiore (sec. XV–XVII)* (Parma, 1992), 97–105.
Boscarelli, Marco. 'Appunti sulle istituzioni e le campagne militari dei ducati di Parma e Piacenza in epoca farnesiana', in *I Farnese: corti, guerra e nobilta in Antico regime*, ed. A. Bilotto, P. Del Negro, and C. Mozzarelli (Rome, 1997), 561–78.
Boutier, Jean. 'Trois conjurations italiennes: Florence (1575), Parme (1611), Gênes (1628)', *Mélanges de l'Ecole Française de Rome: Italie & Méditerranée*, 108 (1996): 319–75.

Brancaccio, Nicola. *L'Esercito del vecchio Piemonte: gli ordinamenti, parte 1: dal 1560 al 1814* (Rome, 1923).
Braudel, Fernand. *The Mediterranean and the Mediterranean World in the Age of Philip II* (New York, 1967), vol. 1, 504–9.
Brnardic, Vladimir. *Imperial Armies of the Thirty Years' War (1): Infantry and Artillery* (Oxford and New York, 2009).
Brnardic, Vladimir. *Imperial Armies of the Thirty Years' War (2): Cavalry* (Oxford, 2010).
Brunelli, Giampiero. *Soldati del Papa: Politica militare e nobiltà nello Stato della Chiesa (1560–1644)* (Rome, 2003).
Brzezinksi, Richard. *Lutzen 1632: Climax of the Thirty Years War*, (Oxford and New York, 2001).
Buono, Alessandro. 'Guerra, Elites locali e monarchia nella Lombardia del Seicento. Per un'interpretazione in chiave di compromesso di interessi', *Società e Storia*, 123 (2009): 3–30.
Caferro, William. *Mercenary Companies and the Decline of Siena* (Baltimore, 1998).
Caferro, William. 'Warfare and economy in Renaissance Italy 1350–1450', *Journal of Interdisciplinary History*, 39 (2008): 167–209.
Canosa, Romano. *I Segreti dei Farnese* (Rome, 2001).
Carra, Ettore. *Le esecuzioni capitali a Piacenza e la Confraternità della Torricella dal XVI al XIX secolo* (Piacenza, 1991).
Castignoli, Pietro. 'Caratteri della feudalità nel ducato di Piacenza durante il secolo XVII', *Archivio Storico per le Province Parmensi*, 18 (1966): 317–24.
Cattini, Marco. 'Congiunture sociali e dinamiche politiche nei consigli municipali di Parma e Piacenza in età moderna', in *Persistenze feudali e autonomie communitative in stati padani fra Cinque e Settecento*, ed. G. Tocci (Bologna, 1988), 47–76.
Cerino Badone, Giovanni. 'Le Seconde Guerre d'Italia (1588–1659): Storiografia, Temi, Fonti' (PhD thesis, Università degli Studi del Piemonte Orientale, 2012).
Cesarini-Sforza, W. 'Il consiglio generale e le classi cittadine in Piacenza nel secolo XVI', *Bollettino Storico Piacentino*, 5 (1910): 71–82.
Chaboche, Robert. 'Les soldats français de la Guerre de Trente Ans: une tentative d'approche', *Revue d'histoire moderne et contemporaine*, 20 (1973): 10–24.
Chaboche, Robert. 'Le recrutement des sergents et des caporaux de l'armée française au XVIIe siecle', in *Recrutement, mentalités, sociétés: Actes du colloque International d'Histoire Militaire* (Montpellier, 1974), 25–44.
Chagniot, Jean. 'Mobilité sociale et armée', *Dix-septième siècle*, 31 (1979): 37–49.
Chagniot, Jean. *Guerre et société à l'époque moderne* (Paris, 2001).
Chauviré, Frédéric. 'Le problème de l'allure dans les charges de cavalerie du XVIe au XVIII siècle', *Revue Historique des Armées*, 249 (2007): 16–27.
Choppin, Henri. *Les origines de la cavalerie française: organisation régimentaire de Richelieu, la cavalerie Weimarienne, le régiment de Gassion* (Paris and Nancy, 1905).
Conforti, Paolo. *Le mura di Parma. II: Dai Farnese alla demolizione* (Parma, 1980).
Contreras Gay, José. 'Aportacion al estudio de los sistemas de reclutamiento militar en la España moderna', *Anuario de Historia Contemporanea*, 8 (1981): 7–44.
Contreras Gay, José. 'El siglo XVII y su importancia en el cambio de los sistemas de reclutamientos durante el Antiguo Regimen', *Studia Historica. Historia Moderna*, 14 (1996): 141–54.
Cornette, Joël. *Le Roi de guerre: Essai sur la souveraineté dans la France du Grand Siècle* (Paris, 1993).

Cornette, Joël. 'La révolution militaire et l'état moderne', *Revue d'Histoire Moderne et Contemporaine*, 41 (1994): 696–709.
Corvisier, André. 'Renouveau militaire et misères de la guerre 1635–1659', in *Histoire militaire de la France*, vol. 1: *Des origines à 1715*, ed. Ph. Contamine (Paris, 1992), 353–82.
Coss, Edward J. *All for the King's Shilling: The British Soldier under Wellington 1808–1814* (Norman, OK, 2010).
Costa, Marco. *Psicologia militare: elementi di psicologia per gli appartenenti alle forze armate* (Milan, 2003).
Coste, Laurent. 'Les malheurs de la Fronde en Entre-Deux-Mers', in *Les Malheurs de la Guerre: de la guerre à l'ancienne à la guerre réglée*, ed. A. Corvisier and J. Jacquart (Paris, 1996), 131–45.
Covini, Maria Nadia. *L'Esercito del duca: Organizzazione militare e istituzioni al tempo degli Sforza (1450–1480)* (Rome, 1998).
Cusatelli, Giorgio and Fausto Razzetti. *Il Viaggio a Parma: Visitatori stranieri in età farnesiana e borbonica* (Parma, 1990).
Cuvelier, Joseph. 'Peeter Snayers peintre de batailles (1592–1667): Notes et documents pour servir à sa biographie', *Bulletin de l'Institut Historique Belge de Rome*, 23 (1944–6): 25–72.
D'Amico, Stefano. 'Rebirth of a city: immigration and trade in Milan, 1630–1659', *Sixteenth Century Journal*, 32 (2001): 697–722.
Dabene, Carlo. 'Cronaca dell'assedio di Valenza del 1635 desunta da diversi antichi scrittori', *Valensa d'na vota*, 4 (1989): 39–49.
De Consoli, Claudio. *Al soldo del duca: l'amministrazione delle armate sabaude (1560–1630)* (Turin, 1999).
De Moor, J. A. 'Experience and experiment: some reflections upon the military developments in 16th and 17th century Western Europe', in *Exercise of the Arms: Warfare in the Netherlands (1568–1648)*, ed. Marco van der Hoeven (Leiden, 1997), 17–32.
De Mouy, Charles. *L'ambassade du duc de Créqui*, 2 vols. (Paris, 1893).
De Mun, Gabriel. *Richelieu et la maison de Savoie: l'ambassade de Particelli d'Hémery en Piémont* (Paris, 1907).
De Rosa, Riccardo. 'Per la storia dello Stato Landi tra Cinque e Seicento: La controversia tra Ippolito e Federico Landi per Borgo Taro', *Bollettino Storico Piacentino*, 96 (2001): 95–114.
De Rosa, Riccardo. 'La congiura di Claudio Landi contro i Farnese e i suoi riflessi sulla questione di Borgo Val di Taro', *Bollettino Storico Piacentino*, 97 (2002): 131–50.
Del Negro, Pietro. 'La Storia militare dell'Italia moderna nello specchio della storiografia del Novecento', *Cheiron*, 22 (1995): 11–33.
Del Negro, Pietro. *Guida alla storia militare italiana* (Milan, 1997).
Delahaye, E. 'Une campagne de l'armée navale sous Louis XIII. La reprise des îles de Lérins et le secours de Parme (1636–1637)', *Revue Maritime*, 115 (1929): 13–37.
Delsalle, Paul. 'De l'interêt anthropologique des rôles de recrutement au XVIIe siècle', in *Hommes d'armes et gens de guerre du Moyen Age au XVIIe siècle: Franche Comté de Bourgogne et comté de Montbéliard*, ed. Arnold Preneel and Paul Delsalle (Besançon, 2007), 177–82.
Delsalle, Paul, François Pernot, and Marie-France Romand. 'Peut-on connaître la vie quotidienne des soldats?', in *Hommes d'armes et gens de guerre du Moyen Age au XVIIe siècle: Franche Comté de Bourgogne et comté de Montbéliard*, ed. Arnold Preneel and Paul Delsalle (Besançon, 2007), 183–200.

Demaria, Giacinto. 'La Guerra di Castro, e la Spedizione de' Presidii (1639–1649)', *Miscellanea di Storia Italiana*, ser. 3, 4 (1898): 191–256.
Devèze, Michel. *L'Espagne de Philippe IV (1621–1665)*, 2 vols. (Paris, 1970).
Deyon, Pierre and Solange Deyon. *Henri de Rohan, huguenot de plume et d'épée* (Paris, 2000).
Di Stefano, Giuseppe, Elena Fasano Guarini, and Alessandro Martinengo, eds. *Italia non spagnola e monarchia spagnola tra '500 e '600: politica, cultura e letteratura* (Florence, 2009).
Dominguez Nafria, Juan Carlos. *El Real y Supremo Consejo de Guerra (siglos XVI–XVIII)* (Madrid, 2001).
Donagan, Barbara. *War in England 1642–1649* (Oxford and New York, 2008).
Donati, Claudio. 'Il "militare" nella storia dell'Italia moderna, dal Rinascimento all'età napoleonica', in *Eserciti e carriere militari nell'Italia moderna*, ed. C. Donati (Milan, 1998), 7–40.
Donati, Claudio. 'The profession of arms and the nobility in Spanish Italy: some considerations', in *Spain in Italy. Politics, Society and Religion 1500–1700*, ed. T. J. Dandelet and J. A. Marino (Leiden, 2007), 314–24.
Drei, Giovanni. *I Farnese: Grandezza e decadenza di una dinastia italiana* (Rome, 1954).
Drévillon, Hervé. 'Vices et vertus du noble exercice de l'escrime au XVIIe siècle', in *A quoi joue-t-on? Pratiques et usages des jeux et des jouets à travers les ages*, ed. M. Pastoureau (Montbrison, 1999), 469–82.
Drévillon, Hervé. 'Le Roi-cavalier: les savoirs du corps dans l'éducation de Louis XIII', in *Le Savoir du Prince: du Moyen-Age aux Lumières*, R. Halévi (Paris, 2002), 147–73.
Drévillon, Hervé. '"Publier nos playes et valeurs". Le fait d'armes et sa notoriété pendant la guerre de Trente Ans (1635–1648)', in *La Noblesse de la fin du XVIe au début du XXe siècle, un modèle social?*, 2 vols., ed. J. Pontet, M. Figeac, and M. Boisson (Anglet, 2002), vol. 1, 289–308.
Drévillon, Hervé. *L'Impôt du sang: le métier des armes sous Louis XIV* (Paris, 2005).
Drévillon, Hervé. *Batailles: Scènes de guerre de la Table ronde aux Tranchées* (Paris, 2007).
Durbec, Joseph-Antoine. 'Un épisode de la guerre de trente ans: l'occupation des îles de Lérins par les Espagnols de 1635–1637', *Bulletin de la Commission royale d'histoire*, 117 (1951–52): 41–74.
Dyer, Gwynne. *War* (2nd edn, Toronto, 2004).
Edwards, Peter. 'Les chevaux et les guerres civiles anglaises au milieu du XVII siècle', in *Le Cheval et la guerre du XVe au XXe siècle*, ed. D. Roche and D. Reytier (Paris, 2002), 243–9.
Elliott, John. *Richelieu and Olivares* (London and New York, 1984).
Elliott, John. 'Managing decline: Olivares and the Grand Strategy of Imperial Spain', in *Grand Strategies in War and Peace*, ed. P. Kennedy (New Haven, 1991), 87–104.
Espino Lopez, Antonio. "La historiografia hispana sobre la guerra en la epoca de los Austrias: un balance, 1991–2000", *Manuscrits*, 21 (2003): 161–91.
Essen, Leon Van der. *Le Cardinal-Infant et la politique européenne de l'Espagne (1609–1641)* (Brussels, 1944).
Externbrink, Sven. '"Le cœur du monde" et la "liberté d'Italie". Aspects de la politique italienne de Richelieu, 1624–1642', *Revue d'histoire diplomatique*, 114 (2000): 181–208.
Fagniez, Gustave. *Le Père Joseph et Richelieu, 1577–1638*, 2 vols. (Paris, 1894).

Ferrari Agradi, Laura. 'Ceti dirigenti urbani nell'Emilia moderna: I consiglieri del Comune di Piacenza (1675–1800)' (Thesis, Università degli studi di Parma, 1983–4).
Fiori, Giorgio. *Le antiche famiglie di Piacenza e i loro stemmi* (Piacenza, 1979).
Fiori, Giorgio. 'Infeudazioni e titoli nobiliari nei ducati parmensi 1545–1859', in *In ricordo di Stefano Maggi* (Piacenza, 1982), 55–105.
Fiori, Giorgio. *Storia di Piacenza*, vol. 4: *T.1: Dai Farnese ai Borbone (1545–1802)* (Piacenza, 1999).
Foa, Salvatore. *Vittorio Amedeo I (1587–1637)* (Turin, 1930).
Foucault, Michel. *Discipline and Punish: The Birth of the Prison* (New York, 1977).
Frezet, Jean. *Histoire de la maison de Savoie*, 3 vols. (Turin, 1826–7).
Frigo, Daniela. '"Small states" and diplomacy: Mantua and Modena', in *Politics and Diplomacy in Early Modern Italy: The Structure of Diplomatic Practice 1450–1800*, ed. Daniela Frigo (Cambridge, 2000), 147–75.
Frigo, Daniela. 'Prudence and experience: ambassadors and political culture in early modern Italy', *Journal of Medieval and Early Modern Studies*, 38 (2008): 15–34.
Fubini, Riccardo. 'Aux origines de la balance des pouvoirs: le système politique en Italie au XVe siècle', in *L'Europe des Traités de Westphalie: Esprit de la diplomatie et diplomatie de l'esprit*, ed. L. Bély (Paris, 2000), 111–22.
Fulaine, Jean-Charles. *Le Duc Charles IV de Lorraine et son armée 1624–1675* (Metz, 1997).
Gaber, Stéphane. *La Lorraine meurtrie* (2nd edn, Nancy, 1991).
Gal, Stéphane. *Lesdiguières: Prince des Alpes et connétable de France* (Grenoble, 2007).
Galletti, Angelo. 'Stato del monastero di S. Giovanni Evangelista di Parma in una relazione del 1650', *Archivio Storico per le Province Parmensi*, 90 (1980): 61–80.
Ghizzoni, Vito. 'Sorprusi dei Farnese ai danni dei Pallavicino nella seconda metà del "500"', *Archivio Storico per le Province Parmensi*, 19 (1967): 149–61.
Giannini, Massimo Carlo. 'Risorse del principe e risorse dei sudditi: fisco, clero e comunità di fronte al problema della difesa comune nello Stato di Milano (1618–1660)', *Annali di Storia moderna e contemporanea*, 6 (2000): 173–225.
Glete, Jan. *War and the State in Early Modern Europe: Spain, the Dutch Republic and Sweden as Fiscal-Military States, 1500–1660* (London, 2002).
Glete, Jan. 'Warfare, entrepreneurship and the fiscal-military state', in *European Warfare 1350–1750*, ed. F. Tallett and D. J. B. Trim (Cambridge and New York, 2010), 300–21.
Gonzalez de Leon, Fernando. '"Doctors of the military discipline": military expertise and the paradigm of the Spanish soldier in the early modern period', *Sixteenth Century Journal*, 27 (1996): 61–85.
Gonzalez de Leon, Fernando. 'Spanish military power and the military revolution', in *Early Modern Military History, 1450–1815*, ed. G. Mortimer (Basingstoke, 2004), 25–42.
Gonzalez de Leon, Fernando. *The Road to Rocroi: Class, Culture and Command in the Spanish Army of Flanders 1567–1659* (Boston and Leiden, 2009).
Greci, Roberto. 'Il castello signorile nei piccoli stati autonomi del contado parmense', in *Corti del Rinascimento nella provincia di Parma* (Turin, 1981), 9–40.
Groebner, Valentin. *Who Are You? Identification, Deception and Surveillance in Early Modern Europe* (New York, 2007).
Gropello, Gustavo di. 'La nobiltà piacentina e la funzione militare', in *I Farnese: corti, guerra e nobiltà in Antico regime*, ed. A. Bilotto, P. Del Negro, and C. Mozzarelli (Rome, 1997), 47–52.

Grossman, Dave. *On Killing: The Psychological Cost of Learning to Kill in War and Society* (Boston and London, 1995).
Gruber von Arni, Eric. *Justice to the Maimed Soldier: Nursing, Medical Care and Welfare for Sick and Wounded Soldiers and their Families during the English Civil Wars and Interregnum, 1642–1660* (Aldershot and Burlington, VT, 2001).
Gruber von Arni, Eric. '"Tempora mutantur et nos mutamur in illis": the experience of sick and wounded soldiers during the English Civil Wars and Interregnum, 1642–1660', in *The Impact of Hospitals, 300–2000*, ed. J. Henderson, P. Horden, and A. Pastore (Frankfurt and New York, 2007), 317–40.
Guéry, Alain. 'Les comptes de la mort vague après la guerre. Pertes de guerre et conjoncture du phénomène guerre, XVIIe–XIXe siècle', *Histoire et Mesure*, 6 (1991): 289–312.
Guill Ortega, Miguel Angel. *Carlos Coloma (1566–1637): Espada y pluma de los tercios* (San Vicente, 2007).
Guill Ortega, Miguel Angel. 'L'Assedio di Valenza del 1635', *Valensa d'na vota*, 23 (2008): 25–52.
Guilmartin, John. 'The logistics of seventeenth-century war at sea; the Spanish dimension', in *Feeding Mars: Logistics in Western Warfare from the Middle Ages to the Present*, ed. J. Lynn (Boulder, CO, 1993), 109–36.
Guthrie, William. *Battles of the Thirty Years War: From White Mountain to Nordlingen* (Westport, CT, and London, 2002).
Guthrie, William. *The Later Thirty Years War* (Westport, CT, and London, 2003).
Gutmann, Myron. 'Putting crises in perspective: the impact of war on civilian populations in the 17th century', *Annales de Démographie Historique* (1977): 101–28.
Haehl, Madeleine. *Les affaires étrangères au temps de Richelieu: le secrétariat d'Etat, les agents diplomatiques (1624–1642)* (Brussels, 2006).
Hanlon, Gregory. 'The demilitarization of an Italian provincial nobility: Siena 1560–1740', *Past & Present*, 155 (1997), 64–108.
Hanlon, Gregory. *The Twilight of a Military Tradition: Italian Aristocrats and European Conflicts, 1560–1800* (London and New York, 1998).
Hanlon, Gregory. 'Infanticidio dei coppie sposati nella Toscana moderna, secoli XVI–XVIII', *Quaderni Storici*, 38/113 (2003): 453–98.
Hanlon, Gregory. 'In praise of refeudalization: princes and feudatories in north-central Italy from the sixteenth to the eighteenth century', in *Sociability and its Discontents: Civil Society, Social Capital and their Alternatives in Late Medieval and Early Modern Europe*, ed. Nicholas Eckstein and Nicholas Terpstra (Turnhout, 2009), 213–25.
Helfferich, Trintje and Paul Sonnino. 'Civilians in the Thirty Years War', in *Daily Lives of Civilians in Wartime Europe, 1618–1900*, ed. L. S. Frey and M. L. Frey (Westport, CT, and London, 2007), 23–58.
Henriksen, Rune. 'Warriors in combat—what makes people actively fight in combat?' *Journal of Strategic Studies*, 30 (2007): 187–223.
Hildesheimer, Françoise. *Richelieu: une certain idée de l'Etat* (Paris, 1985).
Hildesheimer, Françoise. 'Guerre et paix selon Richelieu', *L'Europe des traités de Westphalie*, in *Esprit de la diplomatie et diplomatie de l'esprit*, ed. L. Bély (Paris, 2000), 31–55.
Holmes, Richard. *Acts of War* (2nd edn, London, 2003).
Hugon, Alain. 'Des Habsbourg aux Bourbons: le combat espagnol pour la conservation de l'hégémonie européenne (milieu XVe–fin XVIIe siècle)', *Bulletin de la Société d'Histoire Moderne et Contemporaine*, 3–4 (2000): 34–55.
Hugon, Alain. *Au service du roi Catholique. 'Honorables ambassadeurs' et 'divins espions': Représentation diplomatique et service secret dans les relations hispano-françaises de 1598 à 1635* (Madrid, 2005).

Humbert, Jacques. *Le Maréchal de Créquy, gendre de Lesdiguières, 1573–1638* (Paris, 1962).
Hynes, Laura. 'Routine infanticide by married couples? An assessment of baptismal records from seventeenth-century Parma', *Journal of Early Modern History*, 15 (2011): 507–30.
Israel, Jonathan. 'Olivares, the cardinal-infante and Spain's strategy in the Low Countries (1635–1643): the road to Rocroi', in *Spain, Europe and the Atlantic World: Essays in Honour of John H Elliott*, ed. R. Kagan and G. Parker (Cambridge, 1995), 267–95.
Jaitner, Klaus. 'The popes and the struggle for power during the 16th and 17th centuries', in *1648: War and Peace in Europe*, ed. K. Bussmann and H. Schilling, 2 vols. (Munster-Osnabruck, 1998), vol. 1, 61–8.
Kamen, Henry. *Spain's Road to Empire* (London, 2002).
Keegan, John. *The Face of Battle: A Study of Agincourt, Waterloo and the Somme* (Harmondsworth and New York, 1976).
Keegan, John. *A History of Warfare* (New York, 1993).
Kleinschmidt, Harald. 'Using the gun: manual drill and the proliferation of portable firearms', *Journal of Military History*, 63 (1999): 601–29.
Kroener, Bernhard R. 'Conditions de vie et origine sociale du personnel militaire subalterne au cours de la Guerre de Trente Ans', *Francia*, 15 (1987): 321–50.
Kroener, Bernhard R. 'Le Maraudeur: A propos des groupes marginaux de la société militaire au début de l'époque moderne', in *Nouveaux regards sur la guerre de Trente Ans*, Centre d'Etudes d'Histoire de la Défense (Vincennes, 1998), 167–79.
Kroener, Bernhard R. '"The soldiers are very poor, bare, naked, exhausted": The living conditions and organizational structure of military society during the Thirty Years' War', in *1648: War and Peace in Europe*, ed. K. Bussmann and H. Schilling (Munster-Osnabruck, 1998), 285–91.
La Bruyère, Réné. *La Marine de Richelieu: Sourdis, archévêque et amiral (6 nov. 1594–18 juin 1645)* (Paris, 1948).
Lasagni, Roberto. *Storia demografica della città di Parma dalle origini al 1860*, vol.1: *Fonti Archivistiche e Bibliografia* (Parma, 1983).
Leblanc, Stephan. 'Why warfare? Lessons from the past', *Daedalus*, 136 (2007): 13–21.
Legrand-Girarde, Emile-Edmond. *L'arrière aux armées sous Louis XIII. Crusy de Marcillac, évêque de Mende, 1635–1638* (Paris, 1927).
Leman, Auguste. *Urbain VIII et la rivalité de la France et de la Maison d'Autriche de 1631 à 1635* (Paris, 1920).
Leman, Auguste. *Richelieu et Olivares, leurs négociations secrètes de 1636 à 1642 pour le retablissement de la paix* (Lille, 1938).
Lenihan, Padraig. 'Unhappy campers: Dundalk (1689) and after', *Journal of Conflict Archaeology* (2007): 196–216.
Lloyd Moote, A. *Louis XIII, the Just* (Berkeley and London, 1989).
Loriga, Sabina. *Soldats. Un laboratoire disciplinaire* (Paris, 1993).
Louis, Gérard. *La guerre de Dix Ans, 1634–1644* (Besançon, 1998).
Lovie, Jacques. 'Les fières heures de Madame Royale, duchesse de Savoie (1606–1663)', *Bulletin de l'Académie delphinale*, 5 (1984): 21–35.
Lynn, John. *Giant of the 'Grand Siecle': The French Army 1610–1715* (Cambridge, 1997).
Maffi, Davide. 'Guerra ed economia: spese belliche e appaltatori militari nella Lombardia spagnola (1635–1660)', *Storia Economica*, 3 (2000): 489–527.
Maffi, Davide. 'Confesionalismo y razon de estado en la Edad Moderna. El caso de la Valtellina (1637–1639)', *Hispania Sacra*, 57 (2005): 467–89.

Maffi, Davide. 'Il potere delle armi. La monarchia spagnola e i suoi eserciti (1635–1700): una rivisitazione del mito della decadenza', *Rivista Storica Italiana*, 118 (2006): 394–445.

Maffi, Davide. 'Un bastione incerto? L'esercito di Lombardia tra Filippo IV e Carlo II (1630–1700)', in *Guerra y Sociedad en la Monarquia Hispanica*, ed. E. Garcia Hernan and D. Maffi, 2 vols. (Madrid, 2006), vol. 1, 501–36.

Maffi, Davide. *Il baluardo della corona: Guerra, esercito, finanze e società nella Lombardia seicentesca (1630–1660)* (Florence, 2007).

Maffi, Davide. 'Cacciatori di gloria. La presenza degli italiani nell'esercito di Fiandre (1621–1700)', in *Italiani al servizio straniero in età moderna*, ed. P. Bianchi, D. Maffi, and E. Stumpo (Milan, 2008), 73–104.

Maffi, Davide. 'Le milizie dello Stato di Milano (1615–1700): un tentativo di controllo sociale', in *Las milicias del Rey de España (siglos XVI y XVII)*, ed. D. Maffi and J.-J. Ruiz Ibañez (Madrid, 2009), 245–67.

Magni, Cesare. *Il tramonto del feudo lombardo* (Milan, 1937).

Manfredi, Carlo Emanuele. 'La nobiltà piacentina alla Corte Farenesiana', in *I Farnese: corti, guerra e nobiltà in Antico regime*, ed. A. Bilotto, P. Del Negro, and C. Mozzarelli. (Rome, 1997), 35–46.

Martelli, Francesco and Cristina Galasso. *Istruzioni agli ambasciatori e inviati medicei in Spagna e nell'"Italia Spagnola' (1536–1648)* 2 vols. (Rome, 2007).

Martin, Philippe. *Une Guerre de Trente Ans en Lorraine, 1631–1661* (Metz, 2002).

Martinez-Ruiz, Enrique. 'Los ejercitos hispanicos en el siglo XVII', in *Calderon de la Barca y la España del Barroco*, ed. J. Alcala-Zamora (Madrid, 2001), 17–25.

Martinez-Ruiz, Enrique. 'La eclosion de la historia militar', *Studia Historica, Historia Moderna*, 25 (2003): 17–25.

Martinez-Ruiz, Enrique. *Los Soldados del Rey: los ejércitos de la Monarquìa Hispánica (1480–1700)* (Madrid, 2008).

Mascalchi, Lucia. 'Margherita dei Medici Farnese: Strategie politiche e dinamiche familiari alla corte di Parma e Piacenza', in *Le donne Medici nel sistema europeo delle corti: XVI–XVIII secolo*, 2 vols., ed. Giulia Calvi and Riccardo Spinelli (Florence, 2008), vol. 1, 283–312.

Massa, E. 'Milizie farnesiane', *Rivista di cavalleria*, 26 (1910): 631–48.

Massera, Sandro. 'La spedizione del Duca Henri de Rohan in Valtellina (1635–1637)', in *La Spedizione del Duca di Rohan in Valtellina: Storia e memorie nell'età della Guerra dei Trent'Anni* (Milan, 1999), 21–108.

Masson, Bernard. 'Un aspect de la discipline dans les armées de Louis XIII: la lutte contre la désertion du soldat 1635–1643', *Revue Historique des Armées*, 162 (1986): 12–23.

Matoušek, Vaclav. 'Building a model of a field fortification of the Thirty Years' War near Olbramov (Czech Republic)', *Journal of Conflict Archaeology* (2005): 114–32.

Meier, David A. 'An appeal for a historiographical Renaissance: lost lives and the Thirty Years' War', *The Historian*, 67 (2005): 254–74.

Meli Lupi di Soragna, R. 'Vita di Francesco Serafini, maestro di campo del Serenissimo Duca di Parma', *Atti e Memorie delle R.R. Deputazioni di Storia Patria per le Provincie modenesi e parmensi*, ser. 3, 5 (1888): 1–29.

Meo, Maurizio de. *Le Antiche famiglie nobili e notabili di Parma e i loro stemmi*, 3 vols. (Parma, 2000).

Merlin, Pierpaolo. *Il Piemonte Sabaudo. Stato e territori in età moderna* (Turin, 1994).

Mesa, Eduardo de. *Nordlingen 1634: Victoria decisiva de los tercios* (Madrid, 2003).

Meuvret, Jean. 'Louis XIV et l'Italie', *Dix-septième siècle* (1960): 84–102.

Mohrmann, Ruth. 'Everyday life in war and peace', in *1648: War and Peace in Europe*, ed. K. Bussmann and H. Schilling (Munster-Osnabruck, 1998), 319–28.

Mortimer, Geoffrey. *Eyewitness Accounts of the Thirty Years War, 1618–1648* (Basingstoke and New York, 2002).

Mortimer, Geoffrey. 'Individual experience and perception of the Thirty Years War in eyewitness personal accounts', *German History*, 20 (2002): 141–60.

Mortimer, Geoffrey. 'War by contract, credit and contributions: the Thirty Years War', in *Early Modern Military History* (Basingstoke, 2004), 101–17.

Mozzarelli, Cesare. 'Dall'antispagnolismo al revisionismo', in *Alle origini di una nazione. Antispagnolismo e identità italiana*, ed. A. Musi (Milan, 2003), 385–404.

Mozzarelli, Cesare. 'Nella Milano dei re Cattolici. Considerazioni su uomini, cultura e istituzioni tra Cinque e Seicento', in *Antico Regime e modernità* (Rome, 2008), 321–56.

Mozzarelli, Cesare. 'Principe, Corte e governo tra Cinque e Settecento', in *Antico regime e modernità* (Rome, 2008), 153–65.

Muir, Rory. *Tactics and the Experience of Battle in the Age of Napoleon* (New Haven and London, 1998).

Musi, Aurelio. 'The kingdom of Naples in the Spanish Imperial system', in *Spain in Italy: Politics, Society and Religion 1500–1700*, ed. T. J. Dandelet and J. A. Marino (Leiden, 2007), 73–98.

Muto, Giovanni. 'Il governo dell'Hacienda nella Lombardia spagnola', in *Lombardia Borromaica Lombardia Spagnola 1554–1659*, 2 vols., ed. P. Pissavino and G. Signorotto (Rome, 1995), vol. 1, 303–69.

Muto, Giovanni. 'Pouvoirs et territoires dans l'Italie espagnole', *Revue d'histoire moderne et contemporaine*, 45 (1998): 42–65.

Muto, Giovanni. 'Noble presence and stratification in the territories of Spanish Italy', in *Spain in Italy: Politics, Society and Religion 1500–1700*, ed. T. J. Dandelet and J. A. Marino (Leiden, 2007), 251–97.

Nasalli Rocca, Emilio. 'Il patriziato piacentino nell'età del principato', in *Studi di Paleografia, Diplomatica, Storia e Araldica in onore di Cesare Manaresi* (Milan, 1953), 227–57.

Nasalli Rocca, Emilio. 'Feudi e famiglie feudali nei Ducati di Parma e Piacenza nel secolo XVIII', *Archivio Storico per le Province Parmensi*, 7 (1955): 57–86.

Nasalli Rocca, Emilio. *I Farnese* (Piacenza, 1969).

Noailles, Vicomte de. *Episodes de la guerre de Trente Ans: Le Cardinal de La Valette, lieutenant-général des armées du roi, 1635–1639* (Paris, 1906).

Nosworthy, Brent. *The Anatomy of Victory: Battle Tactics 1689–1763* (New York, 1990).

Nubola, Cristina. 'Supplications between politics and justice: the northern and central Italian states in the early modern age', *International Review of Social History*, 46 (2001): 35–56.

Ochoa Brun, Miguel Angel. 'La diplomatie espagnole dans la première moitié du XVIIe siècle', in *L'Europe des traités de Westphalie: Esprit de la diplomatie et diplomatie de l'esprit*, ed. L. Bély (Paris, 2000), 537–54.

Oresko, Robert. 'The House of Savoy in search of a royal crown', in *Royal and Republican Sovereignty in Early Modern Europe: Essays in Memory of Ragnhild Hatton*, ed. R. Oresko, G. C. Gibbs, and H. M. Scott (Cambridge, 1997), 272–301.

Oresko, Robert. 'The House of Savoy and the Thirty Years War', in *1648: War and Peace in Europe*, ed. K. Bussmann and H. Schilling 3 vols. (Munster-Osnabruck, 1998), 142–53.

Oresko, Robert and David Parrott. 'Reichsitalien and the Thirty Years War', in *1648: War and Peace in Europe*, ed. K. Bussmann and H. Schilling, 2 vols. (Munster-Osnabruck, 1998), vol. 1, 141–60.

Osborne, Toby. *Dynasty and Diplomacy in the Court of Savoy: Political Culture and the Thirty Years' War* (Cambridge and New York, 2002).
Ostoni, Marco. *Il tesoro del Re: Uomini e istituzioni della finanza pubblica milanese fra Cinque e Seicento* (Naples, 2010).
Ottolenghi, Emilio. *Storia di Piacenza, dalle origini sino all'anno 1918* (Piacenza, n.d.).
Outram, Quentin. 'The socioeconomic relations of warfare and the military mortality crises of the Thirty Years' War', *Medical History*, 45 (2001): 151–84.
Outram, Quentin. 'The demographic impact of early modern warfare', *Social Science History*, 26 (2002): 245–72.
Pagès, Georges. 'Autour du "grand orage": Richelieu et Marillac', *Revue historique*, 179 (1937): 63–97.
Panella, Antonio. 'Una lega italiana durante la guerra dei Trent'anni', *Archivio Storico Italiano*, 94 (1936): 3–36.
Paret, Peter. 'The Annales School and the history of war', *Journal of Military History*, 73 (October 2009): 1289–94.
Parker, Geoffrey. 'The etiquette of atrocity: the more things change, the more they stay the same', *MHQ: Quarterly Journal of Military History*, 1993; reprinted in Parker, *Empire, War and Faith in Early Modern Europe* (London, 2002), 143–68.
Parker, Geoffrey et al. *The Thirty Years War* (London, 1984).
Parrott, David. 'Strategy and tactics in the Thirty Years' War: the "military revolution" revisited', *Militargeschichtliche Mitteilungen*, 38/2 (1985): 7–25.
Parrott, David. 'French military organization in the 1630s: the failure of Richelieu's ministry', *Seventeenth Century French Studies*, 9 (1987): 151–67.
Parrott, David. 'The causes of the Franco-Spanish war of 1635–1659', in *The Origins of war in Early Modern Europe*, ed. J. Black (Edinburgh, 1987), 72–111.
Parrott, David. 'A "prince souverain" and the French crown: Charles de Nevers 1580–1637', in *Royal and Republican Sovereignty in Early Modern Europe: Essays in Memory of Ragnhild Hatton*, ed. R. Oresko, G. C. Gibbs, and H. M. Scott (Cambridge, 1997), 149–87.
Parrott, David. 'The role of fortifications in the defense of states: the Farnese and the security of Parma and Piacenza', in *I Farnese: Corti, guerra e nobiltà in Antico Regime*, ed. A. Bilotto, P. del Negro, and C. Mozzarelli. (Rome, 1997), 509–60.
Parrott, David. *Richelieu's Army: War, Government and Society in France, 1624–1642* (Cambridge, 2001).
Parrott, David. 'The utility of fortifications in early modern Europe: Italian princes and their citadels, 1540–1640', *War in History*, 7/2 (2007): 127–53.
Parrott, David. 'Italian soldiers in French service 1500–1700: the collapse of a military tradition', in *Italiani al servizio straniero in età moderna*, ed. D. Maffi, P. Bianchi, and E. Stumpo (Milan, 2008), 15–40.
Parrott, David. 'From military enterprise to standing armies: war, state and society in Western Europe, 1600–1700', in *European Warfare 1350–1750*, ed. F. Tallett and D. J. B. Trim (Cambridge and New York, 2010), 74–95.
Parrott, David. *The Business of War: Military Enterprise and Military Revolution in Early Modern Europe* (Cambridge and New York), 2012.
Pedrazzini, Dominic. 'Opérations Franco-Suisses en Allemagne: la campagne de la Valtelline (1635)', *Revue Internationale d'Histoire Militaire*, 65 (1988): 141–57.
Pedretti, Sara. 'Ai confini occidentali dello Stato di Milano: l'impiego delle milizie rurali nelle guerre del Seicento', in *Alle frontiere della Lombardia: Politica, guerra e religione nell'età moderna*, ed. C. Donati (Milan, 2006), 177–200.

Pepper, Simon. 'Aspects of operational art: communications, cannon and small war', in *European Warfare 1350–1750*, ed. F. Tallett and D. J. B. Trim (Cambridge and New York, 2010), 181–202.
Perjés, Gabor. 'Army provisioning, logistics and strategy in the second half of the 17th century', *Acta Historica Academiae Scientiarum Hungaricae*, 16 (1970): 1–51.
Peschot, Bernard. 'Les "lettres de feu": la petite guerre et les contributions paysannes au XVIIe siècle', in *Les Villageois face à la guerre, XIVe–XVIIIe siècle*, ed. C. Desplat (Toulouse, 2002), 129–42.
Pezzolo, Luciano. 'Nobiltà militare e potere nello Stato veneziano fra Cinque e Seicento', in *I Farnese. Corti, guerra e nobiltà in antico regime*, ed. A. Bigotto, P. Del Negro, and C. Mozzarelli (Rome, 1997), 397–419.
Pezzolo, Luciano. 'La "Revoluzione militare": Una prospettiva italiana 1400–1700', in *Militari in età moderna: la centralità di un tema di confine*, ed. A. Dattero and S. Levati (Milan, 2006), 15–64.
Pezzolo, Luciano. 'Professione militare e famiglia in Italia tra tardo medioevo e prima età moderna', in *La Justice des familles: Autour de la transmission des biens, des savoirs et des pouvoirs*, ed. A. Bellavitis and I. Chabot (Rome, 2011), 341–66.
Picaud, Sandrine. 'La "guerre de partis" au XVIIe siècle en Europe', *Stratégique*, 88 (2007): 101–46.
Piccinini, Giuseppina. *Il Palazzo Gotico: Le vicende del Palazzo Pubblico di Piacenza dal 1281* (Piacenza, 1998).
Pieri, Piero. *Il Rinascimento e la crisi militare italiana* (Turin, 1952).
Pillorget, Réné. 'Populations civiles et troupes dans le Saint-Empire au cours de la Guerre de Trente Ans', in *Guerre et pouvoir en Europe au XVIIe siècle*, ed. V. Barrie-Curien (Paris, 1991), 151–74.
Pinti, Paolo. *L'Armeria di Palazzo Farnese a Piacenza* (Cremona, 1988).
Pinti, Paolo. 'Le Armi dei Farnese', in *I Farnese: corti, guerra e nobiltà in Antico regime*, ed. A. Bilotto, P. Del Negro, and C. Mozzarelli (Rome, 1997), 493–508.
Pithon, Rémy. 'La Suisse, théâtre de la guerre froide entre la France et l'Espagne pendant la crise de la Valtelline', *Schweizerische Zeitschrift fur Geschichte*, 13 (1963): 33–53.
Podestà, Gian Luca. 'Dal delitto politico alla politica del delitto (Parma 1545–1611)', in *Complots et conjurations dans l'Europe moderne*, ed. Y-M. Bercé and E. Fasano Guarini (Rome, 1996), 679–720.
Politi, Giorgio. *Aristocrazia e potere politico nella Cremona di Filippo II* (Milan, 1976).
Porter, Stephen. *Destruction in the English Civil Wars* (Dover, NH, 1994).
Pronti, Stefano. 'Produzione e diffusione delle armi nello stato di Piacenza in età farnesiana: indicazioni per ricerche', in *I Farnese: corti, guerra e nobiltà in Antico regime*, ed. A. Bilotto, P. Del Negro, and C. Mozzarelli (Rome, 1997), 487–92.
Prosperi, Adriano. 'Dall'investitura papale alla santificazione del Potere', in *Le Corti farnesiane di Parma e Piacenza (1545–1622)*, ed. M. A. Romani (Rome, 1978), 161–88.
Quazza, Romolo. *La guerra per la successione di Mantova e del Monferrato (1628–1631)*, 2 vols. (Mantua, 1926).
Quazza, Romolo. 'Il periodo italiano della guerra di trent'anni', *Rivista storica italiana*, 50 (1933): 64–89.
Raudzens, George. 'Firepower limitations in modern military history', *Journal of the Society for Army Historical Research*, 67 (1989): 130–53.
Raudzens, George. 'In search of better quantification for war history: numerical superiority and casualty rates in early modern Europe', *War and Society*, 15 (1997): 1–30.
Redlich, Fritz. *De Praeda Militari: Looting and Booty 1500–1815* (Wiesbaden, 1956).

Ribot Garcìa, Luis Antonio. 'El reclutamiento militar en la España a mediados del siglo XVII', *Cuadernos de Investigacion Historica*, 9 (1986), 63–89.
Ribot Garcìa, Luis Antonio. 'Milano piazza d'armi della Monarchia Spagnola', in *Millain the Great. Milano nelle brume del Seicento* (Milan, 1989), 349–63.
Ribot Garcìa, Luis Antonio. 'Las provincias italianas y la defensa de la Monarquia', in *Nel sistema imperiale l'Italia spagnola*, ed. A. Musi (Naples, 1994), 67–92.
Ribot Garcìa, Luis Antonio. 'Les types d'armée en Espagne au début des temps modernes', in *Guerre et concurrence entre les Etats européens du XIVe au XVIIIe siècles*, ed. Ph. Contamine (Paris, 1998), 43–81.
Riggi, Andrea. 'Le imprese militari di Odoardo Farnese: la campagna di 1635', *Aurea Parma*, 13 (1929): 49–56, 28–36, and 32–8.
Ripetti, Paola. 'Scrivere ai potenti: Suppliche e memoriali a Parma (sec. XVI–XVIII)', *Sogittura e Civiltà*, 24 (2000): 295–358.
Rizzo, Mario. 'I cespiti di un maggiorente lombardo del Seicento. Ercole Teodoro Trvulzio e la milizia forense', *Archivio Storico Lombardo*, 120 (1990): 463–78.
Rizzo, Mario. 'Istituzioni militari e strutture socio-economiche in una città di antico regime. La milizia urbana a Pavia nell'età spagnola', in *Eserciti e carriere militari nell'Italia moderna*, ed. C. Donati (Milan, 1998), 63–89.
Rizzo, Mario. 'Sticks, carrots and all the rest: Lombardy and the Spanish strategy in northern Italy between Europe and the Mediterranean (1550–1600)', *Cahiers de la Mediterranée*, 71 (2005) online journal. <http://cdlm.revues.org/991>.
Rizzo, Mario. '"Ottima gente da guerra": Cremonesi al servizio della strategia imperiale', in *Storia di Cremona: L'Età degli Asburgo di Spagna (1535–1707)*, ed. G. Politi (Cremona, 2006), 126–45.
Rizzo, Mario. '"Rivoluzione dei consumi", "State building" e "rivoluzione militare": La domanda e l'offerta di servizi strategici nella Lombardia Spagnola, 1535–1659', in *Tra Vecchi e nuovi equilibri. Domanda e offerta di servizi in Italia in età moderna e contemporanea*, ed. I. Lopane and E. Ritrovato (Bari, 2007), 447–74.
Robinson, Gavin. 'Equine battering rams? A reassessment of cavalry charges in the English Civil War', *Journal of Military History*, 75 (2011): 719–31.
Roche, Daniel. *Humeurs vagabondes: de la circulation des hommes et de l'utilité des voyages* (Paris, 2003).
Romani, Marzio Achille. 'Finanza pubblica e potere politico: il caso dei Farnese (1545–1593)', in *Le Corti farnesiane di Parma e Piacenza (1545–1622)*, ed. Marzio A. Romani, vol. 1 (Rome, 1978), 3–85.
Rombaldi, Odoardo. *Il duca Francesco I d'Este (1629–1658)* (Modena, 1992).
Roncai, Luciano. 'Sabbioneta dopo Vespasiano Gonzaga', in *La difesa della Lombardia Spagnola*, ed. G. C. Zanella and L. Roncai (Milan, 2004), 265–78.
Rosso, Claudio. *Il Piemonte sabaudo: Stato e territori in età moderna* (Turin, 1994).
Russon, Marc and Hervé Martin. *Vivre sous la tente au Moyen-Age (Ve–XVe) siècle* (Rennes, 2010).
Sabbadini, Roberto. *La Grazia e l'Onore: Principe, nobiltà e ordine sociale nei ducati farnesiani* (Rome, 2001).
Saglio, Pietro. *Notizie storiche di Broni*, 2 vols. (Bologna, 1970).
Sallmann, Jean-Michel. 'Le cheval, la pique et le canon: le rôle tactique de la cavalerie du XIVe au XVIIe siècle', in *Le Cheval et la guerre du XVe au XXe siècle*, ed. D. Roche and D. Reytier (Paris, 2002), 253–67.
Sandberg, Brian. *Warrior Pursuits: Noble Culture and Civil Conflict in Early Modern France* (Baltimore, 2010).

Schaub, Jean-Frédéric. 'La crise hispanique de 1640. Le modèle des "révolutions périphériques" en question', *Annales; Histoire, Sciences sociales*, 49 (1994): 219–40.
Schnettger, Matthias. 'Le Saint-Empire et ses périphéries: l'exemple de l'Italie', *Histoire: Economie et Société*, 23 (2004): 7–23.
Séré, Daniel. *La Paix des Pyrenées: Vingt-quatre ans de négociations entre la France et l'Espagne (1635–1659)* (Paris, 2007).
Showalter, Dennis. 'A modest plea for drums and trumpets', *Military Affairs*, 39 (1975): 71–4.
Shy, John. 'History and the history of war', *Journal of Military History*, 72 (2008): 1033–46.
Signorotto, Gianvittorio. *Milano Spagnola. Guerra, istituzioni e uomini di governo (1635–1660)* (2nd edn, Milan, 2001).
Sodini, Carla. 'L'Italie et la Guerre de Trente Ans', in *Nouveaux regards sur la Guerre de Trente Ans: Centre d'Etudes d'Histoire de la Défense*, ed. Philippe Bonnichon (Vincennes, 1998), 37–56.
Sodini, Carla. *L'Ercole Tirreno: Guerra e dinastia medicea nella prima metà del '600* (Florence, 2001).
Sodini, Carla. *De re militari: War and military culture in the early modern age* (Pisa, 2002).
Soldini, Nicola. 'Strategie del Dominio: la cittadella nuova di Piacenza (1545–1556)', *Bollettino Storico Piacentino*, 86 (1991): 11–69.
Spagnoletti, Angelantonio. *Principi italiani e Spagna nell'età barocca* (Milan, 1996).
Spagnoletti, Angelantonio. *Le dinastie italiane nell'epoca moderna* (Bologna, 2003).
Spagnoletti, Angelantonio. 'Onore e spirito nazionale nei soldati italiani al servizio della monarchia spagnola', in *Militari e società civile nell'Europa dell'età moderna, sec. XVI–XVIII* (Bologna, 2007), 211–53.
Stevenin, Michel. 'Une fatalité: les devastations des gens de guerre dans l'Est de la France (1620–1660). L'exemple de la Champagne', in *Les Malheurs de la Guerre: De la guerre à l'ancienne à la guerre réglée*, ed. A. Corvisier and J. Jacquart (Paris, 1996), 161–79.
Stradling, Robert. 'Spain's military failure and the supply of horses, 1600–1660', *History*, 69 (1984): 208–21.
Stradling, Robert. 'Olivares and the origins of the Franco-Spanish war, 1627–1635', *English Historical Review*, 101 (1986): 68–94.
Subacchi, Paola. 'L'imposizione fiscale in età farnesiana: formazione degli estimi piacentini', *Archivio Storico per le Province Parmensi*, ser. 4, 44 (1992): 151–73.
Subacchi, Paola. *La Ruota della Fortuna: Arricchimento e promozione sociale in una città padana in età moderna* (Milan, 1996).
Susane, Louis. *Histoire de l'ancienne infanterie française*, vol. 4 (Paris, 1852).
Swart, Erik. 'From "landsknecht" to "soldier": the Low German foot soldiers of the Low Countries in the second half of the 16th century', *International Review of Social History*, 51 (2006): 75–92.
Tallett, Frank. *War and Society in Early Modern Europe, 1495–1715* (London, 1992).
Tanzi, Marco. 'La dinamica della popolazione di Piacenza dalla metà del '500 alla peste del 1630' (Thesis, Università degli studi di Parma, 1983–4).
Theibault, John. 'The demography of the Thirty Years War revisited: Gunther Franz and his critics', *German History*, 15 (1997): 1–21.
Thompson, Anthony. 'El soldato del Imperio: una aproximaciòn al perfil del recluta español en el Siglo de Oro', *Manuscrits*, 21 (2003): 17–38.
Tlusty, B. Ann. *The Martial ethic in Early Modern Germany* (Basingstoke and New York, 2011).

Tocci, Giovanni. *Le terre traverse: Poteri e territori nei ducati di Parma e Piacenza tra Sei e Settecento* (Bologna, 1985).

Trombella, Cristina. 'La 'Memoria' di Colorno (1612–1674) di Don Costantino Canivetti; parte prima 1612–1658' (Thesis, Università degli studi di Parma, 1997–8).

Ulbricht, Otto. 'The experience of violence during the Thirty Years War: a look at the civilian victims', in *Power, Violence and Mass Death in Pre-modern and Modern times*, ed. J. Canning, H. Lehmann and J. Winter (Aldershot, 2004), 97–127.

Vignal Souleyreau, Marie-Catherine. *Richelieu et la Lorraine* (Paris, 2004).

Visceglia, Maria Antonietta. 'Il cerimoniale come linguaggio politico: su alcuni conflitti di precedenza alla corte di Roma tra '500 e '600', in *Cérémonial et rituel à Rome (XVIe–XIXe siècles)*, ed. M. A. Visceglia and C. Brice (Rome, 1997), 117–76.

Waquet, Jean-Claude. 'Politique, institutions et société dans l'Italie du "Seicento"', in *L'Italie au XVIIe siècle*, ed. Y.-M. Bercé, G. Delille, J-M Sallmann, and J.-C. Waquet (Paris, 1989), 13–134.

White, Lorraine. 'Spain's early modern soldiers: origins, motivations and loyalty', *War and Society*, 19 (2001): 19–46.

White, Lorraine. 'The experience of Spain's early modern soldiers: combat, welfare and violence', *War in History*, 9 (2002): 1–38.

Wilson, Peter H. 'New perspectives on the Thirty Years War', *German History*, 23 (2005): 237–61.

Wilson, Peter H. *Europe's Tragedy: A History of the Thirty Years War* (London, 2009).

Wright, Robert. *Nonzero: The Logic of Human Destiny* (New York, 2000).

Zannoni, Mario. 'L'esercito parmense nella guerra di 30 anni', *Parma per l'Arte*, 23 (1975): 141–8.

Zeller, Gaston. 'Bresse, Turin et Pignerol', *Revue Historique*, 193 (1942): 97–110.

Index

(Persons in boldface, places in italics)

absolute rule 3, 22, 23, 186
adventurers, companies of, partisans 152, 181
Albornoz, cardinal and governor 38, 39, 90, 104–6, 108
Aldobrandini, cardinal Pietro 18, 31, 33, 212
Alessandria 6, 49, 82, 90, 93, 96, 97, 101, 102, 109, 112, 116–19, 123, 143, 154
Alessandro Farnese, duke 11–13, 15, 21, 49, 211
Anguissola, house of 9, 10, 46, 49, 141
Anne of Austria, queen of France 25, 29, 126
Aragon, don Martin d', general 168–9, 172–5, 178, 198–9
aristocracy 3, 5, 12, 15, 39–40, 42, 44, 45; civil nobility 9, 10, 13, 25, 33, 43, 46–7, 53, 89, 92, 186
armour 48, 56, 79, 80, 82, 85, 105–06, 120, 146, 148
army makeup/recruitment/impressment 42–87
army morbidity, sick leave, attrition 59, 72–7, 192–3
army supply, army impresari, army diet, sutlers 78–87; uniforms 83–4
Army of Flanders, Spanish 2, 11, 23, 45
artillery 36, 82–3, 90, 98, 112, 118, 146, 159–61, 167–8, 173; bombardiers 98, 149, 175, 185
Avogadri, Ricciardo, general 49, 50, 54, 77, 105–8

bandits and outlaws 52, 63, 78, 144, 166, 182
banking fair of Piacenza 14, 31, 132, 139, 211
Barberini, house of 29, 32, 113, 187, 212; **cardinal Antonio** 63, 211
Taddeo 29, 211–12
bastions 9, 16, 96, 130
Berceto 136, 186, 202
Bernhard of Weimar, duke and general 127
Bobbio 143, 205
Borgo San Donnino (Fidenza) 47, 92, 132–3, 176–7, 197
Borgo Taro 10, 152–3, 167, 188
Borso d'Este, prince and colonel 122, 179
Breme 121, 123
Brescello 146
Brescia 49, 77, 78, 82
Broni 93, 124, 157
Busseto 10, 132–3, 172, 177, 188, 197, 202, 203

Calandrini, Ippolito, biographer 20, 21, 145, 152, 182
camerata 57
captains 45, 48, 50–9, 61, 63, 66, 70, 71, 73, 84, 85, 107, 111, 115, 138, 139, 142, 143, 155, 156, 171, 198
Capuchin order 15, 36, 93, 95
Casale Monferrato 19, 26, 27, 29, 34, 48, 53, 54, 86, 89, 90, 96, 101, 104, 117, 121, 124, 139
Casalmaggiore in Lombardy 31, 67, 140, 146, 178, 189
Castel San Giovanni 91, 124, 135, 148–9, 157, 168, 198–200, 205
Castellarquato 201, 205
Castelnuovo Scrivia, action of 95, 123–4
castles 5, 9, 10, 11, 40, 42, 46, 48, 53, 86, 97, 118, 121, 135, 139, 141, 142, 144, 146, 149, 150, 152, 154, 157, 168, 173–7, 181–6, 193, 198
Castro 63, 83, 212–15; Castro War 58, 71n., 212–14
Catholic Church 3, 4, 22, 133, 156, 193
Celada, count 104, 117, 118, 120
census 6, 64, 138, 149, 151, 193, 201
Charles, duke of Mantua 26, 53, 141, 210
Charles IV, duke of Lorraine 27, 34, 59
Charles Emanuel I, duke of Savoy 19, 21, 27, 62, 92
chivalric code 20
Christian war 92–3
citadel of Parma 12, 17, 33, 82, 83, 139, 146; citadel of Piacenza 9, 10, 11, 13, 16–17, 21, 23, 46, 51, 53, 61, 78, 123, 130, 141, 168, 179, 183; citadel Casale 19; citadel Milan 37; citadel Tortona 95
citizen status 9, 15, 24, 45, 73, 79, 82, 86, 130–1, 134–5, 138, 143, 146, 149, 150, 187, 195
coinage, coinage manipulation 132n., 139–40, 208
Coloma, Don Carlos, general 38, 39, 90, 93, 94, 95–8, 104, 107, 112, 117–22, 155
colonel, or maestro de campo 48–56, 62, 63, 71–3, 80, 94, 114, 115, 119, 124, 128, 141, 143, 150, 152, 178, 196
company rosters 5, 46–8, 55–9, 65, 68, 71, 73, 78, 86n., 87, 111, 129, 141, 142, 180, 181, 193, 209
contributions, requisitioning 19, 38, 52, 122, 138, 157, 170–3, 176, 178, 188, 197

Cornetta Bianca horse guard 30, 42, 46, 47, 87, 94, 107
Corsica, Corsican troops 40, 49, 58, 66, 74, 142, 168
Cortemaggiore 132, 134, 173–5, 177, 188, 198, 201, 205, 207
Council of State in Madrid 63, 187
council of war 118
court of Parma 10, 11, 12–15, 20, 21, 42, 43–9, 132, 136, 138, 139, 156, 186, 212; court of France 6, 32n., 125–8; court of Spain 13, 214, court of Turin 35, 38n., court of Mantua 35
Cremona 16, 45, 67, 90, 140, 146, 172, 174, 181, 184, 189, 214
Créquy, marshal of France 26, 29, 30, 33, 35, 36, 71, 89, 90, 95, 96, 101–4, 109, 112, 114, 115–24, 141, 156, 158, 160, 161, 163, 214
Crescenzi Romani, historian 92n., 123n., 144, 169n., 171, 175, 181, 182

devastation 172, 179, 181, 190; atrocities 5, 27, 144, 151, 170, 189–91, 214
Dauphiné, province 27, 35, 50, 67, 88, 114–15
desertion 39, 48, 54, 56–9, 62–70, 72–5, 77, 95, 103, 104, 107–12, 115, 118, 121–3, 135, 142, 155, 158, 166, 169, 179, 181, 209, 213
Doria, Gian Andrea 13, 22, 152–4, 167–8, 188
dragoons 39, 161–2, 174, 178, 189, 197
drill, drill manuals 6, 14, 21, 50, 55, 78–80, 82, 106, 126
Duplessis-Praslin, ambassador 28

earthworks 19, 90, 96–7, 109, 117, 119–20, 130, 133, 135, 138, 149, 152, 158, 161, 185
ecclesiastics 7, 22, 84, 197–9; ecclesiastical immunities 72, 84, 133–4, 172, 197
engineers 16, 40, 90, 96, 98, 135, 158, 160–1
ennoblement 44
equestrian statues Piacenza 14, 33, 91
Este dynasty 8, 12, 22, 28, 122, 145, 146, 154, 179, 214, 215
estimo, or compartito, or cadastre 9, 129–30, 132–3, 137
excommunication 72, 133, 186

famine, hunger as weapon 12, 44, 160, 169–70, 179, 190–6, 207, 208
Farnese dynasty 8, 9, 10–15, 19–23, 31, 42, 43, 82, 85, 129, 154, 155, 167, 174, 177, 186–7, 211, 213
Farnese, don Francesco 16, 49, 51
Farnese troops 16, 40, 94, 102, 144, 146, 151, 170, 179

Ferdinando II, Grand Duke of Tuscany 28, 187
Ferrara 8, 155, 212, 214
Ferriere 82, 154, 175
feudatories 8–15, 20–3, 39, 40, 42–6, 50, 52, 85, 105, 129, 137, 138, 141, 143, 160n., 174, 175
Finale Liguria 37, 39, 96, 117, 118, 154, 166
finance of state 8–12, 30, 114, 132, 134–9, 159, 171, 177, 183, 208, 212; borrowing 137, 139, 151
Fiorenzuola 132, 136, 173, 177, 181, 198, 205
Florence 9, 91, 97, 169, 187, 214
forage and fodder 37, 77, 96, 101, 102, 114, 121, 123, 135, 136, 143, 144, 145, 154, 159, 163, 176, 179, 182, 192, 207
Fornovo 136
fortification 5, 10, 16, 21, 27, 38, 40, 78, 86, 89, 90, 92–7, 117–8, 130, 132–5, 138, 140, 143, 149, 151–2, 156–7, 160, 166, 170, 181, 212
France 2, 8, 11, 12, 15, 21–40, 44, 48, 52–4, 62, 68, 70–2, 87–9, 91, 112, 116, 125, 127–32, 148, 154–6, 159, 165–6, 181–3, 188, 191, 208, 214
Francesco I d'Este, duke of Modena 28, 145–6, 150, 154, 167, 185, 188, 214–15
Franche Comté of Burgundy 25, 36, 62, 68, 142, 183, 190–1
Frascarolo, action at 104, 118
French navy, relief force 166–7
French subsidies 26, 86, 183
French troops 35–6, 53, 86, 88, 91, 95, 107, 109, 115, 117, 122, 139, 142, 143, 157, 159–60, 166, 181, 184, 188–9, 212

galleys 38, 40, 122, 144, 166–7
Gambacorta, general 39, 105, 107, 157, 161–2
Gaston d'Orleans, prince 21, 126, 157n.
gate guards 64, 84, 132
Gaufridy, Jacques 22, 24, 125, 127, 158, 211, 213
Geneva 27, 35
Genoa, Republic 15, 24, 31, 38, 40, 65, 140, 152, 154–5, 164, 166, 215; Genoa city 13n., 14, 16, 24, 28, 32, 35, 37, 67, 90, 96, 117, 121, 152, 155, 159, 165, 166
German troops 10, 19, 39, 49, 70, 76, 84, 88, 97, 113, 117, 122, 142, 149, 152, 154–6, 161, 170, 176, 178–9, 182, 184, 189–90, 197–8
Germany 2, 4, 13, 19, 20, 30–1, 34, 37, 39, 45, 49, 64, 66, 70, 84, 88, 104, 122, 127, 134, 140, 142, 155, 169, 178, 179, 190–3, 207, 208
gift-giving 13, 84, 117, 128
Golden Fleece, order of 13–14, 33, 40, 91, 127, 167, 214

Index

Gonzaga dynasty 12–13, 19, 20, 22
Governor of Milan 6, 10, 30, 38, 90, 121, 124, 143, 187
governor of Parma: civil 11; military 134, 179
governor of Piacenza: civil 132; military 95
grain prices 45, 83, 118, 186, 208, 211
Gran Giustizia of 1612 7–8, 14, 42, 47
Guastalla, town & duchy 1, 13n., 30, 146

Habsburgs of Austria 24, 25, 33, 49, 79, 86, 122, 151
Habsburgs of Spain 2, 18, 21, 24–6, 33, 49, 57, 66, 105, 113–14, 116, 122, 147, 154, 161, 170, 183–4, 186, 196, 214
Haes, Gil de, colonel 155, 170
Hémery, Michel Particelli d', ambassador 35, 36, 109, 112, 122, 125, 141, 144–6, 148, 151, 155, 157–9, 162, 164–6
Holy Roman Emperor 8, 10, 12–13, 19, 36, 52, 88, 122, 167–8
hospital, Piacenza hospital 6, 73–7, 136, 142, 180, 195–6, 198
hygiene, e-coli, typhus, sanitary conditions 73, 120, 163, 184, 192, 195, 201

Imperial army 16, 19, 27, 37, 70, 122, 140, 150, 155, 170, 183, 190
Imperial fiefs 13, 22, 31, 36, 113, 154, 167
infanticide of newborns 201
Intendants, civil 114; army 114–15

Jesuits, Society of Jesus 7, 14–15, 20, 129, 136

Lake Como 88
Lake Maggiore 160
Landi, house of 9, 10, 22, 47, 85, 152, 167–8, 215
Lazio region 13n., 32, 58, 62–3, 137, 187
League of Italian states, French; 28–9, 30, 32; Papal 32, 34, 41
Lérins islands 117, 166
letters patent 15, 44–5, 48, 50, 53–4, 130, 141, 142
Liguria 13n., 21, 27, 28, 35, 37, 58, 66, 118, 122, 142, 166
Lombardy 3, 13, 16, 21, 30, 31, 37, 39, 40, 51, 58, 66, 87, 89, 91, 96, 103, 109, 116, 121, 133, 140, 155, 156, 159, 198
Lomellina district 121
Lorraine, duchy of 25, 27, 34–6, 70, 191; royal Lorraine 70
Louis XIII, king of France 22–30, 32–5, 41, 48, 50, 53–4, 88–9, 91–2, 97, 113, 117, 122, 124–7, 158, 166–7, 183, 187, 210
Lunigiana 22, 31, 152

magazines 17, 96, 138, 143, 179
Mantuan Succession war 26, 215

manufactures, weapons 82
marauders 95, 135, 179
Marazzani, house of 46, 105; Francesco 52, 150
Margherita Aldobrandini, duchess 8, 141
Margherita d'Austria, duchess 8, 11, 14
Margherita de'Medici, duchess 21, 134, 140–1, 143, 145, 150–1, 187
Margherita of Savoy, duchess of Mantua 26, 35, 141
Maria de'Medici, queen 21, 24, 126
Marie-Christine, duchess of Savoy 27, 34, 35
Marques de Leganés, governor of Milan 121–4, 143, 146, 151, 156, 160–3, 168–70, 183–5, 187, 189, 195, 210
Maurizio of Savoy, cardinal prince 35–6
Mazarin, Jules or Giulio Mazzarini 32, 35, 127, 213–15
Medesano, action near 182
Medici dynasty 9, 12, 13, 21, 22, 28
Melo, Francisco de, diplomat 210
merchants 31, 33, 130–2, 136–7, 139–40, 189, 190
Mezzogiorno 3
Milan city 11, 19, 37, 39, 40, 45, 64, 82, 89, 90, 116, 130, 155, 157, 160, 187; duchy of 6, 10, 15, 22–3, 25, 30, 32, 35, 37, 54, 58, 65, 94, 116, 121, 133, 140, 143, 148, 179, 214
military enterpriser, or asientista 2n., 52, 53, 155
military history, vii. 1–3
military justice, or provost, army magistrate 55, 71, 199
militia, Farnese 10, 19, 21, 24, 30, 33, 46, 48–9, 53, 55, 64, 78, 81, 84–6, 104, 109, 133, 135, 138, 140, 142–6, 148–52, 154, 156, 157, 168, 173–6, 180, 182, 184, 193, 208; of Lombardy 40, 89, 90, 94, 95, 97, 102, 113, 116–18, 121, 123–4, 144, 150, 168, 188–9
mills, floating mills 21, 95, 98, 102, 118, 123, 140, 184
Modena, duchy of 13n., 22, 28, 29, 41, 85, 122, 135, 140, 145–6, 150, 154, 158, 159, 167, 169, 185, 208n., 212, 214–15
Monferrato 19, 26, 27, 34, 35, 38, 40, 53, 69, 70, 77, 86, 90, 96, 101, 103, 111–12, 117, 120–3, 139, 141, 147, 157, 159, 164
Montechiarugolo 10, 146, 182, 185, 202
Moralt, Johann Werner, colonel 50, 52–3, 70–1, 73, 109, 111, 142
Mormons, microfilm mission 74n., 193–4, 198
mortality, army fatalities 57, 110, 113, 117, 120, 122, 148, 162, 169, 196
mortality, civilian 191–207
Mortara 89, 90
municipal assembly 9, 44, 172, 188

Index

musketeers, shot 38, 79–81, 106–7, 112, 118, 120, 123, 144, 147, 149, 152, 184

Naples, kingdom of 11, 13, 25, 37, 40, 66–7, 69, 73, 90, 116–17, 122, 154, 159, 169, 187, 188, 215
Neapolitan troops 16, 39, 63–4, 67, 89, 93, 94, 97, 105, 113, 115–20, 147–9, 155, 157, 161, 178, 189, 196, 198
negotiation, negotiators 119, 152, 173–4, 184, 185; safeconducts, passports, ceasefires 105, 108, 181
Netherlands Republic 11, 13, 15, 24, 26, 30, 182; *Spanish Netherlands* 19, 20, 25, 30, 35–7, 39, 62, 68, 211, 214
Nicart, François 51, 93, 109, 132, 141
Nördlingen, battle of 37, 39, 40, 79, 94, 119, 121, 162
Novara 30, 82, 89, 90, 92, 156, 157, 159–60, 163, 178, 198

Odoardo Farnese, duke 4, 6, 9, 19, 21–2, 30–3, 38, 41, 42, 62, 72, 78, 82, 86, 87, 90, 101, 104, 107, 109, 113, 118, 121–2, 132–3, 138, 140, 145, 151, 157–9, 164–5, 167–70, 174, 180, 187, 208, 211–12; personality 20–3, 116, 167, 186, 210; trip to Paris 123–8; unpopularity of 31, 148, 176, 185, 187
Odoardo Farnese, cardinal regent 15–18, 58
officers, army 42–54
officers, non-commissioned 54–8
Olivares, count duke 16, 19, 23, 25–6, 30, 36–8, 40, 122, 183
Ottavio Farnese, bastard 8, 20, 31, 186
Ottavio Farnese, duke 8, 10–11, 14, 84, 129, 187

Pallavicino house 10, 47, 188, 211; Pallavicino state 10, 132, 188
Papacy 32, 63, 78, 113, 156, 187, 211, 212, 215
Papal States 8, 9, 11, 18, 23, 29, 49n., 54, 58, 63, 67, 84, 109, 113, 133, 150, 159, 187, 212–13
parish registers 4, 6, 74n., 113, 191, 193–207
Parma 5–12, 14, 15, 17, 27, 30–3, 42–7, 50–1, 62–4, 67, 70, 78–9, 82–3, 86, 90–1, 122, 132, 134–9, 141, 145–8, 151–2, 164, 170, 176, 178–9, 182, 185–6, 188, 192, 194, 201
Pavia 6, 82, 118
Pax Hispanica 14
pay, army 30, 51–2, 55, 57, 59, 64, 72–3, 76, 78, 85, 109, 114–15, 132, 138–40, 143, 155, 159, 165, 188, 192, 208–9
peace talks 26, 113, 150, 158, 167, 183–5, 187, 188, 210
petitions 45, 48, 208–9

Phillip II, king of Spain 11, 12, 13, 58, 187
Phillip III, king of Spain 12, 13, 35, 39, 58, 167
Phillip IV, king of Spain 25, 30, 35, 37, 40, 66, 92, 188, 214
Piacenza 6, 9, 10, 11, 13–7, 21, 23–4, 31, 33, 38, 43, 44–6, 47, 50–1, 53, 58–9, 61–7, 71–7, 79, 82–4, 91–2, 113, 123, 130–2, 134–5, 137, 141–9, 154–7, 159, 164, 168, 170, 187–8, 194–6, 205–7; blockade of 171–85
Piedmont 3, 13 n.19, 16, 26, 30, 32, 35–7, 49, 68, 77, 84, 90, 115, 141, 156, 160, 163, 179, 182, 188, 215
pikemen 38, 79–80, 86, 107, 112
Pilotta Palace of Parma 14, 31, 146, 182
Pinerolo fortress 26–8, 33–6, 86
plague, bubonic 3, 21, 37, 44, 85, 132, 140, 146, 190–1, 194–5, 198–9, 207
plunder, booty 22, 38, 70, 79, 83, 91, 94, 95, 115, 120, 131, 144–5, 149–52, 155, 171, 174, 177–8, 182–3, 189, 195, 209
Po river 14, 16, 31, 78, 96, 118, 121, 140, 197
Ponte d'Enza, action of 146–7
Pontecurone, action of 93–4, 134
Pontremoli 31
population decline 4, 190–9
prisoners, exchange of 181
processions, religious 134, 156–7, 198
professional soldiers 10, 16, 37, 39, 40, 45, 52, 70, 78, 81, 84, 85, 89–90, 93, 107, 112–13, 116, 123, 139, 140, 142–4, 146, 154, 157, 164, 168, 171, 174, 180–2, 184, 188, 190, 193, 195, 208–9, 213
Protestants 12, 20, 24–5, 27, 30, 32, 34, 37, 38, 40, 52, 71, 77, 79, 88, 122, 132, 151 163
protocol 13, 27, 29, 43–4, 125–7, 166, 188
Provence 27, 40, 114, 117, 166
Pugolotti, Andrea, chronicler 33, 90, 92, 139, 145, 164, 180n.

raiding 40, 135, 137–40, 142–4, 148–52, 164, 171, 174, 178, 188, 198
Ranuccio Farnese I, duke 7–15, 20, 30, 42–4, 130, 133, 167
Ranuccio Farnese II, and prince 44, 47, 82, 156, 212–15
Reggio Emilia 145, 214
religious toleration 34
religious wars 24, 50, 132
Richelieu, cardinal 6, 16, 22–38, 41, 50, 53, 70, 86–9, 103, 113–17, 121, 125–8, 139, 158, 166–7, 169, 183, 187, 188, 192, 210, 215
Rivalta, siege of 168, 184
Rocchetta prison 10, 14, 15, 30, 31, 150
Rohan, duke of 16, 38–9, 82, 86, 88, 104, 121, 151, 157, 159–60, 163, 182, 210

Rome 8, 18, 21, 29, 32–3, 36, 38, 63, 66, 92n., 113, 122, 158, 178, 183, 187, 210–14
Rossi of San Secondo, house of 11, 40, 52, 105–8, 121, 137, 151
Rossi, Pietro, treasurer 139, 208
Rottofreno, action of 149, 156–7, 168–9, 170, 177, 180–2, 196, 199
royal address, royal treatment 31, 35
rules of war, offering quarter 119, 130, 151, 182

Sabbioneta 13n., 20, 23, 27, 31, 53, 159, 168, 188
Saint-Esprit, French Order of the 127
Saint-Paul, comte de 86, 123, 141, 148–50, 157, 165, 168–9, 171, 184
Salsomaggiore, salt pans 82, 176, 208
San Lazzaro, action at 147–8
San Secondo Parmense 151, 178, 189, 196, 202
Santa Cruz, marques de, general 40, 117
Santo Stefano d'Aveto 152, 154, 167
Savoy, duchy 13n., 24, 26, 34, 37, 41, 47, 89, 103, 112, 114, 116, 133, 136, 169, 183; region 25, 34, 35, 36, 183
Savoy dynasty 3, 22, 27–8, 31, 34, 36, 125, 158
Scotti, Fabio 22, 24, 32, 94, 105, 108, 123, 125–8, 133, 158, 164, 167, 213
Scrivia river 95, 123, 158, 168
Serafini, Francesco 49–51, 55, 62–3, 66, 70, 79, 83, 94, 109, 123, 130, 141, 168, 179
Serbelloni, Giovanni, general 88, 104
sergeant-major 33, 48, 50–1, 132, 140
siege tactics 21, 36, 89, 96–113, 117–20, 148–9, 175–82
Siri, Vittorio, historian 32n., 159
smallpox 59, 201
Soragna 137, 151, 172, 178, 196
Sourdis, Henri de, admiral 117, 166–7
sovereignty 4, 13, 22–4, 113, 127, 211, 214–15
Spanish alliance 10, 45
Spanish court 13, 214
Spanish troops 16, 26, 31, 34, 37, 39, 79, 88, 121, 137, 140, 146, 149, 151, 161, 166, 172, 183, 185–6, 188–9, 201, 214
Spinola, Filippo, colonel 93, 94, 105, 119
Stradella 93, 144, 157, 181
Swedish troops 27, 39, 50, 79, 183
Swiss Grison troops 34, 38, 88, 163, 210
Swiss mercenaries 15, 50, 52–4, 70, 73, 89, 109, 111, 113, 126, 142, 155, 181

tactics 78–9; infantry 79, 80–2, 162; cavalry 106–7, 147
tagliateste guerrillas 182, 188, 209

taxation 9, 11, 31, 33, 45, 62, 78, 83, 84, 116, 129–30, 133, 137; chimney tax 132; window tax 137; salt tax 134, 176; surtax 137; corvée 137, 208; flour tax (macinato) 140, 188
tax rebellion 89, 114
tercios 38–9, 50, 66, 68, 85, 93, 105, 111, 118–19, 143, 154, 170
Ticino river 160–1, 165
titles of address and status 13, 27, 28, 31, 35, 145, 158, 214
Toiras, marshal of France 26, 38, 103, 139, 158, 160
Tommaso of Savoy, prince 35, 36
Tornavento, battle of 159–63
Tortona 90, 93–6, 123, 144
Treaty of Cherasco 1631: 26
Treaty of Monzon 1626: 16, 24
Trebbia river 143, 169, 170, 184, 195
Trivulzio, cardinal 39, 90, 91, 111, 143, 170, 172, 181, 184–5
troop lodgings, billeting 6, 48–9, 51, 55, 59, 61–2, 76, 114, 212, 124, 133, 135–7, 140, 144, 173, 189, 191
Tuscan troops 116, 122, 154, 162, 167, 178, 184

Urban VIII Barberini, pope 21, 23, 29, 32, 63, 113, 122, 151, 186, 211–12

Valenza 6, 48, 54, 89, 90, 95–121, 143, 158, 160
Valtellina 16, 38–9, 86, 88, 104, 121, 157, 160, 163, 210
vantaggiati 57–8
Venice, Republic of 13n., 30, 31, 38, 41, 54, 68, 84, 158, 212, 214; city 50, 122; *Venetian Terraferma* 30, 53, 77
Vercelli 49, 103
Verrua, fortress 16, 34, 49
veterans 21, 57–8, 65, 70, 82, 87, 93–4, 119, 146, 189, 213
Victor Amadeus I, duke of Savoy 27, 28, 33–6, 89, 97, 103–4, 112, 115, 118–9, 121, 123–4, 141, 145, 155–6, 158, 160–3, 183
Villa, Guido, general 112, 123–4, 135, 144–8, 150, 154, 157, 159–60, 198–9, 214
Visdomini, Cremona, courtier 20, 21, 48, 107
Voghera 93, 148

winter quarters 121, 133, 135–6, 140–1, 155, 179, 182, 189
women, soldiers' wives 76–7, 136, 155, 178